W9-DGK-551

city baby new york

The Ultimate Parenting Guide
for New York Parents from
Pregnancy Through Preschool
Third Edition

By Kelly Ashton and Pamela Weinberg

Universe Publishing

For our City Babies:
Alexander, Angela, Rebecca, and Benjamin

This edition first published in 2005
by UNIVERSE PUBLISHING
A Division of Rizzoli International Publications, Inc.
300 Park Avenue South
New York, NY 10010
www.rizzoliusa.com

Copyright © 2005, 2003, 2001, 1997 by Kelly Ashton and Pamela Weinberg
First Universe edition published in 2003
Previously published by City and Company
Design by Paul Kepple and Jude Buffum @ Headcase Design
Cover Illustrations by Mary Lynn Blasutta

All rights reserved. No part of this publication may be reproduced, stored in a retrieval system, or transmitted in any form or by any means, electric, mechanical, photocopying, recording, or otherwise, without prior consent of the publishers.

2005 2006 2007 2008 / 10 9 8 7 6 5 4 3 2 1
Third Edition
Printed in the United States

Library of Congress Catalog Control Number: 2005908499
ISBN-10: 0-7893-1348-0
ISBN-13: 978-0-7893-1348-5

Publisher's Note: Neither Universe Publishing nor the authors have any interest, financial or personal,
in the locations listed in this book. No fees were paid or services rendered in exchange for inclusion in these pages.
Please also note that while every effort was made to ensure accuracy at the time of publication, it is always best to call ahead
to confirm that the information is still up-to-date. All area codes are 212 unless otherwise noted.

contents

7 *Acknowledgments*

8 *Preface to the Third Edition*

9 *Introduction by Diane Debrovner*

part one

Preparing for Your New York Baby: Everything You Need to Know!

11 *Chapter One: From Obstetric Care to Childbirth*

12 **THE BIRTH ATTENDANT**

OBSTETRICIANS • MIDWIVES

16 **THE BIRTH PLACE**

HOSPITALS • BIRTHING CENTERS

24 **CHILDBIRTH METHODS**

THE LAMAZE METHOD • THE BRADLEY METHOD HUSBAND-COACHED CHILDBIRTH

WATER LABOR AND WATER BIRTH

25 **CHILDBIRTH EDUCATORS, CLASSES, AND OTHER RESOURCES**

31 *Chapter Two: Taking Care of Yourself*

32 **EXERCISE**

FITNESS/HEALTH CLUBS

38 **YOGA**

41 **MASSAGE**

43 **NUTRITION**

EATING RIGHT WHILE YOU'RE PREGNANT • FOOD DELIVERY

45 **HOME ORGANIZERS**

46 **SPAS FOR BABY AND YOU**

47 *Chapter Three: From Healthcare to Day Care*

48 **PEDIATRICIANS**

50 **BABY NURSES/DOULAS**

52 **NANNIES**

NEWSPAPER ADVERTISEMENTS • AGENCIES • THE INTERVIEW • CHECKING REFERENCES

WHEN THE NANNY STARTS • TAXES AND INSURANCE

59 AU PAIRS

60 DAY-CARE CENTERS

61 BABY-SITTING

Chapter Four: Adjusting to New Motherhood

65

66 NEW MOTHER CLASSES
    HOSPITAL CLASSES • CPR CLASSES • OTHER CLASSES, GROUPS, AND SEMINARS

74 ENTERTAINMENT FOR NEW MOMS

76 HOTLINES, WARMLINES, AND OTHER SPECIAL HELP
    ADOPTION • BREASTFEEDING • HOTLINE HELP
    PREMATURE INFANTS • SINGLE PARENTS • TWINS OR MORE
    SPECIAL NEEDS GROUPS

79 IMPORTANT SUPPLIES
    DIAPER SERVICES • BREAST PUMPS

Chapter Five: Entertainment for Kids and Moms

83

84 MOMMY AND ME CLASSES AND PROGRAMS

99 MOMMY AND ME YOGA CLASSES

99 PLAYGROUNDS
    CENTRAL PARK • OTHER PARKS

103 PUBLIC LIBRARIES

104 OTHER ACTIVITIES FOR YOU AND YOUR CHILD

107 CONCERTS, SHOWS, AND SPECIAL EVENTS

Chapter Six: After-School Activities

109

111 ONE-STOP SHOPPING: AFTER-SCHOOL INSTITUTIONS

112 THE ARTS
    ART • DANCE • DRAMA • MUSIC • POTTERY • COOKING

120 SPORTS
    GYMNASTICS • SPORTS TRAINING • SWIMMING • YOGA

122 PERSONAL ENRICHMENT PROGRAMS
    COMPUTERS • ETIQUETTE • LANGUAGE

Chapter Seven: Kid-Friendly Restaurants

125

    UPPER EAST SIDE • UPPER WEST SIDE • MIDTOWN EAST AND WEST
    CHELSEA/FLATIRON • WEST VILLAGE • EAST VILLAGE • SOHO •

LOWER EAST SIDE • CENTRAL VILLAGE/NOHO

TRIBECA • THE CHAINS • THEME RESTAURANTS

COFFEE BARS

136 **A FEW WORDS ON BATHROOMS . . .**

part two

Shopping for Your New York Baby: Everything You Need

139 *Chapter Eight: The Big Firsts*
140 **BIRTH ANNOUNCEMENTS**
143 **BIRTHDAY PARTIES**

PARTY PLACES AND ENTERTAINMENT • PARTY FAVORS

CENTRAL PARK PARTIES • BALLOONS AND DECORATIONS

BIRTHDAY COOKIES AND CAKES

154 **HAIRCUTS**
156 **SHOES**
158 **PHOTOGRAPHS**
161 **A WORD ON PRESCHOOLS**

163 *Chapter Nine: Maternity Clothing*
164 **SHOPPING TIPS**
165 **THE STORES**

171 *Chapter Ten: Baby Furniture and Accessories*
172 **THE NECESSITIES**

BASSINETS • CRIBS • CHANGING TABLES • GLIDERS

CARRIAGES/STROLLERS • CAR SEATS • BABY SWINGS

BOUNCY SEATS • HIGH CHAIRS • BOOSTER SEATS/

HOOK-ON SEATS • PLAYPENS/PORTABLE CRIBS

BATHTUBS/BATH SEATS • BABY CARRIERS • BACKPACKS

BABY MONITORS • DIAPER BAGS

182 **THE STORES**

SUPERSTORES • SPECIALTY STORES • SUPERSTORES OUTSIDE

OF NEW YORK CITY • FURNITURE, CLOTHING, AND DONATIONS

INTERIOR DESIGN AND DECORATION • BEST PLACES FOR GIFT ITEMS

192 **BABY PROOFING**

195   *Chapter Eleven: Baby and Toddler Clothing*

196   SHOPPING TIPS

198   THE STORES

210   TRUNK SHOWS AND PRIVATE BOUTIQUES

211   RESALE SHOPS

212   MALLS

       NORTHERN NEW JERSEY • WESTCHESTER/ROCKLAND

       LONG ISLAND • CONNECTICUT

217   *Chapter Twelve: Toys, Toys, Toys . . .*

218   AGE-SPECIFIC TOYS

221   THE STORES

229   *Chapter Thirteen: Books, Videos/DVDs, Audios, Catalogs, and Magazines*

230   BEST BOOKSTORES FOR CHILDREN

232   CHOOSING A BOOK FOR YOUR CHILD

234   BEST BOOKS FOR YOUNG CHILDREN

239   BEST BOOKS FOR PARENTS

242   VIDEOS/DVDs

245   AUDIOCASSETTES AND CDS FOR CHILDREN

246   CHILDREN'S CATALOGS

248   MAGAZINES FOR PARENTS

251   WEBSITE DIRECTORY

261   THE CITY BABY YELLOW PAGES

289   INDEX

Acknowledgments

We would like to thank the following people for their encouragement and support in the writing of this book: Carlo Sant Albano and Matthew Weinberg, Susan and Joel Kastin, Sander and Mechele Flaum, Harris and Angela Ashton, Ronni Soled, Susan Barr, and Emerson Bruns.

With great appreciation to Victoria Ashton for assistance in updating each and every entry. With special thanks and gratitude to Kathleen Jayes, Tricia Levi, and Jacob Lehman at Universe, whose invaluable help and advice make this book possible.

Preface to the Third Edition

Can this be New York with strollers everywhere?

Since the first edition of *City Baby* was published in 1997, we've witnessed something of a baby boom here in New York. Now, more than ever, couples are opting to raise their children in the Big Apple. There are indeed strollers everywhere—uptown, downtown and Brooklyn, too. Amazingly, New York has become a kindler, gentler, kid-friendly town, no longer just a stop on the way to the suburbs. Dare we say we told you so?

We knew we were on to something when the first edition of *City Baby* quickly went into second and third printings. The book filled a niche. There was nothing like it, and we were delighted to find parents virtually lining up to buy a copy. We caught the attention of television news shows, newspapers and parenting magazines. The local weekly *Midtown Resident* called *City Baby* "the Fodor's of baby guides," while news anchor Carol Jenkins on Fox News at Noon exclaimed, "Everybody should have a book like this. It's great! What a wonderful idea!" We were hailed as authorities on the awesome experience of childbirth and childcare, as well as on children's shopping and activities in Manhattan. For two years, we wrote a column on kid-friendly restaurants in the city. We spoke at the New York Junior League and at several Jewish centers, and Pamela launched a luncheon series for new mothers. And not incidentally, Kelly gave birth to a second child, bringing our author total to four.

But, being a New Yorker, *City Baby* demanded more: a thoroughly updated third edition, to be exact. Here it is, a new and improved all-purpose parenting guide, with many new sources for you and your child. We have added a wealth of new information on programs for preschoolers; a yellow pages section that serves as a handy phone reference; and an index that puts every major *City Baby* category at your fingertips. So pack us into your baby bag, gear up the stroller, and take us along for the incredible ride called parenthood. Whether you're an experienced mother or new mother, we know that *City Baby* will remain your New York baby "bible."

—Kelly Ashton
Pamela Weinberg

introduction

Unfortunately, when I had my first child eleven years ago, *City Baby* hadn't been published yet. I was twenty-eight years old, had never changed a diaper, and none of my friends had kids. Even though I'd lived in New York City my entire life, I had no idea where to find a Lamaze class, get help with breastfeeding, buy a crib, or meet other new moms. Motherhood was a brand new adventure, and I eventually managed to figure out everything I needed to know. A few years later, my good friend Kelly Ashton teamed up with Pamela Weinberg when they realized that smart, savvy New Yorkers needed a go-to guide about parenthood—and *City Baby* quickly became a must-read for new moms and dads.

Just as I was learning how to parent a preteen, my new husband and I decided to have another child. Despite the fact that I've been an editor at *Parents* magazine for a decade, having a baby is still daunting—and I've been incredibly grateful to have the second edition of *City Baby* as a resource this time around. How things have changed! You can now find great maternity clothes in black, and there's so much new gear. Who knew that one of the first big questions facing expectant parents would be

To Bugaboo or not to Bugaboo? Although my friends wondered how I could go back to diapers and sleep deprivation, I think that being an older mom has helped me relax and relish every day. I've also discovered that New York City is more baby friendly than ever.

Without a doubt, being a parent is the most challenging and rewarding job you'll ever have. Your time is precious, and Pamela and Kelly have done all the research so you don't have to. Having their updated insider information at your fingertips will make motherhood much less stressful; instead of making phone calls to hunt down what you need, you can take a shower or a nap—or just sit on a park bench with your baby. My best advice: Be good to yourself and get all the help you can—from your spouse, parents, friends, lactation consultants, magazines, websites, and other new moms—and don't feel guilty that you're not perfect. What's really important is having patience, perspective, and a sense of humor.

—Diane Debrovner
Senior Editor, *Parents* magazine

part one

Preparing for Your New York Baby: Everything You Need to Know!

Chapter One

from obstetric
care to childbirth

Congratulations! The pregnancy test is positive! Tell the prospective grandparents, aunts, and uncles about the new addition to the clan, then start making the decisions that will keep you busy for the next nine months. First, you will have to consider:

❊ Who will provide you with prenatal care throughout your pregnancy?
❊ Who will deliver your baby?
❊ Where will your baby be born?

Who will look after you and your baby during your pregnancy? Basically, you have two choices: a doctor (who may be the obstetrician/gynecologist you saw in your pre-pregnancy days or another doctor you select at this time) or a midwife. Both of these professionals will essentially perform the same service—meet with you during your pregnancy to monitor your progression and help deliver your baby on the big day.

Where your baby will be born is easy: a hospital, a birthing center, or at home. Yes, the occasional New York City baby has made his or her way into the world via taxi cab in the middle of the Triborough Bridge, but that is a remote possibility. Chances are, you'll make it to the right place at the right time.

You have had the good sense (or blind luck) to be having a baby in a city that seems to have an obstetrician on every other block and some of the best hospitals in the world. Finding excellent care won't be a problem.

This chapter provides everything you need to know about the birthing business in New York—doctors, midwives, hospitals, birthing centers, childbirth preparation classes, labor coaches, lactation consultants, and more.

Looking back on our own birthing experiences with all four of our children, we know that being comfortable with and confident in your doctor is the most important part of a positive birth experience. All of the hospitals and birthing centers we list have the qualifications to provide an excellent birthing experience, whether you choose to deliver with an obstetrician or a midwife.

the birth attendant

Whether it's an obstetrician or midwife, you should choose this person as soon as you discover you're pregnant.

Obstetricians

Most women in New York deliver their babies in a hospital under the care of an obstetrician. You probably already have an obstetrician/gynecologist whom you've been seeing for annual checkups, and you may be perfectly happy to continue together throughout your pregnancy. But you may want to find a new doctor for one of several reasons: your current ob/gyn is fine for the routine checkups, but friends have told you about a wonderful new doctor; your ob/gyn is farther away from your apartment than you'd like; your ob/gyn is affiliated with a hospital that doesn't appeal to you; or you may be over thirty-five years old, considered high risk, and want an ob/gyn who specializes in high-risk pregnancies.

If you're a high-maintenance mom, especially a first-timer, you may want an ob/gyn who is very good at hand-holding, one who gets on the phone to comfort you every time you call, or tells you to come to the office. If you are more laid back, you might want an ob/gyn more in keeping with that style. If you're comfortable and happy with your current ob/gyn, stick with her. If you would like to find someone else, do so. With the large number of good obstetricians in New York, you can afford to pick and choose.

To find an obstetrician:

❊ Ask friends who have had babies or the mother down the hall in your apartment building. A recommendation based on the personal experience of a woman who's already been through what you're just beginning is a good way to go.

❊ Ask your internist or general practitioner to recommend an obstetrician.

❊ Call the hospital where you would like to deliver, and ask for a referral from the obstetrical department. (After you check out the hospital chart starting on page 20, you may find a hospital that is especially suited to your needs.)

❊ Go to the library and look up New York magazine's most recent "The Best Doctors in New York" issue.

❊ Call the New York County Medical Society (684-4670) for a listing of obstetricians who practice in the city.

❊ Log onto www.newyork.urbanbaby.com for an extensive listing of doctors' names and addresses.

Once you have a candidate or two, call for a consultation. Any doctor should be willing to sit down with you and discuss what you can expect over the next nine months and during the birth. Come for your appointment armed with a list of questions, a pen and pad, and your husband or partner—two listeners are better than one.

After this initial consultation, you should be able to decide whether this is the doctor for you. He or she should listen to you carefully, answer your questions thoroughly, and inspire your trust. You need to feel confident that this doctor will be there for you any time night or day during your pregnancy. Feeling confident and comfortable with your ob/gyn is the most important thing.

Here are some questions that you should ask:

❊ Are you part of a group practice? If so, will I see the other doctors in the practice? What is the likelihood that you will deliver my baby, rather than one of your colleagues? (Ask when the doctor typically takes vacation. You will be able to figure out what month you are delivering, so inquire early on. Many doctors take off two weeks in March, when the private schools are on break.) Do you have school-age children?

❊ How often will I need to have an office visit?

❊ What tests should I expect to have and when?

❊ What is the fee for a vaginal birth? cesarean birth? What extra charges should I expect? (Many good doctors now charge the same fee for a vaginal or a cesarean delivery, because they do not want to be accused of performing unnecessary cesareans.)

❊ What are your thoughts on natural childbirth, anesthesia, episiotomy, cesarean section, induction of labor? (Ask these and other questions about the doctor's birthing philosophy that are of concern to you.)

❈ With which hospital are you affiliated? Does the hospital have birthing rooms; labor, delivery, and recovery rooms; rooming-in for baby and husband; a neonatal intensive care unit?

❈ What do you consider "high risk" birth factors?

❈ How do I get answers to my questions between visits? If you are busy, is there another doctor in the office who will take my call?

❈ Do you have nurses trained to answer basic prenatal questions? (Obstetricians spend half their day doing hospital deliveries or patient check-ins, so it is important to know that if your doctor is not there, someone will be available to answer your questions in a timely manner.)

While you're at the doctor's office for your consultation, check out the waiting room. If you can, ask one or two of the pregnant women leafing through the latest *Parents* magazine, how long they usually wait to see the doctor. Routine visits should take about ten minutes, and there is nothing more frustrating than waiting an hour for a ten-minute visit. Also, ask whether the doctor works in a collaborative way with patients, making joint decisions, or whether he likes to call the shots. Again, the doctor's personality must jibe with yours.

The usual schedule for visiting your ob/gyn in a low-risk, normal pregnancy is every three weeks for the first seven months, every two weeks in the eighth month, and every week in the ninth month. Of course, this may vary with different practices, and if your pregnancy is high risk you may see your doctor more often.

Some common tests to expect in the course of your pregnancy are:

❈ *Sonogram.* Typically, a woman has two or three sonograms (ultrasounds) during her pregnancy. The first will be done in the second month (about nine weeks) to date her pregnancy; the second more extensive sonogram will be done in the fifth month (about twenty weeks), sometimes at the hospital, to check the growth and internal organs of the fetus; a third may be done in the ninth month (about thirty-six weeks) to get an idea of the baby's size and position. During Kelly's second pregnancy, her ob/gyn had acquired an in-office sonogram machine. In fact, many New York ob/gyns now have a sonogram machine in their offices and will do sonograms more often.

❈ *MSAFP* (Maternal Serum Alpha-Fetoprotein Screening) The MSAFP screening is performed in the fourth month (sixteen to eighteen weeks). This simple blood test determines the levels of alpha-fetoprotein (blood protein) present in the mother's blood. High or low levels may indicate serious problems in the development of the fetus. If the MSAFP level comes back either too high or too low, the doctor will probably recommend a second test to confirm the results of the first.

❈ *Amniocentesis.* Known to moms as an amnio, this procedure is performed in the fourth month (sixteen to eighteen weeks) of pregnancy. The technician, guided by an ultrasound image of the uterus, inserts a long hollow needle through the woman's abdominal wall and withdraws a small amount of amniotic fluid. Amniocentesis is recommended for women over thirty-five (although many women over thirty choose to have it performed as well) and in cases in which genetic disorders or chromosomal abnormalities might be suspected.

These tests and procedures are routine, and the obstetrician you choose will have conducted, ordered, or overseen them on hundreds of pregnant women before you. But remember: this is your pregnancy. You should feel perfectly comfortable asking what you think are "dumb questions" about the need for tests and what the results mean. If you are thirty-five or older, you are considered high risk in New York City. Statistics show that women over thirty-five have a slightly greater risk of problems during pregnancy. Other circumstances can also determine a high-risk pregnancy—a previous period of infertility, multiple miscarriages, high blood pressure, diabetes, obesity, and other serious health problems. Make sure your doctor knows your full medical history.

A number of obstetricians specialize in high-risk pregnancies. *New York* magazine's "The Best Doctors in New York" issue lists many of them, as does www.urbanbaby.com. Your own ob/gyn can also refer you to such a specialist. Or call the obstetrical department of any of the hospitals (starting on page 20), and ask for a referral based upon your specific needs.

Midwives

A growing number of New York women opt for a midwife, rather than an obstetrician, to guide them through pregnancy and delivery. A midwife may be a good fit for you if you're low risk, and if you like the idea of working one-on-one. A midwife will likely be more available than an obstetrician to talk with you about the emotional aspects of what you're experiencing, and will probably be more oriented toward natural childbirth.

If this sounds good to you, you will want to find a Certified Nurse Midwife (CNM), a registered nurse who has undergone extensive formal training through an accredited nurse-midwifery program. The American College of Nurse Midwives (ACNM), based in Washington, D.C., provides midwife certification nationally and sets the standards for the practice of nurse-midwifery. Only ACNM-certified midwives are able to practice in hospitals. Midwives can prescribe pain medications for women in labor and they can call an anesthesiologist when in a hospital.

Two other categories of midwives are Direct Entry Midwives, often referred to as Lay Midwives, and Physician-Assistant Midwives. The latter may also be certified through the ACNM and therefore can practice in hospitals. Direct Entry Midwives, trained through a combination of coursework and apprenticeship, are not permitted to practice in hospitals but do perform or assist at many home births in the New York City area.

When you choose a CNM, find out about her hospital affiliation. You may prefer to deliver in a birthing center or at home, but in the event of a medical complication, it is critical that your practitioner has access to a hospital nearby. Many CNMs in New York do practice in hospitals and will deliver your baby in the same birthing rooms that the obstetricians use.

With a CNM, you can expect the same schedule you would have with an obstetrician: a visit every three or four weeks at the beginning of your pregnancy, every three weeks in the seventh month, every two weeks in the eighth month, and every week in the ninth month. Like an obstetrician, the midwife will ask how you are feeling and if you have any questions. She will give you an external exam, take your blood pressure and weight, and listen to the baby's heartbeat.

If you would like to check out midwifery, call any of the names listed here, and set up an appointment for a consultation, just as you would for an obstetrician. Use the list of questions we have provided for choosing an obstetrician (see page 12). In addition, you may be especially interested in learning how the midwife will help you through the stages of labor and delivery, the point at which the practices of CNMs and obstetricians usually differ. Many CNMs are skilled at relaxing and preparing the perineum so that anesthesia and episiotomies are rarely necessary.

The following is a list of the hospital-based independent Certified Nurse Midwife practices in New York City:

❊ **Beth Israel Women's Health Center**
16th Street and First Avenue
420-2000

❊ **CBS Midwifery, Inc.**
Barbara Sellars
(affiliated with St. Luke's-Roosevelt)
103 Fifth Avenue at 17th Street
366-4699

❊ **Midwifery Services, Inc.**
(affiliated with St. Luke's-Roosevelt)

135 West 70th Street bet. Broadway and Columbus Avenue
877-5556

Note: You and your doctor or midwife should decide jointly, based on your wishes and her expertise, on a birthing plan for the big day. Sometime after you begin your visits, but well before your due date, decide what will happen regarding anesthesia, IVs, and episiotomies. Your ideal birthing plan (barring any unexpected surprises) should be in writing, in your doctor's file, and on hand at the hospital when you arrive.

the birth place
Hospitals

All obstetricians are affiliated with a hospital, or maybe two, so once you have selected your obstetrician, you will deliver at her hospital.

If you are still in the process of choosing an obstetrician, you may want to work backward—find the hospital you prefer, and then find an agreeable obstetrician who practices there. Knowing as much as you can about the place your baby will be born is very helpful and comforting.

Here's what's important to know about the hospital: the number of birthing rooms, cesarean rate, level of care provided in the neonatal unit, policies on husbands in the delivery room, rooming-in (husband and baby staying overnight in your room), and sibling and family visitors. New York has many hospitals, but some are newer and more comfortable than others. Mount Sinai and Roosevelt hospitals have decorated their labor, delivery, and recovery rooms with Laura Ashley–style touches, so they feel more like a bedroom than a hospital room. While it may be tempting to choose a hospital based upon decor, trust us when we tell you that once you are in labor, the color of the wallpaper in the labor room will be the last thing on your mind.

New York Hospital was one of the last to renovate. When Kelly delivered Alexander it looked like a war zone, but the new wing that was built is state-of-the-art and beautiful, and it continues to provide outstanding care.

We toured all of the private hospitals in New York City where babies are delivered and found them to be similar in many ways. They provide birthing beds, showers, or squatting bars to help your labor and delivery. And in most, if not all, cases, it is your own doctor or midwife—not the hospital or staff—who makes the important decisions concerning your labor.

Other general points to keep in mind:

❊ All the hospitals allow you to preregister. This is a good idea, because once you are in labor, you won't want to fill out forms—registering in advance can keep the paperwork to a minimum upon your arrival.

❊ Be sure to check your insurance company's policy on length of hospital stay permitted for childbirth. Most insurance companies cover either a twenty-four or forty-eight-hour stay for a vaginal delivery and three to four days for a cesarean delivery.

❊ Contact your insurance company when you become pregnant so that later there won't be any problems with the forms you submit. Some

Top Ten Hospital Tips

1. Decide whether you want a private room before you go into labor.
2. Bring a pillow with a colored pillow case from home.
3. Bring your robe and slippers.
4. Bring a bath towel and washcloth. (Hospital towels are tiny!)
5. Bring sanitary napkins.
6. Have a friend or family member present as much as possible to go for drinks, run errands, and get the nurse.
7. Have key phone numbers with you—baby nurse, furniture delivery, hotel, etc.
8. Call your insurance company as soon as possible after the baby is born.
9. Rest as much as possible: you are not going to get much rest for the next ten years.
10. Let the nurse feed the baby at 2 or 3 a.m. if you are not exclusively breastfeeding (and even if you are, one feeding won't cause nipple confusion!). You need your sleep!

insurance companies require notification before you check into the hospital.

❊ Private rooms are available at these hospitals. But keep in mind that the cost of a private room is not covered by insurance—your out-of-pocket expenses will range from $150 to $300 per night. Rooming-in for husbands and newborns is permitted in all hospitals in a private room. (In some hospitals it is also permitted in a semi-private room so long as your roommate doesn't object.)

❋ All the hospitals have twenty-four-hour parking lots nearby and will provide you with a list. Find out which hospital entrance to use in case you arrive in the middle of the night.

❋ All hospitals offer weekly classes for new mothers: bathing the baby, breastfeeding, and basic childcare. If you cannot make it to a class, ask the nurses, who are trained to help. From our own experience, you must ask to have these lessons. You are in charge, so speak up about your needs.

❋ Many of the hospitals have extremely generous visiting hours. The nurse conducting our tour at New York Hospital gave excellent advice in this regard: She said to be selfish and careful about your visitors for your own health and well being and for that of the baby. Use your hospital stay to get some rest, if possible, and to bond with your baby. There will be plenty of time for visitors when you and your baby get home.

❋ Bring two pillows from home for your postpartum room. You will be a lot more comfortable sleeping on your own pillows, as most hospital pillows are flat as a board. Make sure your pillow cases are any color but white so they don't get mixed in with the hospital laundry.

❋ You should also consider bringing towels from home. If you plan to shower at the hospital, the bath towels are the size of face towels, and can barely fit around a postpartum woman's body!

After touring ten hospitals, we became experts at predicting the questions we'd most often hear from fellow expectant parents:

❋ Can we bring music into the delivery room?
❋ Can the baby be wrapped in a receiving blanket that we bring from home instead of a regulation hospital blanket?
❋ Can we dim the lights in the labor room?
❋ Can my husband/partner cut the umbilical cord?

The answer to all these questions is yes, but we can tell you that once labor begins your only concern is delivering that baby any way you can, music or no music.

The chart on the following pages provides information to consider while evaluating the hospital in which you will deliver your baby. It includes:

Hospital: The name, address, key phone numbers, and visiting hours.

Labor rooms: The number and type of delivery rooms. In a labor, delivery, and recovery room, known as an LDR room, you will do just that before you are transferred to a postpartum room. An operating room is where cesareans and complicated vaginal births take place. A labor room is for labor only. A delivery room is where you will be taken when you are ten centimeters dilated and ready to deliver. From delivery you go to a recovery room for one to two hours before going to your own room, where you will stay until you leave the hospital.

Midwives: Hospitals with midwives on staff, and those which allow midwives to deliver babies.

Cesarean birthrate: Numbers indicate the percentage of births by cesarean section each year. The percentages listed are the most recent figures available from each hospital. Generally, hospitals with midwives have the lowest rates; hospitals with a large infertility/high-risk patient base (very New York City) have the highest. The New York cesarean rate for 2004 is 26 percent.

Nursery level: Neonatal intensive care units are classified in Levels I through IV, with Level IV being the most advanced. Choosing a hospital with a Level III or Level IV nursery is recommended, especially for high-risk pregnancies.

Classes: Prenatal classes for women and their husbands or partners, including Lamaze, breastfeeding, and preparation for cesarean birth. These classes are given at the hospital (unless otherwise noted), and you must sign up in advance. For second-time moms, many hospitals offer sibling classes. Pamela took Rebecca to one at Mt. Sinai before Benjamin was born, and it was an excellent way to prepare her for having a new baby at home.

In addition we've included any unique features about the hospital.

Birthing Centers

If you choose a midwife, she may deliver at one of the hospitals listed above or at a birthing center. Many women find the nonhospital-like atmosphere and amenities of the birthing center enormously appealing.

Not only your husband or coach, but your mother, father, best friend, and your new baby's older brother or sister can be with you throughout your birth experience. During your labor you can usually walk around, sip tea, or relax in a Jacuzzi or tub, all of which many women find more labor-enhancing and less alarming than being in a hospital bed hooked up to a monitor. At a birthing center, you can choose to labor and even deliver your baby in a special tub of soothing warm water!

One caveat to delivering at a birthing center: You must be committed to a natural childbirth. No pain relief, such as Demerol or an epidural block, can be administered.

One birthing center exists in Manhattan:

❊ *The Birthing Center*
(attached to St. Luke's-Roosevelt Hospital Center)
1000 Tenth Avenue bet. 58th and 59th streets
523-BABY

If the idea of a birthing center appeals to you, call to schedule a tour and an interview with the director. You also can ask for a CNM referral. Or, call a midwife who is affiliated with it (see pages 15–16) and schedule a consultation.

Hospital	Labor Rms/other	Classes
Beth Israel Hospital 16th St. & 1st Ave. 420-2000 (General) 420-2999 (Classes) 420-2935 (Patient Care) www.bethisraelny.org **visiting hours:** General: 11 a.m.–8 p.m. Fathers: 10 a.m.–10 p.m. 24 hrs. in private rooms	10 LDR (6 recently renovated with showers) 1 Recovery Suite (with 4 beds) 3 Operating Rooms midwives: Yes cesarean rate: 25% nursery level III Has mother/baby nursing (family center-ed—the same nurse takes care of you and your baby). One of the largest mid-wifery programs in the state—over 10% of births are delivered by a midwife. All birthing rooms are private and beautifully decorated, and furnished with an easy chair that can be converted into a bed.	Pregnancy and Beyond Fitness Program (Prenatal Yoga, Pregnancy Exercise and Yoga Shape Up for New Moms); Promoting a Healthy Pregnancy; Childbirth Pre-paration (Lamaze); Prepara-tion for Parenthood; Lamaze Refresher Course; Sibling Preparation; How to Succeed at Breastfeeding; Baby Saver CPR and Child Safety; New Mother's Support Group
Columbia Presbyterian Hospital/Babies Hospital/ Sloane Hospital for Women 3959 Broadway at 166th St. www.nyph.org 305-2500 (General) 305-2040 (Parent Ed.) **visiting hours:** General: 12–8 p.m. Fathers: 8 a.m.–10 p.m. 24 hrs. in private rooms	8 LDR/2 Delivery 2 Operating Rooms midwives: No cesarean rate: 24.5% nursery level III Aesthetically the most impressive. Spacious postpartum rooms are beauti-fully decorated, with bathroom and shower. Moms bring baby to postpartum floor by themselves—provides nice bonding time. On-staff post-natal masseuse available.	Preparation for Childbirth; Breastfeeding; Cesarean Birth; Sibling Tours

Hospital	Labor Rms/other	Classes
Lenox Hill Hospital 100 E. 77th Street bet. Lexington & Park Aves 434-2000 (General) 434-2273 (Parent Ed.) Hospital 434-3152 (Babies' Club) www.lenoxhillhospital.org **visiting hours:** Fathers: 24 hrs. Family: 3–8 p.m. General: 12–1:30 p.m.; 7–8 p.m.	11 LDR/3 Operating 1 Recovery Suite (holds 7) midwives: No cesarean rate: 31% nursery level III LDR in one room. Many of our friends have delivered here over the years. Some of the best child/ birth preparation classes are offered here. Also, we hear great praises for the outstanding nurses in the maternity ward.	Patients are referred to the 92nd Street Y (996-1100). Small group and individual classes are available in Lamaze (434-3512). Classes
The Mount Sinai Medical Center One Gustave L. Levy Place Klingenstein Pavilion 1176 Fifth Ave. at 98th St. 241-6500 (General) 241-7491 (Women's & Children's Office) 241-6578 (Breastfeeding Warm Line) www.mountsinai.org **visiting hours:** General: 11 a.m.–8:30 p.m. Fathers: 11 a.m.–11 p.m.	15 LDR/1 Recovery (holds 5 women) 3 Operating midwives: Yes cesarean rate: 20% nursery level IV LDR rooms are decorated with Laura Ashley in mind and resemble hotel rooms more than hospital rooms. Pam had both her children at Mount Sinai and was thrilled with the care she received. Pam's daughter Rebecca was in intensive care for seven days, and Pam credits Mt. Sinai with saving her life.	Breastfeeding; Lamaze; Weekend Lamaze; Labor and Delivery Sibling Preparation Classes; Sibling Preparation for 3–7 years; Preparation for Cesarean; Infant Massage; Refresher Lamaze
NY Presbyterian Hospital at the NY Weill Cornell Center 525 E. 68th Street bet.	12 LDR/4 Operating Rooms/ 1 Recovery (holds 4) midwives: No cesarean rate: 25–30%	Lamaze; Breastfeeding; Baby Care; Adapting to Parenthood; New Mother Support Group; Cesarean

Hospital	Labor Rms/other	Classes
York Ave. & East River 746-5454 (General) 746-3215 (Parenthood Prep.) www.nyp.org **visiting hours:** General: 12–8 p.m. Partner: 24 hrs.	nursery level IV Semi-private rooms sleep two. Private rooms are lovely and roomy. Kelly delivered Angela and Alexander here and although she was very happy the first time, the new renovations have made this first-class hospital even better.	Preparation Classes; Breast-feeding Consultation Class; Sibling Classes; Multiples Class
New York University Medical Center 560 First Ave. at 32nd St. 263-7300 (General) 263-7201 (Classes) www.nyubaby.org **visiting hours:** General: 8:30 a.m.–8:30 p.m. Fathers, Family: 8:30 a.m.–10 p.m.	10 Birthing (LDR) 3 Delivery and Operating Rooms midwives: Yes cesarean rate: 28% nursery level IV/regional perinatal center One of the first NYC hospitals to reno-vate in style. NYU is pristine. Very modern facilities with TV/VCR/CD Player and shower in each room. Spacious Birthing Rooms (LDR) with rockers, wood floors. Request upon arrival in Labor.	Prepared Childbirth; Pre-pared Childbirth Review, Accelerated Childbirth; Cesarean Birth; Sibling Class Breastfeeding; Breast-feeding Support Group; Father, Family: Infant Care; New Moms Group; Getting a Good Start; Prenatal Yoga; Infant CPR
Roosevelt Hospital 1000 Tenth Ave. at 59th St. 523-4000 (General) 523-6222 (Classes) www.wehealny.org **visiting hours:** General: 11 a.m.–8 p.m. Father: 24 hrs.	12 LDR/3 Operating 1 Recovery/3 Birthing Centers midwives: Yes. Midwives deliver in LDR and Birthing rooms at Birthing Center. cesarean rate: 24.5% nursery level III New and attractive facilities. Only NYC birth center attached to hospital. Center has jacuzzis, kitchen, special meals,fancy decor, allows siblings to observe birth. Private birthing rooms are furnished	Preconception Seminar; Choices in Childbirth; Why Lamaze; Sensuality and Sex-uality in Pregnancy; Prenatal Yoga for Expectant Parents; Preparation for Childbirth Classes; Prepared Parent-hood; Baby Care/Feeding/ Infant CPR; Breastfeeding; Infant CPR; Child CPR; Combined Infant/Child CPR;

Hospital	Labor Rms/other	Classes
	with a rocking chair and an easy chair which converts to a bed.	First Aid, a Primer for Parents; Sibling Preparation Course; Breastfeeding & New Parent Support Group
St. Luke's Hospital 1111 Amsterdam Ave. at 114th St. 523-4000 (General) 523-6222 (Parent/ Family Ed.) www.wehealny.org **visiting hours:** General: 11 a.m.–8:30 p.m. Father: 24 hrs.	5 LDR/2 Operating/1 Recovery midwives: Yes cesarean rate: 26% nursery level III Huge, comfortable private rooms-two-bed rooms used for one woman if requested. Least expensive private room at $100 extra per night. Rooms have own showers, plus a rocking chair and an easy chair which converts to a bed. Two guests are allowed during labor and birth.	All classes given at Roosevelt hospital location.
St. Vincent's Hospital and Medical Center 170 W. 12th St. at 7th Ave. 604-7000 (General) 604-7946 (Maternity Ed.) www.stvincents. healthcentral.com **visiting hours:** General: 10 a.m.–10 p.m. Father: 10 a.m.–10 p.m.; 24 hrs. in private rooms	7 LDR/2 OR/4 Recovery midwives: Yes cesarean rate: 25% nursery level III Sunny and spacious private rooms with two beds. Family-centered care—mom and baby share the same nurse. Birth suites allow single-room maternity care, and feature a love seat that folds out for overnight guests.	Preparation for Childbirth; Childbirth Refresher; Breastfeeding; Newborn Care; Welcome to Parenthood Infant CPR; Sibling Preparation Class

Note: Ask detailed questions about what procedures the center follows should a medical emergency arise at the time of delivery.

childbirth methods

Once the who and the where of your pregnancy and delivery have been settled, you will start to focus—more and more as you grow and grow—on the how of it all. What are the best, easiest, and most pain-free ways to get that baby out?

As you talk with other pregnant women and new mothers, you will hear about the relative merits of one birthing technique over another. Here is a very short course on the three most well-known and popular.

The Lamaze Method

This method, named after its developer, Dr. Fernand Lamaze, head of an obstetrical clinic in Paris in 1950, is popularly, if not entirely accurately, known as childbirth without pain. The method combines learned breathing techniques (the hoo-hoo-hoo, hee-hee-hee) used during contractions, with relaxation exercises designed to help a woman get through labor comfortably.

Most hospitals offer Lamaze classes. Call to sign up. (Also, most of the obstetrical nurses listed are trained in Lamaze and can assist your coach in the labor room if needed.) Couples usually begin Lamaze in the seventh month.

Some large obstetrical practices also offer Lamaze or will make referrals to private instructors, so ask your obstetrician or midwife. Kelly took Lamaze with Fritzi Kallop (517-4488) and was very happy with her. Kallop, formerly an R.N. at New York Hospital, has published an excellent book on Lamaze called *Fritzi Kallop's Birth Book*. Fritzi is very funny and down to earth, answers questions day and night, and is there for you long after the birth of your little one.

The Bradley Method Husband-Coached Childbirth

This method was developed by Dr. Robert A. Bradley, a Toronto-based obstetrician. The Bradley Method is based on a calming pattern of relaxation, deep abdominal breathing, and close teamwork between husband (or partner) and wife. Bradley's goal is a completely unmedicated pregnancy (no aspirin or cold remedies) and labor and birth (no epidural block or Pitocin).

With Bradley, the pregnant woman learns various positions for first- , second- , and third-stage labor. She is encouraged to approach her entire pregnancy as training for labor and to prepare her muscles for birth and her breasts for nursing.

Few New York City hospitals offer Bradley instruction for childbirth. To find the name of a certified Bradley instructor in your area, write to:

✳ *The American Academy of Husband-Coached Childbirth*
 P.O. Box 5224
 Sherman Oaks, CA 91413
 Visit them on the web (www.bradleybirth.com) or call (800) 4-ABIRTH

Water Labor and Water Birth

Water birth, popular in Russia since the 1960s, has attracted a small but enthusiastic number of supporters in the United States. Studies have shown that warm water can reduce the hours and stress of labor, offers support to the laboring woman, and helps relax blood flow, making the baby's journey into the world easier.

Some women use this method's water-filled tub only as a comfort during labor. Others deliver while still in the tub, and the baby takes his first breaths while most of his body is submerged in water, a gentle and familiar medium from his time in the womb.

The Birthing Center at Roosevelt Hospital makes water labor and water birth available as an option. Our friend Judy delivered her daughter there with Judith Halek attending (see page 26) and was thrilled with her experience. Should you wish, you can rent a birthing tub and have a water birth at home with the help of a midwife.

childbirth educators, classes, and other resources

If you are having a normal pregnancy, you're happy with your OB or CNM, and you've signed up for childbirth education/Lamaze classes through your doctor's office or hospital—congratulations! You are in good shape for a successful pregnancy and delivery.

If you want to know even more about what's going on with your body and what's to come during pregnancy, labor, delivery, and after, New York has many experts who work on a one-on-one basis or in a small group.

Here is a list of resources. These private practitioners specialize in a variety of birth-related areas: Lamaze, Bradley, water birth, labor support, and childbirth education. Some practitioners offer more than one kind of service; make some phone calls, and you may find just the right match for you.

Class lengths vary, but most childbirth series cost between $200 to $400 per couple. If you use more than one service from a practitioner, you can probably negotiate a package deal.

The following are specialists in pregnancy and childbirth education:

�֎ *Ellen Chuse, C.C.E.*
718-789-1981
www.ellenchusechildbirth.com
Ellen Chuse has been working with birthing women and their families since 1984. She has served as president of the Childbirth Education Association of Metropolitan New York, and remains active on the Board of Directors. Her childbirth preparation series includes information on labor, birth, postpartum, breastfeeding, and newborn care; classes are held in lower Manhattan locations and cost $350 per couple. These classes fill up quickly, so call early. Ellen also maintains a private practice as a pregnancy and birth counselor at Realbirth in Manhattan. Realbirth is a resource center for prenatal and postpartum women. Please call 367-9006 for specifics. Ellen is the mother of two daughters herself.

Choiceful Birth and Parenting

Ellen Krug, CSW, CCE

718-768-0494

www.members.aol.com/choiceful

A certified social worker and childbirth educator, Ellen Krug has been offering childbirth classes and counseling since 1984. Ellen offers a class on natural childbirth for pregnant women and their partners. Classes cover birth planning, labor support techniques, and relaxation; private classes are available, as well as counseling on any pregnancy, birth, or parenting issues. Ellen also runs a New Mom/Newborn circle, a support group for new moms and their babies that meets weekly. Parenting issues, adjustment to new family roles, sleeping issues, health care, and ways to balance work and parenthood are among the topics discussed. All classes and counseling are offered at a Park Slope, Brooklyn, location.

Fern Drillings, RN, MSN, CCE

East and West Side locations

744-6649

Fern is a well-known name around town. She is an excellent Lamaze/childbirth instructor and a faculty member at NYU School of Nursing. Many of my friends have used her for childbirth classes and think she is terrific. She also teaches CPR/Baby Saver classes and does lactation consulting.

Fritzi Kallop, RN, BS

517-4488

Fritzi Kallop is a certified childbirth educator and a registered nurse with years of experience in assisting with labor and delivery. She offers a childbirth class that includes body changes in late pregnancy, the labor and delivery process, the father's role as coach, pain relief, and Lamaze breathing techniques. Kelly took Fritzi Kallop's childbirth class and really loved her and the class.

Mary Lynn Fiske, CCE, AAHCC

718-855-1650

Mary Lynn Fiske has been teaching the Bradley method for over ten years. She offers an eight-class series at a few locations in Cobble Hill, Brooklyn, and also teaches privately in her own and her clients' homes. Classes focus on pain coping techniques, good birth planning, coaching tools for partners, and what to expect during labor and birth. Classes include labor rehearsals and role-play, discussion of interventions and cesarean, videos, and relaxation practice. Mary Lynn is an open and generous instructor; she makes her clients feel comfortable with the decisions they reach about their pregnancy and birth.

Judith Elaine Halek
Birth Balance

309 West 109th Street

bet. Broadway and Riverside Drive

222-4349

www.birthbalance.com

e-mail: judith@birthbalance.com

One of the first labor support doulas in New York City, Judith is a fitness instructor, birth counselor, and specialist in pre- and postnatal massage, as well as the director of Birth

Balance. She writes and speaks nationally on birth issues. She attended the first New York City water birth in 1987, currently runs the East Coast Resource Center for Water Birth, and is a water birth consultant. Judith also is a photographer/videographer in New York who specializes in pregnancy, labor, birth, and postpartum documentation. She works with clients in their home, birth center, or hospital.

❖ Realbirth

54 West 22nd Street
off Sixth Avenue, 2nd Floor
367-9006
www.realbirth.com

Erica Lyon, an experienced childbirth educator, opened Realbirth about a year ago as a stand-alone, comprehensive center for expectant and new parents. Realbirth offers childbirth classes that explore the many labor methods and pain management options available to pregnant women. The center also offers classes in CPR, breastfeeding, and much more. Realbirth offers drop-in classes every day of the week for new moms, too. It is also one of the few places in the city to run drop-in postpartum groups.

❖ Expectant Parenting Seminars Ronni Soled/Pamela Weinberg

744-3194
http://newmothersluncheon.com

Ronni Soled (founder of New Mothers Luncheons and parent educator) and Pamela Weinberg have created a series of unique seminars for expectant parents. Their most popular is a two-hour seminar that covers "Getting

Ready: What you need to buy, borrow, or don't need for your new baby" and "Adapting to Parenthood—the first three months." They also do a seminar called "Help!: Choosing a childcare provider, doula, baby nurse, and pediatrician." These popular seminars are given on the East and West sides of Manhattan monthly. Call for seminar dates and times.

❖ The Jewish Community Center in Manhattan

334 Amsterdam Avenue at 76th Street
646-505-4444
www.jccmanhattan.org

The JCC offers a plethora of classes for expectant parents. It offers an eight-week series that includes everything from how and where to purchase your layette (taught by Pamela), to planning your baby's bris or baby naming and everything in between. It also offers pre- and postnatal swim and yoga classes. Check out the schedule online.

❖ Mama Nurture

West Park Presbyterian Church
165 West 86th Street
877-2005

Mama Nurture is a resource center for expectant and new parents. The center offers classes in natural childbirth and breastfeeding support, as well as mommy and me classes for older babies. Mama Nurture also rents breast pumps and sells supplies for nursing moms.

Risa Lynn Klein

1490 Second Avenue bet. 77th
and 78th streets
249-4203
email: rlkbirth@aol.com

Risa Lynn Klein is a certified Bradley childbirth educator who has been teaching group and private classes, as well as refresher classes, for over fifteen years. Risa is a certified nurse and midwife. Risa herself took Bradley classes and gave birth to her daughter (now fifteen) naturally. The experience changed her life; she left a career in television production for one in birth production. She also gives a three-part workshop to help couples prepare for birth, and serves as a breastfeeding consultant.

Diana Simkin

Upper East Side locations
348-0208

A certified personal trainer, Diana has been offering one-to-one fitness for pre- and postnatal women for over twenty years. She gives private or group Lamaze classes. Diana has also written three books on pregnancy: The Complete Pregnancy Exercise Program, The Complete Baby Exercise Program, and Preparation for Birth: A Complete Guide to the Lamaze™ Method.

Tara Fallin

917-282-1699
www.doulafallinhouse.com
email: doula@fallinhouse.com
or tarabrooke@fallinhouse.com

Tara Fallin is a DONA-trained doula who lives in Manhattan. She has over three years of experience, first with the Philadelphia Alliance for Labor Support and now with the Metropolitan Doula Group. Her background enables her to empower and support women, during and after the birth of a child. Tara specializes in creating a secure and safe birth experience. She doesn't promote a particular birthing method but helps you choose to make an informed and individually suitable decision that is right for you. She is available for full-time work days, part-time work days, or overnights if you contact her in advance.

Martine Jean-Baptiste, CNM, CCE

769-4578
email: midwife@classicsoul.com

A certified nurse midwife, registered nurse, and certified childbirth educator, Martine has worked in women's health since 1986. She has served on the Childbirth Education Association of Metropolitan New York (CEA/MNY) board since 1993. In June 2000, she established a homebirth practice, JBB Midwifery. Together with her husband, she provides gynecology, contraception, and homebirth services. They also offer counseling and prenatal care. She would be happy to talk with you and discuss questions about pregnancy or childbirth options.

Gayatri Martin, RN

Choices for Childbirth
220 East 26th Street
725-1078
email: info@celebratetango.com

Gayatri has been teaching yoga for over ten years and Co-operative Childbirth Preparation classes for over eight years. Her classes encourage expectant mothers to be central to the experience of planning and preparing for birth. Gayatri is also a certified Prenatal Holistic Counselor and uses body-centered hypnosis to help women address the emotional and psychological aspects of birth. She conducts private and group classes.

❊ Marcy Perlman Tardio, CNM

718-788-9139

email: marciu@verizon.net

She is a home-birth midwife based in Park Slope, Brooklyn, and can be reached for a free consultation by telephone. She serves women in all five boroughs, lower Westchester, and parts of New Jersey that are close to New York City. Marcy focuses on gentle births, including water birth, and she does prenatal and checkups in the privacy of women's homes.

❊ Wellcare Center

161 Madison Avenue

bet. 32nd and 33rd streets

Long Island College Hospital

349 Henry Street, Brooklyn

696-9256

Wellcare has been providing comprehensive services for expectant and new mothers since 1995. Laura Best-Macia, IBCLC, and Ilana Taubman, RN, IBCLC, are the core lactation consultant staff (both previously coordinated the breastfeeding program at Beth Israel Medical Center). The center offers lactation consulting seven days a week, childbirth education classes that combine the Lamaze and Bradley approaches, breastfeeding, and childcare. It also provides continuing education courses on lactation management for lactation consultants and other health-care providers. Wellcare is also a resource for pump rentals/sales and nursing bras and pillows.

If you are looking for more information on nontraditional childbirth educators/labor support practitioners, here are two organizations that can help:

❊ Association of Labor Assistants

and Childbirth Educators (ALACE)

P. O. Box 382724

Cambridge, MA 02238

(888) 22ALACE

www.alace.org

This is a nonprofit educational organization that offers parents and professionals referrals for both childbirth preparation classes and professional labor support. It also provides information on pregnancy, childbirth, and breastfeeding.

❊ Doulas of North America

www.dona.org

Doulas of North America is an international association of doulas who are trained to provide quality labor support to birthing women and their families. The website provides general information on the role of the doula, and information on locating a labor support doula or postpartum doula in your area.

It has come to our attention that there is another new choice that expectant parents are faced with: whether or not to store the baby's umbilical cord blood. Umbilical cord blood has been used with much success to treat over forty diseases (blood and marrow diseases, e.g. leukemia) and is expected to be used more and more. There are a few different resources for private blood banking. The cost is approximately $1,500, with a fee of $125 per year to store the blood. Your OB/GYN will most likely discuss this option with you. If you want to research it yourself, one of the companies, Viacord, has a comprehensive website that explains the options: www.viacord.com.

taking care
of yourself

Once you have assembled your support team, from Lamaze instructor to lactation consultant, checked out the hospital room or birthing center in which your baby will first set eyes upon the world, it's time to be good to yourself. Since the first edition of *City Baby*, being pregnant has become truly chic. Like so many supermodels and Hollywood actresses, many New York women have discovered the benefits, physical and emotional, of staying fit during the whole nine months.

Pamela's friend Debby didn't even appear pregnant until her seventh month. She had perfect skin and hair that got thicker and shinier. She looked and acted as if she felt like a million bucks. She may be the luckiest woman we know. If you are like the rest of us, however, the weight gain, the bulging belly, and the exhaustion might make you feel unattractive on occasion. Now is the time to pamper and indulge yourself. Take advantage of some of the terrific body-strengthening and spirit-lifting services New York has to offer. Treat yourself to a manicure when you're in your ninth month and feel as though you can't stand to be pregnant for one more day.

Most importantly, get involved with a physical fitness program early on. It will help you feel your best throughout your pregnancy and prepare you for labor. Our friend Matty worked until ten days before her delivery, taking the subway from her Upper West Side apartment to her downtown East Side office and back again every day. She said climbing up and down all those stairs, carrying what turned out to be her ten-and-a-half pound son, gave her legs of steel. This is good. Strong leg muscles are useful for getting you through the last months of pregnancy, as well as labor and birth.

You can do even more for yourself by checking out one or another of the facilities described in this chapter. You'll find information about health clubs, exercise studios, and private practitioners that offer pre- and postnatal exercise classes, fitness training, yoga, and massage, all fine-tuned and appropriate for pregnant women.

Kelly swears by the Medical Massage Group; the massages she had there relaxed her and the foot reflexology helped her morning sickness. The second time around Kelly tried massage more frequently, worked out regularly, and had a much easier pregnancy.

exercise

Most experts agree that exercising throughout your pregnancy is safe, healthy, and beneficial to your overall well being. If your pregnancy is low risk and normal, you can participate in a moderate exercise program throughout your nine months. If you're a long-time jock or have exercised regularly prior to pregnancy (at least three times per week), you should be able to safely maintain that level of activity, with some modifications, throughout pregnancy and postpartum. Of course, check with your obstetrician or midwife before starting or continuing any exercise regimen, whether you are low- or high-risk. Also, be aware of the following recommendations adapted from guidelines issued by the American College of Obstetricians and Gynecologists (ACOG):

❖ Regular exercise (at least three times per week) is preferable to intermittent activity.

❖ Avoid exercise that involves lying flat on your back after the fourth month. Lying on your back is associated with decreased cardiac output in pregnancy. Also avoid prolonged periods of standing.

❊ During pregnancy, you have less oxygen available for aerobic exercise. Modify the intensity of your exercise. Stop exercising when fatigued, and never exercise to the point of exhaustion.

❊ Weight-bearing exercises, such as jogging, may be continued throughout pregnancy, at lower intensities. Nonweight-bearing exercises, such as cycling and swimming, minimize risk of injury.

❊ During exercise, be sure that your heart rate does not exceed 140 beats per minute.

❊ Avoid exercise that could cause you to lose your balance, especially in the third trimester. Avoid any type of exercise with the potential for even mild abdominal trauma.

❊ Be sure to eat enough prior to your workout. Pregnancy requires an additional 300 calories a day just to maintain your weight.

❊ Drink water and wear comfortable clothing to augment heat dissipation during exercise.

Many of the body changes of pregnancy persist four to six weeks postpartum. After your baby is born, resume your pre-pregnancy routines gradually, according to how you feel.

Fitness/Health Clubs

If you don't already have an exercise routine and want to get started, walking is a safe way to stay in shape. For those who desire a more structured workout environment, the following health clubs offer

Top Ten Tips for Prenatal Exercising

1. Do it!
2. Try as many classes as necessary until you find one you like.
3. Remember to do your kegels.
4. Don't lie on your back after the fourth month.
5. Drink plenty of water.
6. Don't exercise on an empty stomach; make sure to have a snack first.
7. Exercise with other pregnant women; you won't feel as big.
8. Try yoga for excellent stretching and relaxation.
9. Don't let your heart rate exceed 140 beats per minute.
10. Consult your obstetrician before starting any kind of new exercise.

special classes and/or training for pregnant women. Many personal trainers in these health clubs are certified to work with pre- and postnatal women; just inquire. (In many clubs, pregnant women work out right next to their non-pregnant counterparts.)

Membership fees in most full-service health clubs (Equinox, New York Sports Club, New York Health & Racquet Club, Reebok Sports Club, and David Barton) range from $900 to $2,000 per year, with a one-time initiation fee between $200 and $500. These fees are often negotiable and may be discounted if you join with a friend or spouse, or pay the entire amount upon joining, or work for an affiliated company. The fee for a personal trainer varies from club to club, but is normally $55 to $100 per hour. With some club memberships, you can use all locations in the chain; others limit workout locations.

Private clubs offer pleasant accoutrements: roomy changing areas, lots of towels, and nice snack bars. Check your local Y classes as well. They are the most economical and offer a wide range of classes and equipment.

❋ *Bally Total Fitness*
45 East 55th Street
688-6630
144 East 86th Street
722-7371
641 Sixth Avenue
bet. 19th and 20th streets
645-4565
While Bally has no childcare facilities it does offer personal trainers with experience in pregnancy exercise and postnatal workouts. As we feel location, i.e. proximity to home, is the key to many successful workout regimens, we have listed Bally's three NYC locations in the hope that one of these may be on your doorstep. Please visit the club nearest you for more information.

❋ *David Barton*
30 East 85th Street
bet. Madison and Fifth avenues
517-7577
215 West 23rd Street bet. Seventh and Eighth avenues
414-2022
David Barton offers personal trainers who are specialists in working with pre- and postnatal women and will design a regimen that is right for your level of fitness. For postpartum women, Barton offers Strollercize classes in which women bring their babies in strollers and perform a series of exercises using the strollers as resistance. These classes are included in the membership fee.

Barton is small and tightly packed with equipment so it is difficult to move around. The design and low lighting give it a nightclub feel. There is no baby-sitting available.

❋ *Body by Baby*
Jane Kornbluh
535-1904
344 East 14th Street
780-0800, ext. 236
www.bodybybaby.com
Body by Baby offers prenatal and postpartum exercise classes throughout Manhattan. Prenatal exercises help you stay fit and comfortable during pregnancy, while mommy/baby workouts help you and your baby get strong together. There are tons of yoga classes offered here, from prenatal yoga to soothe the aching muscles of moms-to-be, to postnatal yoga classes, where moms can work out with their babies. Aquatic prenatal classes, which focus on aerobic training and delicate stretching, are also offered.

❋ *Core Fitness*
12 East 86th Street bet. Fifth and Madison avenues
327-4197

email: MichaelYaleMargulies@yahoo.com
Owners Michael and Denise Margulies are probably the most fit husband and wife team in New York City! They are both excellent trainers and have clients coming back for years and years. They run a personal training facility that has all of the weights you need plus cardio machines. Denise and Michael both train pre- and postnatal women and have lots of experience doing so. A ten-pack training session is $800, which also allows you to use the gym for aerobic exercise any time during the week, even when you are not training. Both Kelly and Pam have trained with Denise and believe she is a great trainer and motivator.

❈ Equinox

10 Columbus Circle at 60th Street
871-0425
1633 Broadway at 50th Street
541-7000
420 Lexington Avenue at 44th Street
953-2499
97 Greenwich Avenue (West Village)
620-0103
14 Wall Street at Nassau (Wall Street)
964-6688
54 Murray Street at West Broadway (Tribeca)
566-6555

The Equinox clubs offer a few pre- and postnatal exercise classes but recommend using a personal trainer certified in pre- and postnatal fitness to work with you. There are many trainers available, but you must be a member of the club to hire one, and the cost is not included in the membership fee. Equinox is known for its outstanding instructors and offers a wide range of exercise classes, including spinning. Their locker rooms are immaculate. The Tribeca, Columbus Circle, and Broadway at 92nd Street Equinox locations have childcare facilities for an additional fee. Kelly exercised at the East 85th Street location before and after both her pregnancies and lost 25 pounds with Equinox after each birth. (She had gained 50 to 55 pounds with each baby.) The full-service spa is great; it offers manicures, pedicures, facials, and massage.

❈ JCC of Manhattan

The Jewish Community Center in Manhattan
334 Amsterdam Avenue at 76th Street
646-505-4444
www.jccmanhattan.org

The JCC offers lots of classes: it's like a modern-day "Y." There are exercise programs for infants, kids, and everyone in the whole family, with a complete gym, pool, and changing facilities. The JCC has exercise classes too. Membership fees vary and you can buy ten- and twenty-week passes based on the different classes. There's swimming, basketball leagues for boys and girls, and all the same activities you find at a local YMCA.

❈ Maternal Fitness

108 East 16th Street, 4th Floor, bet. Park Avenue and Irving Place
353-1947
www.maternalfitness.com

Developed by Julie Tupler, this unique fitness program physically prepares women for labor and teaches them to exercise safely throughout their pregnancies. All instructors are RNs and Certified Personal Trainers. Small groups or individual sessions focus on strengthening the abdominal muscles with the safe and effective "Tupler Technique" exercises. Kelly took five classes at the end of her first pregnancy and found them very helpful. Maternal Fitness offers a variety of other classes and services, including prenatal yoga, prenatal massage, infant massage, mother/baby exercise classes, and classes on breastfeeding and babycare. This program is also taught at Reebok Sports Club/NY, New York Sports Club, New York Health & Racquet Club, and other fitness centers. Individual sessions are $115 to $200, and a six-week workshop is $325.

New York Health & Racquet Club

Various locations in all boroughs
(800) HRC-BEST to find the club nearest you
www.hrcbest.com
New York Health & Racquet Club offers prenatal lectures and exercise classes through the Maternal Fitness program. Call Maryanne Donner (802-5198) to find out when and where classes are available. Lectures are free to members, and the six-week workshop is about $350 for members, $375 for nonmembers. Lecture topics include safe exercise during pregnancy, aerobic dos and don'ts, muscle strengthening, and flexibility. NYHRC offers baby-sitting at the York Avenue location only.

New York Sports Clubs

Various locations in all boroughs
(800) 796-NYSC to find the club nearest you

www.nysportsclubs.com
The New York Sports Club offers two programs for new mothers, both taught by Maternal Fitness trainers. "Preparing for the Marathon of Labor" is a six-week prenatal class that helps women maintain their fitness during pregnancy. The cost is $160 for members, and $220 for nonmembers. A six-week postnatal class for new moms and their babies (from age six weeks to four months) focuses on light weights, dynabands, and exercises you can do with your baby. This class is $275 for members, and $295 for nonmembers. Many of the over sixty NYSC locations offer baby-sitting for a nominal fee. We like New York Sports because it provides more value than some of the more chic athletic clubs.

92nd Street Y

1395 Lexington Avenue at 92nd Street
415-5729
415-5722 exercise class listings
www.92ndsty.org
This is one of the most complete Y's in the city with everything imaginable! The Pregnancy Exercise class is fifty-five minutes, helping expectant moms ease the discomfort of pregnancy, develop body awareness, and maintain fitness through yoga and dance exercises. A five-session class is $110 for nonmembers and $90 for members. Pick up a catalog; you will definitely want to sign up for a Mommy and Me class here as well. Its baby-sitting fees are nominal.

Peggy Levine

2726 Broadway bet. 104th and 105th streets, 3rd Floor

222-3637

www.peggylevinefitness.com

Peggy Levine's Upper West Side studio closed this year, but she is still teaching prenatal and postnatal fitness classes at Bridge for Dance Studio on Broadway between 104th and 105th streets. You can also contact Peggy for private training lessons.

Pure Power Boot Camp

38 West 21st Street, 2nd Floor

414-1886

Lauren Brenner runs the only indoor obstacle-style confidence course in New York City and caters classes to new mothers. Her class "Me Time for Mommies!" offers moms a chance to do something positive for themselves, while getting back into their pre-pregnancy shape. This high-energy workout is a lot of fun and guaranteed to get results.

Reebok Sports Club NY/ Sports Club LA

160 Columbus Avenue at 67th Street

362-6800

330 East 61st Street bet. First and Second avenues

355-5100

45 Rockefeller Plaza bet. 50th and 51st streets, and Fifth and Sixth avenues

218-8600

www.thesportsclubla.com

Reebok offers low-impact water aerobic classes and personal trainers who specialize in working with women during and after their pregnancies. All sorts of yoga—prenatal, postnatal, etc.—classes are offered. Prenatal exercise classes focus on the key physical toning, stretching, and breathing that pregnant women need to do; this class covers kegels, stretching, and, of course, moderate resistance training to keep pregnant women in shape. All pregnant women participating in this program wear heart-rate monitors.

Once your baby is six months old, you can leave him in the state-of-the-art Kids Club while you exercise. Mommy, Daddy and Me classes are held Sundays throughout the day. This is probably the largest and most expensive health club in the city; a yearly membership costs over $2,000. Pamela, an exercise guru, has worked out and tried everything Reebok has to offer. And if her figure has anything to do with Reebok, they're doing something right!

Diana Simkin

348-0208

For ten years, Diana was the pre- and postnatal exercise instructor for the Marymount Manhattan Fitness Certification Program, and she is also the author of The Complete Pregnancy Exercise Program and Preparation for Birth. She is a Certified Personal Trainer with a Master's degree in dance education and a specialty in pre- and postnatal exercise. She offers in-home, one-on-one fitness classes for women. Diane travels to Upper East Side and Upper West Side locations only.

Strollercize, Inc.

(800)Y-STROLL

www.strollercize.com

Created by Lizzy Trindade, Strollercize is a terrific way to meet other new moms, spend time with your baby, and have a great workout all at once. This is a fun, interactive fitness program incorporating strollers and babies into the new mother's workout. Pre- and postnatal classes are held in various parks and gyms throughout the city, and personal training programs are also offered. Workouts are safe, tough, and effective, and create a great atmosphere for both baby and mom. Strollercize offers 150 classes per month, year-round, throughout Manhattan. Discounted memberships are available. Call for locations and times; and check out workshops and weekly new mother gatherings, "Margarita Moms."

Vanderbilt YMCA

224 East 47th Street bet. Second
and Third avenues

756-9600

www.ymcanyc.org

The YMCA's Vanderbilt location has a forty-five-minute prenatal exercise class, which includes a combination of aerobics and stretching and toning exercises. Classes are held twice a week; an eight-week series is free for members and $130 for nonmembers. A physician's approval is required. Individual membership to the Y is $993 a year (which can be paid in monthly installments) with a one-time initiation fee of $125. Family memberships are also available.

YWCA

610 Lexington Avenue at 53rd Street

735-9750

www.ywcanyc.org

The YWCA offers a forty-minute Water Exercise for Pregnancy and Postpartum class twice a week, from 11:40 a.m. to 12:20 p.m. Mondays and Thursdays. The class is a combination of water aerobics and stretching. The price is $90 for an eight-class card, plus $60 for the annual YWCA membership. Individual classes are $10 for members, $15 for nonmembers. A doctor's note may be required.

Private Trainers

Here are four personal trainers who offer pre- and postnatal private training at your home, gym, or office: Jane Kornbluh, 677-6165; Ana Lerner, 355-3109; Debby Peress, 249-3972; and Diana Simkin 348-0208. Their fees range from $60 to $100 per hour.

yoga

There has been a huge yoga explosion since our first book. (Madonna's yoga practice throughout her pregnancies surely didn't hurt any.) But yoga is great exercise for pregnant women—aiding relaxation, maintaining flexibility, and providing an excellent way to work out without risking injury.

Many health clubs have yoga classes. If you have taken yoga before your pre-pregnant days and want to continue, do so. Make sure you tell your instructor you are expecting, however, and ask for alternatives that will be safer and more comfortable.

Yoga instructor Gayatri Martin tells us that prenatal yoga emphasizes the strengthening of pelvic floor muscles to get women ready for pregnancy and birth. Prenatal classes usually allow more time than traditional yoga for resting and relaxation. You'll learn breathing and postures that are helpful for birth and labor.

The following yoga instructors or studios specialize in pre- and postnatal yoga classes:

❊ Mary Ryan Barnes Yoga for Two

175 West 93rd Street at Amsterdam Avenue
666-2237
www.yogafortwo.com
Mary Barnes has created her own style of teaching called The Barnes Method, which combines anusara yoga, breath work, alignment, sound vibration, strength training, and therapeutics. Her prenatal yoga method also aids in the birthing process, helping women feel centered and strong during labor and delivery. Postpartum women can enjoy Mommy & Baby Yoga for Two™ classes, New Mom & Baby Yoga Sanctuary with mothering expert guests, and yoga with baby-sitting. (Pamela has been a student of Mary's for some time and believes she is truly terrific!)

❊ Beth Donnelly Caban

718-604-0104
www.yogabethbkny.com
email: yogabeth@earthlink.net
An integral yoga instructor and co-author of *New York's 50 Best Places to Keep Your Spirit*

Alive, Beth Donnelly Caban teaches pre- and postnatal yoga around New York. Beth teaches mostly in Brooklyn but will do private instruction. She teaches a yoga class for labor and delivery. Private classes are around $80 an hour. Call for more information.

❊ Integral Yoga Institute

227 West 13th Street
bet. Seventh and Eighth avenues
929-0586
www.iyiny.org
The Integral Yoga Institute offers a multitude of classes for all levels, including prenatal and postpartum yoga, at various times throughout the week. The prenatal class focuses on movements, postures, and practices especially beneficial to pregnant women. Soothing and relaxation practices are emphasized. Postpartum classes are for moms and newborns ages one month to one year, and include one hour of gentle stretching, chanting, breathing, and a half hour of sharing and discussion. Each class is ninety minutes. A single class is $13; ten classes are $115; and twenty classes are $220. Also there are classes for babies and toddlers up to eighteen months.

❊ Iyengar Yoga Institute of New York

150 West 22nd Street, 11th Floor
bet. Sixth and Seventh avenues
691-9642
www.iyengarnyc.org
Iyengar Yoga Institute offers prenatal, gentle, and restorative classes that focus on postures for the physical and psychological aspects of

women's health. Prices per class range from $15 to $20.

✳ Jivamukti Yoga Center

404 Lafayette Street, 3rd floor,
bet. Astor Place and East 4th Street
353-0214
853 Lexington Avenue, 2nd Floor,
bet. 64th and 65th streets
396-4200
www.jivamuktiyoga.com

The Jivamukti Yoga Center offers two classes for soon-to-be and new moms. Prenatal Yoga meets Mondays through Thursdays from 10 a.m. to 11:35 a.m. Jivamukti focuses on breathing, stretching, and strengthening, as well as adapting yoga postures to the needs of the changing pregnant body. Baby and Me, a postpartum class for moms and dads with babies six weeks to twelve months, meets on Mondays, Wednesdays, and Thursdays at 10 a.m. This class emphasizes postures, and is designed to realign the inner body and tone the abdominal muscles. Special postures are taught for infants, and the class addresses postpartum issues. Each class costs $17, and is available as a series.

✳ Gayatri Martin, RN
Choices for Childbirth

220 East 26th Street
725-1078

Gayatri, a registered nurse, has been a Certified Childbirth Educator and yoga teacher since 1988. Her private classes emphasize "discovering your strengths, feeling your flexibility, and

experiencing breath as the bridge between body, mind, baby, and heart." Gayatri is available for in-home instruction for a cost of $90 per hour.

✳ Mikelle Terson

37 West 76th Street
bet. Central Park West and Columbus Avenue
362-4288
www.yogablossom.com

Mikelle is available for private yoga instruction at your home for $175 per seventy-five-minute session.

✳ Be Yoga

Locations downtown, midtown, Upper East and Upper West sides
www.beyoga.com

Be Yoga evolved from Alan Finger's Yoga Zone studios in 2001, with co-owners Beverley Murphy and Bob Murphy. Alan Finger has been at the forefront of expanding yoga in the West and is considered one of the leading yogis. Alan founded Yoga Zone in 1990. Under the Yoga Zone™ name, Mr. Finger opened five studios, and created over fifty videos and a national TV show. He has been practicing and teaching for over forty years. All the teachers at Be Yoga have been trained to work with pregnant women. Senior instructors prepare women for the deep internal work of pregnancy and postpartum life, concentrating on breath and unique physical characteristics. Be Yoga offers prenatal yoga classes at most locations as well as age-appropriate yoga programs for babies five months to crawlers and kids ages three to teens. Log onto the Be Yoga website to get schedule information on the studio nearest your home or office.

✳ *Baby Om*

9 locations in Brooklyn and Manhattan;
call for the location nearest you
Karma Yoga (main location)
37 West 65th Street, 4th Floor
bet. Broadway and Central Park West
615-6935
www.babyom.com

A unique yoga experience for moms and their babies, parents bring baby and participate in a yoga class run by Sarah Perron or Laura Staton, the founders of Baby Om. Baby Om is a challenging yoga class designed to stretch and tone the postpartum mom, while providing a playful and stimulating atmosphere for baby. Baby Om also offers prenatal yoga and yoga for all stages of motherhood.

✳ *Prenatal Yoga Center*

251 West 72nd Street, Suite 2F
bet. Broadway and West End Avenue
362-2985
www.prenatalyogacenter.com

The Prenatal Yoga Center specializes in pre- and postnatal. Run by the dynamic Debra Flashenberg, this studio offers fabulous classes for pregnant/postnatal women, plus seminars and workshops on a variety of pregnancy/baby-related topics. The prenatal yoga classes help to strengthen your body and works toward alleviating many of the discomforts of pregnancy. The postnatal class helps women regain strength

and energy while providing a great opportunity to meet other new moms. Classes are purchased in eight-week sessions. (Pamela's friend Abby swears by the Pilates class here too!)

✳ *Elana Weiss*

917-882-1643
452-2922
www.freetobeyoga.com
email: freetobeyoga@yahoo.com

Elana Weiss is a private yoga instructor and special education teacher who has been teaching children and adults Hatha yoga for over five years. She can come to your apartment and work with you, your baby, or you and your baby together!

massage

Many pregnant women suffer from back pain and strain, especially during the later months. Why not get a massage?

A massage therapist should be licensed by New York State, certified in prenatal massage, or have experience working with pregnant women.

Communication with your therapist is critical. If you feel lightheaded, short of breath, or uncomfortable, let the practitioner know. Many women feel uncomfortable lying on their backs after the fourth month (remember, ACOG recommends that you do not lie on your back after this time), so prenatal massages are often given to a woman as she lies on her side with pillows between her legs. The Medical Massage Group has a special table with a cut-out middle so that you can lie on your stomach when you might be uncomfortable on your side.

Every massage therapist listed is licensed by the state of New York. Some specialize in prenatal massage, and many will come to your home for an additional fee. All work is by appointment only, so call ahead.

❋ *Carapan**
5 West 16th Street bet. Fifth and Sixth avenues
633-6220
www.carapan.com
Want a vacation right in the heart of the city? Try one of Pamela's favorite places. Carapan is a Zen-like massage center, with some practitioners experienced in prenatal massage. The atmosphere here is sublime. Fees are $100 for an hour and $135 for ninety minutes.

❋ *Laura Favin, LMT, LCSW*
220 West 71st Street, Suite 2A
bet. West End Avenue and Riverside Drive
917-209-6534
501-0606
Laura has been a Licensed Massage Therapist, specializing in massage for pregnant women and new moms, for over eighteen years. She charges $85 for a one-hour massage, $140 if she travels to your home or office. She also teaches infant massage—a lovely way to bond with your new child.

❋ *The Quiet Touch*
317 West 35th Street
bet. Eighth and Ninth avenues
246-0008
800-946-2772
www.massageinc.com

The Quiet Touch is a national service that provides a licensed, insured, and fully equipped massage therapist at your door within a few hours. It has specialists in all types of massage, including prenatal. Massages are $120 per hour; membership packages are available for a discounted rate, and there is a 10-percent discount for first-time clients.

❋ *Wellpath*
1100 Madison Avenue at 83rd Street
737-9604
www.thewellpath.com
Wellpath approaches women's medical health with holistic and Western techniques in order to treat women, especially pregnant women, for various health issues. It offers photo rejuvenation, laser hair removal, Epicurean facials, and endermologie, the process that reduces cellulite and increases blood circulation. It has a private Pilates studio and medical consultations with Dr. James Heskett are also available.

❋ *Mother Massage and More*
Janet Markowitz
108 East 16th Street, Suite 401
bet. Union Square East and Irving Place
533-3188
Elaine Stillerman, a licensed massage therapist since 1978, began her pioneering work with expectant women in 1980. She is the author of Mother Massage: A Handbook for Relieving the Discomforts of Pregnancy and The Encyclopedia of Bodywork, and she also developed the course "Mother Massage®: Massage During Pregnancy," which certifies massage

therapists and childbirth educators in prenatal massage. Now Janet Markowitz has assumed the Mother Massage mantle, offering prenatal and postpartum massage therapy (using the bodyCushion™ system for moms-to-be), baby massage classes, and private labor support classes for partners. Each hour massage is around $100.

❋ *The Medical Massage Group**

328 East 75th Street, Suite 3
bet. First and Second avenues
472-4772
www.medicalmassagegroup.com
The Medical Massage Group is run by Donna and Harvey Manger-Weil. The practice is mostly pre- and postpartum medical massage and staffed with massage therapists. It has specially designed massage tables for pregnant women: tables that have a hole in the center so pregnant women can lie down comfortably and their stomachs are supported by adjustable slings. We highly recommend this group of licensed physical therapists. Kelly has had massages with both Donna and Harvey and they are superb!

❋ *Prenatal Massage Center*

123 West 79th Street, Suite LL2
330-6846
www.prenatalmassagecenter.com
The Prenatal Massage Center is run by Anne Heckheimer, a New York–licensed massage therapist, who has specialized in prenatal and postpartum massage for over five years. After receiving her massage license, Anne became

additionally certified as a prenatal and labor massage therapist through the Mother Massage® method of prenatal and postpartum massage therapy.

nutrition

You know that good nutrition is a critical part of producing a healthy baby, and there are many books available addressing this subject. Two of the best are: *What to Expect When You're Expecting*, the pregnant woman's bible, which has an excellent section called the "Best Odds Diet," with guidelines on how to eat every day; and *What to Eat When You're Expecting*. Your OB or CNM should talk to you about nutrition, but if he or she doesn't, bring it up yourself.

If you are underweight, overweight, diabetic, or need extra help managing your diet, you can consult a nutritionist to set up a diet that meets your needs. Weight Watchers also offers a healthy plan for overweight pregnant women. You might want to keep them in mind for after the pregnancy, too . . . We sure did.

Eating Right While You're Pregnant

What you should know about nutrition during your pregnancy:

❋ *Eat regularly and well.* This is no time to diet. You will gain weight, and most obstetricians today say a gain of 25 to 35 pounds or more is normal. Increase your calorie intake by about 300 calories a day during the last two trimesters, as you will need more energy during this time.

✳ *Eat healthy foods.* That means ample daily servings of grains (cereal, whole-grain bread, crackers), fruits, vegetables (steamed are best), protein (eggs, meat, fish, peanut butter), and calcium (milk, cheese, yogurt, tofu).

✳ *Avoid junk food.* When you want sugar, reach for fresh fruit, which will also help you avoid the ubiquitous affliction of pregnancy: constipation.

✳ *Drink water.* Your core body temperature is higher than normal when you are pregnant and you need to take in at least two quarts of liquid a day, especially before, during, and after exercise.

✳ *Do not drink alcohol.*

✳ *Don't drink caffeinated beverages* (coffee, tea, colas) during your first trimester, and restrict intake to one cup a day after that. Caffeine reaches the baby through the placenta.

✳ *Listen to your body.* Those infamous cravings for pickles and peanut butter may have a basis in physiology. Your body may need a little extra salt.

The following nutritionists have worked with pregnant women. Initial consultations cost around $125, with follow-up visits ranging from $50 to $85. You can also call the New York State Dietetic Association for certified dietitian nutritionists (CDNs) in your area at 691-7906. Or, send a self-addressed, stamped envelope to the American Board of Nutrition (1675 University Boulevard, University of Alabama, Birmingham, Alabama 35294-3360; 205-975-5564; email: joness@shrp.uab.edu). It can provide you with a listing of board-certified nutritionists with MDs or PhDs in your area.

Nutritionists

✳ *Joanne Diamond, RD*
Women's Health Beth Israel
844-8620

✳ *Allyson Mechaber*
718-797-0310
201-615-6143
email: AMechaber@nyc.rr.com
Allyson specializes in pre- and postnatal nutrition as well as nutrition for children. Allyson comes to your home and works with you one-on-one. She will look through your pantry and offer healthy suggestions (she will even take you food shopping). She will also advise you on a vitamin program.

✳ *Lauren Slayton*
Food Trainers
769-4300
www.foodtrainers.net
A mom herself, Lauren knows the issues facing pre- and postnatal women—and her practice has many of them. For her prenatal clients, she does a consultation in the third trimester going over all the things to keep in the house and stock when the new baby arrives. She of course sees many postnatal women who want to get back to their pre-pregnancy weight too. Her practice has recently started Family Foodtraining where they see Mom or Dad and discuss a family meal plan complete with recipes/items for each family member. Lauren will also send weekly care packages of "afternoon ammunition" to your home or office complete with healthy low carb/high-fiber snacks.

Pamela speaks from experience in saying that Lauren is a terrific nutritionist who truly gets results!

✣ Bonnie Taub-Dix, MA, RD, CDN

Practices in New York City and Long Island:
737-8536
516-295-0377
Bonnie is the spokesperson for the American Dietetic Association, the organization that helps people to eat in a healthy and realistic way.

Food Delivery

If you are too tired to cook and prepare your own food (and your baby's food when the time comes) there are solutions besides that take-out Chinese menu by the phone. For (an often high) price the following outfits will cook and deliver your food to your door fresh and healthy.

✣ Baby Time Chef

592-3077
www.babytimechefs.com
Baby Time Chef's personal chef service offers healthy, home-cooked meals to enjoy at your leisure. A week or more of meals from this professional service is a popular shower or baby gift for new parents. New parents also can treat themselves to these great meals by the week or month. Baby Time Chefs will do the shopping, cooking, and clean up in your home too.

✣ Mothers & Menus

646-522-9591
www.mothersandmenus.com

Mothers & Menus is a food delivery service that customizes organic, gourmet meals around your nutritional needs and food cravings. The goal is to provide increased energy and optimum nutrition for your postnatal needs. The one-week cost for three meals per day and one snack is approximately $500. One new mom that we know found out that her baby was allergic to wheat and dairy, and Mothers & Menus was able to prepare her great food to eat that wouldn't upset that baby's allergies.

✣ Evie's Organic Edibles

544-2122
www.eviesorganicedibles.com
Evie provides homemade baby food for babies 4 to 11 months. She is a new mom who had a hard time finding healthy food for her colicky child, and began a business by cooking food for her own child out of her kitchen. She shops and cooks for her clients in their home and will also deliver her healthy food to moms all over New York City. She charges $45 per hour plus the price of groceries.

home organizers

You may be feeling overwhelmed at this point with all of the "stuff" you are getting for your new baby. With a typical city apartment, it is often difficult to find room to store all of your gear and still have the baby's room be tidy and organized. A home organization specialist may be the answer. We think highly of Sonya Weisshappel, who is a new mom herself and well-suited to the challenges of new parents.

Sonya Weisshappel

Seriatim, Inc.

115 Central Park West, Suite 2G

877-3267

The owner of Seriatim (a professional organization firm), Sonya Weisshappel is a new mom herself. She has specific services that are particularly beneficial for new moms everywhere. Seriatim can prepare a room for the new baby, sort out gifts from the baby shower, and organize toys and clothes. Another terrific service is photo album organization and upkeep.

spas for baby and you

In Manhattan, there are spas everywhere but now there are two that we can recommend taking your baby to and that were created specifically with baby and mommy in mind.

The Gravity Fitness & Spa

at the Le Parker Meridien Hotel

119 West 56th Street

708-7340

This spa can supply guests with special diapers for the pools and cribs. The postnatal massage is $110 and is great to help restore energy to sleep-deprived moms. It's one of the few New York City spas that allow you to bring your infant in and take a day of relaxation. For those who want a quick way to relax, the Water Babies 101 tutorial for kids and parents in the indoor pool is great and it's only $75.

The Greenhouse Spa

Arlington, Texas

817-640-4000

www.greenhousespa.com

The Greenhouse Spa in Texas began offering its now twice-a-year Baby and Me week two years ago, and it has proven to be quite popular. For $3,850, new mothers can take their infants to a postnatal yoga class, get a daily fifty-minute Swedish massage and three European facials, and listen to lectures about children's health and development. The spa provides nannies to watch babies while mom has treatments.

Kidville, NY

163 East 84th Street

848-9415

It's the place families can go with small children for haircuts, shopping, and classes all under one roof. Kidville is the creation of Shari Misher Stenzler, who decided to establish this everything-for-mommy-and-baby emporium shopping center/combination "Y" in a great Upper East Side location. It has an indoor playground so kids can play, parenting classes, exercise classes, and Mommy and Me programs! You can pay as you go or join for a year. Call for more information.

from healthcare
to day care

Sometime toward the end of your pregnancy, you should begin searching for the people who will help care for your little one. This is a toughie. The very idea of entrusting your baby to another person can be terrifying. You'll feel more comfortable with the idea if you take the time to do the necessary research—scout around, ask questions, make phone calls, pay visits.

First, you will need to find a pediatrician. Your goal is to find one you and your husband or partner connect with and who can provide your baby with the best available medical care. But, that is just the beginning. You may wish to hire a baby nurse or doula (see page 50) to help out in your home the first few days or weeks after your baby is born. After that, your childcare needs depend on what else is going on in your life. If you are returning to a job after a maternity leave, you will probably require full-time help, either in your home or elsewhere. If you work at home or are involved in activities that will take you away from your child a period of time each day or week, you will need childcare part-time. Also, if you simply want to get out of the house now and then, sans baby, you should have one or two reliable baby-sitters to call upon. If you have family nearby, you may be lucky enough to have occasional free baby-sitting come your way.

We have each changed nannies several times since the first edition was published in 1997. The transitions were difficult both for our kids and ourselves, but we learned a valuable lesson: the most important person in your child's life is you, the parent. Kids eventually adjust to a new nanny or caregiver. That said, get the best nanny you can find, and keep looking until you find that person.

In this chapter, we'll show you how to find reliable childcare. To help get the ball rolling, we'll give you names and numbers and our impressions.

pediatricians

You should begin looking for a pediatrician during the last few months of your pregnancy. Your baby's doctor will be noted on the record form that your obstetrician will send to the hospital about a month prior to your due date, and the pediatrician will then come by the hospital to examine your baby before the two of you are released.

Here's how to find a pediatrician, and what you should look for:

❉ Ask your obstetrician for a recommendation. If your doctor lives in the city, whom does she use for her own children? This is how Pamela found her pediatrician.

❉ Ask relatives, neighbors, and friends about pediatricians they use.

❉ Call any of the hospitals in the city, and ask for a referral from the pediatric department.

❉ Go to the New York Public Library and look up listings in the American Academy of Pediatrics directory. *New York* magazine's yearly edition of "The Best Doctors in New York" is a great resource as well.

❉ Consider location. Your newborn will be going to the doctor often, and having a pediatrician with an office near your home is practical, especially during an emergency or nasty weather.

❉ Consider whether you place importance on the doctor's age, type of practice (group, partnership, or solo practitioner), or gender (some parents prefer to have a pediatrician the same sex as their baby).

Once you have the names of two or three pediatricians who sound promising, set up a consultation. Most will agree to make appointments in the early evening after regular office hours. Good doctors should be willing to take the time to meet with you and your husband or partner. Kelly requested consultations with five pediatricians. One did not conduct prenatal interviews; the other four were happy to meet with her and her husband to answer their questions and give them a brief office tour. It was time-consuming, but Kelly has been very happy with her pediatrician, and has never had to change. (If your prospective pediatrician is part of a group practice, it's a good idea to meet with most of the doctors; chances are each one will be treating your child at one time or another.)

Prepare a list of questions in advance and write down the doctors' answers. That way, you can compare pediatricians and discuss everything with your husband/partner, who may not be with you at each consultation. And, while you are waiting, take a look around the waiting room.

❋ Is it child friendly, with enough toys, pictures, and books to keep a baby or toddler busy during the wait to see the doctor?

❋ Is the receptionist friendly, or does she seem curt and harried?

❋ If you're visiting during office hours, ask parents in the waiting room about their experiences with the doctor; have they been positive?

❋ Find out how long they typically wait to see the doctor. A forty-five minute wait with a sick toddler is no fun.

❋ Do sick and healthy children wait in the same waiting room? Kelly's pediatrician has eight

Top Ten Things to Look For in a Caregiver

1. Track record and references (strong ones!). How long does she stay in a job?
2. The ability to speak and read English or your native language.
3. Personality—it's hard to be around someone who never smiles.
4. Experience—especially with children the same age as your own.
5. Honesty—this is fundamental to any relationship between employer and employee, and particularly in regard to someone hired to watch your children.
6. Patience.
7. Positive attitude.
8. Nice appearance.
9. Reliability and responsibility.
10. Instinct—trust your gut.

examination rooms, and babies under one year old automatically go into one of these. The office tries to keep only healthy children in the waiting area.

❋ Is there an on-site lab for quick blood tests, earwave sonograms, etc.?

When you sit down with the doctor, be sure to ask the following questions:

❋ How does the doctor answer parents' nonemergency calls throughout the day? Is there a call-in hour or does the doctor take calls all day and return them intermittently between patients? Is there a nurse who can answer questions?

- How are emergencies handled? Is the doctor affiliated with a nearby hospital? Is the practice affiliated with more than one hospital? (A good pediatrician will meet you at the hospital or have a specialist meet you there in case of an emergency.)
- How does the pediatrician feel about breastfeeding? (Whether or not you choose to breastfeed, you will want a pediatrician who is supportive and encouraging of your decision.)
- What are the pediatrician's views on circumcision, nutrition, immunizations, and preventive medicine? (It is important that you and your doctor are in sync on most of these issues.)
- If the pediatrician is a solo practitioner, who handles phone calls when she is on vacation?

If you don't feel rushed during the consultation, and the pediatrician is patient with you, these are good indicators of how the doctor will be with your baby. Again, don't be afraid to ask any questions. Even after you select a pediatrician don't be afraid to change. We've had many friends do just that, and it is worth it! There are hundreds of pediatricians in New York, so just persevere. Like all aspects of childcare, the right one for you is out there.

baby nurses/doulas

Immediately after the birth of your baby, you may wish to have a baby nurse or doula.

Baby nurses usually come the day you bring the baby home and live with you in your apartment for a week or two or longer. An in-home nurse works twenty-four hours a day, seven days a week. She cares for the baby, gets up in the middle of the night to change and feed him or bring him to you for breastfeeding, and generally allows you to sleep late and rest up. Baby nurses are expensive, costing from $125 to $180 a day. Some live-out and work for shorter periods (not a full day).

A doula comes to your home for a few hours each day and almost always lives out. She helps and pampers you: she does the grocery shopping, laundry, and fixes meals, so you have more time with your baby. She may also assist you in taking care of your baby by bathing or changing him, and she should be able to answer questions regarding breastfeeding.

When you hire a doula, typically you buy a set block of visits or hours with a fifteen-hour minimum. Each visit is at least three hours, and costs approximately $21 to $30 an hour.

The best way to find a baby nurse or doula is through a trusted friend who has used one herself. Or call one of the many agencies that has baby nurse divisions. Kelly hired her nurse, Olga, through an agency and was extremely pleased. Olga had been taking care of babies for more than twenty years, and her references were impeccable. So good, in fact, that one family kept her for five years! Pamela hired a baby nurse that she found through a friend, and she is so great, she continues to work for the family one day a week.

An agency will send three or four candidates for you to interview while you are pregnant. You may then reserve the baby nurse or doula of your choice, and the agency will try not to place her for two weeks around your due date. If you are late or early, the nurse you've requested may be on another job, but this rarely happens. Agencies are very good at monitoring their baby nurses' schedules.

Baby nurses get booked way in advance, so plan early. Kelly started asking friends for recommendations when she was five months pregnant, and three of the names she received were already booked.

Of course, your mother or mother-in-law may offer to come stay with you. If you feel comfortable with a family member living in and helping out, great. However, we've found that many new parents prefer to hire short-term professional help, which allows them to get the rest they need without having to impose on—or be nice to—a relative.

The following is a list of baby nurse and doula agencies in the New York area.

❋ *Absolute Best Care*
850 Seventh Avenue at 55th Street
481-5705
www.absolutebestcare.com

❋ *All Metro Health Care*
50 Broadway
Lynbrook, NY 11563
516-887-1200

❋ *Beyond Birth (Doulas)*
1992 Commerce Street, Suite 40
Yorktown Heights, NY 10598
914-245-2229
888-907-BABY

❋ *Bohne's Baby Nursing*
16 East 79th Street, Suite G4
879-7920

❋ *Doula Care*
Ruth Callahan
70 West 93rd Street
749-6613
www.doulacare.com
e-mail: Callahan@webspan.net

❋ *Fox Agency*
30 East 60th Street, Suite 904
753-2686

❋ *Frances Stuart Agency*
1220 Lexington Avenue, Suite 2B
439-9222
www.francesstewartagency.com

❋ *In a Family Way*
124 West 79th Street, Suite 9B
877-8112
www.inafamilyway.com
email: christinekealy@kealy.com

❋ *Mother Nurture*
Doula Service
P.O. Box 284
Glen Oaks, NY 11004

718-631-BABY (718-631-2229)
www.mothernurture.com
e-mail: doulacomp@aol.com

nannies

Hiring someone to look after your child while you're at work or away is stressful and nerve-racking. You want someone who is good, kind, smart, honest, sober, reliable, loves kids, knows infant CPR, bakes cookies, and is going to think your baby is the most adorable child she's ever seen. You want another you.

Of course, you won't find another you, but if you're determined and keep your ears open, you will locate someone who will be an affectionate, caring, responsible childcare provider for your youngster.

You may want a nanny who lives with you or one who comes to your home each morning and leaves each evening. You may need this person's help on a part-time or full-time basis. There are several ways to go about finding her. As is true for so many services, word of mouth is the best place to start. Ask friends who have childcare whether their nannies have friends looking for work. When we were in search of help, we stopped nannies in the park, talked to mothers and nannies at the classes we took with our children, and looked at bulletin board notices in child- and religious-oriented institutions and at our pediatricians' offices. Many schools as well as the Parent's League also post nanny information on their bulletin boards.

If you get nowhere by word of mouth, try the newspapers. Many parents have successfully found childcare by advertising in newspapers or by answering an ad. We'll show you how to do that shortly. Finally, a number of agencies specialize in nanny placement. We list those agencies as well.

We cannot sufficiently stress the importance of checking references and thoroughly questioning candidates. On more than one occasion, we have heard stories of falsified references in which nannies listed friends or relatives instead of former employers. Toward the end of this section, we'll give you a list of some of the most important questions to ask your future nanny. You may also want to read *How to Hire a Nanny* by Elaine S. Pelletier. This step-by-step guide helps you through the nanny search. Another excellent resource, written by two experienced British moms, is *The Good Nanny Guide* by Charlotte Breese and Hilaire Gomer. Although geared to the English nanny system, it is full of practical advice and guidelines.

Prices for nannies varies according to experience, education, checkable references, and legal status, but start at around $500 a week. For an experienced, educated caregiver, you can expect to pay as much as $600 or $700 per week.

Newspaper Advertisements

Placing a classified ad can be an excellent way to find a nanny. The *Irish Echo*, the *Irish Voice*, and *The New York Times* are popular nanny-finding papers. A number of newspapers are published for various nationalities and many nannies look in them for jobs. Explore them if you would prefer a nanny from a specific country, would like your child to learn a foreign language, or if your spouse is from another country.

When you place an ad, be as specific as possible. If you must have a nonsmoker, live-in help, or someone with a driver's license, say so. If you need someone to work on Saturdays or stay late in the evening, state it. Check the classified sections to see examples of help-wanted ads, or follow the sample we've provided here:

Upper East Side Nanny Needed.

Live-in nanny needed for a two-year-old boy. Light housekeeping, shopping, and errands. Must have two years experience with toddlers and excellent checkable New York references. Nonsmoker. Must swim, drive, and cook. Must have legal working papers. Willing to travel with family. M-F, weekends off. Own room, TV-VCR, A/C. Call 555-5555.

When Kelly ran an ad similar to this one in two newspapers three weeks before Christmas, her phone began ringing at 6 a.m. the Wednesday morning the *Irish Echo* came out and she had received sixty calls by 11 a.m.

Interview candidates on the phone before you bring them to your home. Tell them about the job, find out what they are looking for, and ask about their past work experience. Screen them carefully; it will save you time later. Kelly needed a caregiver who could work on Saturdays and travel with the family, and she was able to eliminate a number of candidates who could not fill those requirements over the phone.

We recommend making a list of the three most appealing and the three least appealing aspects of your job. Discuss them with the applicant over the phone. Start with the three worst aspects: she must arrive at 7:30 every morning, she must baby-sit three nights a week, and she will be expected to work on Saturdays. If the applicant is still interested and if you are pleased with her responses to your key questions, proceed from there with an interview in your home or office.

The following four newspapers are reliable and frequently used. When you call, check their deadlines. Ads can be phoned or faxed, and can be paid with a credit card.

❋ Irish Echo

14 East 47th Street, 6th floor
New York, NY 10017
686-1266, ext. 112 (fax: 683-6455)
www.irishecho.com
The *Irish Echo* comes out once a week on Wednesdays. Ads must be submitted before 2 p.m. the Friday before you run the ad. Three lines cost $21 and each additional line is $7.

❋ Irish Voice

875 Avenue of the Americas, Suite 2100
New York, NY 10001
684-3366, ext. 22 (fax: 244-3344)
www.irishvoice.com
email: classifieds@irishvoice.com
The Irish Voice comes out Wednesdays and accepts ads up to the previous Monday. Thirty words cost approximately $38; that's four lines approximately.

❋ The New York Times

229 West 43rd Street
New York, NY 10036
354-3900
www.nytimes.com
Ad rates vary per day. Call for details. The deadline is 5 p.m. Friday for Sunday's paper.

Deadline for a weekday ad is 1 p.m. the day before the ad is to run.

❉ The Polish Daily News

Contact person: Nowy Dziennik
333 West 38th Street
New York, NY 10018
594-2266, ext. 31 (fax: 594-2374)

This daily paper (except Sundays) is written in Polish, but many of the classifieds are in English. Ads must be submitted by noon to run in the next day's paper. A thirty-five word ad running for one week costs $50; for Monday through Wednesday, $30; on Thursday, $12; on Friday, $13; and on Saturday, $18. For an additional $5, your ad is translated into Polish.

Agencies

On one hand, good word-of-mouth and a sterling reputation keeps a service business alive. On the other hand, the more people they place, the more money agencies make; high turnover is oddly beneficial to their business. This is contrary to what you are looking for—someone who will stay with you a long time. So, a few words of caution when using an agency. Although agencies claim they check references, many have been known to send a candidate on an interview with skimpy or weak references. Some have never even met the candidate face to face. Be on guard if, for example, a nanny's previous employer has moved and now has an unlisted phone number somewhere in Florida, or if the applicant hands you a hand-written letter of reference with grammatically incorrect sentences and misspelled words.

Although we can't personally endorse any of the agencies listed here, we know people who have found good help through them. We suggest you read the forty-two-page report on placement agencies entitled "Who's Watching Our Kids?" published by the Department of Consumer Affairs. You can write to the Department of Consumer Affairs, 42 Broadway, New York, NY 10004, and request a copy. The report lists fifty agencies investigated by the department and any violations filed against them. You can also call the office, at 487-4444, to check whether a particular agency is licensed and whether it has received any complaints, or to file a complaint yourself.

❉ A Choice Nanny

850 Seventh Avenue, Suite 305
246-KIDS

❉ Absolute Best Care

850 Seventh Avenue at 55th Street
481-5705
www.absolutebestcare.com

This is a well-run agency that specializes in placing families with highly qualified nannies in New York, New Jersey, and Connecticut. Absolute Best Care's goal is to match families with caregivers who are highly qualified, capable and sensitive to the needs of children. It also offers nanny training classes and workshops.

❉ Best Domestic Placement

10 East 39th Street at Fifth Avenue, Suite 1118
683-3060 (fax: 683-3239)
www.bestdomesticplmt.com
email: bestdomesticplmt@aol.com

Domestic Job Picks
545 Fifth Avenue, Suite 309
986-2102
www.domesticjobpicks.com

Fox Agency
30 East 60th Street, Suite 904
753-2686

Frances Stuart Agency
1220 Lexington Avenue, Suite 2B
439-9222
www.francesstewartagency.com

Greenhouse Agency
55 West 39th Street bet. Fifth and Sixth avenues
889-7705 (fax: 889-3673)

The London Agency
767 Lexington Avenue
755-5064

My Child's Best Friend
35 West 35th Street at Sixth Avenue
396-4090
email: mychild98@aol.com

Nannies Plus
P.O. Box 603
Chester, NY 10918
800-752-0078
845-469-5130
www.nanniesplus.com
email: staff@nanniesplus.com

Pavilion Agency
15 East 40th, Suite 400
889-6609
www.pavilionagency.com
email: seth@pavilionagency.com

Professional Nannies Institute
501 Fifth Avenue, Suite 908
692-9510
www.profnannies.com
email: pni@msn.com

Robin Kellner Agency
2 West 45th Street
997-4151
www.robinkellner.com
email: robin@robinkellner.com

Sitter City
213 West Institute Place, Suite 410
Chicago, IL 60610
888-211-9749
www.sittercity.com

Sittercity.com is America's largest database for baby-sitters and nannies. It has over 50,000 caregivers in fifteen major markets (including New York, of course), and provides an alternative to agencies or message boards as a way for parents and caregivers to contact each other and set up childcare jobs. All of its sitters are over the age of seventeen, and are skilled in areas like pre-med, early childhood education, CPR, first aid, disability, and more. Most sitters are college students, but there are also nannies and other childcare providers posted. Membership costs $39.99 for the first month,

$5 each month after that. Parents pay the sitters themselves on an hourly basis. Sittercity.com does not screen its applicants, so you must check references carefully.

- ***Town and Country***
  250 West 57th Street
  245-8400

The Interview

Nothing is as important as the interview to determine whether a candidate is the right person to take care of your little one. Be conscious of the atmosphere you create. Are you interviewing potential nannies at your office, in your formal living room, in the playroom, family room, or at the kitchen table? Are you looking for someone to join the family, or will this person be more of an employee with a formal working arrangement?

Pamela always likes to interview nannies with her husband present. It's useful to get a second opinion, and to have another person asking questions you might forget to ask. It's also good to have your child nearby so you can see how the potential candidate interacts with him.

Here's our suggested list of interview questions:

- Tell me about yourself. Where are you from? Where did you grow up? How many brothers and sisters do you have? Did your mom and dad work?
- Why do you want to be a nanny? What is it you like about being a nanny?
- What previous childcare experiences do you have? Tell me about those jobs.
- What was a typical day like? What did your duties/responsibilities include? (Look for someone who has held a childcare position similar to the one you are offering. If she cooked and cleaned on the last job and you are looking for light cooking and cleaning, she probably won't be upset if you ask her to grill a chicken breast or wipe off the kitchen counter.)
- How many children did you take care of in your previous positions? How old were they?
- Do you have children of your own?
- What did you like best about your previous jobs? What did you like least?
- Why did you leave your last job(s)?
- Did Mrs. X work? How did you two interact on a daily basis?
- Do you smoke?
- Do you have CPR or first-aid training?
- Can you stay late during the week or work on weekends if necessary?
- Describe an emergency or stressful situation in your past job? How did you handle it?
- What are your child-rearing philosophies or views on discipline? Do you believe in spanking and time-outs?
- What are your interests? What do you like to do when you're not working?
- Do you have any health restrictions or dietary preferences I should know about?
- What are you looking for in a family?
- Would you travel with the family if needed?
- Do you know your way around the city?
- Do you drive, swim, bicycle (or whatever else is important to you)?
- Do you like to read? What is your favorite

children's book? (Some nannies can't read well in English.)

* When could you start? What are your salary requirements?

Checking References

Checking references with previous employers can be one of the most challenging parts of finding childcare. Who are you calling? How can you be sure the name you have been given is not a candidate's friend or relative? And then, some people just aren't very talkative on the telephone. They reveal very little that can help you reach a decision.

Use your common sense and intuition; be open and friendly; and identify yourself in detail. For example: "Hello Mrs. X, this is Mrs. Y, and I am calling to check a reference on Susan Jones, who told me she worked for you. My husband and I live in New York City on East 53rd Street and we have a three-year-old daughter." Tell her a little about your family. This will help break the ice and allow you to ask about her family and work situations. It's important to know the kind of household in which your potential nanny has worked, because it may be very different from your own. If Mrs. X had a staff of three, and Susan had no household duties, she may not be happy in your home if you ask her to cook, clean, and do the laundry. Be realistic.

Here are some questions you may want to ask:

* How did you meet Susan? (agency, friend, ad?)
* How long was Susan with you?
* Why did she leave?
* How many children do you have? How old are they?

* Do you work? What do you do? Were either you or your husband home during the day or was Susan pretty much on her own?
* What were Susan's responsibilities?
* What were her hours?
* Was there ever an emergency or difficult situation that Susan had to handle on her own?
* How would you describe her overall personality and attitude?
* Was it easy to communicate with her? Did she give you daily feedback on your children? Did she take direction/instruction well?
* Did she cook, clean, drive, run errands, swim, iron (or whatever you need most)?
* Did you trust her? Did you find her reliable and honest?
* How did your children like her? Did you like her?
* Would you hire her again?

Several agencies verify references on nannies. Documented Reference Check (800-742-3316 or 909-629-0317, www.badreferences.com) investigates employment references and sends a report to you for $87.95. American International Security in Virginia (276-346-3400) charges $95, for which you obtain a motor vehicle record, a New York City criminal convictions record, and a social security number track report. A credit check is an additional $35, and other services are available, including National Criminal Check Only, $150; National Criminal Check with DMV and SSN, $195; and Criminal Check in a Foreign Country, $95.

When the Nanny Starts

After you have found the right person, it is important to watch how she and your baby and/or children interact in order to make sure they are comfortable with each other. It's a good idea to have prepared a typewritten list of duties as well as what is expected of the nanny on a daily basis aside from childcare, such as cooking, cleaning, laundry, and grocery shopping. Be specific. Sit down and go over everything again within the first few days to make sure she understands and accepts the responsibilities of the job. Set a date for a follow-up meeting in two weeks to discuss how things are going, what's working well, and what is not.

We are big on giving the nanny a "trial" period. We try her out for a week or so and see if it's a match hiring her full time. If you are going back to work, it is a good idea to have your new nanny begin at least two weeks before you start. This will give you an opportunity to observe her with your baby and to show her around your neighborhood. Take her to your supermarket, dry cleaner (or to whatever other places she may need to visit while working for your family), as well as to the pediatrician's office so that she can feel comfortable going there without you, if necessary.

You may also want your nanny to have a physical examination. Certainly, inquire about her health and vaccinations. Depending on where your nanny is from and how long she has been in this country, she may not be vaccinated against measles, mumps and rubella, or chicken pox. If she's not, arrange with your doctor for her to get these shots.

Once a nanny is on the job, you may want to monitor her activities in your absence. Parents who have had to hire a caregiver very quickly and have little time to train and supervise may find that this service provides peace of mind.

Care Check, created by Lori Berke and Gail Cohen, offers videotaping as a learning tool for better communication between you and your caregiver. Care Check has state-of-the-art equipment and will rent or sell any customized surveillance system you need. A two-day video surveillance rental costs around $350. Care Check can also help you with the prescreening process, including interview techniques and questions, and for $200 will conduct a check on your applicant, confirming previous employment, education, passport, and other records. International credit checks may cost more. Care Check can be reached at 360-6640; 1056 Fifth Avenue, New York, NY 10028.

Babywatch is a service that has been in business for over twelve years. The New York provider is Lori Shecter. With a wide variety of equipment available, Babywatch will install a monitoring device in your home to evaluate your nanny's performance. The cost is approximately $399 for a five-day rental, or you can purchase the alternative digital, hardwire, or wireless equipment. You can reach Babywatch at 889-1494 or e-mail lorishecter@yahoo.com.

The following is a list of additional companies that provide video surveillance and other nanny-related services. In addition, backyard swimming pools or outdoor areas can be monitored too. Some companies now have remote monitoring packages that allow parents to view their children via the Internet.

❊ *Care Check*
1056 Fifth Avenue
360-6640

(800) 624-2930
www.carecheck.net
email: loriberke@nyc.rr.com

❖ *Homestep*
760-5959
(516) 375-8492
www.homestepsafety.com
email: info@homestepsafety.com

❖ *Kid View*
(800) 624-2930 (Code 00)
www.kidview.com
email: info@kidview.com

❖ *Mind Your Business*
P.O. Box 4434
Warren, NJ 07040
888-869-2462 (fax: 732-302-9104)
www.mybinc.com
email: mcagnetta@mybinc.com

Taxes and Insurance

Remember that once you hire a nanny, you have become an employer. In a 1995 *New York* magazine article, CPA Stuart Rosenblum, provided a list of responsibilities as an employer. You must:

1. Apply for an employer identification number with the IRS using form SS-4 (www.irs.gov).
2. File Schedule 1040H (a tax form that replaced Form 942). Employers should report wages paid to household workers or nannies on their income tax returns. Schedule H, which is filed with your 1040, simplifies the work of calculat-

ing social security, Medicare, and federal income taxes.
3. Give your nanny a W-2 form, listing total wages and taxes paid, by January 31.
4. File a W-3, a summary of all your W-2s, by February 28. File quarterly and annual state reports.

Other forms to fill out include federal unemployment and state unemployment tax forms. These cover anyone who earns more than $100 a quarter. The federal unemployment tax form 940 can be obtained from the IRS; the New York State Labor Department supplies state unemployment forms.

Other areas of concern are compensation and disability policies. If you employ a childcare provider for more than forty hours a week, you should buy a workers' compensation and disability policy. These start at around $300. Call the State Insurance Fund for more information (312-9000). The IRS publishes two booklets to help employers through this maze: "Employment Taxes for Household Employers" (Book 926) and "What You Need to Know If You Hire Domestic Help" (Book 27). To receive these booklets, call the N.Y.S. Department of Taxation and Finance at (800) 462-8100. Call the New York State Department of Labor (265-2700) to request the "Employer's Guide to Unemployment Insurance." The best phone number at the moment for the IRS is (800) 829-4933.

au pairs

Hiring an au pair is a childcare option many parents find practical and economical.

Au pairs come to the United States from various countries, but they are usually European. They can remain in this country legally for one year and work a forty-five-hour week. Generally, an au pair has a weeklong orientation just after she arrives in this country, and she takes one academic course during her stay. In addition, she is provided with support counselors and a health plan by her umbrella organization.

Au pairs are not permitted to care for babies younger than three months, and must have two hundred hours of childcare experience to care for children younger than age 2. Current wages for an au pair are $139.50 per week plus room and board. Families also pay $500 toward academic coursework for the au pair. Au pairs can work forty-five hours per week, no more than ten hours per day. Always interview a prospective au pair over the phone or in person if possible. Most agencies provide background information on several candidates.

Au pairs tend to be inexperienced childcare providers. They most often work in homes with stay-at-home mothers. They are not allowed to remain alone with children overnight, so an au pair is not a good option for parents who travel. Pamela's friend Margot has employed close to half a dozen au pairs in seven years. She was extremely satisfied with one out of six; the rest were mediocre to decent, but none fabulous. One drawback with au pairs is that they are young, and many of them want an active social life. In New York, that is not always compatible with childcare.

If you are interested in an au pair, contact the following agencies:

❊ *Au Pair in America*
River Plaza
9 West Broad Street
Stamford, CT 06902
(800) 9AU-PAIR (800-928-7247)

❊ *Au Pair Childcrest*
111 East 12700 South
Draper, UT 84020
(800) 574-8889
(888) 287-2471
www.goaupair.com
email: info@goaupair.com

❊ *Au Pair USA/Interexchange*
161 Sixth Avenue, 10th Floor, at Spring Street
New York, NY 10013
(800) AU-PAIRS (800-287-2477)
www.interexchange.org

day-care centers

New York City has more than twenty-five hundred day-care centers where you can bring your child each morning and pick him or her up by 6 p.m. Centers must meet rigid requirements in order to be licensed by the State of New York.

One of the best professionally run day-care centers we know is the Bright Horizons Center at 435 East 70th Street (746-6543). This nationwide chain has an excellent reputation as a leader in upholding stringent day-care standards. In addition, there are approximately fifty-three hundred in-home care centers or family day-care providers in the city. In family day care, an individual takes care of a few children (by law, no more than twelve) in her home.

The provider must be licensed by New York State and must register with the Department of Health. Even so, be cautious. Pay a personal visit to the center, speak with other parents, and trust your instincts.

Investigate options offered by your employer. More and more companies are offering on-site day care, or are willing to contribute to day-care costs.

✳ *Love A Lot Preschool*
99 Suffolk Street (bet. Delancey and Rivington streets)
529-2650
email: info@lovealotpreschool.com
Ages: 2 months to 5 years old
Love A Lot preschool is a combination preschool/day-care center and it provides all-day care, following a preschool curriculum. Love A Lot takes children as young as two months old. It offers full, partial, half, or extended-day options, two to five days a week. Love A Lot is licensed by the NYC Department of Health and is a great new day-care option for downtown families.

For more information contact:

✳ *The Department of Health:* This city agency regulates day-care centers and will tell you whether a specific center is licensed. Call 676-2444 and ask for the childcare bureau.

✳ *The Daycare Council of New York:* The Council will refer you to twenty-five centers free of charge. Centers are listed by zip code, and you can request referrals in three zip codes.

The Daycare Council of New York is located at 12 West 21st Street, 3rd Floor, New York, NY 10010. The phone number is 206-7818. You probably want to look at centers that are in your home and office zip codes to compare and contrast.

✳ *Child Care Inc.:* Located at 322 Eighth Avenue, 4th Floor, New York, NY 10001, 929-4999, this nonprofit organization serves as an information and referral resource for New York parents. Its excellent guides include "Choosing Child Care for Your Infant or Toddler," "Choosing an Early Childhood Program," and "In-Home Care." Other handouts cover finding and working with in-home care or nanny agencies, and it has samples of contracts for household employment. Child Care will also prepare lists of day-care centers and in-home care providers by zip code.

baby-sitting

You may be a stay-at-home mom who requires only a little childcare on a Saturday night or a few afternoons a week. The solution here is a baby-sitter. Ask your doorman, superintendent, or neighbor whether there are teenagers in the building available for baby-sitting, or check out colleges that have baby-sitting services or a baby-sitting agency. Each service works differently; often there is an initial registration fee between $25 and $50. Many require a two-hour minimum and have varying rates, starting at $9 an hour. Look for a sitter who has experience with children the same age as your child, and check references. Don't assume that just because some-one is enrolled in a local college she is trustworthy.

Finally, tell everyone you know that you're look-ing for a sitter. Ask other baby-sitters or nannies for recommendations; check bulletin boards at your pediatrician's office and play spaces. Pamela has used Barnard Baby-Sitting Service and always finds the students reliable and competent.

You may want to consider having a sitter come for an afternoon when you are at home to watch how she interacts and plays with your child. It is bet-ter for your child to have regular sitters whom she knows and you trust.

Baby-sitting services include:

❊ Absolute Best Care
481-5705
(NJ Office: 732-972-4090)
www.absolutebestcare.com
email: info@absolutebestcare.com

❊ Baby Sitters Guild
60 East 42nd Street
682-0227
babysittersguild.com
babysittersguild@cs.com
It has been in business for over fifty years and can send you a sitter who is bilingual. The com-pany has sitters who speak over sixteen differ-ent languages. Rates start at $20 an hour.

❊ Bank Street College
610 West 112th Street
bet. Broadway and West End Avenue
875-4400 • 875-4404

(fax: 875-4678)
Bank Street College will post baby-sitting employment positions for graduate students for free. It is open Monday through Friday from 9 a.m. to 5 p.m.

❊ Barnard Baby-Sitting Service/
Barnard College
11 Millbank Hall
3009 Broadway at 119th Street
854-2035
854-7678
Families are required to cover all meal expenses incurred and transportation after 9 p.m., i.e. cabfare, to ensure the safety of the student. Rates are between $10–$12 an hour.

❊ NYC Babysitters Club
239 East 73rd Street, Suite 2E
396-4090 (fax: 717-0182)
www.nycbabysitters.com
email: mychild98@aol.com
Unlike other baby-sitting services in the New York metro area, the NYC Babysitters Club (a division of My Child's Best Friend) offers a cost-effective program that is still one of the best-kept secrets in NYC! Parents can join the NYC Babysitters Club for an annual membership of $99 and rest assured that each sitter referred is carefully screened by the agency (a reference check and thorough criminal background check are conducted). A list of five sitters with age-related experience will be given to the family. These baby-sitters are available for the occa-sional evening (after 5:30 p.m.) and weekend baby-sitting and ready for the family to contact

them directly for work. The hourly rates vary and are determined by each baby-sitter ($10–$20 an hour) depending on their experience.

❈ New York City Explorers

244 Fifth Avenue, Suite 2545
591-2619
This baby-sitting service provides New York City parents with some wonderful options, such as Sleep-In Saturdays ($15 per hour), where the baby-sitter stays over to watch the children, then feeds them breakfast, and takes them out to do an educational activity. Its sitters will take your kids to nearby neighborhood places, such as zoos, museums, and parks. Discovering NY Daytrips are age-specific excursions that are also available. Baby-sitters have current, checkable references and are experienced caregivers or educators.

❈ Pinch Sitters

799 Broadway bet. 10th and 11th streets
260-6005
email: pinchsitters@yahoo.com
$16 an hour, four hour minimum. After 9 p.m. you must provide cab fare home.

❈ Sitter City

213 West Institute Place, Suite 410
Chicago, IL 60610
888-211-9749
www.sittercity.com
email: comments@sittercity.com
Sittercity.com is America's first website for parents and college baby-sitters. Now over three years old, Sittercity.com has aided more than 50,000 sitters in fifteen major markets to find local jobs in their area. Parents joining Sittercity.com get access to local sitters for a subscription fee of $39.99 for the first month, and $5 a month after that. Baby-sitting rates vary by location.

adjusting to
new motherhood

After you bring your newborn home, your bulging belly won't be the only thing missing— all semblance of control over your life will have vanished too . . . but that's okay.

The first few weeks at home are going to be turbulent. Many new mothers feel a bit blue or depressed. Having a baby is an emotionally draining experience, and to complicate things, those hormones really kick in after the birth. You may feel tired all day. Life will seem to be reduced to baby feedings, diaper changing, and laundry, laundry, laundry. The state of your apartment will deteriorate right before your very eyes.

Our advice? Let the place get messy. Use the time between feedings, changes, and naps to take care of yourself, rest, and think about what an adorable child you have. Allow willing friends and grandparents to throw in a load of laundry for you or pick up your dry cleaning.

If you actually cook, forget about it now. Order in. New York is take-out heaven, and there is wonderful prepared food all around you. Come to think of it, order all your necessities! Most pharmacies will take phone orders and deliver. The big drugstore chains, such as Duane Reade and Rite Aid, all deliver formula by the case, disposable diapers, and baby wipes by the package. Or get online and order formula and diapers from one of the sites listed in the Website Directory. Have your food and supplies delivered from your local supermarket. Make it easy on yourself.

This book suggests dozens of places to meet new mothers and learn from the experts. We can't say enough about forming or joining a playgroup, or a group of moms with babies who are the same age as your own. Playgroups usually meet once a week in rotating homes. If you don't have friends with babies your age, don't worry, you'll meet some. Take a Strollercize class, attend a New Mothers Luncheon, sign up for a hospital class—before you know it, you will have friends all over town.

Joining a playgroup was a lifesaver for Pamela, whose children were both born in the winter. The women she met in Rebecca's group twelve years ago are some of her best friends to this day. A playgroup should have four to six moms and babies and meet at a specific time each week. You can serve lunch, or just cold drinks, and let the babies do their thing while the moms discuss everything from breastfeeding to sleep deprivation and more. These get-togethers become vital to a new mother's sanity, and definitely will become one of the highlights of your week.

new mother classes

Once your baby is a few weeks old and you have settled into something of a routine, you'll enjoy swapping baby stories with other mothers and sharing advice on caring for your infant.

A number of hospitals offer classes you can attend with your baby. They provide an opportunity to hear from pediatricians, child psychologists, child-safety experts, and other skilled professionals. Plus, you'll be able to ask questions and meet other new parents.

When Alexander was six weeks old, Kelly attended the five-week New Mother Discussion Group at New York Hospital. This class, led by Jean Schoppel, RN, and Ronni Soled, became the highlight of her week. Pamela took the New Mother/New Baby class, for mothers with children newborn to twelve months, offered by the 92nd Street Y, and loved it.

Hospital Classes

The hospitals listed below offer new mother classes. Fees vary from hospital to hospital and change frequently; most range from $20 to $75 for one-time classes or workshops, and $200 to $300 for a series of classes or new mother support group meetings. Most hospital classes and support groups are open to all women, not just those who delivered at that hospital. So, if you want to take a class at New York Hospital but deliver at Beth Israel, just call New York Hospital to sign up. New moms are encouraged to bring their babies to all classes.

❋ Beth Israel Hospital

16th Street at First Avenue
420-2000 (General)
420-2999 (Classes)
www.wehealny.org/familyed
email: lmanigo@bethisraelny.org
Beth Israel offers a variety of classes for the new mother, including a CPR course, a class in child safety, a breastfeeding class, and a New Mother's support group.

❋ Columbia Presbyterian Hospital

Babies Hospital/Sloane Hospital for Women
Broadway at 166th Street
305-2500 (General)
305-2040 (Parent Education Program)
Columbia Presbyterian offers classes in breastfeeding, baby care, and parenting.

❋ The Mount Sinai Medical Center

One Gustave L. Levy Place
Klingenstein Pavilion
Fifth Avenue at 98th Street
241-6500 (General)
241-7491 (Women & Children's Office)
241-6578 (Breastfeeding Warm Line)
Mount Sinai offers classes in caring for newborns, CPR, and breastfeeding. Its New Mother's support group meets once a week.

❋ New York Hospital/ Cornell Medical Center

525 East 68th Street
746-5454 (General)
746-3215 (Preparation for Parenthood Office)
New York Hospital offers a Multiples Class, for women delivering twins or multiple babies; a baby care class; and a New Mother's Discussion Group that meets once a week. The Preparation for Parenthood staff maintains a telephone information line for new mothers.

❋ New York University Medical Center

560 First Avenue at 32nd Street
263-7300 (General)
263-7201 (Classes)
New York University Medical Center offers a breastfeeding support group for new mothers that meets once a week.

❋ Roosevelt Hospital

1000 Tenth Avenue at 58th Street
523-4000 (General)
523-6222 (Parent/Family Education)
Roosevelt Hospital offers classes in baby care, infant CPR, child CPR, and breastfeeding, and has a New Mother's support group.

Top Ten Things to Keep You Sane with a Newborn

1. Stock the freezer before the baby is born—lasagna, soup, etc.
2. Get help—a friend, mother, sister, or baby-sitter, if possible. Remember: any relief is better than no relief at all.
3. Sleep when the baby sleeps.
4. Order take-out food the first few weeks; it's too tiring to cook.
5. Buy in bulk and have it delivered— a case of formula, a box of diapers, and several packages of baby wipes will make life much easier.
6. Open up charge accounts at stores in the neighborhood that will deliver.
7. Let the house get messy.
8. Make friends with other new moms, and call them.
9. Try to go outside every day.
10. Attend a New Mothers Luncheon or class.

✻ St. Luke's Hospital

1111 Amsterdam Avenue at 114th Street; same phone numbers as Roosevelt Hospital All classes are given at Roosevelt Hospital.

✻ St. Vincent's Hospital and Medical Center

153 West 11th Street
604-7000 (General)
604-7946 (Maternity Education)

St. Vincent's offers classes in newborn care and breastfeeding and it has a breastfeeding support group.

CPR Classes

✻ Downtown Babies

Locations in Tribeca and Soho
217-2716
email: Maria@downtownbabies.com
Downtown Babies is a parent education resource and social club for parents, caregivers, and children (birth to 5 years). Downtown Babies also offers creative play packages for infants, toddlers, and preschoolers that focus on a variety of areas important to a child's physical growth and development (feelings, sharing, caring, pretend play, music, creative movement, and so on).

✻ Fern Drillings, RN, MSN, CCES

East and West Side locations
744-6649
Besides being a childbirth educator, Fern also gives infant CPR and baby safety classes. Contact her to get the schedule for the East and West Side locations, or put together your own group and inquire about private sessions.

✻ GotCPR.com

691-5989
email: Class@GotCPR.org
CPR/baby safety classes from GotCPR are held on the Upper East Side, Upper West Side, Downtown, and Brooklyn. Classes are available daytime, evening, and weekends too, so there

is no excuse not to take a class! If getting a babysitter is not possible, young babies are also welcome.

❊ *Mindful Parenting:*

A RIE-Inspired Playgroup
for Parents and Their Babies
Exhale Spa
980 Madison Avenue
(bet. 76th and 77th streets)
561-6400
email: jsherwitz@verizon.net

Johanna Herwitz, PhD, leads this parent and baby playgroup and encourages moms to trust their instincts, do less, and observe their child more. The RIE method (popular in L.A. and meaning "Resources for Infant Educators") teaches parents how to recognize the unique needs of their baby and how to have realistic expectations for themselves and their child in fulfilling those needs. Johanna also sees moms and dads through her private practice.

Other Classes, Groups, and Seminars

There are excellent non-hospital-based support and discussion groups throughout the city. Many of them, like the hospital classes, teach infant CPR, which every new parent should learn. Some of the classes listed are fun to take with your child.

Schedules and fees are always subject to change. Call for the most up-to-date information.

❊ *Save-A-Tot*

317 East 34th Street

725-7477

Save-A-Tot offers private or group infant/child CPR at your home or in midtown Manhattan. Private childbirth education classes are also available.

❊ *Tot-Saver*

5 East 98th Street
241-7491

Conducted at Mount Sinai Hospital, these classes teach CPR techniques for infants and children as well as safety and injury prevention. The fee is $75 per person or $135 per couple per two-session course. Class is limited to six participants. Call for further information and registration.

❊ *The Parent Child Center*

Alice Rosenman
247 East 82nd Street
879-6900

The Parent Child Center, affiliated with the New York Psychoanalytical Society, offers weekly learning-while-playing groups to parents and children (from birth to three years). These groups are limited to seven or eight families in order to provide an intimate and cohesive environment. This side-by-side program costs about $650 for eighteen classes (from either September through February or from February through June).

❊ *Parenting Horizons**

Julie Ross/Carolyn Meyer
765-2377
St. Bartholomew's Church

109 East 50th Street and Park Avenue
West Park Presbyterian Church
165 West 86th Street at Amsterdam Avenue
www.parentinghorizons.com
Julie Ross teaches "Practical Parenting," which covers how to handle tantrums, and how to help children sleep at night, learn to brush their teeth, get dressed for school, and perform other daily tasks. Julie works to build parental confidence and gives practical examples of what to do when a particular situation arises. Kelly and Pam have both had wonderful experiences with Julie Ross. She is an excellent resource. Classes meet weekly for eight weeks, three semesters per year. Fees are $395 per person and $725 per couple. This is an excellent class for parents of toddlers. Private instruction is also available.

❖ The SoHo Parenting Center

568 Broadway, Suite 205
334-3744
www.sohoparenting.com
The Parenting Center, a respected downtown resource for new moms, organizes various mother/infant support groups during the day and in the evenings. The center offers a second-time mother's group and both private and group parent counseling sessions. It also offers mother/toddler programs, sleep counseling, and pre- and postnatal yoga. The directors of the center—Jean Kunhardt and Lisa Spiegel—along with Sandra K. Basile, have written *The Mother's Circle*, which is about the first year of motherhood.

❖ Elizabeth Bing Center for Parents

164 West 79th Street
362-5304 • 646-456-3266 • 718-856-5677
email: lamaze@wonderwomen.com
The Elizabeth Bing Center conducts several classes for new moms and dads, including seminars on parenting, baby safety, and breastfeeding. Elizabeth is a much-loved teacher who has been doing this for over thirty years. Each seminar is approximately one and one half hours and costs $75 (varies by seminar). The center also offers a Lamaze refresher class for second-time parents for $250.

❖ Colleen K. Campo
More than a Moms Group
Institute for Psychological Change

744-3700, ext. 49
Nationally certified counselor Colleen Campo specializes in supporting mothers as they transition into motherhood. She sees women privately, but is now forming groups that will support new moms and give them a forum to explore the conflicts and challenges new motherhood brings and learn practical coping skills for this transitional time. The groups will meet for six weeks and the cost is $60 per session.

❖ The Early Childhood Development Center

163 East 97th Street
360-7803
The center conducts one-hour weekly meetings to discuss sleeping, feeding, crying, and other early child-raising issues. Twenty sessions cost $400.

❋ Educational Alliance Parenting and Family Center at the Sol Goldman YM-YWHA*

344 East 14th Street bet. First and
Second avenues
780-0800, ext. 236
www.14streety.org

The Educational Alliance, a nonprofit organization, is a great city resource with a variety of wonderful workshops for parents and classes for children of all ages. For new moms, the Alliance offers New Moms Stroll-In, an open discussion led by the director of the Parenting and Family Center, Kiki Schaffer. The groups are ongoing. It's five sessions and it costs $50 for members, $65 for nonmembers. A trial class costs $15. (Ms. Schaffer, a CSW, is available for private counseling sessions as well. She can be reached at 529-9247.) The Alliance also offers a workshop entitled Preparing Your Marriage for Parenthood, counseling groups for mothers suffering from postpartum depression and mothers returning to work; classes in infant massage, and prental, postnatal, and mommy/baby yoga. Kiki Schaffer is a consummate professional, and we only wish we lived closer to the Sol Goldman Y.

❋ Sandra Jamrog

866-8527
jjamrogbirthbaby@earthlink.net

A mother of four, Sandra Jamrog has been a childbirth educator for over thirty years. She has been teaching pre- and postnatal classes for more than thirty years. She also teachers childbirth education. She is a New York State–licensed massage therapist. She still offers childbirth classes, parent education classes, and massage therapy. She also teaches infant movement sessions, which stimulate appropriate infant development, with the caretakers' cooperation. This helps parents understand their infants better.

❋ Jewish Community Center

on the Upper West Side
334 Amsterdam Avenue at 76th Street
646-505-4444 • membership: 646-505-5700
www.jccmanhattan.org

The 120,000-square-foot JCC offers a wide range of classes for new parents, including New Moms, New Babies, Infant/Child First Aid/CPR, Baby Teeth Basics, Postpartum Depression, and Massage for Babies: Connecting to Your Child. The JCC is a valuable local resource for parents.

❋ Kiki Schaffer, CSW

Mother/Infant Counseling
529-9247

Kiki offers short-term psychotherapy for new moms and their babies to promote healthy interaction and to safeguard the relationship from potential early problems. She also will counsel women on postpartum depression.

❋ 92nd Street Y "New Parents' Get Together"*

92nd Street YM-YWHA
1395 Lexington Avenue
996-1100
www.92ndsty.org

New Parents' Get Together features speakers

who discuss topics including working and parenting, childcare, sleep, babies, and your marriage ($5 for members of the Y's Parenting Center, $10 for nonmembers; annual membership is $175). There is a New Parents' Get Together on Sunday mornings for moms and dads who can't make it during the week. Other classes for new moms include postpartum exercise, caring for a newborn, and a breastfeeding workshop. The Y also offers a New Mother/New Baby class that tackles different topics each week. The Y offers baby-sitting for children four months to four years; $11/hour for nonmembers and $10/hour for members. For more information on baby-sitting, please call 415-5617; this is a separate line just for baby-sitting rates. For the parenting center, call 415-5609 or 415-5611.

✳ Rhinelander Children's Center

350 East 88th Street bet. First
and Second avenues
876-0500
www.rhinelandercenter.org
The Rhinelander Center is part of the Children's Aid Society. For expectant or new moms, classes include Enhanced Lamaze, Lamaze Refresher, and Infant Massage. Rhinelander is also an early childhood center and offers a full nursery school. For parents of older children, there are daytime and evening discussion groups, with topics that include gaining cooperation, calming temper tantrums, learning to share, and reducing sibling squabbles. Kelly has had positive experiences over the years at Rhinelander.

✳ New Mothers Luncheons*

1 West Side and 2 East Side locations
Ronni Soled
744-3194
www.newmothersluncheons.com
email: ronninml@aol.com
The New Mothers Luncheons, now in its fifteenth year on the East Side and its sixth year on the West side, is truly the "First Thing to Do with a Baby in NYC!" as its slogan says. The luncheons are geared for moms with babies newborn to six months or so (the younger the better) since it is really an event for the moms to get out of the house, have lunch in a restaurant, listen to a parenting expert, and socialize with other moms. Ronni Soled started the luncheons on the East Side in 1990, and Pamela Weinberg has been the leader of the West Side luncheon since its inception in 2000. The East Side luncheons meet on Tuesdays and Thursdays, and the West Side luncheon meets on Wednesdays. All luncheons begin at 11 a.m.

✳ New Mommies Network

Lori Robinson
769-3846
www.newmommies.com
Lori Robinson organizes lunches, brunches, and occasional dinners several days a week at different restaurants. Get-togethers range in price from $10 to $40, last two hours, and attract twenty to twenty-five moms with babies (newborn to one year). Lori holds separate events for moms of toddlers (ten to twenty-four months) called the Graduate Group and also organizes events for working mothers and

expectant parents. Past speakers have addressed sleep problems, second babies, pediatric care, eating habits, and schedules. Dads are always welcome.

⁂ The Parent's League*

115 East 82nd Street
737-7385

The Parent's League, a nonprofit organization founded thirty years ago, is a vital resource for New York parents. For a $90 annual fee, you'll have access to lectures, literature, and counseling services, plus a calendar and guide to city-wide events and programs for children, a birthday party reference guide, a list of emergency telephone numbers, a newsletter, and information on schools and after-school activities. The league maintains an advisory service for schools and camps, as well as a listing of nannies, mother's helpers, and baby-sitters. You'll also receive the *Parent's League Toddler Book*, which contains information on classes you can take with a toddler. The Parent's League sells a guidebook to private schools that describes all of the Independent Schools Admissions Association of Greater New York (ISAAGNY) member schools. It's $23 by mail.

⁂ The Parenting Program

Temple Shaaray Tefila
250 East 79th Street at Second Avenue
535-8008, ext. 248

The Parenting Program provides social interaction for you and your toddler (dads and grandparents, too). There are daytime classes for parents and toddlers, evening classes for toddlers and employed mothers, and evening playtimes for dads and toddlers. Classes offer children between ages sixteen and thirty-six months (classes are divided by age) developmentally appropriate challenges that foster self-confidence and curiosity in the world around them. This unique program incorporates Sabbath celebrations, Hebrew songs, and holiday rituals. Classes cost around $45 per session.

⁂ Elizabeth Silk, MSSW, CSW, BCD

873-6435

Elizabeth Silk, a psychotherapist with expertise in womens' reproductive issues, postpartum depression, and mothering, holds weekly groups for new mothers. The women focus on adding new dimensions of motherhood to their identity. Individual and couples sessions are also available.

⁂ Mindful Parenting: A RIE-Inspired Playgroup for Parents and Their Babies

Exhale Spa
980 Madison Avenue
(bet. 76th and 77th streets)
561-6400
email: jsherwitz@verizon.net

Johanna Herwitz, PhD, leads this parent and baby playgroup and encourages moms to trust their instincts, do less, and observe their child more. The RIE method (popular in L.A. and meaning "Resources for Infant Educators") teaches parents how to recognize the unique needs of their baby and how to have realistic expectations for themselves and their child in fulfilling those needs. Johanna also sees moms and dads through her private practice.

❄ *Phyllis LaBella, CSW, BCD*

Adoption Specialist, Domestic and International
987-0077
Phyllis treats an entire range of emotional problems and issues affecting adopted children, adoptive couples, and birth moms.

❄ *Nancy Samalin, MS*

787-8883
www.samalin.com
Nancy has worked with parents, educators, and health-care professionals since 1976, teaching positive discipline and improved communication skills for toddlers through teens. She is also a prolific author of parenting books such as *Loving Your Child Is Not Enough: Positive Discipline that Works.* She is a former contributing editor to *Parents* magazine, and her newest book is *Loving Without Spoiling.*

❄ *Lisa Schuman, CSW, CASAC*

590 West End Avenue, Suite 1A
874-1318
Lisa Schuman is a psychotherapist who specializes in family issues. She works with couples, individuals, and groups on child-rearing issues, relationship difficulties, and a wide range of parenting questions. She also works with parents in the area of infertility and adoption.

❄ *Uptown Mommies*

Sarah Klagsbrun, MD
996-4300
email: kw@bway.net
Sarah Klagsbrun, a child psychiatrist and mother of two, runs new parent discussion groups on the Upper East Side. The groups help new moms learn about their child's social, emotional, cognitive, and language development so they can parent with confidence. Topics include establishing sleeping and eating patterns; temper tantrums; limit-setting; self-esteem; toilet training; sibling relationships and more. A six-week session is $290.

entertainment for new moms

❄ *Metropolitan Moms*

799-3748
www.metropolitanmoms.com
email: msnyder@metropolitanmoms.com
Molly Snyder (a New Mothers Luncheon alum) has created Metropolitan Moms. MMs offers a series of once-a-week classes for new moms, to be taken with or without your baby. Series prices range from $375 to $475 per multi-week class. Each class in the series takes place at a different museum, gallery, or neighborhood. Recent classes have included a walking and architectural tour of Greenwich Village and a gallery tour of Chelsea. Classes are led by experts and mom and baby classes include baby-sitters.

Mamallama Munch

Christina Soto

646-488-8542

email: CSoto@mamallama.CityMax.com

Mamallama Munch runs luncheons and events for new mothers downtown. Each luncheon features a speaker and costs $35.

Big City Moms

917-488-8542

www.bigcitymoms.com

Big City Moms was started over a year ago by Risa and Leslie, two sisters who believe that new moms need a night away from their babies to socialize with each other and just have fun. It offers a different kind of moms-night-out adventure every Tuesday night at a variety of locations around the city. It also does special kid-centered weekend events that the whole family can enjoy—a recent Valentine's Day party at a New York hotel was a big hit. A lifetime membership to Big City Moms is $300, and nonmembers pay $40 per outing.

Divalysscious Moms

917-601-0068

www.divalyssciousmoms.com

Divalysscious was started by Lyss Stern, a dynamic new mom who wanted to enjoy all of the exciting things that NYC had to offer—but found that most movie premieres, day spas, and cooking schools weren't baby friendly at all. Divalysscious Moms offers all sorts of lifestyle events throughout the city for moms, babies, and grandmas too. Recent events have included parties at Dylan's Candy Bar, a shop-ping outing at Barneys, and moms-night-out at a fun hotel. Prices vary by event.

Reel Moms

www.enjoytheshow.com

Reel Moms (held at Loews Cineplex theaters around the city) offers the opportunity for moms to bring their babies to the movies. Tickets to all Reel Moms events go on sale at the box office the day of the show. Stroller check is available; admission for grown-ups is regular ticket price, babies are free. The movies are tailored to meet the needs of moms and babies, and include dimmed lights and reduced sound levels so you can hear your infant's every sound during the presentation.

Cry Baby Matinee

City Cinema

86th Street bet. Second and Third avenues

www.crybabymatinee.com

Like Reel Moms, Cry Baby matinee offers movies for moms and babies with a semi-darkened theater, stroller valet, etc. Admission is regular price for adults, free for babies. Movies are shown Wednesdays at 11 a.m.

hotlines, warmlines, and other special help

There may be times during your baby's first few weeks or months when you need more specialized help or support than your pediatrician, mother, or friend can provide.

During these weeks it is a good idea to keep handy the telephone number of the nursery of the hospital in which you delivered. Often, the nurses can easily answer your questions and help you through a minor crisis. Some hospitals also have special telephone numbers set up to assist new moms. Inquire about your hospital's policy for new mother call-ins. Following are a variety of additional support groups and referral programs, as well as some important numbers to have in case of an emergency.

Adoption

❋ *Adoptive Parents Support Group*
475-0222
A support group for adoptive parents.

❋ *Adoptive Parents Committee*
304-8479
An adoptive parents support group with chapters in New York, Long Island, and Westchester.

Breastfeeding

❋ *La Leche League*
794-4687
www.lalecheleague.com
A worldwide volunteer organization founded by a group of mothers to support other moms who choose to breastfeed their babies. La Leche's services are free, nonsectarian, and supported by membership fees. La Leche has group leaders in various parts of New York who run monthly meetings to discuss breastfeeding. It also provides a valuable telephone help service. When you call, a recording gives you the name and number of a woman who can be reached that day. A new mother who couldn't figure out how to work her electric breast pump called La Leche, and a volunteer spent twenty minutes on the phone explaining it to her.

❋ *Beth Israel Medical Center*
Lactation Program
420-2939
A warmline to answer breastfeeding questions and provide support for nursing mothers.

❋ *Màire Clements, RN, IBCLC*
The Breastfeeding Salon
595-4797
www.thebreastfeedingsalon.com
Màire Clements (pronounced "Moira"), RN, is a breastfeeding expert and lactation consultant who teaches women how to breastfeed correctly. She gives breastfeeding classes at St. Luke's-Roosevelt Hospital and other locations. She also sponsors luncheons where she speaks, offering mothers additional support and guid-

ance about breastfeeding and other issues concerning new mothers. Màire offers a working mother's group and a breastfeeding Toddler Teas group, all of which she personally caters at mothers' homes (locations rotate).

❋ The National Association of Mothers Centers

Levittown, NY
516-520-2929
www.motherscenter.org
email: info@motherscenter.org
A referral service for mothers' groups in your area.

Hotline Help

❋ Child Abuse and Maltreatment Reporting Center

(800) 342-3720
A hotline to report cases of suspected child abuse.

❋ Emergency Children's Service

341-0900 (general)
966-8000 (nights, weekends, holidays)
Emergency assistance for abused, assaulted, mistreated, or neglected children.

❋ National AIDS Hotline

(800) 342-AIDS
www.cdc.gov
Trained specialists answer questions about HIV infections and AIDS.

❋ New York Foundling Hospital Crisis

Intervention Nursery
472-8555
An emergency placement for a child up to the age of ten whose parent is under stress. This free service provides some cooling-off time for parents, for a period of one day up to three weeks.

❋ Poison Hotline

(800) 222-1222
A service that offers immediate advice and direction in cases of poison ingestion.

Premature Infants

The best place to get advice and counseling or to find out about support groups for parents of premature babies is through your hospital's Intensive Care Nursery. Many ICNs automatically provide such support. If yours does not, ask the staff to direct you to a group in your area.

❋ First Candle/National SIDS Resource Center

(800) 221-SIDS (800-221-7437)
703-902-1249 • www.firstcandle.org
This center provides Sudden Infant Death Syndrome (SIDS) information to parents.

Single Parents

❋ Parents Without Partners

(800) 637-7974
www.parentswithoutpartners.org
A self-help group providing support and information about single parenting issues.

Single Mothers by Choice
988-0993
www.singlemothersbychoice.com
A support group for women who have had a baby on their own.

Single Parents Support Group
780-0800, ext. 239
This group meets at the Parenting Center at the 14th Street Y. Baby-sitting is available with advance reservation.

Twins or More

M.O.S.T. (Mothers of Super Twins)
631-859-1110
www.nomotc.org • email: info@nomotc.org
A support group for parents of triplets, quadruplets, or quintuplets. Also offers information and support for parents of premature babies.

National Organization of Mothers of Twins Clubs, Inc.
877-540-2200
This club provides information on local twin, triplet, and quadruplet (or more) support groups.

Special Needs Groups

The Lighthouse/New York Association for the Blind
821-9200
www.lighthouse.org
The Lighthouse works with blind children throughout the city and provides comprehensive services and resources for them and their families.

Cerebral Palsy
United Cerebral Palsy of New York City
677-7400 • 683-6700
www.ucpnyc.org
email: pjohnson@ucpnyc.org
This organization offers comprehensive services for children and their families, beginning at infancy.

Cystic Fibrosis Foundation
986-8783
A foundation providing advice, counseling, and hospital referrals for families of children with Cystic Fibrosis.

National Down's Syndrome Society
460-9330
This society offers general information, parent support, and assistance with identifying programs at local hospitals for Down's Syndrome babies and children.

League for the Hard of Hearing
www.lhh.com
Provides information on speech and hearing programs and clinics.

Pregnancy and Infant Loss Center
(Bereavement Group)
612-473-9372
This center provides information on local support groups for women or couples recovering from a miscarriage or the loss of an infant.

❈ Educational Alliance

780-0800

Educational Alliance runs workshops to help parents through pregnancy loss.

❈ Resources for Children with Special Needs

677-4650

www.resourcesnyc.org

email: info@resourcesnyc.org

An information, referral, advocacy, and support center for parents of children with special needs.

❈ Spina Bifida Information and Referral

(800) 621-3141

www.spaa.org

❈ Williams Syndrome Hotline

P. O. Box 297

Clawson, MI 48017-0297

(800) 806-1871 • 248-244-2229

www.williams-syndrome.org

email: info@williams-syndrome.org

The Williams Syndrome Association was formed in 1982 by, and for, families of individuals with Williams syndrome. The WSA is the only group in the US devoted exclusively to improving the lives of individuals with Williams syndrome. The WSA supports research into all facets of the syndrome, and the development of the most up-to-date educational materials.

❈ YIA Early Intervention Program

418-0335

Called Life Start now, YIA Early Intervention Program is a federally funded agency that has an agreement with New York City to run Life Start for children under the age of three who have mental, physical, emotional, social, or cognitive development difficulties. All sorts of physical, speech, and occupational therapies are available free of charge to children in New York State.

important supplies

Diaper Services

In our environmentally conscious age, some people may want to use cloth diapers to help the earth. Since our last edition, many diaper services have closed down or consolidated. There is only one diaper service in the tristate area that still provides cloth diapers. We have also included the Walgreens website for easy online ordering of disposable diapers; see below.

www.walgreens.com

❈ Tidy Diapers

50 Commerce Street

Norwalk, CT 06850

(800) 852-7638

(800) 732-2443

email: tidydiapers@aol.com

$16.95/week

Breast Pumps

For breastfeeding working moms or other women who would like their husbands or caregivers to feed baby an occasional bottle of breast milk, an electric breast pump is a wonderful convenience. Electric pumps are faster and easier to use than manual or battery-operated pumps. If you plan to breastfeed for three months or less, we recommend renting an electric, hospital-grade pump. Pumps can be rented by the day, week, or month. They can also be purchased through The Right Start catalog. Buying is a good idea if you plan to breastfeed for an extended time or if you are planning to have more children. The Medela Lactina is a good one to rent or purchase. For the nearest outlet, call Medela at: (800) TELL-YOU. The La Leche League, 794-4687, can also tell you where to rent a breast pump.

Prices for pump rental range from $65 to $80 per month. Most places sell an accompanying kit that contains sanitary accessories to be used with the pump. The kit is priced at about $40 for the single pump and $65 for the double. The single pump allows you to pump milk from one breast, and the double from both breasts at the same time.

Breast pumps can be rented at the following locations in Manhattan:

upper east side

❖ *Caligor Pharmacy*
1226 Lexington Avenue at 83rd Street
369-6000

❖ *Cherry's Pharmacy*
207 East 66th Street

bet. Second and Third avenues
717-7797
www.cherryspharmacy.com
Cherry's Pharmacy is unique, as it is the only pharmacy in the city that caters directly to kids and families. Cherry's pharmacists prepare children's medication with flavors that actually taste good, and good tasting medicine is easier to administer. You will find all children's medication and products here, even some toys and gifts. Delivery is free.

❖ *Falk Drug*
259 East 72nd Street at Second Avenue
744-8080

❖ *Goldberger's Pharmacy*
1200 First Avenue at 65th Street
734-6998

❖ *Timmerman Pharmacy**
799 Lexington Avenue bet. 61st
and 62nd streets
838-6450

upper west side

❖ *Apthorp Pharmacy**
2201 Broadway bet. 78th and 79th streets
877-3480

❖ *Chateau Drug*
181 Amsterdam Avenue bet.
68th and 69th streets
877-6390

Joseph Pharmacy
216 West 72nd Street and West End Avenue
875-1718

Planet Kids
2688 Broadway bet. 102nd
and 103rd streets
864-8705
Sells pumps only. Electrics range from $70 to $289, and manual pumps from $44 to 50.

Suba Pharmacy
2721 Broadway at 104th Street
866-6700

midtown

NYU Medical Center
560 First Avenue at 32nd Street
263-BABY

St. Luke's-Roosevelt Hospital Center
1000 Tenth Avenue at 58th Street
523-4000

downtown

Barren Hospital Medical Center
49 Delancey Street bet. Eldridge
and Forsyth streets
226-6164

C.O. Bigelow Apothecaries
414 Sixth Avenue bet. 8th and 9th streets
533-2700

Elm Drugs
298 First Avenue bet. 17th and 18th streets
777-0740

Kings Pharmacy
5 Hudson Street
at Reade Street
791-3100

Little Folks
123 East 23rd Street bet. Park
and Lexington avenues
982-9669

Miriam Goodman
Home Delivery
219-1080

entertainment for kids and moms

You've survived the first couple of months; you have packing the diaper bag down to a science, you're getting a handle on this motherhood business—it is time to venture out with your little one and have some fun!

You and your baby can roll around on a mat together at the 92nd Street Y, get some culture at the Temple of Dendur at the Met, relax at an outdoor cafe, or stroll to a neighborhood playground and meet other moms and their babies.

In this chapter, we'll give you a rundown of the Mommy and Me classes and activities available in the city. (Unless otherwise indicated, caregivers, dads, or grandmas are also welcome to take their young charges to these classes.) Then we'll turn to New York's playgrounds and parks, museums, and other special spaces where you and your baby can have a good time.

Given our considerable experience with all of these classes and activities, we have a few thoughts on monitoring your child's schedule. With our first kids, we both overdid it with classes. Beginning at three months old, Rebecca and Alexander "learned" music, art, gym, French, ballet, tumbling, soccer, swimming—you name it. You get the idea; we overbooked them. The second time around, we were smarter and realized that playgroups and time with mom in the park are just as valuable as Gymboree.

Once Benjamin was a year old, he and Pamela began a gym and music class. It paid to wait because he enjoyed it much more at one year than Rebecca had at six months. Angela took her first music class with Kelly at age one and she is more advanced and talkative now at age two than her brother was at that age, although he had been introduced to everything under the sun by the time he was two years old.

mommy and me classes and programs

As your child grows, she is going to learn to run, jump, tumble, sing songs, and scribble pictures all on her own. But classes can help her develop social skills, learn how to function in groups, be disciplined, and acquire a host of other skills. Above all, children enjoy themselves in these programs, and it's nice to have some places to go during New York winters.

All these places and programs offer classes for children age three and under. Some take babies as young as three months. However, you and your child will find an organized class much more enjoyable if she is able to sit up on her own, so it's a good idea to wait until your baby is at least six to nine months old before signing up.

Here are some guidelines to follow as you check out these programs:

❋ Take a trial class or attend an open house before you sign up. You may have to pay for it, but you'll have a better sense of what you are getting into.

❋ Look for classes with children the same age as your own.

❋ Look for big, open, clean rooms with plenty of space and light, accessible by elevator or ramp. You should not have to walk up five flights of stairs carrying your baby, diaper bag, and stroller.

❋ Equipment should be scaled down to small-child size, and any gymnastic-type facilities should include lots of mats and other safety features.

❋ Small- to medium-size classes are best. Do not be too concerned if a class is very big on the first day, because everyone is not there every week. Illnesses, naps, and vacations normally account for a quarter of a class being absent in any given week.

❊ The teacher makes all the difference; some are better than others. The other children and their mothers and nannies also can affect the atmosphere of a class. If you are the only mom in attendance, for example, you may feel awkward spending time with ten nannies every Thursday afternoon at two o'clock. (You can always ask to switch to a class with more moms.)

❊ Location is important. Enroll in a class near your home. If you can push your baby in a stroller less than ten blocks, you will be more likely to attend and to make it there on time.

Prices and schedules change almost every semester, so call ahead for the latest information. Classes often run in sessions of seventeen to nineteen weeks; prices range from $300 to $475. During the summer, many places—Jodi's Gym and the 92nd Street Y, for example—offer four-, six-, and nine-week sessions that cost from $95 to $200.

❊ *Aha! Learning Partners*

1624 First Avenue bet. 84th and 85th streets

517-8292

www.ahalearning.com

Age: 6 months to 3 years

Developed in conjunction with child development experts from Harvard and The Brazelton Institute, Aha's philosophy is that children learn best through open-ended play. The unstructured Aha! classes are child-directed and let children play and discover at their own pace

Top Ten Things to Do with Your Family on the Weekend

1. Visit Chelsea Piers (skating, gymnastics, bowling, etc.).
2. Go to Central Park to watch the rollerbladers and feed the ducks (mid-park at 72nd Street).
3. Go to dinner at the restaurant at the 79th Street boat basin (79th Street and the Hudson River). Eat good food in a kid-friendly environment and watch the boats.
4. Go down to Battery Park City. Stroll by the water, eat ice cream cones, and people-watch.
5. Visit the Brooklyn Botanic Garden. It has a great kiddie area with all types of hands-on activities.
6. Invite a few other families to a potluck picnic in Central Park. Bring bubbles, balls, and blankets.
7. Take a drive out into the country for fall apple-picking/pumpkin-picking.
8. Visit the penguins in the Central Park Zoo (infants love to look at black and white).
9. Form a "daddy" playgroup—dads get to bond with other dads and babies, and you get some time off.
10. Go to a playground in a neighborhood other than your own.

with a variety of different sensory stimuli. Every two weeks, it creates a different "immersive play environment" around a theme such as paper, clay, or foam. Aha! also believes that parents need to take an active role in their children's learning and development and thus provides parents with biweekly play diaries, parent-only group discussions, and in-home play suggestions; $400 for ten weeks. Sample classes are offered prior to each semester.

✽ The Art Farm in the City

419 East 91st Street bet. York and First avenues
410-3117
www.theartfarms.org
Age: 8 months to 7 years
In each week's forty-five-minute class the children are visited by a live animal such as a rabbit, frog, or pig and learn about the animal's habitat, eating habits, etc. Classes alternate each week between music and art (music only for six- to fourteen-month-olds). At the end of class, the children have fifteen minutes to visit all of the animals in the 1,000-square-foot indoor "farm." Kids three to seven years old can take animal care classes. Classes are $420 plus a $25 annual registration fee for 14 weeks. Trials cost $30.

✽ Asphalt Green Inc.

The A.G.U.A. Center
1750 York Avenue at 91st Street
369-8890
Age: 4 months and up
Swimming classes for young children at Asphalt Green, a huge fitness and sports complex, are held in the warm water teaching/exercise pool (not the Olympic-sized pool) under excellent supervision. Water Babies is for four- to eighteen-month-olds. It accustoms them to being in the water through soothing games and songs. Water Tots, for children eighteen to thirty-six months, teaches kicking, arm movements, prone floating, and safety jumps. The curriculum incorporates the teaching methods of both the American Red Cross and the American Swim Coaches Association. Adults must go in the water with children under three. Asphalt Green also hosts parties and offers delightful puppet shows for children eleven months and older, as well as various art and fitness classes such as Toddlercise, Tumble Tots, and Kindermusik. This is one of the best places for swimming lessons in the city, and parents travel from across town to downtown so their kids can swim here. Book your classes early!

✽ Baby Fingers

West Park Presbyterian Church
165 West 86th Street at Amsterdam Avenue
Ballet Hispanico
167 West 89th Street
bet. Amsterdam and Columbus avenues
and Upper East Side and Murray Hill locations
874-5978
www.mybabyfingers.com
Age: newborn to 6 years
A unique program for children ages one month to six years old offering sign language instruction through the arts. Classes involve music, signing, and singing. Founder Lora Heller is certified in early childhood education, special

education, and speech therapy. She is also a musician with a magical voice.

✻ Bloomingdale School of Music

323 West 108th Street bet. Broadway
and Riverside Drive

663-6021

www.bsmny.org

Age: 6 months and up

Bloomingdale's preschool programs are an ideal way to introduce children to the world of music. Baby's First Music Class offers a wealth of fun activities like singing, dancing, rocking, and exploring instruments, and shows adults how to help their children develop musically. While Music and Movement encourages children age eighteen months to three years to improvise and stretch their imaginations through music. It also offers classes—Musical Adventures and More Musical Adventures—for three- and four-year-olds, respectively. A number of private and group classes are offered for older kids, too, without parents or caregivers, including Musical Adventures, Dalcroze Eurythmics, Guitar, Keyboard, Violin, and more.

✻ Broadway Babies

St. Jean's Community Center

184 East 76th Street at Lexington Avenue

Reebok Sports Club/NY

160 Columbus Avenue

Citibabes

52 Mercer Street

472-0703

www.broadwaybabies.com

Age: 6 months to 12 years

Each week, a different Broadway musical sets the stage for this energetic, interactive, and educational Mommy and Me class. Four professional teacher/performers along with a live pianist sing out the show tunes in harmony while everyone performs and plays along with different props, toys, and musical instruments. Guided by highly accredited teachers and pediatricians, owner Audrey Kaplan's curriculum weaves educational activities such as Pre-K development of motor skills, color and letter recognition, counting, and socialization through the stories and songs of each musical.

✻ C.A.T.S. (Children's Athletic Training School)*

131 West 86th Street, 5th Floor,
bet. Amsterdam and Columbus avenues

877-3154

235 East 49th Street bet. Second and Third avenues

832-1833

Ages: 1 year and up

CATS is the only comprehensive children's sports training program for one- to twelve-year-olds in the United States. Baby CATS and Kiddie CATS meet once a week in a large auditoriumlike space; children under two years play on gym equipment such as slides and tunnels. Classes are large, eighteen toddlers with moms or caregivers, with three coaches for each session. Many children stay with the program for years, going on to take lessons in tennis, soccer, golf, hockey, basketball, dance, and martial arts. Alexander loved CATS and even participated in CATS summer programs for two years.

Chelsea Piers

Pier 62, 23rd Street at Twelfth Avenue
336-6500
Age: 6 months and up

In addition to its extensive adult offerings, Chelsea Piers, the largest sports complex in New York, offers various programs and facilities for very young children. Tiny Tots, for ages fifteen months to three years accompanied by caregivers, uses directed play such as games, art, and drama to encourage children to share and ask questions. For physical activity, enroll your child in the preschool gymnastics program (seventeen months to five years), or take her to the toddler gym, where she can crawl, roll, and jump on mats and equipment designed to help develop basic skills. Chelsea Piers also offers an excellent introduction to soccer for three- to five- year-olds. Benjamin was recently enrolled, and learned all the soccer moves and about teamwork. One session at the toddler gym is $10; call for other prices.

The Children's Studio

307 East 84th Street
bet. First and Second avenues
737-3344
www.thechildrensstudio.com
Age: 6 to 34 months

The Children's Studio offers a clean, cheerful space where babies can play with a variety of age-appropriate toys. An early education specialist provides a gently structured class with music, story time, parachute play, and more. Buy a package of fifteen visits and come at any of the scheduled times for your age group

($300 for 6- to 10-month-olds; $375 for 11- to 34-month-olds). Free trial classes. The Children's Studio space can also be rented for birthday parties.

Child's Play

Central Presbyterian Church
593 Park Avenue at 64th Street
838-1504
Rutgers Presbyterian Church
236 West 73rd Street at Broadway
877-8227, ext. 204/879-2019
www.rutgerschurch.com
Age: 6 months to 5 years

Child's Play offers a combination of story-time, gym play, singing, and art projects for parents and children (no caregivers). It also offers a nursery program for three- to five-year-olds, where parents stay with the children. A program is available for children being home schooled as well, providing a forum for parents to exchange ideas and a place for children to interact.

Children's Tumbling

Suellen Epstein
9 Murray Street
East Entrance, at City Hall
233-3418
www.childrentumbling.com
Age: 16 months to preteen

Downtown moms think highly of this tumbling and gymnastic program for children over eighteen months. Classes are a special combination of dance, gymnastics, and theater. The culmination of each semester is a show, with dramatic lighting, music, and stilt walking, in which the children showcase what they've learned. Classes for toddlers are kept small (six or seven children), last an hour, and meet once a week.

❈ Church Street School for Music and Art

74 Warren Street at West Broadway
571-7290
www.churchstreetschool.org
Age: 16 months and up
This well-regarded program teaches music, movement, art, and instruments. Church Street School features the Dalcroze method of music instruction, which combines music awareness and movement.

❈ Circus Gymnastics

2121 Broadway at 74th Street
799-3755
Age: 11 months to 12 years
Mommy & Me is a forty-minute class that includes circle games, supervised instruction on gymnastic equipment, a parachute, a ball pit, and a trampoline. The classes are for children ages eleven months to three years. All instructors are particularly skilled in working with young children. You and your little one can have a great time here.

❈ Columbus Gym*

606 Columbus Avenue bet. 89th and 90th streets
721-0090
Age: 12 months and up
The facilities at Columbus Gym are some of the nicest and cleanest in the city; there are tunnels, trampolines, balance beams, and hills to climb over and through. Gymnastic classes for toddlers twelve to eighteen months are with mom or caregiver. For older toddlers, there's P.E.P. (Preschool Enrichment Program), a ninety-minute mini-preschool class including gym, arts and crafts, painting, music, and story time. Pamela and Rebecca (and Pamela and Ben) took the P.E.P. class for a year and enjoyed it tremendously.

❈ Diller-Quaile School of Music

24 East 95th Street bet. Madison and Fifth avenues
369-1484
www.diller-quaile.org
Age: about 1 year and up
Diller-Quaile is a New York institution. There are music classes for toddlers and moms, as well as private instruction on different instruments. Classes begin in September and run until June. Music Babies, for those ages twelve to fifteen months, teaches lullabies, finger plays, nursery chants, and a variety of playful rhythmic activities. Music for Nearly Twos uses movement activities, games, and percussion instruments to guide classroom play. There are ten to twelve children in a class, with three instructors for children under eighteen months. Note: The application process begins one year in advance of classes. Call for more information. Classes start at $1,000 for thirty sessions.

Discovery Programs

251 West 100th Street at West End Avenue
749-8717
www.discoveryprograms.com
Age: newborn to 14 years
Discovery Programs is a popular uptown option for families. It has recently added a Parent Education Center to its mix, which hosts professionally led discussion groups for parents. Mommy and Me classes include Baby Massage and Music, Mommy Friends and Baby Friends, and My Grandparent and Me. These classes complement the already packed class offerings of dance, music, gymnastics, and art classes. A new On My Own program for two-year-olds has also been added, which features a gradual separation process based on each child's needs.

Do Re Mi

504 East 63rd Street at York Avenue
35 West 26th Street bet. Fifth and Sixth avenues
505-3456
Age: 4 months and up
This is a new class that was started by Leanne DeCamp, a popular former teacher at Gymboree and Curious Apple. Do Re Mi provides a fresh approach to early childhood music and movement education in a class that both explores rhythm and pitch development, and allows the children to experience the joy of movement in a positive, nurturing environment. Classes are forty-five minutes in length. Parents and caregivers actively participate. Call for a free trial class. Leanne is also a popular and experienced birthday party entertainer.

The Early Ear

48 West 68th Street bet.
Central Park West and Columbus Avenue
353 East 78th Street bet. First
and Second avenues
110 West 96th Street bet. Amsterdam
and Columbus avenues
877-7125 (for all locations)
www.theearlyear.com
Age: 4 months to 5 years
The Early Ear is a highly regarded introduction to music for babies as young as four months. Each class has ten children, with two teachers, one to accompany and another to demonstrate. Classes are forty minutes and incorporate sing-a-longs, games, play activities and mini musical instruments. The cost of each fifteen-week session is $435 with a registration fee of $35. From Pamela's own experience with Benjamin, it's best to start when the child is a year old.

Educational Alliance Parenting and Family Center at The Sol Goldman YMHA*

344 East 14th Street bet. First
and Second avenues
780-0800 ext. 239
Age: newborn to 36 months
The Educational Alliance Parenting Center offers Mommy and Me Two x Two play classes that concentrate on play, music, and art, and Tykercise, a sensory-movement course for children three to eighteen months. There is also a variety of multicultural classes, such as Chinese for Children (ages three to four) for adopted chil-

dren, French lessons, Judaica programs, and even a Japanese parenting center. Classes last from forty-five minutes to two hours and are limited to twelve children and adults. It also has a monthly Daddy and Me group (birth to one year), a three-session workshop for new parents called From Pair to Parent, evening groups for working and single parents, and other parenting classes. You can join the 14th Street Y for a yearly fee, which entitles you to program discounts, special events, priority registration, and pool and gym facilities. Classes have member and non-member fees. Kiki Schaffer, the director, creates a special sense of community and is an encyclopedic resource for the downtown parent.

❊ Funworks for Kids

201 East 83rd Street at Third Avenue
917-432-1820
Age: 9 months to 3 years
Funworks has existed for over seventeen years and offers sixty- or ninety-minute classes—a preschool-type program—of combined music, art, and movement. Classes feature free play that includes a ball pool and air mattresses, and circle time with singing, dancing, and the use of many props such as puppets, parachutes, and balls. Plus there's an art project and story time. This program has a loyal following and moms praise the extended program, especially the one for toddlers. Funworks also hosts birthday parties and play-time hours.

❊ Free to Be Under Three

24 St. Mark's Place, Suite 8
New York, NY 10003

988-1708/253-2040
www.freetobeunderthree.com
This very popular class was started a few years ago by Joe Robertson. It incorporates music, story time, and free play hour in a preschool-like environment. There are at least two teachers—with high energy and an understanding of early development issues—in each class. Register at birth, as the wait list is long and it can take a year or more to get a spot.

❊ Gymtime/Rhythm and Glues

1520 York Avenue at 80th Street
861-7732
Age: 6 months to 12 years
Gymtime offers organized play classes that feature songs, games, and circle time for mother and child in clean, bright rooms with gymnastic-style equipment. You'll also find a variety of classes, including cooking, sports, tae kwon do, and art for toddlers. There can be up to ten children in a class with two instructors; classes meet once a week for forty-five minutes to one hour. Gymtime will prorate its prices for latecomers.

❊ Hands On! A Musical Experience, Inc.

1365 First Avenue bet. 73rd and 74th streets
628-1945
529 Columbus Avenue bet. 85th
and 86th streets
496-9929
www.handson4music.com
Age: 4 months to 5 years
Samari Weinberg (no relation to Pamela), a seasoned

early-childhood music teacher, uses a specially formatted program, Hands On!, to present musical activities that also enhance other types of learning such as the acquisition of language, listening skills, auditory discrimination, social understanding, and personal discovery. Young students learn to listen and sing everything from popular American folk songs to Broadway tunes. Classical themes are introduced as well. Classes are approximately $480 for a fifteen-week session, plus a $30 yearly fee. Samari is a former Early Ear instructor, and is wonderful with children.

❋ Imagine Swimming

253-9650

www.imagineswimming.com

Age: 18 months and up

Classes by Imagine Swimming are $40 per session and have a very small (one to four) teacher/student ratio. Locations around the city include Hunter College, Twenty-fifth Street at First Avenue, and North Moore Street in Tribeca. Call for schedules or check it out online.

❋ JAMS

Ansche Chesed Synagogue

West 100th Street bet. Broadway

and West End Avenue

165 West 91st Street

www.jamsnet.com

Age: newborn to 6 years

JAMS is offered for children ages newborn to five years old. Founded by Jay Danzig, a music teacher with twenty years of experience, JAMS helps to cultivate a love and understanding of music in a unique way. Your child will be intro-

duced to international songs, dances, chants, rhythms, and more. Jewish JAMS is also offered, with an emphasis on teaching children Jewish songs and dances.

❋ The Jewish Community Center

334 Amsterdam Avenue at 76th Street

646-505-4444

www.jccmanhattan.org

Age: newborn and up

What doesn't the JCC have for kids? With arguably the best swimming pool in Manhattan (with a hydraulic floor!), new facilities, and top-notch instructors, the West Side truly got lucky when the JCC opened a few years ago. Now in full swing, classes include: gym, swim, art, music (the ever popular Little Maestros), dance, cooking, Jewish culture, and more. Grab a catalog, or get your name on the mailing list so you and your baby can sign up.

❋ Jodi's Gym*

244 East 84th Street bet. Second

and Third avenues

772-7633

Age: 6 months to 12 years

Classes in this brightly colored, well-padded facility feature free playtime, singing, stretching, and an obstacle course. Jodi personally trains all her instructors, who are certified by the USA Gymnastic Federation. Classes for children under three feature slides, ladders, tunnels, balls, and parachutes that are just right for tiny hands and feet. Classes are forty minutes, and there is a maximum of sixteen children to a class with two instructors.

Judy Stevens Playgroup*

77 Franklin Street at Church Street
941-0542
email: judy.stevens@mindspring.com
Age: 2 to 3 years
Judy Stevens, an artist and a mother, started forming playgroups for downtown moms more than seventeen years ago. And what special playgroups they are! Judy does art projects and activities with lots of music, movement, and free play in a warm, child-friendly loft. There are only six toddlers in a class. Classes meet three times a week. There is always a waiting list.

Kidville

163 East 84th Street
bet. Third and Lexington avenues
848-9415
www.kidville.com
Age: newborn to 5 years
Kidville has been the talk of the town since it opened in January 2005. It is a four-story entertainment complex with over one hundred classes for kids and grown-ups, plus a cafe, toy and clothing boutique, kid's hair salon, and movie theater. Enrollment in a class gives you automatic Silver membership, which provides discounts at the cafe and boutique and other perks. You can upgrade your membership to Gold or Platinum for an additional cost, which entitles you to additional discounts and a list of other goodies. Classes are $595–$895 for seventeen weeks. Kidville also has many birthday party packages that are proving to be quite popular.

Kids Co-Motion

Rebecca Kelly Dance Studio
579 Broadway bet. Prince and Houston streets
The Soundings
280 Rector Place
Stepping-Out Dance Studios
37 West 26th Street, east of Sixth Avenue
431-8489
www.rebeccakellyballet.com
Age: 12 months to 6 years
Choreographer Rebecca Kelly and her husband, dancer Craig Brashear, founded this popular, unique, and creative program in 1991. It provides a joyous atmosphere with motion, tumbling, song, and music for young children with their caregivers. Kids Co-Motion emphasizes a productive, positive learning experience. Classes run in twelve-week sessions, in fall, winter, spring, and in an extended summer program. Class prices vary with the length of the session. There is a one-time registration fee of $25 per family.

Kindermusik

The Greenwich Village Center
(a.k.a. The Children's Aid Society)
219 Sullivan Street at West 3rd Street
254-3074
Age: newborn to 7 years
Kindermusik is an international music program with more than twenty-one hundred teachers. This introductory music class gets toddlers singing, chanting, dancing, and playing simple instruments like rhythm sticks, bells, and drums. The sessions are forty-five minutes to an hour long, and children can participate with either a

parent or caregiver. Kindermusik also holds classes at Asphalt Green.

The Language Workshop for Children

888 Lexington Avenue at 65th Street

396-0830

Age: 6 months to 5 years

François Thibaut created the Language Workshops for small children in 1973, and today they are more popular than ever. In the Just for Tots program you'll find a variety of age-appropriate forty-five-minute classes for toddlers, including arts and crafts, music and movement, and gymnastics, in addition to the French and Spanish language workshops.

Life Sport Gymnastics

West Park Presbyterian Church

165 West 86th Street at Amsterdam Avenue

769-3131

Age: 12 months to adult

Rudy Van Daele has been teaching gymnastics for over twenty years. Classes here are small, with seven to eight students, and include activities on mats, trampolines, beams, and horses. Children are encouraged to try whatever interests them, from cartwheels to flips and more. Yoga classes are also offered.

Little Maestros*

344 East 69th Street

bet. First and Second avenues

347-400-3977

Age: 3 months to 3 years

This music class seems to be the most popular

class around right now. Each class has four teachers singing everything from "Bach to Rock" with guitar, piano, and percussion accompaniment. Every week there is musical story time, language development activities, a puppet show with an ongoing story, instruments, bubbles, and much more. There is often a guest musician as well. Evening classes are offered and are ideal for working parents; $455 plus one-time $30 registration fee for a thirteen-week semester. It does not offer trial classes at this time.

The Lucy Moses School for Music and Dance

129 West 67th Street bet. Broadway

and Amsterdam Avenue

501-3360

Age: 12 months and up

In Music Mates, toddlers sing, dance, and learn about different instruments with teachers Anna Rodriguez and Michael Glick. The school offers a class that combines rhythm games, creative movement, and dramatic play; and there are a number of music, movement, and dance classes for older preschoolers as well. Children attend with parents or caregivers.

Mary Ann Hall's Music for Children*

The Church of Heavenly Rest

2 East 90th Street bet. Madison

and Fifth avenues

(800) 633-0078

Age: infants, toddlers, and up

Mary Ann Hall's Music for Children is nationally

acclaimed. This early childhood program nurtures young children in a musical environment, "connecting the art of the music with the heart of the child." Children discover, explore, and develop natural musical abilities. Mary Ann and Emily Hall play the piano as children walk, march, gallop, and run to the appropriate accompaniment. They lead the group in various songs and free play with a variety of musical instruments. Weekly forty-five-minute classes, not exceeding ten children, run from October to May. Kelly has used this program with both of her children.

❋ Mama Nurture

West Park Presbyterian Church
165 West 86th Street
877-2005
www.mamanurture.com

Mama Nurture is a great new resource for Upper West Side parents. It offers playgroups in Spanish and French (as well as English, of course). In addition, it has Mommy and Me sign language, music, and creative play classes too. Call or check the website for schedules.

❋ The Mixing Bowl

243 East 82nd Street
585-2433
www.themixingbowlusa.com
Age: 30 months to 10 years

The cooking classes here a fun, hands-on affair where little "chefs" learn how a dish is prepared, prepare it, and eat the finished product. The classes also teach children about healthy snacks and nutrition.

❋ Mommy and Me
The Greenwich Village Center

(a.k.a. The Children's Aid Society)
219 Sullivan Street at West 3rd Street
254-3074, ext. 19
Age: 10 months to 3 years

Children play outdoors in an enclosed playground, sing songs, listen to stories, and do art projects. Toddler Time, Toddler Gymnastics, and Kindermusik are among the featured classes. There is also a variety of classes for children up to five years old, in subjects such as woodworking, pottery, ballet, and Kung Fu. There are ten children and two teachers in every class.

❋ Music Together*

Various locations
244-3046 (for all East Side locations)
219-0591 (for all West Side locations)
358-3801 (for all Lower Manhattan locations)
www.musictogether.com
Age: newborn to 4 years

Music Together is a forty-five-minute class for mommies and children (or caregivers/fathers), where they sing, dance, chant, and play with various instruments. At the beginning of the program, parents receive a cassette tape, a compact disc, and a charming illustrated songbook. They are encouraged to play the tape at home and children come to know and love the songs. Music Together has ten to twelve children per class. There are classes for babies and toddlers separately and classes for infants and toddlers mixed together. Tuition is $185 ($175 for returning families) for ten weekly 45-minute classes. Additional siblings are $150 each. Pamela has taken many classes at various Music Together locations with Rebecca and Ben. Instructors do vary with each location, so we recommend a trial class before signing up.

❊ Musical Kids

1296 Lexington Avenue
bet. 87th and 88th streets
996-5898
www.musicalkids.net
Age: newborn to 7 years
Music classes with two teachers and a pianist leading children in singing, dancing, and playing musical instruments.

❊ New York Kids Club

265 West 87th Street
bet. Broadway and West End Avenue
721-4400
www.nykidsclub.com
Age: 6 months to 12 years
The New York Kids Club recently expanded to the West 68th Street location and now has two locations on the Upper West Side, with a downtown location coming soon. It is a premier facility for children's gymnastics, rock climbing, and martial arts, and also offers classes in dance, drama, music, art, and cooking. Call for schedule information on classes at both locations.

❊ New York Swims

75 West End Avenue at 63rd Street
265-8200
The swim classes here take place at a clean pool in this high-rise building. Many of Pamela's friends' kids have taken classes here and have been very happy. Call for details.

❊ Once Upon a Baby

Various locations
769-3670
email: rl@onceuponababy.info
Age: newborn to 12 months
This innovative class led by Rebecca Lindenbaum, a former elementary school teacher wth a master's degree in education, is designed to help foster a lifetime love of reading and encourage development of language and motor skills. Parents will learn how to pick quality, age-appropriate books and to make reading to infants enjoyable and rewarding. Classes are $160 for five weeks. No trials offered.

❊ Rhinelander Children's Center

350 East 88th Street bet. First
and Second avenues
876-0500
Age: 6 months to 4 years
Rhinelander is a very popular Upper East Side community center. Mommy and Me classes, early childhood development programs, and evening parenting seminars are all taught here. The Baby Fingers class teaches sign language to six- to twelve-month-olds. Children twelve to eighteen months old can enjoy Steppin' Out, an hour of free play, music, art, stories, bubbles, and snacks. Toddler Time, for eighteen- to twenty-four-month-olds and thirty- to thirty-six-month-olds, and Kiddie Crafters, an art class for toddlers age two and a half to three and a half years, are also offered. Classes usually have fif-

teen children with two instructors. Classes fill quickly, so apply promptly.

❋ 74th Street Magic

510 East 74th Street bet. York Avenue
and the East River
737-2989
www.74magic.com
Age: 6 months and up

Seventy-Fourth Street Magic is held in a clean, bright, and large play space made up of two gyms. The gym for children over one year has padded tunnels, bridges, and houses, while the baby gym, for children under a year, is filled with a bubble pen and big balls. Classes focus on music, art, and gymnastics, and run from forty-five minutes to an hour. There are usually ten children per class with three instructors. Seventy-Fourth Street Magic also offers a large variety of cooking, drama, science activities, and birthday parties.

❋ Sokol New York Gym

420 East 71st Street bet. First
and York avenues
861-8206
Age: 10 months and up

Founded in 1867, Sokol New York offers Mommy and Me classes for infants, and a toddler gym class for one- , two- , and three-year-olds. Classes consist of free play, circle time, parachute play, bubbles, and more, with a different theme every few weeks. This is one of the most reasonably priced programs in New York—$495 for a once-a-week, forty-five-minute class—and it runs from September through May.

❋ The Sports Club/L.A. Fun 'n' Fit programs

330 East 61st Street
bet. First and Second avenues
917-286-9730
www.thesportsclubla.com
Age: 6 months to 13 years

Classes include Mush & Music, art, active playtime, cooking, dance, yoga, and a preschool alternative. Classes for non-club members start at $465 for eighteen weeks. Swimming classes for kids ages six months to three years cost $375 for ten weeks. Club members get roughly a 5-percent discount. Free trials.

❋ The Sunshine Kids' Club: A Preschool of Music

230 East 83rd Street bet. Second
and Third avenues
439-9876
Age: 6 months to 3 years

The SKC strongly believes that music expands a child's horizons intellectually, and strives to provide a curriculum that uses music to promote each child's individuality. Children are divided into six age groups and each class is limited to ten children. It also offers art classes for toddlers to three-year-olds. All classes are forty-five minutes and a parent or caregiver must accompany children. The space is small, but founder Trish Bolton is a gifted and talented teacher, and she spent many years at Diller-Quaile. These classes are hot right now, and tough to get into, so reserve your place early.

❄ Swim Jim

749-7335

www.swimjim.com

Age: 6 months and up

Swim Jim is a proven name in swim instruction in NYC. It offers group, semi-private, and private lessons in a variety of locations, including Fiftieth and Park, Seventy-second and York, and Forty-ninth and Tenth Avenue. Group classes are thirty minutes and a twelve-week session costs $300.

❄ Take Me to the Water

828-1756

www.takemetothewater.com

Age: 6 months and up

Heather Silver teaches private, semiprivate, and group swimming classes. Classes at Take Me to the Water can be as small as three babies and mothers with one instructor, and are taught at various public and private pools around the city. Classes parallel the school year; none are held in the summer.

❄ Tumble Town

118 East 28th Street bet. Lexington and Park Avenue South, Room 708

889-7342

www.tumbletownofnyc.com

Ages: 6 months to 6 years

Tumble Town is a gymnastics program for children six months to six years old. It offers Mommy and Me tumbling classes for the three-year-and-under set, and afterschool gymnastics classes for children three to six years old.

❄ Turtle Bay Music School

244 East 52nd Street bet. Second and Third avenues

753-8811

www.tbms.org

Age: 18 months to adult

Turtle Bay, founded in 1925, is a full-service music school offering private music classes in all instruments. Music and movement classes start for toddlers at eighteen months, and there are programs for two- and three-year-olds as well. The Mommy and Me classes focus on movement, song, and percussion instruments. This warm and friendly school is ideal for midtown families.

❄ YWHA 92nd Street*

1395 Lexington Avenue at 92nd Street

415-5600

www.92ndsty.org

Age: newborn to adult

The 92nd Street Y's Parenting Center has a variety of activities and outstanding programs for parents and children, making it a nationwide model. Classes include Lamaze, Caring for a Newborn, Breastfeeding, Baby Massage, Rock 'n' Roll Baby, Little Explorers, Kids in the Kitchen, and Parkbench. A $175 membership in the Parenting Center allows you priority registration, special prices for every class, invitations to New Parent and Toddler-Parent Get-Togethers, members' rates for baby-sitting ($10/hour), and special discounts at children's stores around the city.

Each of the following Y Associations offers a variety of classes for your baby, from gymnastics to music and swimming. Call your nearest Y for information, or go to www.ymcanyc.org.

❊ *YWCA of the City of New York*
610 Lexington Avenue at 53rd Street
755-4500

❊ *Vanderbilt YMCA*
224 East 47th Street bet. Second and Third avenues
756-9600

❊ *West Side YMCA*
5 West 63rd Street bet.
Central Park West and Broadway
875-4101

❊ *McBurney YMCA*
124 West 14th Street at Sixth Avenue
741-9210

mommy and me yoga classes

Since our first *City Baby* edition came out, there has been an explosion of yoga studios all over the city. There is probably one on your corner that has Mommy and Me classes but, if not, here are some good ones to check out. We have just listed them with web addresses, because many places have multiple locations and schedules change frequently.

❊ *Be Yoga*
www.beyoga.com

❊ *New York Yoga*
www.newyorkyoga.com

❊ *Prenatal Yoga Center*
www.prenatalyogacenter.com

❊ *Yoga for Two*
www.yogafortwo.com

❊ *Baby Om*
www.babyom.com

playgrounds

New York's parks and playgrounds provide just about every activity you can think of. The park is a great place for your baby or toddler to explore, swing, slide, and climb, and for you to meet other moms with children close in age to yours. And when the weather's nice, you'll love going out, enjoying a change of scenery, and taking in some fresh air.

The Department of Parks and Recreation oversees some 1,578 parks and 862 playgrounds around the city. In the past few years, many playgrounds have been renovated and now have soft rubber mat surfaces, brightly colored metal bars for climbing, and sprinklers for cooling. One of the city's most original playgrounds is the Rustic Playground at East 67th Street, a perfect stop before or after a visit to the Central Park Zoo.

You can call the Parks Department at 360-8111 (www.nycgovparks.org) for information on events in any of the city's parks. For older children, call the department's recreation office at 24 West 61st Street, 408-0243, to find out about playground programs, sports, and Arts in the Park, a summer series of free activities and performances for children. Playground Partners is a wonderful organization dedicated to fund-raising to help maintain the playgrounds within Central Park. Its annual spring parties in the Park are not to be missed!

Central Park

You can easily spend a leisurely day in Central Park (www.centralpark.org). Walk around the Boat Pond (72nd Street at Fifth Avenue), or sit in an outdoor cafe and watch the miniature boat enthusiasts sail their remote-controlled beauties across the pond. Run through the Sheep Meadow (69th Street at mid-park) or Strawberry Fields (72nd Street at Central Park West); bring a ball for a game of catch and some nibbles for a picnic lunch. Or buy one from a nearby concession stand.

Some of our favorite Central Park spots include:

* ❋ **Alice in Wonderland statue** (74th Street at Fifth Avenue). As soon as your youngster is moving around comfortably on her own, this huge bronze statue, full of nooks and crannies to climb on, will captivate her. There are always lots of kids, with moms and caregivers sitting on the nearby benches keeping an eye on things.

* ❋ **James Michael Levin Playground** (77th Street at Fifth Avenue). This newly reno-

vated playground has a padded gym/slide good for eighteen-month-olds and up; space to run, play, or ride a tricycle; an enclosed swing area; a big, roomy sandbox; and a toddler-friendly water sprinkler system for those hot summer days.

* ❋ **Spector Playground** (85th Street at Central Park West). A West Side favorite, this playground has an area for children under two, with a sandbox, slides, climbing equipment, and a blacktop space for tricycles and toy cars. For children over two, a sandy section of the playground has tire and rope swings, climbing chains, and more.

* ❋ **Adventure Playground** (next to Tavern on the Green, West 67th Street at Central Park West). Divided into two sections, a lower play area has baby swings, a sandbox, slides, and a bridge, while the hilltop playground, for older kids, resembles an Egyptian park. Perfect for "imagination" games!

* ❋ **Diana Ross Playground** (81st Street at Central Park West). This is the perfect place to go with your new baby or visiting five-year-old niece; it has baby swings as well as great climbing equipment for older kids.

* ❋ **East 96th Street Playground** (at Fifth Avenue). This large, well-laid-out playground is the East Side stomping ground for the four-to-six-year-old set. After preschool it is the place to meet, complete with swings, sandbox, climbing gym, and fort.

You'll undoubtedly find your own favorite parts of Central Park. And, of course, you'll pay many visits to these two special attractions:

❊ The Central Park Carousel

Middle of Central Park at 64th Street
879-0244

The Central Park Carousel is one of this country's great antique carousels. Each ride lasts about five minutes and is accompanied by calliope music. Your baby can ride with you on a horse that moves up and down, on a stationary horse, or in one of two chariots. Each ride costs one dollar per person.

❊ Central Park Wildlife Conservation Center (Zoo)

Fifth Avenue at 64th Street
439-6500

Officially called the Central Park Wildlife Conservation Center, this zoo provides natural habitats for mostly small (with the exception of the polar bear) animals. Visit the rain forest, complete with monkeys; the penguin house; and, of course, the sea lions' circular pool with see-through sides. The daily sea lion feedings are sure to delight your youngster. You'll find plenty of places to sit, as well as a cafeteria.

There are scheduled tours and activities each day (story hours, arts and crafts, and animal feedings), so call ahead. Adult admission is $6, $1.25 for seniors, children three to twelve years pay $1, and children under three are free. These prices include admission to the newly renovated Tisch Children's Zoo's Enchanted Forest and Domestic Animal Area.

Other Parks

While Central Park is the biggest and best, New York has a variety of parks where your child can have some outdoor fun. Here are some favorites, by neighborhood:

East Side (East River)

❊ **Carl Schurz*** (East End Avenue at 84th Street). This popular Upper East Side park has something for everyone: for infants, there is a play area with swings, bridges, and slides; for toddlers, there is an enclosed sandbox with climbing and sliding jungle gyms; and for adults, there is a superb riverside promenade. A paved pavilion with a sprinkler fountain running in the summer is used for ball play and tricycles in the fall and spring.

❊ **John Jay*** (FDR Drive at 76th Street). This big, clean enclosed playground has slides and moving bridges, a good central sprinkler system, a sandbox with swings for all ages, and benches all around. From the Fourth of July to early September, a large swimming pool is open from 11 a.m. to 7 p.m., and there are free swimming lessons for children ages three and up. Sign up early; the playground and pool get busy and crowded in the summer months.

You might also check out these parks:

❊ **St. Catherine's Playground**
(First Avenue at 67th Street).
Sutton Place Park

(FDR Drive at 57th Street).
MacArthur Playground
(FDR Drive at 48th Street).

West Side/Riverside Park

❄ *Hippo Park Playground at Riverside Drive and 91st Street.** This is one of our favorites, with adult and baby hippo statues ideal for climbing. It's extremely clean, and monitored by a parents' association as well as by the Parks Department. Picnic tables, benches, slides, a sandbox, seesaws, swings, and climbing equipment are shaded by fifty-year-old oak trees. This playground was specially designed for kids ages two to seven.

❄ *P.S. 87 Playground* at 77th Street and Amsterdam. This playground was completely gutted and redone recently. What a clever place! Lots of interesting structures to climb on, monkey bars for kids of all sizes—even pretend kiosks for kids who want to play "store."

❄ *Riverside Drive at 76th Street.** Here you'll find nicely divided sections for infants and toddlers, plenty of climbing equipment, swings, and a gentle circular sprinkler system. There is a separate sandbox, a nice grassy area, and a basketball court for older children nearby. Bring your sunscreen; there isn't a lot of shade.

❄ *River Run Playground at 83rd Street and Riverside.** This playground was recently renovated, and true to its name has a "river" running through the center (with about an inch of water in it). The water is turned on in this park if the temperature reaches 75 degrees. The playground also features a sandbox with faces sculpted into the perimeter, tons of climbing equipment for all ages, a mini carousel, and swings for all sizes.

A friend of Pamela's held her daughter's third birthday party here, and the kids had a blast! You must call the Parks Department for a permit, but it's free, and there are three picnic tables there to hold your pizza and cake. And remember this is New York—you can get pizza delivered directly to the playground!

Other Riverside Park playgrounds are located at:

❄ *Riverside Drive at 97th Street*

❄ *Riverside Drive at 110th Street*

❄ *Riverside Drive at 123rd Street*

Downtown

❄ *Hudson River Park Playground** (Chambers at Greenwich Street). A thriving downtown favorite, this clean, enclosed playground sits across from the esplanade of the Hudson River. All the equipment is labeled by age group, and there's a separate section with tables. There are swings, a sand table, a sliding bridge, climbing structures, sprinklers, and some of the most imaginative play equipment in the city.

❄ *Battery Park** (Battery Park City). Located at the tip of Manhattan, this park attracts a number of tourists. While the swings and slides (across from the entrance to the Staten Island Ferry) are old and outdated, the grassy park itself has a fabulous view and is a pleasant place for picnicking.

Also for downtown parents and tots:

❃ *P.S. 40*
(Second Avenue at East 19th Street)

❃ *Union Square Park*
(Broadway at East 16th Street)

❃ *Washington Square Park*
(West Fourth and MacDougal streets)

❃ *Duane Park*
(East Stuyvesant High School)

❃ *Abingdon Square Park*
(Bleecker and Bank streets)

❃ *James J. Walker Park*
(Leroy Street and Seventh Avenue)

public libraries

Beginning at six months, children are good candidates for short library visits. Sit and relax while your toddler listens during story time, watches a short film with popular characters, or participates in an arts and crafts project.

The New York Public Library system puts out a free booklet every month listing each branch's activities for children, but proximity to your home is the key in choosing what to do. Stop in or call and see what's going on.

Library branches with children's activities are listed below, by neighborhood.

Upper East Side

❃ *96th Street*
112 East 96th Street bet. Park and Lexington avenues
289-0908

❃ *67th Street*
328 East 67th Street bet. First and Second avenues
734-1717

❃ *Webster*
1465 York Avenue bet. 77th and 78th streets
288-5049

❃ *Yorkville*
222 East 79th Street bet. Second and Third avenues
744-5824

Upper West Side

❃ *Bloomingdale*
150 West 100th Street at Amsterdam Avenue
222-8030

❃ *Columbus*
742 Tenth Avenue bet. 50th and 51st streets
586-5098

❉ *Riverside*
127 Amsterdam Avenue at 65th Street
870-1810

❉ *St. Agnes*
444 Amsterdam Avenue at 81st Street
877-4380

Midtown

❉ *Donnell Library Center*
20 West 53rd Street bet. Fifth and Sixth avenues
621-0636
This special branch boasts the largest collection of children's and young adult books in the city. Moreover, it houses Christopher Robin's original Winnie-the-Pooh stuffed animals (Pooh, Tigger, Eeyore, Piglet, and Kanga), who live in the second floor children's room.

❉ *Epiphany*
228 East 23rd Street bet. Second and Third avenues
679-2645

❉ *Kips Bay*
446 Third Avenue at 31st Street
683-2520

Downtown

❉ *Hudson Park*
66 Leroy Street at Seventh Avenue South
243-6876

❉ *Jefferson Market*
425 Sixth Avenue at 10th Street
243-4334

Lower East Side

❉ *New Amsterdam*
9 Murray Street bet. Broadway and Church Street
732-8186

❉ *Tompkins Square*
33 East 10th Street bet. Avenues A and B
228-4747

Indoor Play Space

❉ *Sydney's Playground*
66 White Street at Broadway
431-9125
www.sydneysplayground.com
Downtown families have it made with this tremendous indoor playground located in Tribeca. This play space is great for kids newborn to age ten, and even offers a special space for nursing moms. There are age-appropriate toys all around and a jungle gym for older children.

other activities for you and your child

Everything in this section is definitely worthy of a gold star.

American Girl Place

609 Fifth Avenue at 49th Street
(877) AG-PLACE
www.americangirlplace.com
Ages: 2 to teen

The American Girl Place has been a great addition to New York. It is an entire four-story emporium dedicated to American Girl dolls. Little girls can shop, see a show, get their doll's hair done, and have lunch all in one place with their American Girl doll in tow. Just be warned: this place gets really crowded. It is best to reserve in advance for lunch and a show. This is also a popular place to celebrate a little girl's birthday. When Rebecca and Pamela dined there, birthday cakes came out of the kitchen at record speed.

The American Museum of Natural History

79th Street at Central Park West
769-5100
www.amnh.org

Even when the American Museum of Natural History fills with toddlers and their parents, it's so huge and full of hands-on exhibits and fascinating things to see that you'll hardly notice the crowd. Little children stare in wonder at the life-like dioramas and those spectacular dinosaurs. Parents love bringing their children to the Whale's Lair, where little ones can run around on the huge floor under the giant blue whale. And for your convenience, there's a child-friendly cafeteria, located in the basement. Adult admission is $13, children are $7.50, and seniors and students are $10.

Barnes & Noble/Barnes & Noble Junior

Locations throughout the city

These are more like community centers than bookstores. Introduce your children to the kids' sections, where they can listen to you read a story or lie on the floor to look at books by themselves. In addition, the stores have special scheduled readings, Gymboree story time, and bedtime stories. Schedules change weekly, so call ahead or drop by for a listing of events. Most Barnes & Noble stores are open from 9 a.m. to 10 p.m.; all events are free.

The Bronx Zoo

185 Street at Southern Boulevard
718-220-5100

At the Bronx Zoo, the largest in the United States, animals roam in large, natural settings. The Sky Ferry takes visitors through the park—a nice rest for a tired toddler and his exhausted parent. Visit the children's area, a petting zoo where youngsters can pet and feed some smaller animals and go on rides. Admission is $8 for adults and $6 for seniors and children two to twelve. Children under two are free and Wednesdays are free for everyone. Admission to the children's zoo is an additional $3.

The Children's Museum of Manhattan

212 West 83rd Street bet. Broadway and Amsterdam Avenue
721-1234

This interactive museum allows young children to explore, touch, and investigate its various exhibits. Its size has doubled since our first edition and the museum offers more than ever before for children of all ages. The Creative Corner is an early childhood center (for ages four and under) where children can paint, color, and play with educational toys in a specially designed kids' room. Exhibits change yearly, but you will always find something geared toward the under two set here. Story hours, puppet shows, and other activities are offered throughout the museum. It also offers terrific birthday parties that are popular for two and three olds. Admission is $8 for adults and children over one; children under one are free; seniors 65 and over are $5. Strollers or carriages must be folded up and checked at the door.

❊ The Children's Museum of the Arts

182 Lafayette Street
bet. Broome and Grand streets
274-0986
www.cmany.org

You can spend an entire afternoon at this hands-on museum, which offers exhibits as well as activities for children. You and your child can do arts and crafts, make a poster for Dad, or create a T-shirt design. Slides, climbing equipment, and a dress-up corner are also available. Two- and three-year-olds love this museum. Ages eighteen months and over: $6 per person.

❊ Dahesh Museum of Art

580 Madison Avenue
bet. 56th and 57th streets
759-0606
www.daheshmuseum.org

The Dahesh Museum has developed some nice programs for kids. One is their story time offered on Thursdays from 11:15 to 11:45 a.m., geared for children three to five years old with a parent or caregiver. It also has a Teddy Bear Tea in its Opaline Cafe each day from 2:30 to 5:00 p.m. The Tea features all kinds of kiddy foods served in a very grown-up setting. There are many hands-on art programs for older kids on weekends too.

❊ Metropolitan Museum of Art

Fifth Avenue at 82nd Street
535-7710

There are times you just need a good place to take a sleeping baby while you stroll around by yourself or with a friend. And even when your toddler is awake, the Met does have some open spaces, such as the reflecting garden, where the little one can roam. Strollers are not allowed on Sundays, but the museum will provide you with a backpack for your child when you check your stroller. We found that our toddlers were good for about an hour. Suggested donations are $15 for adults, $7 for students, and $10 seniors, but you can give whatever you want. Children under twelve are admitted free.

❊ Scandinavia House

58 Park Avenue bet. 37th and 38th streets
879-9779
www.amscan.org

Scandinavia House and its Heimbold Family Children's Center offers regular programs and activities for children and families. Scandinavia House provides a cultural link between the U.S.

and five Nordic countries. It's definitely worth checking out.

concerts, shows, and special events

When your child is between two and three years old, he may be ready to enjoy one of the city's many shows, concerts, or special events that are produced especially for children. Watch for:

❋ Performances of The Big Apple Circus (at Damrosch Park behind Lincoln Center from October through December), Sesame Street Live (at The Theater at Madison Square Garden in February), the Madison Square Garden Ice Shows (throughout the winter), and Barney, Baby Bop, and the gang (at Radio City Music Hall in January). Blues Clues, Rugrats, and Pokemón at Radio City at various times during the year. Call Ticketmaster or Telecharge for ticket prices and purchases.

❋ Children's theater shows are offered throughout the year by The Puppet Company (741-1646), Puppetworks (718-965-6058), TADA! (252-1619), The Paper Bag Players (633-0390), and Tribeca Performing Arts Center (220-1460).

❋ Call for prices, schedules, and information; some shows are for children ages three and over.

❋ The Lolli Pops Concert Series introduces children to classical music and the orchestra at hour-long concerts. Produced by The Little Orchestra Society (971-9500), the concerts are wonderful for children ages three to five.

❋ The Swedish Cottage Marionette Theater produces children's classics at the theater in Central Park at West 81st Street (988-9093). Kid favorites here have included Cinderella, Rumpelstiltskin, and Gulliver's Travels. Tickets are $5 for children, $6 for adults. Call ahead for reservations.

❋ New York Theatre Ballet's "Once Upon a Ballet" Family Series at the Florence Gould Hall (355-6160) is ballet made for children. Though the offerings change each year, The Nutcracker is always included in the package.

after-school activities

Preschoolers are tremendously curious about the world and have a great capacity to learn. Today many children ages three and younger are enrolled in programs designed to expand creativity, enhance social skills, and improve fitness. They might take violin lessons, attempt computer games, or plunge into the muddy delights of clay. Many toddlers enjoy tumbling or the challenge of martial arts classes, while others study languages, take ballet, and learn to swim.

Never before have there been so many choices for your child. But a word of caution: beware of over-scheduling. Every city baby, no matter how bright, needs some free time to play with friends or simply to be alone.

Choosing a Program

The hardest part of choosing a program is determining the best, most wonderful activity for your child when there are so many great options available. It's easy to become overzealous in your approach to your child's happiness and well-being, but you have to keep your perspective. Remember to be light-hearted about your child's free time. You're not sending him off to become a neurosurgeon or master violinist, but exposing him to activities that may or may not become large parts of his life. Finding a program ultimately should be a child-directed process. Rebecca tried ballet, gymnastics, soccer, and modern dance before falling in love with ice skating; now she's been skating for three years. Alexander tried acting, soccer, and tae kwon do, among other activities, and still hasn't settled on one "thing." Ideally, you want your child to experiment and learn, and have a great time, too!

Most classes are offered once a week on a year-long, semester-long, or per-class basis. A more intensive class, like a violin class, might meet twice a week. Our kids have enjoyed taking up to three or four classes per week, but don't push; you don't want to force anything, or you'll end up making a chore out of what should be a fun, passion-driven experience. In this chapter you'll find classes in art, dance, music, pottery, and theater, as well as a number of sports and personal enrichment programs, language and computer classes, and other programs like chess.

Whatever you choose, be sure to take convenience into account. We recommend choosing classes within ten blocks of your home.

Here are a few more things to think about when choosing a class or program:

* How long has the school/gym/academy been in business?
* How large are classes?
* How many teachers/coaches are there?
* Must you commit to a full year, by the semester, or by the class?

To make the process as easy as possible for you, we have listed classes in every subject appropriate for your city baby. Our kids and our friends' kids have tried many of these programs with happy results. But be sure to check out each program carefully yourself. Notice how the afternoon is structured, and how the teachers interact with the children.

You can also contact the Parent's League (at 737-7385) for more information on after-school activities available throughout the city. Good luck—and remember to have fun!

one-stop shopping: after-school institutions

Our "after-school institutions" really are one-stop shopping meccas, offering a multitude of programs for children of all ages—everything from art, music, gymnastics, and cooking, to science and Jewish culture. As your child gets older, he can even join a swim team or basketball league. These all-purpose after-school institutions make your life easy (always a plus for city moms), providing everything your child could need. The following are the best of these super schools with programs for children up to three years old.

❊ Asphalt Green
555 East 90th Street at York Avenue
369-8890 for catalog
www.asphaltgreen.com
This huge, modern fitness complex has an extensive Youth Aquatics program for children eighteen months and up; the instructor ratio is five to one. There is also a variety of gymnastics, indoor/outdoor soccer, and basketball classes, as well as instruction in karate and chess. It has one of the best pools in the city for learning to swim.

❊ Carmine Street Recreation Center
1 Clarkson Street
242-5228
Ages: 4 and up
Downtown families swear by the Carmine Street Recreation Center as a terrific, inexpensive place

for kids from Pre-K and up that's actually run by the City! Its after-school program is only $5/day, and it also has sports leagues (soccer, T-ball, baseball) which involve a nominal fee. It has both an outdoor pool (open from the Thursday before July Fourth weekend until the Friday before public schools open) and an indoor pool that is open all year and is free for children under thirteen.

❊ Chelsea Piers
Pier 62, 23rd Street and Twelfth Avenue
336-6500
www.chelseapiers.com
This enormous sports complex has it all: huge two-level gym, an entire track, a sand volleyball court, a climbing wall, a three-level driving range, twin hockey rinks, soccer fields, roller hockey rink—you name it. Tumbling classes are offered for children ages three and up.

❊ Discovery Programs
251 West 100th Street at West End Avenue
749-8717
Discovery Programs offers a range of interesting, creative classes for children from toddlers to age seven. The Young Leonardos class brings together artistic creativity and scientific problem solving by exploring the outside world, while the Young Explorers class learns about cultures throughout the world. Tae kwon do, ballet, and acting classes are also offered.

❊ Jewish Community Center
334 Amsterdam Avenue at 76th Street
646-505-4444

www.jccmanhattan.org

Age: newborn to adult

The after-school programs here are abundant and include everything from swimming, art, pottery, music, dance, gymnastics, and more. After-school sports are also popular here and kids can play soccer, basketball, and more, depending on the season.

❋ *92nd Street Y*

1395 Lexington Avenue at 92nd Street

996-1100

www.92ndsty.org

Here classes include tennis, circus arts, chess, cooking, computers, science, soccer, tae kwon do, gymnastics, swimming, music (including guitar and piano instruction), and dance (including ballet, Isadora for Children, and modern dance classes). Art classes include Learning from the Masters, in which kids create original artwork based on the media and techniques of famous artists; and A Course of a Different Color, in which children explore their ideas, dreams, and fantasies through mask making, book making, clay sculpting, painting, collage, and more. Kelly and Alexander have taken many classes here over the years.

❋ *Rhinelander Children's Center*

350 East 88th Street bet. First
and Second avenues

876-0500

www.rhinelandercenter.org

In Rhinelander's After School Arts & Smarts club, kindergartners and first-graders take part in the KinderClub, exploring art, music, and

computers, and engaging in dramatic play, dance, outdoor play, and cooking. In The After School Visual & Performing Arts Program, kids can take classes in art, music, fashion design, cooking, singing, dance, computers, ceramics, pottery, sculpture, woodworking, chess, and much more.

❋ *74th Street Magic*

510 East 74th Street bet. York and the East River

737-2989

www.74magic.com

74th Street Magic offers a wealth of activities for kids. There are music classes that explore the sounds of reggae, jazz, and more; science and exploration classes; Kindermusik classes that take kids on musical adventures with song, dance, stories, and games; various Tumble Time classes that provide gymnastics instruction for kids of different ages; and Magical Movement classes that integrate dance! Your child can also take art and music classes, as well as classes that incorporate stories, puppets, science activities, games, and more.

the arts

Art

❋ *After-School Art, Inc.*

510 East 74th Street
bet. York Avenue and the East River

431-1026

In Mark Rosenthal's After-School Art program,

children explore different media, create their own projects, work on fine motor skills, and have fun in general. A professional painter and former medical illustrator, Mark has taught art for over twenty years. He often tells fairy tales and myths during class. This is Rebecca's favorite art class. Each class is limited to fifteen children, and with ten or more children a second teacher is present.

✳ ARTKIDS
Museum Adventures NYC
646-201-9168
www.museumadventuresnyc.com
Age: 3.5 to 12 years
Mother of three Natasha Schlesinger started ARTKIDS a few years ago when she wanted to combine her passion for art with her love of kids. Her classes take moms and kids to a variety of museums and galleries all over the city to view art and do hands-on projects that coordinate with a theme. She also offers moms-only classes during school hours.

✳ Art-N-Orbit
Reebok Sports Clubs, East and West
160 Columbus Avenue at 67th Street
330 East 61st Street bet. First and
Second avenues
Jewish Community Center
of the Upper West Side
334 Amsterdam Avenue at 76th Street
The Children's Museum of Manhattan
212 West 83rd Street bet. Broadway
and Amsterdam Avenue
and other select locations

www.artnorbit.com
420-0474
Art-N-Orbit offers art and science programs for children ages eighteen months to ten years old. Classes last between forty-five minutes to an hour once a week, and are offered on a semester basis (September to December, January to March, April to June); summer classes are offered as well. Classes are $400 per semester, and are limited to fifteen children. Rebecca really enjoyed the class she took here. Art-N-Orbit also does fabulous birthday parties.

✳ Gymtime/Rhythm & Glues
1520 York Avenue at 80th Street
861-7732
Kids can take art, music, cooking, and dance classes, as well as combination classes like music/art, music/cooking, gym/cooking, and music/gym in this popular East Side program.

✳ Hi Art!
362-8190
www.hiartkids.com
Hi Art! is an ambitious ten-week series of workshops designed to introduce children ages two to twelve to "real" art in highly imaginative and creative ways. Classes are held in galleries and museums throughout the city as well as in a midtown studio, where children study opera, ballet, theater, and symphonies, and engage in ongoing art projects designed to help them understand how actual artists work. Each class series is centered around a contemporary musical work.

❋ *Kids at Art*

1349 Lexington Avenue at 89th Street

410-9780

www.kidsatartnyc.com

Age: 2 to 11 years

This bright, sunny art studio is a lovely place to take art classes, which are offered for kids two and up. Classes are creative, and kids are encouraged to use their imaginations to produce masterpieces "their" way. Kids at Art also has birthday parties.

Dance

❋ *The Ailey School*

405 West 55th Street

405-9143

The official school of the Alvin Ailey American Dance Theater offers a First Steps program for children ages three to six. Ballet is taught in graded levels, and classes incorporate other forms of dance (Dunham, Graham-based modern, Horton, and Limon techniques; West African, Spanish, and East Indian dance, mime, and floor gymnastics for boys) as children progress through the curriculum.

❋ *American Youth Dance Theater*

434 East 75th Street, #1C, bet. First and York avenues

717-5419

www.americanyouthdancetheater.com

Kids ages two and older learn ballet and creative dance, tap, and jazz.

❋ *Ballet Academy East*

1651 Third Avenue, 3rd Floor

bet. 92nd and 93rd streets

410-9140

email: info@baenyc.com

Age: 2 years to adult

Ballet Academy East offers mommy and me classes for girls two years and up, and pre-ballet, drama, and tap classes for girls three and up. The classes here are very structured and excellent. It is a must for all East Side little girls.

❋ *The Bridge for Dance*

2726 Broadway, 3rd Floor, at 104th Street

749-1165

www.bridgefordance.com

Children ages three and up learn expressive movement, while ages six and up begin studying ballet, tap, and pre-jazz.

❋ *Broadway Dance Center*

221 West 57th Street at Broadway

582-9304, ext. 25

www.bwydance.com

Broadway Dance Center offers children ages three to fourteen fun, creative, and challenging classes in ballet, tap, jazz, hip-hop, creative movement, pre-dance, voice, acting, and theater performance. It also has a youth performance company, A.I.M., or Arts in Motion, providing an opportunity for young dancers to perform in the community. Past students at the Broadway Dance Center have performed in *Miss Saigon*, *Annie Get Your Gun*, *Lion King*, and other Broadway plays.

Chinese Folk Dance Company

New York Chinese Cultural Center

390 Broadway, 2nd Floor, bet. Walker
and White streets

334-3764

In this Chinatown cultural center, children ages three and older can study Chinese language, Chinese dance, Chinese acrobatics, Chinese opera, and Chinese painting. All nationalities are welcome.

Dance for Children

Murray Street Studio

19 Murray Street bet. Broadway
and Church Street

608-7681

www.murraystreetdance.com

Children ages three and older explore the basic vocabulary of movement in the Creative Movement class, exercising their imaginations through ideas, images, and stories.

Djoniba Dance and Drum Center

37 East 18th Street, 7th Floor, bet.
Broadway and Park Avenue South

477-3464

www.djoniba.com

Children ages three to sixteen can take classes in African dance, African drums, capoeira, and ballet at this downtown studio.

The School for Education in Dance and the Related Arts

254-3194

Taught in schools and day-care centers throughout the city, this is an interrelated arts program that includes movement, music, theater games for self-esteem, exposure to visual quality arts, and tumbling as it applies to dance—all combined in one class. The purpose is to deal with the creative process at the earliest possible moment of a child's development, for lifetime use. If this program is not available in your child's school, you can call to discuss ways to bring it into your child's school.

In Grandma's Attic

Locations on the Upper West Side, Washington Heights, and special outreach classes for students attending St. Hilda's and St. Hugh's School and Chabad ELC

726-2362

www.ingrandmasattic.com

This is a fantasy-based creative dance program for children ages two to twelve. In Budding Ballerina (2–3 years) children dance to nursery rhymes and favorite stories; in Fairies and Fantasy (4–6 years) children revisit favorite fairytales and learn new tales and stories.

Greenwich House Music School

44–46 Barrow Street bet. Bleecker
and Bedford streets

242-4770

www.gharts.org

Greenwich House Music School has been providing high quality, affordable music education since 1902. Children ages two and older can choose from classes in music, art, ballet, and musical theater.

❋ Judy Lasko Modern Dance

West Side Cats
131 West 86th Street, 5th Floor
Studio School
124 West 95th Street
bet. Amsterdam and Columbus avenues
864-3143
This school offers modern dance classes for children ages three and up. Judy Lasko has been teaching for thirty-five years, and is both a dancer and Orff music teacher.

❋ Kids Co-Motion

Rebecca Kelly Dance Studio
579 Broadway bet. Prince and Houston streets
The Soundings
280 Rector Place
37 West 26th Street, east of Sixth Avenue
www.rebeccakellyballet.com
431-8489
Choreographer Rebecca Kelly and her husband, dancer Craig Brashear, founded this unique creative program in 1991. Kids Co-Motion emphasizes a productive, positive learning experience. In the after-school program kids ages three to seven are introduced to ballet and modern dance with emphases on creative movement and active listening to music.

❋ Kinderdance®

579-5270
www.kinderdance.net
Kinderdance® is a developmental dance, movement and fitness program for children ages two to eight. Classes are a combination of warm-up, motor skills, ballet, gymnastics, creative movement, and tap dance. This is a popular program taught in thirty different elementary schools throughout the city; outside students are accepted at some Upper West Side and Chelsea locations. You can also call about getting Kinderdance® into your own child's school.

❋ Manhattan Ballet School

149 East 72nd Street bet. Lexington
and Third avenues
535-6556
www.manhattanballetschool.org
At this forty-year-old neighborhood school children are taught classical ballet in a traditional manner. Children from ages three and up study creative movement and pre-ballet.

❋ The Lucy Moses School for Music and Dance

129 West 67th Street bet. Broadway
and Amsterdam Avenue
501-3360
www.ekcc.org/lucy.htm
For over fifty years, The Lucy Moses School has offered a variety of classes in dance, music, theater, and the visual arts for children ages eighteen months and up. A nurturing faculty makes learning the arts a very positive experience for children.

❋ Perichild Program

132 Fourth Avenue, 2nd Floor,
bet. 13th and 12th streets
505-0886

www.peridance.com

Located at the Peridance Center, the Perichild Program offers technique classes in ballet, modern, jazz, tap, hip-hop, and tae kwon do for children ages eighteen months and up.

✤ Shake, Rhythm and Roll

West Side Dance Project
357 West 36th Street, 3rd Floor
563-6781
www.westsidedanceproject.com

The West Side Dance Project offers dance and music education programs for children ages three and up. Classes are offered in instrumental music (on all instruments), music introduction, voice, creative movement, classical ballet, modern jazz, and tap. Classes are also held at an Upper West Side location.

✤ Steps on Broadway

2121 Broadway at 74th Street
email: info@stepsnyc.com
Age: 2.5 to adult

Like Ballet Academy East on the East Side, Steps is the West Side place to get your little ballerina started. Girls (or boys) start with Little Steps and can move up to pre-dance, pre-tap, or pre-ballet classes. The program here is very structured and serious. It is a real treat to watch the older kids and adult classes here too.

Drama

✤ The Drama Zone

220 East 86th Street
bet. Second and Third avenues
917-690-0789
www.dramazonenyc.com
Age: 4 months to adult

The Drama Zone offers classes in art, dance, music, or drama for babies as young as four months to kids ages thirteen and up. It offers morning classes for the youngest babies and after-school classes for kids three and up. Classes for toddlers include Let's Pretend, MusicZone, DanceZone, and DramaZone. Drama Zone also has summer camp programs and dramatic birthday parties. Call or check website for class times and schedules.

Music

✤ Bloomingdale School of Music

323 West 108th Street bet. Broadway
and Riverside Drive
663-6021
www.bsmny.org

Bloomingdale School of Music offers a variety of children's classes, including, keyboard, guitar, violin, recorder, chamber music, and Musical Adventures and More Musical Adventures, in which kids develop music skills through song, creative movement, listening, and playing.

✤ Campbell Music Studio

305 West End Avenue at 74th Street
436 East 69th Street bet. First and York
avenues
496-0105
www.campbellmusicstudio.com

Felicia and Jeffrey Campbell have been teaching

music to children for almost twenty years. Music classes for children ages eighteen months and up include live music, singing, movement, solfege, stories, notation, and original songs (Felicia writes them all).

❖ Church Street School for Music and Art

74 Warren Street at West Broadway
571-7290
www.churchstreetschool.org
This school offers a variety of classes in music and art for children ages sixteen months and older. Classes are offered in everything from music and movement to visual art, with an emphasis on the process of making art in a relaxed setting. A children's chorus, private lessons, and music therapy are also available.

❖ Diller-Quaile School of Music

24 East 95th Street bet. Madison
and Fifth avenues
369-1484
www.diller-quaile.org
Diller-Quaile is a New York institution. Through their Early Childhood program this family-based school offers a number of music classes for children from two to seven years, including Music and Movement, Dalcroze Eurythmics, Story Dramatization, Chorus, Creative Movement, Meet the Instrument, and Instrument Making. Classes meet for a full year. A forty-five-minute Rug Concert is given once a month, on Friday afternoons and Saturday mornings, for children both enrolled and not enrolled in school; concerts introduce

children to all the instruments of the orchestra, plus additional instruments (a tabla player comes once a year), and all kinds of singing voices. The concerts also involve singing, movement, and the opportunity for audience members to play rhythm instruments. This is one of the most established music schools on the Upper East Side.

❖ Family Music Center

Various locations
864-2476
Colleen Itzen was the first Kindermusik® teacher in Manhattan, and still offers the program to children ages newborn to seven years. In these music and movement classes children enjoy singing, rhyming, instrument playing, dancing, and composing. Private instruction on the piano is also available.

❖ The French-American Conservatory of Music

154 West 57th Street, Suite 136
(Carnegie Hall), at Seventh Avenue
246-7378
www.facmusic.org
The French-American Conservatory of Music, located in the historic Carnegie Hall studios, offers Kindermusik® classes for children ages three years and up, as well as private instrumental and vocal instruction for ages four and older.

❖ Greenwich House Music School

44–46 Barrow Street bet. Bleecker
and Bedford streets

242-4770

www.gharts.org

See entry on page 115.

✱ Mary Ann Hall's Music for Children

2 East 90th Street bet. Fifth and

Madison avenues

(800) 633-0078

These creative classes for kids ages two to eight weave music in and out of poetry, books, dance, drama, and art. Kelly has taken many classes here with Alexander and Angela, and always finds them to be warm and upbeat.

✱ Mozart for Children

129 West 67th Street bet. Broadway

and Amsterdam Avenue

15 Gramercy Park on 20th Street

off Park Avenue

120 East 87th Street bet. Lexington

and Park avenues

942-2743

www.mozartforchildren.com

Debbie Surowicz's popular classes introduce children ages one and a half to seven to classical music through singing, rhythmic instruments, and choreographed dances. Classes include live music and visits from various musicians. Private mini-group classes are also available at your own location.

✱ Music, Fun & Learning

339 East 84th Street bet. First and

Second avenues

263 West 86th Street at West End Avenue

717-1853

At Music, Fun & Learning children four months to six years enjoy instruments, movement, stories, and singing in spirited classes featuring live music and colorful props (toddlers come with a parent or caregiver). Teacher and director Barbara Frankel helps kids develop their imagination, coordination, and listening skills while learning about different musical qualities. She also offers private classes in piano and flute, provides entertainment at birthday parties, and demonstrates instruments and songs from around the world in a participatory song and story hour called Tuneful Tales, held several times a year. Call for details.

✱ The School for Strings

419 West 54th Street bet. Ninth

and Tenth avenues

315-0915

This Suzuki-based school teaches violin, cello, and piano to children ages sixteen months and up. Beginners take a full course of study, which includes a weekly individual lesson, musicianship class, group class, and parent class (in which parents learn the rudiments of the child's instrument). After the first year, parents are no longer required to take classes, but are expected to remain actively involved in the child's instruction. As children advance, study of orchestra and, eventually, chamber music is incorporated into their routine. The School for Strings is also one of the leading teacher-training schools for violin, cello, and piano in the United States.

❈ Third Street Music School Settlement

235 East 11th Street bet. Second
and Third avenues
777-3240

This school was founded in 1894 as a settlement house for anyone interested in art and music, regardless of talent or ability to pay. In addition to being a fully licensed preschool with an arts focus, the school also offers a variety of music classes in voice, and various instruments and forms of performance (chamber music, ensemble, etc.) for children ages eighteen months and up. Some dance and art classes are also offered.

❈ Turtle Bay Music School

244 East 52nd Street bet. Second
and Third avenues
753-8811

Turtle Bay, founded in 1925, is a full-service music school that offers private music classes in all instruments for children ages eighteen months and older. This warm and friendly school is ideal for midtown families.

Pottery

❈ Greenwich House Pottery

16 Jones Street bet. Bleecker
and West Fourth streets
242-4106

This long-established school offers classes exclusively for children, and also classes in which children ages two and a half to five collaborate with parents or caregivers to create imaginative clay works.

Cooking

❈ The Miette Culinary Studio

109 McDougal Street, Suite 2
460-9322
www.cookingwithmiette.com
Age: 4 months to 11 years

The Miette Culinary Studio has classes for children as young as four months! For the youngest babies, class offerings include an organic baby foods class while older children learn real cooking techniques and skills and use a large variety of kitchen equipment and tools. All children learn knife skills, such as chopping, mincing, and slicing. The Miette studio also offers weekend workshops (such as chocolate making) and custom birthday parties.

sports

Gymnastics

Gymnastics is a popular after-school activity, especially for girls. If your daughter is an avid gymnast, many of these facilities also have teams.

❈ Asphalt Green

555 East 90th Street bet. York
and East End avenues
369-8890 for catalog
www.asphaltgreen.com

❈ Chelsea Piers

Pier 62, 23rd Street at Twelfth Avenue
336-6500
www.chelseapiers.com

�֍ *Circus Gym*
2121 Broadway, 2nd Floor, at 74th Street
799-3755

�֍ *Columbus Gym*
606 Columbus Avenue bet. 89th and 90th streets
721-0090

�֍ *Gymtime Gymnastics*
1520 York Avenue at 80th Street
861-7732

�֍ *Jodi's Gym*
244 East 84th Street bet. Second
and Third avenues
772-7633

�֍ *Life Sport Gymnastics*
West Park Presbyterian Church
165 West 86th Street at Amsterdam Avenue
769-3131

�֍ *Sokol New York*
420 East 71st Street bet. First and York avenues
861-8206

�֍ *Tumble Town Gymnastics*
Baruch College Early Learning Center
104 East 19th Street
387-1420

�֍ *Wendy Hilliard Foundation-Rhythmic Gymnastics NY*
792 Columbus Avenue,
Suite 17T, at 100th Street
646-587-5421

Sports Training

✖ *The Baseball Center NYC*
202 West 74th Street
bet. Broadway and Amsterdam Avenue
www.thebaseballcenternyc.com
Age: 1 to 12 years
The Baseball Center NYC (formerly Frozen Ropes) offers baseball and softball programs for kids as young as one year old. The Baseball Center instructors teach the kids all aspects of baseball and softball including: hitting, pitching, fielding, catching, throwing, base running, confidence, visualization, breathing, focus and concentration, and goal setting. Pamela's son Benjamin has taken classes here for years and loves the small class size and individualized attention.

✖ *Super Soccer Stars*
877-7171
www.supersoccerstars.com
Age: 30 months to 12 years
Super Soccer Stars is all the rage with the five-and-under set. Super Soccer Stars features skilled coaches who work with small groups of boys and girls to develop self-confidence and teamwork in a fun, non-competitive environment. It is a great after-school sports program that is held at dozens of locations around the city. Check the website for locations and class schedules.

Swimming

These locations offer individual and group lessons. A special favorite here is Take Me to the Water; many New Yorkers have taught their children to swim through this program.

✳ Asphalt Green
555 East 90th Street bet. York
and East End avenues
369-8890 for catalog
www.asphaltgreen.com
This huge, modern fitness complex has an
extensive Youth Aquatics program for children
eighteen months and up; the instructor ratio is
seven to one for kids five years and older, and
five to one for younger.

✳ New York Health and Racquet Club
60 West 23rd Street
989-2300
Private swim classes

✳ Take Me to the Water
10 locations
828-1756
www.takemetothewater.com

Yoga

As yoga gains popularity with moms and dads, kids
want to join in the fun, too. Here are some studios
that offer yoga for kids.

✳ B.K.S. Iyengar Yoga Association
150 West 22nd Street, 11th Floor
bet. Sixth and Seventh avenues
691-9642

✳ Goodson Parker Wellness Center
30 East 76th Street, 4th Floor,
at Madison Avenue
717-5273

personal enrichment programs

Computers

✳ Futurekids Computer Learning Center
1628 First Avenue bet. 84th and 85th streets
717-0110
www.futurekidsnyc.com
At Futurekids Computer Learning Center, children ages three to fifteen learn the latest technology. Children are introduced to animation,
graphics, operating systems, word processing,
the Internet, and more—all incorporated with
themes and subjects kids love.

✳ The Techno Team
Reebok Sports Club
160 Columbus Avenue at 67th Street
501-1425
Provided by Radicel Education Technology,
these classes introduce children ages three and
older to the use of computers in daily life, and
focus on enhancing and enriching academic
and creative skills. Classes are small with individualized programs for each child.

Etiquette

✳ Nicole De Vault, Etiquette Consultant
415 East 37th Street, Suite 22J,
bet. First Avenue and the FDR Drive
481-7280
Nicole De Vault offers private lessons for chil-

dren ages four years and older, and will make house calls to work with families in their homes. Parents and children can formulate their own curricula, focusing on table manners, social skills (introductions, eye contact, posture, conversation), phone manners, cross-cultural etiquette, or any combination of the above.

Language

❋ Big Apple Kids
221 West 82nd Street
579-0301
email: info@bigapplekidsnyc.com
Age: 6 months and up
Big Apple Kids offers French and Spanish language classes for babies (six months and older) and children in a playful and comfortable setting. These are playgroups in which French and Spanish are spoken with moms and caregivers.

❋ China Institute in America
125 East 65th Street bet. Park
and Lexington avenues
744-8181, ext. 142
www.chinainstitute.org
Children ages three to ten gain familiarity with Chinese language and culture through active classroom instruction. Songs, games, and art add to the linguistic and cultural experience.

❋ La Croisette French Language Center
861-7723
La Croisette offers three separate programs in which children learn French through a range of fun, creative activities. In the regular classes, children ages two and a half to nine learn through songs, poems, creative projects, stories, games, and educational videos, while in the Art/French class kids ages five to seven focus on painting, collage, printing, stencils, and more. A Puppetry at La Croisette class centers around puppet making, puppet "discussions," and a small puppet show kids put on for parents—all in French, of course!

❋ La Escuelita
302 West 91st Street
877-1100
www.laescuelitanyc.org
Age: 2 to 9 years
La Escuelita was founded in 2002 by two parents, both professional educators, who wanted bilingual play and preschool experiences for their children. Their mission is to promote bilingualism in children from a very young age. Their programs include both a Bilingual Preschool for children ages two to five years old, and an after-school program that's for children ages five and up.

❋ Language Workshop for Children
888 Lexington Avenue at 66th Street
396-0830
Children ages three to ten learn French, Spanish, or Italian in an active environment, filled with songs, play, sports, gymnastics, cuisine, and dance.

kid-friendly
restaurants

Yes, dining out with your new baby or toddler can be an enjoyable experience; the choice of restaurant is critical and must meet your needs. They are as follows:

When your child is still an infant, under one year, you want a restaurant that provides stroller or carriage space and a staff that doesn't mind babies.

When your child is a toddler, an understanding staff is even more important since your youngster may knock over a glass of water, rip up the sugar packets, or throw flowers on the floor. Also, the restaurant should provide adequate booster seats and quick service (so you can be in and out of the restaurant in an hour).

Certainly, if you have favorite neighborhood spots with food you already love, you can always look around to see if children are dining there and whether there is adequate space next to tables for a stroller holding a sleeping infant.

But what do you do when you are in an unfamiliar neighborhood? Look for kid-friendly clues: paper rather than cloth table covering, crayons, children's menus, booster seats, high chairs, and interesting sights such as fish tanks, rock pools, gardens, shopping areas, and the like. New York's ethnic restaurants can be wonderful for children. The owners usually like kids; waiters will bring them something to eat right away; and they can be flexible about menu offerings. Coffee shops are good, too, but not necessarily during a frantic lunch hour.

But what about the food? We are not restaurant critics, but we do know what we like where family dining is concerned. Good food for everyone is integral to the dining experience. Out of two zillion options, we are including our favorites for you to dine en famille.

Before you go out, consider your child's ability to sit still and eat in a somewhat mannerly fashion. Some days it might be better to stay home and order in.

Upper East Side

✳ Barking Dog Luncheonette

1453 York Avenue at 77th Street
861-3600
1678 Third Avenue at 94th Street
831-1800
These are cozy spots with cozy food like meat loaf, pot roast, mashed potatoes, and all-day breakfast stuff. The decor is comfortable, too, with a dog motif.

✳ California Pizza Kitchen

201 East 60th Street bet. Second
and Third avenues
755-7773
With all of the great New York pizza in this city, who would have thought that California Pizza Kitchen would be so popular? People like California Pizza Kitchen for its unique style of pizza and for its tremendous variety of toppings. Proximity to Dylan's Candy Bar doesn't hurt either. The restaurant is kid friendly and offers yummy pizzas and pastas for the little ones, as well as high chairs and crayons.

✳ China Fun

1221 Second Avenue at 64th Street
752-0810
246 Columbus Avenue at 71st Street
580-1516

These restaurants are big and noisy and just our style, with inexpensive, generous portions that kids love. In fact, we know a couple of kids hooked on the steamed vegetable dumplings.

Googie's
1491 Second Avenue at 78th Street
717-1122

Incredibly popular with moms and babies during the week, this is also the spot for Sunday brunch on the Upper East Side. The crowds come because the diner food is decent and well priced and the service is pretty speedy. You will feel comfortable here with your screaming baby because yours won't be the only one.

Hi Life Bar and Grill
1340 First Avenue at 72nd Street
249-3600
477 Amsterdam Avenue at 83rd Street
787-7199

Yummy bar food and burgers—and now sushi, too! It is reasonably priced, and the waitstaff friendly. Take advantage of the kid-appealing early-bird specials every weeknight until seven. Don't forget the fries—they're fabulous!

Il Vagabondo
351 East 62nd Street bet. First
and Second avenues
832-9221

Haven't been here for a while? Remember the bocce court? Kids love it, of course. They don't have to concentrate on eating but can look at an actual ball rolling on a floor really made of

dirt . . . in a restaurant! This restaurant is crowded and loud, with Italian fare everybody likes.

Lili's Noodle Shop and Grill
1500 Third Avenue
bet. 84th and 85th streets
639-1313

Lili's is a favorite with Pamela's kids who are picky when it comes to Chinese food. Lili's food is always delicious and fresh—the chicken and broccoli is a winner. It offers all of the food kids like, such as dumplings, spare ribs, and noodles too. New to Lili's are the Bubble Tea drinks, which can keep kids occupied at the table for the entire meal.

Nick's
1814 Second Avenue
bet. 93rd and 94th streets
987-5700

Nick's has some of the most delicious thin-crust pizza on the East Side. It is a friendly restaurant, too, with yummy pastas and salads. Much of the food is served family style, so it is a great place to go with a crowd. Kids will love the pizza and pasta and you will too. The back room is a great place for a birthday party.

Serendipity 3
225 East 60th Street bet. Second
and Third avenues
838-3531
www.serendipity3.com

A classic. Your child's not a New York kid until he's had a foot-long hot dog (which he'll never finish) and a frozen hot chocolate (which you will finish quite easily). Lots of great stuff to look at here, from the offerings near the front door to the giant clock and colorful stained glass lampshades. It's also fun to walk up and down the spiral staircase. No strollers or carriages!

❊ Tony's Di Napoli

1606 Second Avenue at 83rd Street

861-8686

This spacious Italian restaurant is a favorite of East Side families, with enormous portions served family style. Strollers are not permitted at the tables, so bring a car seat. Families should come early for best service.

Upper West Side

❊ Alice's Tea Cup

103 West 73rd Street at Columbus Avenue

799-3006

www.alicesteacup.com

This charming spot is a great addition to the Upper West Side. With its Alice in Wonderland theme, there is plenty to look at in the shop area in the front of the store. In the restaurant, you'll find scones, soups, sandwiches, and a full morning or afternoon tea—served on eclectic china. The children's menu includes sandwiches of granny smith apple slices and peanut butter or Nutella, grilled cheese, homemade Graham crackers, and pureed baby food. Pamela's friend Vicky had her daughter's birthday party in the back room at Alice's and it was terrific.

❊ @SQC

270 Columbus Avenue

bet. 72nd and 73rd streets

579-0100

www.sqcnyc.com

Owners Linda and Scott Campbell (the restaurant's name is based on Chef Scott's initials) have created a restaurant for grown-ups, but also cater to kids with a special kids' menu, including gourmet, homemade baby food (also available to take home). The decadent hot chocolate and delicious French fries are not to be missed.

❊ Fairway Cafe

2127 Broadway at 74th Street

595-1888 ext. 145

Upstairs from the market (there is an elevator) you will find the Fairway Cafe. Breakfast is served here all day, or kids can opt for burgers, soup, veggie platters, or sandwiches. Fairway Cafe is mommy central—especially during the week. Pamela is a big fan of the omelettes here and her kids love the milkshakes, which are huge! Booster seats and high chairs available.

❊ Firehouse

522 Columbus Avenue at 85th Street

595-3139

www.therestaurantgroup.com

This is a great place to take your kids: the Firehouse menu has burgers, fries, chips, guacamole for grown-ups and kids' pizza (plus five different styles of pizza for adults). Firehouse has always been popular with the post-college crowd for its inexpensive chicken wings and beer, but before the twentysomethings arrive, families rule.

Fred's

476 Amsterdam Avenue at 83rd Street

579-3076

1649 Third Avenue bet. 92nd and 93rd streets

While there is no kids' menu here, kids love Fred's because of its dog theme. There are photos of dogs all over the walls and plenty to look at for the young ones. Kids dig the hamburgers and French fries here, as well as the pasta and chicken. The weekend brunch menus feature French toast, pancakes, and eggs, which are good options too. High chairs are available.

Gabriela's

685 Amsterdam Avenue at 93rd Street

961-0574

It's big, bustling, open all the time from breakfast until dinner so you can eat at odd hours, and the place is filled with kids of all ages. Authentic Mexican fare (downright cheap) from tacos to quesadillas, enchiladas, and rice and beans for the kids, to more exotic house specialties for you. Be extra early for dinner, or you'll wait.

Josephina

1900 Broadway bet. 63rd and 64th streets

799-1000

If you're near Lincoln Center and if you're in the mood for healthy, organic California-style eating, this is the place. It's airy, roomy, and kids like it.

Louie's Westside Cafe

441 Amsterdam Avenue at 81st Street

877-1900

This comfortable neighborhood place will prepare anything your kids want. The staff is happy to push tables together for bigger parties.

Popover Cafe

551 Amsterdam Avenue at 87th Street

595-8555

Children love the teddy bears that live all around this restaurant; kids can "adopt" one while you enjoy the wonderful food. Freshly baked popovers with strawberry butter are the main attraction here, and well worth waiting for.

Ruby Foo's

2182 Broadway at 77th Street

724-6700

1626 Broadway at 49th Street

489-5600

www.brguestrestaurants.com

While Ruby Foo's does not have a kids' menu per se, kids really enjoy the decor and vibe here. The restaurants are theatrical and boisterous with delicious Pan-Asian cuisine. Even picky eaters will like the noodles, rice and spare ribs, and dumplings all served family style. The Ruby Foo's in the theater district is the perfect place for a pre-theater dinner or lunch for the family.

Sambuca

20 West 72nd Street

bet. Central Park West and Columbus Avenue

787-5656 • 799-9052

This dinner-only restaurant offers all the traditional Italian dishes, such as penne pasta, ravioli, and chicken and veal parmigiana, so it's not difficult to find something here you and your kids will like. While there is no kids' pizza, there are plenty of good pasta dishes and classic italian ice creams and desserts to please any toddler. Moreover, Sambuca is reasonably priced and offers takeout and delivery for Upper West Siders in this neighborhood.

Midtown East and West

❈ Benihana

120 East 56th Street bet. Park and Lexington avenues
593-1627
47 West 56th Street bet. Fifth and Sixth avenues
581-0930
www.benihana.com
Kids adore Benihana. Watching the chefs cook at your table provides hours of entertainment. Even the pickiest eaters will enjoy the delicious steak, chicken, and shrimp here. The chefs are usually pretty friendly and put on quite a show with slicing, dicing, and tossing the food. Benihana is a popular spot for kids' birthday parties.

❈ Broadway Diner

590 Lexington Avenue at 52nd Street
486-8838
This upscale diner is better than most but remains easy on the pocket. The food is typical American fare, including sandwiches, salads, grilled burgers, eggs, and pancakes. This is a good choice if you're in a hurry; you'll have no problem getting in and out in less than an hour.

❈ Ellen's Stardust Diner

1650 Broadway at 51st Street
956-5151
www.ellensstardustdiner.com
This fifties-style diner features milkshakes, burgers, chicken, and tuna melts, as well as some Mexican dishes and an assortment of salads. The waiters sing and entertain; the kids will enjoy it as much as you will.

❈ Hamburger Harry's*

145 West 45th Street bet. Broadway and Sixth Avenue
840-2756
Known for big burgers, Harry's is casual and friendly. The menu has chicken and eggs, too, but this is a place for a burger fan.

❈ Metropolitan Cafe

959 First Avenue
bet. 52nd and 53rd streets
759-5600
Metropolitan is large, busy, and kid friendly, and its main attraction is the beautiful outdoor garden. The menu reflects Indonesian, French, and Chinese, but mostly American influences.

Chelsea/Flatiron

❈ America

9 East 18th Street bet. Fifth Avenue and Broadway
505-2110
On weekends this huge, friendly restaurant sets up a kids' reading area with little tables, chairs, and books. A balloon artist wanders

through on Saturday and Sunday afternoons making balloon hats and animals. There are lots of high chairs and good food that appeals to the whole family.

❈ Chat 'n' Chew

10 East 16th Street
bet. Union Square West and Fifth Avenue
243-1616

It feels like you're in a tiny town in the South in the 1950s, but you could only find a place like this in New York. There's plenty to look at in this crowded restaurant, from antique advertising signs to old jukeboxes. If you can take it, there are great deep-fried dishes, too. Chat 'n' Chew is best for booster-seat kids.

West Village

❈ Arturo's Pizzeria

106 West Houston Street at Thompson Street
677-3820

Here's a neighborhood place with a low-key atmosphere friendly to kids. The brick oven pizza, their specialty, is delicious, and the service is quick. Arturo's also serves all types of salads, pastas, and chicken dishes.

❈ Cowgirl Hall of Fame

519 Hudson Street at West 10th Street
633-1133

Li'l pardners from all over come to see the Western memorabilia in this cool little shop that stocks everything from sheriff badges to squirt gun holsters, bandanas, and rawhide vests. The food appeals, too, with a perfectly messy Frito

pie (a bag of chips split open, topped with chili) and a baked potato dessert (vanilla ice cream rolled in powdered cocoa and topped with "sour cream," or whipped cream that sits on a hot fudge pond).

East Village

❈ Miracle Grill

112 First Avenue bet. 6th and 7th streets
254-2353
415 Bleecker Street between Bank Street and West 11th Street
924-1900

This comfortable and reasonably priced restaurant serves excellent black bean soup, lamb, and pork chops. Dine in the garden at the East Village location, if possible—it's beautiful; a nice place to relax when you've been on the go all day.

❈ Two Boots

37 Avenue A bet. 2nd and 3rd streets
505-2276

❈ Two Boots to Go-Go

74 Bleecker at Broadway
777-1033

❈ Two Boots to Go West

201 West 11th Street at Seventh Avenue
633-9096

❈ Two Boots Pizzeria

42 Avenue A at 3rd Street
254-1919

The "boots" of Italy and Louisiana kick in for great pizza with creative toppings. Great decor, lots to look at, and a great party atmosphere that's enhanced by lively music.

SOHO

❊ *Peanut Butter & Co.*

240 Sullivan Street

677-3995

Peanut Butter & Co. is a fun place to go with the peanut butter lover in your family. It doesn't serve mere out-of-a-jar peanut butter here, of course. This peanut butter is ground fresh daily and is served on fresh bread with a tremendous variety of options on top. The peanut butter comes in six varieties: creamy, crunchy, spicy, cinnamon raisin, chocolate chip, and white chocolate.

❊ *Tennessee Mountain*

143 Spring Street at Wooster

431-3993

Be prepared for messy fingers and faces at this BBQ joint. Bringing your children is encouraged here—they get a chef's hat and crayons. You can find some of the best barbecue ribs in the city here; and parents will go for it, too.

Lower East Side

❊ *Grilled Cheese NYC*

168 Ludlow Street (near Stanton Street)

982-6600

www.grilledcheese.com

There are so many choices of grilled cheese at this tiny cafe that you will be dazzled. You can conjure up your own sandwich variety here, or have them make one of their eight different grilled cheeses with a variety of toppings such as Canadian bacon, turkey, or ham, and cheeses such as American, cheddar, and mozzarella. Obviously, this is a kids' paradise but some days, even parents want to feel like a kid again. Here they do.

Central Village/NOHO

❊ *Noho Star*

330 Lafayette Street at Bleecker Street

925-0070

A standard for some Manhattanites, this restaurant has a casual and comfortable atmosphere that easily accommodates kids. You'll find interesting Chinese and Thai food here, as well as kid favorites like pasta, burgers, salad, and chicken.

Tribeca

❊ *Bubby's*

120 Hudson Street at North Moore Street

219-0666

The menu at this kid-friendly restaurant is standard diner fare but better, with a gourmet twist. Bubby's is best known for its delicious breakfasts; it's a popular brunch spot on weekends.

❊ *The Odeon*

145 West Broadway bet. Duane and Thomas streets

233-0507

Popular with celebrities for years, this restaurant has gained a following among downtown families. It is a cozy spot, with great food and good people watching. Don't skip the fries! The Odeon gives out crayons, too.

The Chains

Somedays you will just need a reliable restaurant where you can have a decent meal with the kids. Special menus, reasonable prices, and high chairs are all to be expected at local and national chains. Popular national chains include Pizzeria Uno and T.G.I. Friday's.

❉ Carmine's
2450 Broadway at 91st Street
362-2200
200 West 44th Street bet. Broadway and Eighth Avenue
221-3800
Popular, family-style southern Italian food is the specialty here. Carmine's is bustling, fun, and noisy but the wait can be long. If you go with at least six people, you can make a reservation (and you'll be able to sample more dishes).

❉ Dallas BBQ
Various locations including:
1265 Third Avenue at 73rd Street
772-9393
27 West 72nd Street bet. Columbus Avenue and Central Park West
873-2005
132 Second Avenue at 8th Street
777-5574

Inexpensive, big portions of kid favorites from ribs to burgers and corn on the cob make this a great standby.

❉ EJ's Luncheonette
1271 Third Avenue at 73rd Street
472-0600
447 Amsterdam Avenue bet.
81st and 82nd streets
873-3444
432 Sixth Avenue bet. 9th and 10th streets
473-5555
Tons of families come for the children's menu featuring everything from PB&J to scrambled eggs. Breakfast is served all day long, an interesting concept. (We call it brinner.) Lines are long for weekend brunch.

❉ Jackson Hole Burgers
1611 Second Avenue bet. 83rd and 84th streets
737-8788
232 East 64th Street bet. Second and Third avenues
371-7187
517 Columbus Avenue at 85th Street
362-5177
521 Third Avenue at 35th Street
679-3264
1270 Madison Avenue and 91st Street
427-2820
This traditional burger joint has every kind of burger and topping you could ever want, as well as great fries, salads, omelettes, Tex-Mex stuff, and fantastic chocolate cake and sundaes. Kids love it!

John's Pizzeria

260 West 44th Street bet. Broadway
and Eighth Avenue
391-7560
408 East 64th Street bet. First
and York avenues
935-2895
278 Bleecker Street bet. Sixth
and Seventh avenues
243-1680

Some New York parents we know swear these thin-crust pies from a wood-burning oven are the best in the city. The service is fast; there's pasta for the rare child that does not eat pizza; there's plenty of room around the tables; and it's noisy, so your child won't stand out among the loud voices of all the other children. Another plus: your child can watch the chefs prepare your pizza.

La Cocina

217 West 85th Street bet. Broadway
and Amsterdam Avenue
874-0770
2608 Broadway bet. 98th and 99th streets
865-7333

La Cocina features moderately priced but quite generous single tacos, burritos, enchiladas, and more, including large, well-deserved margaritas for the adults. There's plenty of room around the tables. Kids get to choose a marble to take home for their collections.

Ollie's Noodle Shop & Grille

200 West 44th Street at Seventh Avenue
921-5988
1991 Broadway bet. 67th and 68th streets
595-8181
2315 Broadway at 84th Street
362-3712
2957 Broadway at 116th Street
932-3300

Early every evening, Ollie's is filled with children who love the soups, noodles—from soft to crispy; from hot to cold—and all the other classic Hong Kong–style dishes. Huge portions, moderate prices, and the fastest service a parent could ever hope to find are all huge plusses.

Patsy's

Seven locations throughout Manhattan
688-9707 (East Side location)

Families love Patsy's and for good reason. The pizza is delicious, the service is fast, and the prices reasonable. With seven locations around Manhattan, there is surely a Patsy's near you. They don't take reservations, and waits can be long, so go early if you are bringing hungry kids along. They don't have a kids' menu, but pizza and pasta do the trick.

Theme Restaurants

The West fifties now offer big blaring restaurants of all varieties and gimmicks that are sure to attract visitors. Amid the tourists, you won't find a whole lot of New York parents popping in (waiting in line is more like it) as their first choice for dining. However, you may find yourself in that neighborhood or planning a birthday party, and these places do come up in conversation. So here goes:

Hard Rock Cafe
221 West 57th Street bet. Broadway
and Seventh Avenue
489-6565

Jekyll & Hyde
91 Seventh Avenue South
bet. West Fourth and Barrow streets
989-7701

Mars 2112
1633 Broadway at 51st Street
864-2553
www.mars2112.com
Creatures from all planets are welcome at this
Times Square restaurant. This restaurant's
theme, celebrating all things from the Red
Planet, is wacky and fun. It serves the standard
kids' fare, such as hamburgers and chicken fingers, but also has adult entrees, such as
salmon, for parents. Dancing martians and
other aliens will keep your little ones entertained while you dine. Mars 2112 has an arcade
and a gift shop.

Mickey Mantle's
59 Central Park South
bet. Fifth and Sixth avenues
688-7777

Planet Hollywood
1540 Broadway at West 45th Street
333-7827

Coffee Bars

It is amazing that we once lived without double iced-
mocha lattes. Even more important, that hit of caffeine, administered at opportune moments during
the day, does a lot for a mother who has been called
into action during the wee hours. Here are two of
our favorite places to swill coffee, accompanied by
babies and toddlers.

DT:UT
1626 Second Avenue
bet. 84th and 85th streets
327-1327
41 Avenue B
bet. East 3rd and 4th streets
477-1021
This coffee bar/lounge has plenty of space for
strollers. The coffee, including delicious lattes
and cappuccinos, is good, and the food selection is appealing. Menu items include sandwiches (ham & cheese, tuna fish, and more), as
well as delicious chocolate fondue and make-
your-own s'mores. Lots of quiet corners and
tables with sofas and comfortable chairs make
this feel like your own living room. A relaxing
place for breakfast, lunch, or just a snack—the
staff never rushes you.

Starbucks
For branches, call 613-1280
Atmosphere and ample space at Starbucks
make it a good choice for a group of stroller-
clad moms. You can sit for hours and chat over
a coffee. (That is, if your munchkin will allow it.)
And, if you're hungry, Starbucks offers a nice
selection of breakfast foods all day, plus

prepared sandwiches for lunch. We couldn't live without our their tall skim lattes. In fact, we wrote the bulk of *City Baby* at various Starbucks around town.

a few words on bathrooms...

We can't even begin to tell you how important this topic is. Once you begin to venture into the world with your child, you'll soon realize the challenge of finding a decent bathroom in the city. New York can frustrate even the most formidable city moms searching for a clean place to change a diaper. To aid you in this important mission, here are some good bathrooms in a variety of neighborhoods. Keep them in mind in case you suddenly find yourself in a bathroom bind. We've noted the best places for diaper changing and nursing; all bathrooms include a handicapped stall unless otherwise noted.

❋ *Barnes & Noble*

Locations throughout the city
All the Barnes & Noble stores have bathrooms, and the stores with a Junior section have an oversized stall with a changing station inside.

❋ *Starbucks*

Locations throughout the city
All Starbucks have large bathrooms. Most have a diaper deck inside.

See the lists below for some of the nicest spots in town, but remember any hotel will suffice! If you are

desperate McDonald's and Burger King have bathrooms, but they are rarely the cleanest. We suggest scoping out your neighborhood for kid-friendly restaurants that will let you use their bathrooms when needed. This will come in handy for potty training, too!

East Side

If you're anywhere in midtown on the East Side, you're near a number of department stores that provide comfortable, clean bathrooms. Barneys (Madison Avenue at 61st Street), Bergdorf Goodman (Fifth Avenue at 57th Street), Bloomingdale's (Third Avenue at 59th Street), Bendel's (Fifth Avenue at 55th Street), Lord & Taylor (Fifth Avenue at 39th Street), and Saks Fifth Avenue (Fifth Avenue at 50th Street) all have bathrooms with enough stalls so that there's usually not a line; all include diaper changing areas and/or couches or chairs nearby or in the stalls that are suitable for diaper changing or for nursing.

Here are some other facilities you'll want to know about:

❋ *FAO Schwarz*

767 Fifth Avenue at 58th Street
644-9400
Location: second floor

❋ *The Hotel Pierre*

2 East 61st Street bet. Madison
and Fifth avenues
838-8000
Location: main floor

The New York Palace Hotel*
455 Madison Avenue at 50th Street
(800) 697-2522
Location: second floor (take stairs up one flight
or the elevator)

The Regency Hotel
540 Park Avenue at 60th Street
759-4100
Location: main floor lobby

Tiffany & Company*
727 Fifth Avenue at 57th Street
755-8000
Location: mezzanine

The Waldorf-Astoria
301 Park Avenue at 50th Street
355-3000
Location: main floor lobby

West Side

Macy's
151 West 34th Street at Herald Square
695-4400
Locations: cellar, second, sixth,
and seventh floors

Manhattan Mall
100 West 32nd Street at Sixth Avenue
465-0500
Locations: second, fourth, sixth,
and seventh floors

New York Hilton
1335 Sixth Avenue at 53rd Street
586-7000
Location: second floor on
the 54th Street side of hotel

Time Warner Center
59th Street at Columbus Circle

Downtown

ABC Carpet & Home
888 Broadway at 19th Street
473-3000
Location: second and fourth floors

Bed, Bath & Beyond
620 Avenue of the Americas at 18th Street
255-3550
Location: main floor

SoHo Grand Hotel
310 West Broadway bet. Grand
and Canal streets
965-3000
Location: main floor

South Street Seaport
(The Fulton Market)
11 Fulton Street
732-7678 (general information)
Location: mezzanine

Tribeca Grand Hotel
2 Avenue of the Americas
bet. White and Walker streets

519-6600
Location: lower level past the concierge desk

✳ *World Financial Center*

The Winter Garden
West Street bet. the World Trade
Center and the Hudson River
945-0505
Location: main floor

the big firsts

A baby is to celebrate! First you mark the new arrival with a printed birth announcement, something special, of course, but where do you find exactly the right thing? In the ensuing months, as you watch your baby grow, there will be many joyful and singular moments to celebrate. We call them "the big firsts." For each, New York can provide an expert who will help you make the most of these once-in-a-lifetime occasions. This chapter lists what we've discovered to be the best stationers for buying ready-made or personalized birth announcements; the most fun and unusual party places; the absolute best bakeries for ordering that first—and second, and third—birthday cake; the most skillful and entertaining hair cutters; the most reliable shoe stores; and the most artful photographers for that important first portrait.

Of course, you will be taking hundreds of your own photos as your child grows. For Rebecca and Alexander, we always had a camera at hand to record such things as haircuts and parties. But with the second and third child, we found it was easy to overlook either photographing or videotaping their big firsts. To make sure you never miss a special moment, do what lots of moms do: keep a disposable camera in your stroller.

You will be amazed at how fast your baby grows. Just when you are wondering when your baby will ever have enough hair to warrant a real haircut, it will be time to consider another important first: preschool. This is a rite of passage in New York, or anywhere, and we conclude with a few suggestions on how to start exploring the options.

birth announcements

Even in this day of e-mail and websites, printed birth announcements are still the most popular way to get the word out about the new addition to your family.

There are several options available. You can purchase ready-made cards at a stationery or party store and fill in your new baby's name, weight, size, and birth date.

Or you can order through a catalog, such as K & T birth announcements—(800) 964-4002; www.kandtannouncements.com. The price for 100 announcements and plain envelopes is $99 ($79.20 online); envelopes printed with the return address are an additional $24 ($19.20 online). Most parents we know order pre-printed cards. Another alternative, economical too, is to buy plain cards and print announcements from your computer at home. If you have a digital camera, you can even print a snapshot of your little bundle of joy on the card. Kelly did this the second time around, believing that everyone who knew her well already knew about Angela's arrival, and that it was unnecessary to spend hundreds of dollars on birth announcements.

It's a good idea to choose your announcements a month or so in advance of your due date. If you are ordering from a store or catalog, plan on two weeks for printing. Get your envelopes early, and address them in advance. Then, after the baby is born, call the shop with all the details, such as height, weight, sex, and date and time of birth.

New York stationers have everything you could possibly want, and they will ship your selection directly to you. Below, we list the best. These are also great sources for special birthday party invitations for the years to come.

❋ Blacker & Kooby

1204 Madison Avenue at 88th Street

369-8308

www.blackerandkooby.invitations.com

With more than seventy companies to choose from, the selection at Blacker & Kooby is outstanding. It ranges from well-known lines like Crane's, Regency, and William Arthur, to smaller, more creative ones like Blue Mug and Stacy Claire Boyd. At this Carnegie Hill spot, an order for 100 baby announcements starts at $150.

❋ Hudson Street Papers

At time of publication, this store was in the process of relocating to the East Village, so check local information for new details.

Hudson Street Papers is a legendary West Village shop where parents can create the announcements of their dreams. In addition to name-brand cards like William Arthur, it offers a choice of 450 varieties made from their unique in-store computerized lettering and design system. With a turn-around time of one week, it is a terrific alternative to more traditional cards. One hundred birth announcements start at $180 to $250.

❋ Hyde Park Stationers

1070 Madison Avenue at 80th Street

861-5710

In comfortable surroundings, you can sit and look at a variety of manufacturer's lines, including Crane's, William Arthur, Chase, Elite, and Regency. Prices for an order of 100 cards range from $100 to $700.

❋ Jamie Ostrow

54 West 21st Street, 2nd Floor

734-8890

Beautiful announcements, as well as personal stationery and invitations, designed by Jamie Ostrow fill this lovely store. There are many other lines to choose from, including Crane's. An order of 100 announcements starts at around $200.

❋ Jill M. Cooper
Personalize it!

799-8317

email: jillcoops@aol.com

Jill is also a new mom who does great business with birth announcements, stationery, and more. She carries tons of stationery lines and party favors too. She offers different specials each month, so contact her website for sales and promotions on announcements.

❋ Kate's Paperie

561 Broadway at Prince Street

941-9816

8 West 13th Street at Fifth Avenue

633-0570

1282 Third Avenue at 74th Street

396-3670

These crème de la crème of paper stores carry an outstanding selection of baby announcements, including unusual and hard-to-find manufacturers, such as Sweet Pea, Indelible Ink, Blue Mug, and Stacy Claire Boyd. Working with an experienced staff person, customers can also design their own cards and choose from dozens of papers and type styles. Announcements can then be printed by letterpress if so desired. An order of 100 cards starts at $200. Kate's hands-on approach and the store's very welcoming atmosphere make new moms feel right at home.

❋ Laura Beth's Baby Collection
321 East 75th Street bet. First and Second avenues
717-2559
Laura Beth, a former buyer in the Baby Department at Barneys New York, meets one-on-one with stylish moms-to-be to help them select their birth announcements as well as linens and accessories. She offers high-end cards, both whimsical and classic, at prices 20 percent below retail—or 100 cards for $150. Lines include Stacy Claire Boyd and more.

❋ Lauren Wittels
Excellent Paper Place
235 West 76th Street, apt. 4A
580-0921 (fax: 703-832-2193)
email: lauren@excellentpaper.com
www.excellentpaper.com
Excellent Paper offers all of the latest and greatest options in baby announcements and stationery. Check out the offerings online, or call for an appointment to view the extensive card lines. It also offers 20 percent off retail prices on all orders.

❋ Lincoln Stationers
1889 Broadway at 63rd Street
459-3500
Lincoln Stationers is a wonderful resource for

the Upper West Side. It carries all major brands, or you can create your own card with the staff.

❋ Little Extras
676 Amsterdam Avenue at 93rd Street
721-6161
Little Extras carries many of the top lines, such as Stacy Claire Boyd, Regency, Sweet Pea, Encore, Indelible Ink, and Lalli, all discounted. Orders of $200 or less are discounted 10 percent, and orders over $200 are discounted 15 percent. An order of 100 cards costs anywhere from $100 to $300. This comfortable store delivers for free if you live on the Upper East or Upper West Side.

❋ Mrs. John L. Strong
Barneys
660 Madison Avenue at 61st Street, 2nd Floor
833-2059
Elegant and exquisite, this stationer is one of the few in New York that still practices the art of hand engraving. Prices start at $500 for 100 announcements and go up according to style and detail. Mrs. John L. Strong is the engraver of choice to the city's socially prominent; she is a favorite of Martha Stewart Living. You may see her showroom by appointment. Some of her cards are also sold at Barneys.

❋ Papyrus Cards & Stationery
1270 Third Avenue at 73rd Street
717-1060
852 Lexington Avenue bet. 64th
and 65th streets
717-0002

107 East 42nd Street at Lexington
Avenue (Grand Central Station)
490-9894
2157 Broadway bet. 75th and 76th streets
501-0102
www.papyrusonline.com

Papyrus is an upscale chain of fine papers and cards, with lines like William Arthur, Crane's, Stacy Claire Boyd, Cross-My-Heart, and Carlson Craft. An order of 100 announcements costs between $240 and $500, and is usually shipped to the customer within seven to ten days. Papyrus can be found in malls around the tri-state area. This is also a great place to find special gift items.

❖ *Rebecca Moss, Ltd.*

510 Madison Avenue at 53rd Street
832-7671

This handsome store sells some prepackaged birth announcements but focuses on big manufacturers' books, including those of Crane's, William Arthur, Stacy Claire Boyd, and Cross-My-Heart. An order of 100 announcements costs approximately $200.

❖ *Tiffany & Co.*

727 Fifth Avenue at 57th Street
755-8000

Tiffany & Co. has a large stationery department offering both the Tiffany brand and some Crane's lines. The Tiffany cards are simple, elegant, engraved, and pricey. The average cost for 100 announcements is more than $500. It also has contemporary lines of cards that are a bit more fun.

❖ *Venture Stationers*

1156 Madison Avenue at 85th Street
288-7235

One of the most popular East Side shops for stationery and announcements, Venture carries a large selection of manufacturers, including Stacy Claire Boyd, Sweet Pea, Crane's, Lalli, and Regency. The average price for 100 announcements is $150 to $200. Venture is also a great place to pick up a quick birthday gift, with a nice selection of craft kits and other items. Pamela often shops here when she is in the neighborhood.

birthday parties

Many parents love extravagant birthday parties, especially their child's first one. When your baby hits the magic age of one, the birthday party is mostly for Mom, Dad, grandparents, and friends. A cake and a few balloons will make most one-year-olds very happy, and you'll get great photos of your baby mushing up his icing.

We like the idea of having the first birthday at home, but this may not be possible if you have a big family, many friends, and a small apartment. Happily, New York is full of places that organize parties for one-year-olds. Keep this list handy for future reference—two- through six-year-olds can have even more fun at a party place.

Most of these sites will host a party seven days a week. They offer catering services that supply everything down to the cake and party favors, though all will let you bring your own. Prices are noted, but this is New York, so they may change over time. Call ahead. The Parent's League at 115 East 82nd Street (737-7385) has more party information; however, you must be a member ($90 annual fee) to use their files. Many of the below listings are great for older kids' birthdays, too. We've had and attended many second, third, fourth, and even seventh birthdays at several of the places mentioned below.

Party Places and Entertainment

❖ *Chelsea Piers Gymnastics**

Pier 62, 23rd Street at Twelfth Avenue

336-6500

www.chelseapiers.com

Little ones, ages six months to three years, spend thirty minutes in a party room and an additional hour or more in the baby gym, where they can crawl, explore, play in a ball pit, and be entertained by an instructor. For $350, ten kids can play for one and a half hours ($15 for each additional child, per hour). Older children, ages three and four, have a more advanced gymnastics experience in which they play on rope swings and a trampoline. Chelsea Piers also offers theme Barbie or Batman party packages. For older kids, Chelsea Piers offers parties of all types, including bowling, ice-skating, roller-blading, and basketball. Catering is additional. The bowling parties are a lot of fun—Kelly can attest to this.

❖ *Circus Gymnastics*

2121 Broadway at 74th Street

799-3755

Circus Gym offers fun gym-based parties for kids ages one and up. Children can jump on the trampoline, go through obstacle courses, and play on and under a parachute. Each party is one and a half hours long, and includes at least two instructors for the group. Circus Gymnastics provides coffee for the grown-ups, and you provide everything else—paper goods, food, drinks, cake, etc. A party for ten children is $475 ($18 for each additional child). Pamela held Rebecca's first birthday party here with much success. Catering from Fairway (downstairs) makes it easy. Space is available Friday afternoons, Saturday, and Sunday.

❖ *The Craft Studio*

1657 Third Avenue at 92nd Street

831-6626

The Craft Studio is one of our favorite birthday party spots. The staff is superb and the craft choices for parties are endless. You can choose from a wide array of parties, including pottery painting, cookie decorating, gingerbread houses, chocolate houses, decorating picture frames, and much more. The parties are held in the back room, where there is fun music and games are played when the little ones are done with their projects.

❖ *Eli's Vinegar Factory**

431 East 91st Street at York Avenue

987-0885, ext. 4

www.elizabar.com

Eli's Vinegar Factory offers a wide variety of party options in their own setting on the second floor of the store. Spacious and comfortable, this is a terrific place to hold large birthday parties for any age. The basic party package costs $25 per child (with a minimum of twenty-five kids), and another $300 for staffing. Clearly this is not a bargain, but we've never tasted better food at a birthday party! This price includes a two-hour party, tables and chairs, balloons, snacks, juice, and two kiddie entrees—with options like chicken fingers, mini pizzas, and PB&J. Eli's does not provide entertainment, but you are free to hire your own entertainers and have them perform in the space. For an additional charge, Eli's will host a pizza-making party or a cookies-and-cake-decorating party. Eli's offers a full adult catering menu as well, so if you'd like to offer food for adults, they can do it all.

❋ Gymtime*

1520 York Avenue at 80th Street

861-7732

Partygoers can play in the padded big or mini-gym spaces. Kids enjoy tumbling and crawling in the gym spaces, and participating in activities involving a trampoline, a parachute, a ball pit, and bubbles. There are also circle songs. Helium balloons are provided, along with coffee and tea for adults. The space is available Friday, Saturday, and Sunday during the school year, and Monday and Wednesday in the summer. The cost is $550 for ten children ($17 for each additional child, up to twenty-five children) for one and a half hours.

❋ Jodi's Gym*

244 East 84th Street bet. Second

and Third avenues

772-7633

The Five Best Places to Have a Two-year-old's Party

1. Your home, if you have room, or a common space in your apartment building.
2. Any place with Bobby DooWah, a musical entertainer (917-762-2421)
3. Columbus Gym (721-0090)
4. Kidville New York
5. Children's Museum of Manhattan (721-1234)

Jodi's Gym is very popular among the two through four crowd. This bright and spacious facility provides a young child with gym equipment all scaled down to just the right size. Birthday party kids play for forty-five minutes with an obstacle course, air mattress, balance beams, bars, mats, slides, parachutes, bubbles, and much more. They then have thirty minutes for cake and ice cream. A party for ten children costs $525 ($16 for each additional child). Food packages are available. Jodi's is available Monday through Friday in the summer, and Monday, Friday, Saturday, and Sunday during the school year.

❋ Linda Kaye's Birthday Bakers PartyMakers

195 East 76th Street bet. Third

and Lexington avenues

288-7112

www.partymakers.com

Linda Kaye offers children's birthday parties at a

most unique location, The Central Park Wildlife Center. For children ages one to four, she offers two themes: Animal Alphabet Safari, where children learn about animals through the alphabet. The cost for 15 children is $560 to $660 for an hour to one and a half hours, respectively. Linda Kaye offers an extensive party selection for older children as well, both at the zoo and at the Museum of Natural History.

❊ Our Name Is Mud

1566 Second Avenue bet. 81st and 82nd streets
570-6868
506 Amsterdam Avenue bet. 84th and 85th streets
579-5575
59 Greenwich Avenue
at Seventh Avenue and 11th Street
647-7899
www.ournameismud.com
Our Name Is Mud is a great place to have a birthday party for children ages three and up. Each party guest chooses a piece of pottery to paint and have fired in the kiln. These parties can be costly depending on which piece the children choose, but Our Name Is Mud has a good selection of reasonably priced pieces. For parties of fewer than twenty-five people, you will share the space with others, but will have hands-on attention from the staff, plus balloons and other goodies.

❊ Party Poopers*

100 Greenwich Street
274-9955
www.partypoopers.com
Party Poopers creates zany and original theme parties at its various locations throughout the city. It has a large selection of costumed characters to choose from, as well as magicians, clowns, storytellers, puppeteers, and other entertainers. Prices start at $339 for one character at your own location for half an hour, and go up to $2,300 and more for full-service party packages at its place that include costumes, dancing, snacks, soda and juice, balloons, and paper goods. Kids can also have fun with a closet full of costumes, a tiny castle, toys, a moonwalk, and face painting. Check out the online store, Pooper Cavern, or its Reade Street location, both of which offer paper goods, balloons, favors, costumes, and everything else you could need for parties.

❊ The Regency Hotel

540 Park Avenue bet. 61st and 62nd streets
339-4132
www.loewshotels.com
The swanky Regency Hotel has recently started doing birthday parties. It has several lovely rooms available depending on size of the party and budget. Call Tara Newman for more information.

❊ 74th Street Magic*

510 East 74th Street bet. York Avenue
and the East River
737-2989

www.74magic.com

Seventy-Fourth Street Magic has a big and beautiful indoor play space, and holds parties on Friday, Saturday, and Sunday. Toddlers spend one hour in the baby gym with a supervisor/teacher who helps them with the equipment, swing, and ball pit, and then another thirty minutes in the party room. One and a half hours for twelve children costs $475 ($15 for each additional child), and includes balloons, as well as coffee and tea for the grown-ups.

If you're having a party at home and want to hire entertainment, check these out:

- **Arnie Kolodner** (best for three and up; most popular with the four- to six-year-old crowd, with wonderful Cinderella and Peter Pan parties!), 265-1430.

- **Bobby DooWah*** (music with instruments and dancing or a puppet show; fabulous for first and second birthdays! A favorite of Pamela's and Kelly's—between the two of us, we've used him five or six times), 914-762-2421 or through 772-7633 (Jodi's Gym).

- **Clown Magic Party Entertainment** 544-8153, www.clownmagicnyc.com. Clown magic has any kind of entertainment you can possibly imagine for your child's birthday. It features clowns, costumed characters, magicians, face painters, balloon sculptors, puppet shows, pony rides, petting zoos, storytellers, and sing-alongs.

- **Hollywood Pop Gallery** (all kinds of costumed characters), 777-2238, www.hollywoodpop.com

- **Leanne DeCamp** 971-8765. Leanne DeCamp is a professional singer, an early-childhood development teacher, and creator of her own music program called Do Re Mi. She offers engaging and appropriate party entertainment for one- to four-year-olds. Activities include puppets, bubbles, the Birthday Band, instruments, and balloon animals. The fee is $225 for one hour.

- **Little Maestros** Ronni Soled, Party Coordinator, 744-3194, www.littlemaestros.com. Add parties to the list of Little Maestros credentials. It does birthday parties as well as all "special event" parties for ages one to six. The parties are forty-five-minute performances and can be anything from one teacher (with guitar) to "full band." Prices vary accordingly for these fun-filled parties.

- **Madeleine the Magician** 475-7785, or www.madeleinethemagician.com

- **Magical Marion** (costumed character and music), 917-922-9880.

- **Marcia the Musical Moose** (costumed moose character, puppet show, and sing-along; did Alexander's second birthday with great success), 567-0682 or 914-358-8163.

❋ *New York Sketches.com* 646-452-9946, www.nysketches.com. This all-purpose birthday party entertainment company can provide invitations, party favors, and a plethora of entertainers for your soiree. Entertainers include balloon artists, face painting, magicians, and costumed characters.

❋ *Only Perfect Parties* (variety of theme characters and shows), 869-6988 www.nycparties.com

❋ *Send in the Clowns** (variety of theme characters and shows; Kelly has used Gary for years and has had Barney, Baby Bop, and BJ, Batman and Robin, and the Power Rangers come visit her!), 718-353-8446.

❋ *Silly Billy* (magic, comedy and fun; he's a legend among kids ages four to seven), 645-1299.

Party Favors

❋ *HomeFront Kids*
202 East 29th Street, 3rd Floor
bet. Second and Third avenues
545-1447 ext. 1302
This store carries a large selection of educational toys that make special party favors. The staff is very knowledgeable and will help you find age-appropriate items to fit your theme and budget. They will also personalize and wrap them in cellophane at no extra charge and deliver them for free in Manhattan.

❋ *Jill M. Cooper Personalize it!*
799-8317
email: jillcoops@aol.com
Jill Cooper has been selling hand-painted baby gifts, stationery, party favors, and more since before she had baby Marielle. Now that she is a mom herself, she is carrying even more terrific gift items at Personalize it! Adorable, personalized, and reasonably priced party favors are hard to find in this city, and Jill has many!

❋ *Party Gifts by BETHiE*
(877) 371-0932
www.bethiegifts.com
This Internet company custom-makes unique favors to go with your party theme. You tell them your theme and budget and they put together a little package for each guest filled with fun, age-appropriate items like a mini bowling bag filled with a toy bowling set and a pizza puzzle or a gold treasure bag filled with pirate gear and booty. This is a great service for parents who don't have the time to do it themelves.

Central Park Parties

Central Park offers a myriad of party opportunities and is reasonably priced! Hurray! Here you are only limited by your imagination. To begin, for parties of more than twenty people, you need a permit from the City Parks and Recreation Department (360-8111 or www.nyc.gov/parks). A permit costs $25, payable to the city by check or money order.

Central Park parties have to be planned with a rain date or a backup (indoor) plan in case of inclement weather. That aside, plan for lots of outdoor games, such as circle time for younger kids, hot potato, freeze dance (bring batteries for your portable radio), or have a friend (or Bobby DooWah) play guitar. Any entertainers you would hire for indoors—clowns, costumed characters, and so on—can be hired for outdoors as well.

Pamela's friend Esther planned a softball party for her son's sixth birthday, and it was a huge success. She got a permit for a softball field, provided each child with a team T-shirt, and had a real game.

Some popular party locations in Central Park include:

* ❊ *The Great Lawn*
  mid-park, between 79th and 86th streets

* ❊ *Sheep Meadow*
  mid-park, between 66th and 69th streets

* ❊ *Strawberry Fields*
  west side, between 71st and 74th streets

* ❊ *Any playground with a picnic table*

Make sure to mark your area by balloons (The Balloon Man is a great resource; Kelly has used him for years, and he will deliver everywhere. Call Harvey at 268-3900), streamers, etc. Bring lots of blankets, paper tablecloths, and napkins. A folding table for food and cake is a good idea, too.

If you want a more organized party in the park, the Central Park Carousel is a lot of fun for kids ages two to five. Call 736-8700 (or go online at www.centralparkcarousel.com) to book a party there.

Parties start at $21.95 (Mondays–Fridays) or $27.95 (weekends) per child, and include four carousel rides per child, plus one hour in the picnic area. The carousel staff supplies paper goods, hot dogs or pizza, and juice, plus a small party favor and a helium balloon for each child. All you need to bring is the birthday cake. For an additional fee, you can also request a face painter, clown, magician, or costumed characters. Parties are held April through November, seven days a week, weather permitting.

Balloons and Decorations

* ❊ *Balloon Bouquets of New York*
  457 West 43rd Street
  265-5252
  www.balloonbouquetsnyc.com
  This balloon decorating service can provide anything from a bunch of plain, loose latex balloons to elaborate Mylar bouquets and large-scale decorations like centerpieces, arches, and banners. If you prefer, you can rent a helium tank and do it yourself. Thirty latex balloons cost $53. Free delivery Monday–Saturday; $10 to deliver on Sunday.

* ❊ *Balloon Saloon*
  133 West Broadway at Duane Street
  227-3838
  www.balloonsaloon.com
  This full-fledged party-supply store, which sells paper goods, favors, and piñatas, also sells balloons in all shapes and sizes. In addition to the basic loose latex balloons and Mylar bouquets they do elaborate party decorations. Thirty latex balloons cost $60. Delivery below Sixtieth

Street is free and costs $5 above Sixtieth Street. It also rents helium tanks for do-it-yourselfers.

❊ Birthday Express

(800) 424-7843

www.birthdayexpress.com

This catalog/Internet company sells all sorts of paper goods, decorations, favors, balloons, piñatas, party crafts and activities, costumes, and cake-baking supplies for children's birthday parties. Its themed party kits, which cost around $25, have everything you need to throw a party for eight children including invitations, tableware, table cover, and balloons. Deluxe versions for $30 to $40 and "ultimate" versions for $130 and up include extras like decorations, candles, favors, piñata, and thank-yous.

❊ Party City

38 West 14th Street bet. Fifth and
Sixth avenues
271-7310

This huge chain store is worth traveling to and has tons of party supplies for every occasion at bargain-basement prices.

❊ State News

1243 Third Avenue bet. 71st and 72nd streets
879-8076
151 Amsterdam Avenue bet. 67th and
68th streets
875-9654

These stationery stores have some of the biggest selections of party paper goods and tableware in the city, including over eighty children's birthday party patterns. They also have a nice selection of Mylar balloons, invitations/thank-you notes, favors, and cake/cookie baking and decorating supplies.

Birthday Cookies and Cakes

Everybody has a bakery in the neighborhood that makes perfectly fine, even fabulous birthday cakes. Explore your neighborhood, and be sure to ask other moms where they get cakes. Heck, you can probably get a cake from the supermarket complete with your baby's name and ubiquitous frosting flowers. But for your child's first birthday, you may want to go all out. We've listed some makers of outstanding (though sometimes outrageously priced) birthday cakes, and clued you in on which ones will incorporate themes such as Superman, ballerinas, or Peter Rabbit. Don't panic, though. For Angela's first birthday (Kelly's second child), she had an Entenmann's chocolate cake at home with big brother Alexander, and she was perfectly happy! Entenmann's can be quite good when they're fresh, and for $3.99, who's complaining?

❊ BeautifulCookies.com

(866) FUN-GIFT (386-4438)

www.beautifulcookies.com

These adorable hand-decorated cookies are great to serve at a party or to use as favors. Choose from dozens of designs on the website or provide the company with a photo and it will scan it on in edible ink. The cookie-decorating kits make great kids' birthday and holiday gifts.

Cakes 'N' Shapes, Ltd.

403 West 39th Street bet. Ninth
and Tenth avenues
629-5512

For $110, Edie Connolly can create a unique cake in the character or design of your choice. She can sculpt everything from a ballerina to a teddy bear, Batman, or Superman. Give her a favorite picture, and she will scan it onto a cake. A simple round cake for twenty-five costs $75. For Rebecca's Cinderella party, she designed a 3-D cake with Cinderella's gown as the cake, and a Barbie doll as Cinderella. Order at least one week in advance. Delivery available.

CBK Cookies of New York*

226 East 83rd Street bet. Second
and Third avenues
794-3383
www.cbkcookies.com

You can order chocolate or vanilla single-sheet or double-layer cakes in various styles, including cakes baked in the shape of a character of your choice. A basic decorated cake that serves approximately twenty people costs $75. These cakes are so special, CBK makes only two a day, so order at least two weeks in advance. It makes wonderful cupcakes and cookies, too, in every shape and style. Delivery is extra. By appointment only. For years Kelly has used CBK for birthdays, baby showers, and Halloween parties.

Creative Cakes

400 E. 74th Street bet. First and York avenues
794-9811

Creative Cakes hand-sculpts 3-D cakes to look like a fire truck, barnyard, basketball court, or anything you can imagine. Its smallest cake serves twenty-five people and ranges from $300 to $325. Make sure to call two to three weeks ahead to place your order. Delivery costs $50. By appointment only.

Crumbs

3211/2 Amsterdam Avenue at 75th Street
712-9800
1371 Third Avenue at 78th Street
www.crumbsbakeshop.com

Crumbs bakeries (locations on the Upper East and Upper West sides) offer to make your own cupcake or cookie parties (to go). The bakery supplies cookies with edible color markers or cupcakes with choices of frosting, sprinkles, and edible cake toppers. These provide a fun alternative to birthday cakes and an activity for partygoers too. If you just want to buy cupcakes as part of your birthday celebration, the cupcakes here are delicious and come in creative varieties such as Oreo cookie and Snickers.

Cupcake Cafe*

522 Ninth Avenue at 39th Street
465-1530

Cupcake Cafe is one of our favorites! A round cake serving fifteen to twenty-five people with flowers and an inscription costs $55. A theme cake with Big Bird or Barney, serving twenty-five people, is $65. Call two to three days in advance to pick up a cake Monday through Saturday; call Thursday for a cake to be ready on Sunday. Delivery is about $25. No credit cards; cash, money order, or company check only.

Dean & Deluca

1150 Madison Avenue

717-0800

560 Broadway at Prince Street

226-6800

www.deananddeluca.com

Dean & Deluca's chocolate cake is phenomenal. A layer cake that serves approximately twenty-five people starts at $50. Order two days ahead—although some moms have been lucky enough to walk in and find one already made. D&D also carries fantastic cupcakes as well as adorable large character cookies. Delivery is free in the neighborhood with $25 minimum.

Flour Girl

87th Street and Columbus Avenue

595-9505

www.flourgirlbakery.com

Flour Girl makes adorable cakes decorated with cookies instead of icing. It can make a cake to coordinate with any party theme and can even match your invitation or a photograph. Cakes cost $6 per portion and include a cookie for each person. The minimum size is for twenty people. Ten- to fourteen-day lead time is required. It will deliver cakes of $200 or more for $40 per hour.

Grace's Market Place

1237 Third Avenue at 71st Street

737-0600

www.gracesmarketplace.com

Grace's has a wide selection, including carrot and chocolate mousse cakes. Some are beauti-fully decorated with flowers and scrolls of dark chocolate. A cake serving twelve people costs $25. You can stop by Grace's on the spur of the moment and find a cake, perhaps its delicious $17.50 American Beauty chocolate cake. Can you tell we like chocolate? This cake is one of our favorite chocolate cakes in New York City. It will customize with three days' notice. Delivery is $4 within eight blocks.

Lafayette Bakery

26 Greenwich Avenue

between Tenth and Charles streets

242-7580

anycbakery@aol.com

Lafayette Bakery will custom make a cake with a simple design for an extra $5 to $15 over the regular price of $69 for a cake serving twenty-five. Its cakes have fruit, custard, or mousse fillings, and can be topped with whipped cream or a variety of icings. Order a week in advance. No delivery, but open seven days a week.

Magnolia Bakery

401 Bleecker Street at 11th Street

462-2572

Specializing in old-fashioned, homemade cakes, Magnolia Bakery offers delicious yellow or chocolate half-sheet cakes. A $60 cake serves twenty-five to thirty-five. It won't custom-make a cake, but with a day's notice, it will personalize one. Call one to two weeks in advance. The cupcakes here are famous—don't leave without one. No delivery.

My Most Favorite Dessert Company

120 West 45th Street bet. Sixth Avenue
and Broadway
997-5032/997-5130

Well known for delicious kosher food and desserts, Dessert Company sells a two-layer round cake (chocolate or vanilla) that serves twenty-five people and costs $75. A beautifully decorated kids' theme cake is about $95. Call three to four days in advance. Delivery is $12.

The Perfect Cake

481-7467

www.theperfectcake.com

The Perfect Cake will custom-design a birthday cake in the shape of your child's favorite character, animal, sport, hobby, or object. A 10-inch cake for fifteen to twenty people starts at $125. Pick a design from the website or have the bakery create something just for you. Not only are these cakes beautiful, but they are delicious too.

Soutine*

104 West 70th Street bet. Columbus
and Amsterdam avenues
496-1450

www.soutine.com

Pamela buys wonderful cakes at this tiny bake shop. A two-layer round cake serving twenty people costs $45, and a cake with special decoration costs an additional $10 to $15. You can customize designs and flavors. Through a computer graphics program, kids can design their own cake online and Soutine will make the cake of your child's dreams. Order one to two days in advance. Delivery costs $15 to $20 in

Manhattan. Cupcakes are also available, made to order with sprinkles.

Sylvia Weinstock Cakes

273 Church Street bet. White
and Franklin streets
925-6698

www.sylviaweinstockcakes.com

Known in New York as "the cake lady," Sylvia creates masterpieces that range from castles for birthdays to fantasies for brides. She is known around the world for her wedding cakes. Her concoctions start at about $350 for a cake that will serve thirty-five people. Give at least three weeks' notice. Delivery within Manhattan is $50; outside depends on mileage.

Veniero Pasticceria

342 East 11th Street bet. First
and Second avenues
674-7264

Famous not just for fantastic cannoli, it also makes light and creamy cakes for kids. A round cake that serves up to thirty people costs $40. Bring in a postcard-size picture of anything you want on the cake, and it'll copy it for an additional $20. Order two days in advance. Delivery is $10 in Manhattan.

William Greenberg Desserts

1100 Madison Avenue bet. 82nd
and 83rd streets
861-1340

Another baker well known for elaborate designs and decorations, Greenberg's produces a beautiful baby carriage cake for baby showers. It made President Clinton's fiftieth- birthday American flag cake. A two-layer round cake serving twenty-five costs $130 to $150; decorated cakes go up to $265. Call at least two days in advance; longer for more elaborate creations. Delivery with one day advanced notice.

With many birthday cakes under our belt, we've discovered there is nothing better than an ice-cream cake from Haagen-Dazs or Carvel, especially in the spring and summer months. These cakes are usually two layers of chocolate and vanilla ice cream with cookie crunch and icing on the sides and tops. These bring us back to our own childhood birthdays, and you can never discount nostalgia as a good reason to buy one; your kids will love it as much as you did. If you call in advance, you can choose your child's favorite ice cream flavors.

There are Haagen-Dazs stores throughout the city, so they are ideal places to pick up a quick birthday cake. Cakes range in prices—cakes that serve twenty to twenty-five people are around $50 to $70, depending on the decoration. Here are two Haagen-Dazs locations:

187 Columbus Avenue bet. 68th
and 69th streets
787-0265

33 Barrow Street bet. Seventh Avenue
and Bleecker Street
727-2152

There are fewer Carvel locations in the city (now some supermarkets carry the cakes), but they are good and inexpensive. For approximately twenty-five people, an ice-cream cake will cost around $43.

1091 Second Avenue bet. 57th
and 58th streets
308-4744
Call (800) 322-4848 for other locations

haircuts

Many New York moms take their babies to their own hair salon, or attempt to give that first trim themselves. But we think you'll want to try one of these shops that specialize in children's haircutting. Little kids are notoriously bad at sitting still, and most of these places offer fun distractions like *Barney* or *Sesame Street* videos to watch, and toy cars for your child to sit in. You might even come away with a first haircut diploma, a lock of hair, or a balloon. Bring some toys from home, so your child won't badger you to buy one of the pricey toys for sale in some of these salons.

❊ Astor Place Hair Designers

2 Astor Place bet. 8th Street and Broadway
475-9854
Nothing special here for children: no cars to sit in or balloons, just a cheap haircut, good people watching, and a friendly staff downtown. A kid's cut is $13.

❊ Cozy's Cuts for Kids*

1125 Madison Avenue at 84th Street
1416 Second Avenue at 74th Street
448 Amsterdam Avenue at 81st Street
585-COZY
www.cozyscutsforkids.com
This newest Cozy's location appeals to babies as well as older kids with new styling chairs. In

addition, check out the new hair-care products called "So Cozy" that smell yummy. The Seventy-fourth Street location also offers mini-manicures and the same great glamarama birthday parties.

The Hair's Castle

1470 York Avenue at 78th Street
744-2177

Built by Broadway set designers, The Hair's Castle offers lots of brightly colored diversions, including a gigantic pocket watch on the wall with a tortoise and a hare as hands. Each station is equipped with a television and VCR, and Sony PlayStation or Nintendo 64. A child's haircut is $25. Appointments are recommended.

Jennifer Bilek

Get Conveniently Coiffed
718-335-1078 or 917-548-3643
email: getcoiffed@msn.com

If you want an alternative to the frenetic kiddy salon, Jennifer Bilek will come to your home to cut your child's hair for about the same price as the salons. Her services also include haircutting house calls for adults, "glamour" parties for girls, and hair and makeup for weddings and special occasions.

Kids Cuts

201 East 31st Street bet. Second
and Third avenues
684-5252

This store provides a great experience for your child's first haircut. While the haircutter snips away, your child can watch movies and sit in a miniature car. After the cut, you receive a certificate with a lock of your child's hair for your album, as well as a pinwheel for the little one. Haircuts here cost $25.95. Kids Cuts also has a boutique that sells toys for both entertainment and educational purposes. This boutique tends to be pricey, so the pinwheel may have to suffice as a post-cut treat.

Paul Molé Haircutters

1031 Lexington Avenue at 74th Street
988-9176

Paul Molé has been around "forever" but has kept up with the times. Your child can watch a video, eat a lollipop, and go home with a toy. Children sit in an old-fashioned kid-sized barbershop chair, and will receive a special certificate for their first haircut. Cuts are $30.

SuperCuts

For branches in your area,
call (800) SUPERCUT
Here are some locations:
440 Third Avenue at 32nd Street
447-0070
1149 Second Avenue at 60th Street
688-8883
2481 Broadway at 92nd Street
501-8200
69 University Place at 10th Street
228-2545
378 Sixth Avenue at Waverly Place
477-7900

All the salons in this chain cut infants' and toddlers' hair, and award a diploma for the first haircut. Salons are clean and designed to provide quick, easy-in/easy-out service. Haircuts for toddlers cost around $15. Appointments aren't required but, if you wish, you can make one with your favorite stylist.

Whipper Snippers

106 Reade Street
bet. West Broadway and Church Street
227-2600

Whipper Snippers is a downtown kids-only hair salon and toy store. It is a great place to get your little one's first haircut or trim. The shop also specializes in party favors and has a nice selection of toys too.

shoes

Buying your child's first walking shoes is an exciting and important task. Because your one- or two-year-old can't tell you whether the shoes are comfortable, watch carefully as she is being fitted. If it seems difficult to get the shoes on and off, they are probably too small. Shoes should generally last at least two months: if they seem small three weeks after you bought them, go back and have them checked.

The salesperson at the shoe store should measure your child's foot while he is standing toes uncurled. Ask about the width of your child's foot and don't buy a shoe that narrows greatly at the toes. Also, look for a soft, flexible sole. A soft sole is necessary for the first year. After that, when your child is really walking and running, you can buy any shoe except slip-on penny loafers. Your youngster won't develop the gripping action that a slip-on shoe requires until he is four or five.

East Side Kids Inc.*

1298 Madison Avenue at 92nd Street
360-5000

East Side Kids has a wide selection of American and European shoes for first walkers. It also carries such popular brand-name sneakers as Nike, Reebok, and Keds. Other excellent brands include Sonnet (English), Elefanten (German), and Aster (French). The salespeople are some of the best in the city. Leon is Kelly's favorite! Service is on a first-come, first-serve basis, but you can call ahead and have your name put on a waiting list. Free popcorn helps pass the time if there is a wait.

Great Feet*

1241 Lexington Avenue at 84th Street
249-0551
www.striderite.com

This big, bright store has areas carved out for different age groups. It carries brands like Stride Rite, Nike, Reebok, LA Gear, Elefanten, and a wide variety of styles. Prices are among the best around, and the staff are generally quite knowledgeable about little feet. This store gets a star because it stands behind what it sells, exchanges mistakes readily, and has great sales!

Harry's Shoes

2299 Broadway at 83rd Street
874-2035
www.harrys-shoes.com

An Upper West Side fixture, Harry's carries a wide selection of American and European brands, including Stride Rite, Elefanten,

Jumping Jacks, Shoo Be Doo, Nike, Reebok, New Balance, and Enzo. This place can get very crowded, especially on the weekends and after school.

Ibiza Kidz

42 University Place at 9th Street
505-9907

This small downtown store is part shoe store, part toy store, and part clothing store. It carries a large line of shoes with brands such as Aster, Baby Botte, Elefanten, Mod 8, Superga, and Venettini. In the toy section you can find educational toys, Gund and Russ plush toys, and much more. This comfortable neighborhood store has great service and a very loyal customer following. There are good seasonal sales at the end of summer and winter.

Lester's

1522 Second Avenue at 80th Street
734-9292

This Manhattan branch of the Brooklyn chain has an impressive shoe department tucked behind the clothing. Lester's is a discount store carrying a good selection of European and American brands; there's a wide variety of styles that you wouldn't expect a discounter to stock, and friendly service, too!

Little Eric*

1118 Madison Avenue at 83rd Street
717-1513

A wide selection of shoes for children ages six months to seven years. Brands include Nike, Keds, Converse, and Kangaroos, with styles

from sneakers to high-end imported designer shoes. The Little Eric store brand makes up the majority of its stock and is excellent and very fashionable. This is a child-friendly store, with plenty of space, and toys to keep children busy as they are fitted. It has a loyal following, but a limited selection of shoes for wide feet.

Shoofly

42 Hudson Street at Duane Street
406-3270
www.shooflynyc.com

This is one of the most stylish kiddie shoe stores in the city, carrying all the high-end brands for boys and girls such as Aster, Baby Botte, and Deoso. There's also an excellent selection of purses, hats, barrettes, and other accessories. It has extra-special shoes for girls; it was Rebecca's favorite shop when she was little. Try to shop during the week; weekends are quite busy.

Tip Top Kids*

149 West 72nd Street
874-1004
www.tiptopshoes.com

This store is nicely laid out, with plenty of space for walking around and trying on shoes. The staff is friendly and helpful, and kids are kept occupied by a supply of toys and movies. Tip Top has shoes for every occasion, with prices ranging from $20 to $80. Popular brands include Stride Rite, Monroe Kids, Nike, and New Balance. This is a welcome addition to the neighborhood, which truly lacked a "basic" shoe store for kids!

photographs

It doesn't take long for your drawers to become stuffed with photos taken of your adorable baby by you and your relatives. But there's a reason you've left them in the drawer. When you want a picture to put in that beautiful silver frame you got as a baby gift, it's time to go to a professional. A real photographer can work in your home, the park, or her studio, and can include parents or grandparents in the shots, as well as props such as stuffed animals, antique toys, costumes, and more.

If you don't know a photographer, here are some places to start. These are fairly traditional professionals who are experienced in photographing children (it's an art, truly). Ask to see their portfolios, and if you don't see the kind of work you want, ask your friends for some recommendations. Also, look for photo credits in parenting magazines. There's a good chance the photographers live in New York.

❋ A Perfect Portrait

Principal Photographer: Nancy Ribeck
476 Broome Street, Suite 6A
bet. Wooster and Greene streets
534-3433
www.nanchanpartners.com

Nancy Ribeck's studio photography is often classically lit but casually designed. This combination gives her portraits the beauty of traditional portraiture mixed with a contemporary look. A basic sitting fee is $550 and includes an assistant's fee, film and processing, and contact sheets. Each additional roll costs $45. Photos are taken at the studio at 476 Broome Street, or at a location of your choice for an extra fee. Sessions last two or three hours. Print photos are an additional fee.

❋ Barry Burns

260 West 36th Street, 2nd Floor
bet. Seventh and Eighth avenues
713-0100
www.barryburnsphotography.com

Barry Burns captures the spontaneity of the moment. He takes seventy pictures of your child, and you receive three 8 x 10" prints. His shoots run from $400 to $600. Family portraits can also be made in color or black-and-white film. Most work is done in his studio in the heart of the theater district, but an outside location is possible for a negotiable additional fee.

❋ Brian Kao

646-552-8965 or 201-583-1003
www.captureyourself.com

Brian Kao is a photographer with a portfolio of artistic baby and family portraits. He features nature in a lot of his themes, and provides a creative edge for your child's photos. Contact Brian for prices.

❋ Fromex

182 East 86th Street
bet. Third and Lexington avenues
369-4821

Tucked in the back of this average-looking "one hour" photo place is a photo studio with a photographer on staff. Fromex offers many packages that range in price from $49.95 to $249.95. A standard package is $100 and includes a sitting fee, one set of proofs, and one 8 x 10" print. It's best to call ahead for an appointment, but walk-ins are possible. We both have had good results with Fromex.

Gail Sherman

88 Central Park West at 69th Street

877-7210

email: gail@gailsherman.com

Gail Sherman's work is dramatic. Her photographs are printed in black and white, then hand-colored with oil paints. Her photographs are works of art, not just "pictures." Gail Sherman charges $500 for a sitting. The price per hand-colored portrait is $500. If you want only black-and-white prints, the cost is $100 per print, and digital is $200 per print.

Jami Beere Photography

646-505-5636

917-903-4212

www.jamibeere.com

Jami is a talented photographer who is well-known for her exquisite children's portraits. She is expensive, but many parents believe she's worth it because of the beautiful work she does. Her sitting fee is $975. Once the client chooses the image she wants, Jami hand prints it. Prices vary with size of the print.

Jennifer Lee*

40 West 72nd Street, Suite 53,

bet. Central Park West and Columbus Avenue

799-1501

www.jenniferleephotography.com

Jennifer Lee has been photographing kids for four years. She enjoys shooting on location in people's own homes, where kids are most comfortable. (She will also shoot in the Hamptons.) A new mom herself, Jennifer is adept at capturing the best moments with your new baby. Her prices start at $265 for a sitting, and she will keep shooting until she believes she has numerous good shots in a variety of poses. Jennifer will also shoot your child's birthday party—Kelly had her photograph Angela's second birthday.

JordanElyse Photography

917-757-0703

www.jordanelyse.com

Photographer Jordan Rosner specializes in birth announcements (with your baby's picture on them), holiday cards, and also does great photo shoots of your baby alone or with the whole family. Contact Jordan for her price list or check out her comprehensive website.

Karen Michele

721 Fifth Avenue at 56th Street

355-7576

www.karenmichele.com

Karen Michele will design a backdrop for your photo shoot using colorful balloons or anything else you want. She operates from a full retouching production facility, where she personally works with on-film retouching for each portrait. Her photos can be seen in the children's section of Barnes & Noble. There is a shooting fee of $250; a 5 x 7" print costs $125; an 8 x 10" print costs $150; duplicates are 50 percent off. Parents make a selection from approximately thirty proofs. By appointment only.

Kate Burton Photography

316 East 84th Street

717-9958

www.kateburton.com

Kate Burton has been photographing children for over eight years in New York City. Her work has been featured in the *New York Times* and *Time Out New York*, and is frequently displayed in children's stores such as Shoofly, Little Eric, and Bu & the Duck. Kate Burton shoots in her own full-service studio, but will also go on location to the park or your home. Studio sitting is $575 and local park sitting packages start at $675; in-home sessions begin at $775. A number of Pamela's friends have used Kate, and all of them attest that Kate does beautiful work and is a pleasure to work with.

❊ Kate Engelbrecht Photography

55 Washington Street, Brooklyn

718-858-5165

www.kateengelbrechtphotography.com

While her studio is located in Brooklyn, this documentary-style photographer will come to Manhattan to photograph your children at home or in the park. Her specialty is the family docu-portrait, a still photo essay that captures individual personalities and tells an honest and intimate story. Kate's sitting fee starts at $450 and includes the proofs.

❊ Nancy Pindrus Photography

21 West 68th Street bet. Central Park West and Columbus Avenue

799-8167

Nancy has been a professional photographer for twenty-five years. She is both patient and accommodating. Her basic price is $325 for black-and-white contact sheets or $345 for color contact sheets, with an additional charge for the prints selected. Prints cost $35 for black-and-white photos up to 8 x 10". Color photos are $45 any size up to 8 x 10". She works from her studio. Other locations, such as Central Park, are negotiable.

❊ Nina Drapacz

500 East 85th Street, Suite 4C

at York Avenue

772-7814

www.fotonina.com

Nina Drapacz apprenticed with Richard Avedon, has been working for over twelve years in Manhattan, and specializes in hand-colored black-and-white photos. She offers a black-and-white or color package for $575. The enlargements are all done by hand and include three 8 x 10" and two 5 x 7", and a set of contact sheets. Additional prints are available. She does fabulous work and is extremely accommodating and patient. Pamela's friend Marty used her twice for family photos. Nina will do studio or outdoor shoots.

❊ Paloma Sendrey

917-428-2843

718-432-2365

www.palomasendrey.com

Paloma Sendrey shoots beautiful family and maternity photographs in sepia, black and white, and color. A full session lasts ninety minutes to two hours, resulting in two rolls of film at a cost of $350. She also shoots photo "playdates" in Central Park and will shoot holiday cards in thirty-minute sessions.

Rachel Klein*

595-1444

www.rachelkleinphotography.com

Rachel Klein is a New York City photographer who specializes in black-and-white family portraits. A typical sitting with Rachel resembles a play date in the park or at home. Rachel photographs families in familiar settings with natural light only. It is this formula that makes her work distinct. Her fee is $325, which includes ninety professionally printed 4 x 6" proofs. Rachel is a pleasure to work with and is extremely easygoing and flexible.

Sarah Merians Photography & Company

104 Fifth Avenue, 4th Floor, at 16th Street

633-0502

www.sarahmerians.com

Sarah Merians Photography has been photographing children and families for fifteen years. She employs thirteen child-experienced photographers, so the company can easily accommodate your family's schedule. The starting price for an in-studio photo shoot is approximately $200 to $300, which includes two rolls of film—color and/or black and white. Sarah Merians will also shoot on location. Prices vary according to the locale you choose. Pamela used them to photograph her wedding, with wonderful results.

a word on preschools

As you begin to check out preschools—sometime between your child's first and second birthday—you will probably be subject to intermittent panic attacks. You'll hear rumors that this or that school is "hot" this year. You'll be baffled by the complexity of the admissions process. You'll feel as though you're trying to get an eighteen-year-old into Harvard, not a two-year-old into a sweet little place where she'll play and eat crackers and juice. Try to relax. Things will work out.

Here are some basic facts to keep in mind as you and your child march on toward preschool:

* Many children begin preschool at age three or three and a half years old; others begin as early as two years and four months old. Schools decide on cutoff ages for admission and often change these arbitrarily—a one-year-old born before March 15 can apply for admission for the following September; the next year, perhaps, a child born before March 31 can apply. Schools hold tight to their birth date policies, and there are few exceptions.

* There are many excellent preschools in New York. Pick up a copy of the Manhattan Directory of Private Nursery Schools by Linda Faulhaber. This book describes all the private preschools in New York by neighborhood, with pertinent information from phone numbers to cutoff dates. Or look through the New York Independent Schools Directory, published by the Independent Schools Admission Association of Greater New York (and available through the Parents League). But remember,

there are excellent schools that are not members of the Parents League, and are therefore not listed in the League guidebook.

❉ As you begin your search, look for a school in your neighborhood, if possible. Try to keep your travel distance to about ten blocks. Otherwise, you'll spend all your time getting there, when the school time itself is only two or three hours a day twice a week for children under three. Three-year-olds may go every day, and they'd rather spend their time at school than traveling to it.

❉ Talk to friends about their experiences with preschools. Make arrangements to visit the schools you're interested in; tours usually take place from October through January. You must call the day after Labor Day to make an appointment for a tour and/or request an application. Some schools will not schedule a tour until they receive a completed application; others supply applications only after you have toured the school.

❉ Apply promptly. Schools have been known to stop sending applications by the second week of September, when they have already received enough applicants to fill their classes three times over. Apply to four or five schools. If you have a first choice, indicate it in a letter to the director of admissions of that particular school. It also helps greatly if you know families that attend the school you're most interested in. If possible, have them write or call for you.

Your child will almost surely find a place in a preschool you like, and you will almost surely wonder a year from now what all the fuss was about.

Note: Each spring the 92nd Street Y offers a workshop called "Planning Your Child's Early School Years," conducted by Beth Teitelman and Barbara Katz who run the Parenting Center. The Parents League at 115 East 82nd Street (737-7385) runs one-on-one advisory sessions for school and summer programs; it will give you the names and phone numbers of parents at various preschools who have agreed to talk to interested prospective parents. You can also find this and other information at the website: www.parentsleague.org.

There are a few professionals who specialize in helping parents through the nursery school and (in some cases) the ongoing school process. They will meet with families to discuss their needs and will try to steer them toward schools that will be a good fit. Of course, there are no guarantees for admission. One recommendation:

❉ *Nina Bauer, M.A.*
Ivy Wise Kids
262-1200

maternity clothing

Whatever clothing your lifestyle demands, you can find it in New York's maternity stores. From Veronique Delachaux for sophisticated French clothing, rental gowns from Mom's Night Out, office wear at Mimi Maternity, or the hippest Madison Avenue has to offer at Liz Lange, these stores have everything you need to stay comfortable and look great.

We shopped every maternity store in New York, and tried on dozens of items. We tested oversized and large-cut non-maternity wear by well-known designers such as Joan Vass, Tapemeasure, Eileen Fisher, and Victoria's Secret. We discovered which designers make maternity lines, and which stores carry them.

If you're not much of a shopper, or if you're sticking to a budget, the Belly Basics Pregnancy Survival Kit can be a staple of your wardrobe from day one of your pregnancy. The kit includes boot-cut leggings, a skirt, a long-sleeved tunic, and a baby-doll dress, all of which are made of black cotton and lycra. You can mix and match the pieces or wear them with non-maternity clothes. Kits are available at Bloomingdale's and Lord & Taylor; some pieces are sold separately. Pamela bought the leggings when she was pregnant with Benjamin and found them so comfortable she practically lived in them.

This chapter describes the New York maternity scene—its focus, style, quality of merchandise, price range, and level of service. Most of these stores hold their sales in January and July.

shopping tips

Before you shop, here's some advice from two women who have learned a lot by trial and error.

❖ Hold off on buying maternity clothes for as long as you can. Remember, nine months is a long time, and you'll need new and different things as you grow bigger.

❖ In the first and second trimester, shop in regular clothing stores for larger sizes and items with elastic waists. The Gap, The Limited, and Victoria's Secret often offer inexpensive, machine-washable items with elastic waists. Buy one or two sizes larger than you usually do.

❖ Don't buy shoes in your first trimester; your feet will probably expand. Kelly had to buy two more pairs of shoes in her eighth month because she had only one pair that fit her.

❖ Buy fabrics you are used to and comfortable with. If you never wear polyester or rayon, there's no need to start now. Stick to cotton or other natural fabrics that breathe, such as heavy-weight cotton blend suits you can wear when you go to a business meeting or out to dinner.

❖ Buy new bras, pantyhose, and maternity panties. You may go up as many as three cup sizes during your pregnancy, and bras with good support are essential. (Can you imagine going from an A to a D? We can.) Maternity pantyhose by Hue and underwear by Japanese Weekend are two of our favorites.

❖ For the last two months, invest in a maternity support belt, sold at every maternity store. The belt is a large, thick band of elastic that closes with Velcro under your belly to help hold it up. You will be able to walk more comfortably and for longer periods of time.

❖ A pretty vest is an easy way to dress up an oxford shirt and a skirt or pair of leggings. Kelly loved to wear an oversized black turtleneck with black pants and a bright vest.

❋ Look in your husband's closet. A man's oxford shirt over a long elasticized skirt or leggings provides comfort and a clean, crisp look. Kelly bought some men's sweaters and shirts during her winter pregnancy—now her husband Carlo wears them.

❋ Don't be afraid to wear fitted clothes. As more and more fashion models become pregnant, it's become the trend to wear form-fitting tops and dresses! Feel sexy and be pregnant at the same time. Liz Lange Maternity specializes in that sophisticated pregnancy look.

❋ Pregnant women are more fashionable than ever these days. If the thought of traditional maternity clothes makes you shiver, Dynasty Tailors (679-1075) can turn your own wardrobe into a maternity wardrobe by adding elastic triangles or panels to any items of your own clothing you wish.

Top Eight Alternatives to Maternity Stores

1. Your husband's shirts and sweaters
2. A friend's maternity clothes
3. Eileen Fisher stores
4. Jumpers and waistless dresses in Victoria's Secret catalogs are perfect and affordable, with clothes at $59 or less
5. The Pregnancy Survival Kit
6. Leggings and sweaters
7. Rent clothing—check out Mom's Night Out
8. Secondhand stores

toys, birthday parties, and more. There are over sixty ways to save and new places are added every couple of months. The list of participants includes popular merchants like OneStep Ahead, Jacadi, Little Eric, Bookberries, and The Art Farm in the City.

The Card

❋ **BabyBucks Card**

Susan Barr

646-284-2333

www.babybucksnyc.com

The clever "BabyBucks" card (created by new mom Susan Barr) is a must-have for anyone who wants to save money and the cost of raising children in the city. When you purchase a BabyBucks card ($40 per year) and show it at participating merchants, you are entitled to a 10- to 20-percent discount on items like birth announcements, children's furniture, clothes,

the stores

❋ **A Pea in the Pod***

860 Madison Avenue at 70th Street

988-8039

www.apeainthepod.com

Return Policy: Exchange and store credit only.

This is a top-of-the-line maternity store. It carries its own exclusive line and also commissions suits, dresses, and weekend wear by Carole Little, Joan Vass, David Dart, Shelli Segal, ABS, Lou Nardi, and Adrienne Vittadini. Amenities abound—big bathrooms, extra-large dressing rooms with space to sit down, bottled water, toys for kids, and magazines to occupy husbands and friends. The sales people are extremely helpful and are trained to fit you with the maternity and nursing bras you'll need. Prices run in the $175 to $225 range for most designer pieces. Denim jeans are $175; leggings $15; and bras range from $36 and up.

❊ A Second Chance

1109 Lexington Avenue bet. 77th
and 78th streets, 2nd Floor
744-6041
Return Policy: All sales are final.
A Second Chance offers previously owned clothing for resale. Prices are about one quarter of the cost of a new item, and most of the pieces are in good shape. Although maternity wear is only a small segment of the inventory, the store stocks many basics you might be looking for. A Second Chance is hit or miss, so you'll probably have to go more than once.

❊ Barneys New York Maternity Department

660 Madison Avenue at 61st Street, 7th Floor
826-8900
www.barneys.com
Return Policy: Refund with receipt within 30 days.
A recently opened department of Barneys, focusing on the basics for the quintessential Barneys customer. Barneys has its own maternity label, Procreation. It is a great line with tons of modern, luxurious basics, like cashmere sweaters, capri pants, knit dresses, and cotton button-down shirts—all in a variety of colors. For Barneys, the Procreation line is moderately priced, ranging from $175 to $300 per item. Barneys also carries L'Atessa, a sexy, daring brand with a fun selection of slim-fitting tops, bikinis, leather pants—even vintage Levi's with elasticized tummy panels sewn in. A third brand, Mamma Luna, is a bit dressier, made up mostly of brightly colored raw silk jackets, dresses, skirts, and pants.

❊ Cadeau Maternity

254 Elizabeth Street
994-1810
Cadeau offers simple, stylish designs from stretch denim to silk prints. It is a good place to shop for dressier clothing such as satin dresses. The Cadeau line is made to last for your entire pregnancy with waistbands and a button-out system that adjusts for all three trimesters. Its lingerie collection includes lace slips, camisoles, thongs, and hip-hugger briefs.

❊ Eileen Fisher

521 Madison Avenue bet. 53rd
and 54th streets
759-9888
1039 Madison Avenue bet. 79th
and 80th streets
879-7799
341 Columbus Avenue at 76th Street
362-3000
103 Fifth Avenue bet. 17th and 18th streets
924-4777
314 E. Ninth Street bet. First
and Second avenues
(Outlet Store) 529-5715
395 West Broadway bet. Spring

and Broome streets
431-4567
www.eileenfisher.com
Return Policy: Money is refunded within two weeks of purchase with a receipt; after two weeks a store credit is issued.
Eileen Fisher sells a range of wonderful full-cut separates, including elasticized pants with full legs, loose tunic-type sweaters, roomy skirts, vests, and empire-waist dresses. Most of it is machine washable. This is not a maternity store, but the clothing is perfect for your first or second trimester.

❊ H&M
1328 Broadway
646-473-1164
Only this H&M location has a maternity department, but it is worth checking out. It carries its own private-label maternity line called MAMA. Maternity styles range from casual to office attire; prices are moderate.

❊ Jelly Bean Maternity and Children
2449 Broadway at 90th Street
769-9099
www.mommychic.com
Return policy: Exchange or store credit only.
Formerly called Mommy Chic, this store sells career, casual, sports, and evening maternity wear and nursing wear that is stylish and comfortable. Brands sold include Mommy Chic, Belly Basics, Fleurville, Lilly Pulitzer, and Caden Lane.

❊ Liz Lange Maternity*
958 Madison Avenue bet. 75th and 76th streets
879-2191
www.lizlange.com
Return Policy: Money is refunded for unworn items within two weeks of online purchase; store credit within two weeks of store purchase.
Liz Lange has taken the maternity business by storm. Chic, trim, and sophisticated, her sweater sets and Pucci-style prints are the rage for hip, well-to-do moms. Most of Liz's separates mix and match very well, allowing both the working and non-working mom to achieve varied looks with just a few pieces. Prices start at $75 for the basic white stretch cotton T-shirt, and go to $375 for a blazer. Our friends rave about the stretch pants. At Liz's sleek, modern Madison Avenue shop, you can find diaper bags, shoes, purses, bathing suits, and hand-knit baby blankets. We love Liz's clothes—the perfect gift for the expecting mom-to-be.

❊ Maternity Basics
(877) E-STYLES (877-378-9537)
www.nystyle.com
Along with the Pregnancy Survival Kit, it offers other stylish and comfortable maternity items. Everything from twin sets in bright colors to swimwear and its own diaper bag (in basic black, of course), can be ordered directly from the company. It is also sold at Bloomingdale's and Lord & Taylor.

Maternity Works Outlet

16 West 57th Street bet. Fifth and Sixth avenues
399-9840
www.maternitymall.com
Return Policy: Store credit only, exchange within 10 days.

This third-floor store is a clearinghouse for Mimi Maternity, Maternité by Mother's Work, and A Pea in the Pod. It features sale, off-season, and discontinued items year-round. If you don't mind sewing on a few buttons, there's also an "as is" and "sample" section with some real bargains—you just may find a $200 dress for $20. Check out the Maternity Works Outlet if you're a midtown working mom-to-be. You'll find everything you need.

Michele Saint-Laurent

1028 Lexington Avenue
bet. 73rd and 74th streets
542-4200

Michele Saint-Laurent is a Parisian-born fashion designer who has been creating maternity clothing for over six years. Her shop is unique and it specializes in French casual wear, swimwear, lingerie, and custom evening wear. Ms. Saint-Laurent's collection is very fashionable; it is not your typical oversized maternity wear.

Mimi Maternity*

1021 Third Avenue bet. 60th and 61st streets
832-2667
2005 Broadway bet. 68th and 69th streets
721-1999
www.mimimaternity.com

Return Policy: Within 10 days with receipt, store credit only.

These comfortable stores carry a large and fashionable assortment of career suits, daytime and evening dresses, and casual clothing by Mimi, Mother's Work, BCBG, Paris Blues, and other labels. Most of them are designed exclusively for Mimi Maternity. Average prices: dresses, $150; a plain, elastic waist black skirt, $80; suits, $200 and up. Mimi's stylish black stretch pants with either bead or embroidered trim ($108), remain a best-seller. The Mimi Essentials line is a recent addition, offering inexpensive active wear like cotton tanks, T-shirts, shorts, and jeans for prices ranging from $18 to $54. You'll also find an impressive selection of lingerie and sleepwear, including top brand-name bras and panties.

Motherhood Maternity

The Manhattan Mall
32nd Street bet. Sixth and Seventh avenues
564-8813
1449 Third Avenue bet. 82nd and 83rd streets
734-5984
16 West 57th Street bet. Fifth and Sixth avenues
399-9840
641 Avenue of the Americas at 20th Street
741-3488
Catalog: (800) 4MOM2BE
www.motherhood.com
Return Policy: Store credit only.

Motherhood Maternity has recently changed its line and reduced its prices, and now carries trendy, inexpensive maternity clothes, many of which are 100-percent rayon. Most suits and dresses cost less than $80. Jeans range from $15 to $35; black leggings are $13 and up; and a three-piece navy suit was $44 when we visited the store. The 32nd Street store is small, but there are three large, well-lit dressing rooms with good mirrors. The sales staff is friendly and helpful.

❊ Old Navy

150 West 34th Street
594-0049
Return Policy: Lenient.
Besides offering reasonably priced kids clothing, the Old Navy on Thirty-fourth Street also carries trendy maternity styles at reasonable prices.

❊ Veronique Delachaux

1321 Madison Avenue at 93rd Street
831-7800
www.veroniquematernity.com
Return Policy: Store credit only.
Veronique Delachaux carries its own chic line of imported French-designed maternity wear. These clothes give pregnant women a tailored look, focusing on casual business attire: pants, blazers, and tops, with some special-occasion items. The clothing is French-cut and may not be suitable for tall or larger-sized women. The sales staff is knowledgeable and helpful. Prices are steep; a suit usually costs between $400 and $500, and a pair of jeans can be $140.

baby furniture
and accesories

Walk into any baby furniture store in this city and you'll face a sea of cribs, changing tables, and strollers. A year from now you'll be an expert on all of these items—but, for new moms, some advice is in order. This chapter tells you what you need and why you need it.

While cost and style will influence your choice of your baby's new stroller, crib, or changing table, New York mothers-to-be must also consider space. Is your apartment a roomy two-bedroom plus dining room, or is it basically a large studio? Portability will also be a consideration. Do you have any idea how hard it is to maneuver a super-deluxe stroller in and out of a city bus or taxi?

Don't run out and buy everything at once. You'll need the crib and stroller immediately, but wait until after the baby is born for the rest. You may receive useful gifts. Also, try to borrow some things, such as bouncy seats and swings. When you are ready to shop, read through our listings. Baby "superstores" carry almost everything you will need; the information here will give you an idea of what you want before you go shopping.

Think about purchasing the *Consumer Reports Guide to Baby Products* as well. This guide lists basic products by manufacturer and notes the pros and cons of each. While the information can sometimes seem outdated, you will be able to see pictures of some of the products you're interested in.

If you're of a mind and pocketbook to go all out and fix up a splendid room for your little one, New York has decorators and design consultants at your service. Several interior designers who specialize in children's rooms are listed below. They can help with choosing paint colors, wallpaper, and furniture, and can also contribute great space-saving ideas for city apartments. While you're planning the decor, don't forget to make sure everything is baby-safe. Check here for tips and resources.

A few last bits of advice, however. Order your furniture at least twelve weeks before your due date. Kelly ordered her crib well in advance, and Alexander still arrived first. Also, many items can be called in and ordered by phone or through the Internet. It saves time and anything that saves time helps—especially if this is your second or third child. Finally, if you are a second-time parent, be aware that many car seats and toys have been recalled in the past four years. Please call the Consumer Products Safety Commission (800-638-2772) to find out if your old infant car seat is still okay, before you use it.

the necessities
Bassinets

A bassinet is a lovely basket for a newborn to sleep in. It is usually used for about three months. It can be handy if you want your baby to sleep in your bedroom, or if a full-sized crib seems too big for that tiny infant. There are a lot of styles—from bassinets with wheels, to those that rock and those that lift off the stand—and some come with full bedding ensembles, including linens, coverlets, and fitted sheets. Prices generally range from $50 to $130, though you can pay up to $700 for a full, top-of-the-line bassinet set. Our favorite is the Kids Line bassinet, featuring carry straps on the detachable basket for portability, and full bedding. The unit collapses for easy storage or travel and the bassinet linens (available in a variety of different colors and patterns) are removable for washing.

Just a word about co-sleepers: This is a growing trend among nursing moms and those who practice "attachment parenting." A co-sleeper attaches to an adult mattress so your child can be next to you in bed without being in your bed. It is used instead of a bassinet. The most popular model in New York is the Arm's Reach, sold for about $60.

Here are some of the popular brands of bassinets in New York:

* *Badger*
* *Kids Line**
* *Lee Hy*
* *Century*
* *Graco*

Cribs

There are so many choices of styles, colors, and finishes, it can be overwhelming. And, since the first edition of *City Baby*, new crib manufacturers have entered the marketplace—most of them high-end, offering designs, styles, and colors that reflect trends in the adult market. You can find cribs in sleigh-bed styles and distressed wood finishes, in traditional styles or sleek, modern designs, but in almost all cases, the choices you're making are purely aesthetic. Don't worry, however—there's no need to be concerned about safety issues. All cribs sold today are certified by the Juvenile Products Manufacturers Association (JPMA), which develops standards for many baby products, including strollers/carriages, high chairs, and playpens. JPMA safety specifications require that the space between crib bars is no more than two and three-eighths inches apart, all crib mattresses fit snugly, and all cribs have firmly locking dropsides and childproof lock-release mechanisms.

There are some new and trendy crib models that are not widely carried in the city, but may be worth seeking out. They include:

* Cribs by the Netto Collection, which can be found at www.nettocollection.com.
* Cribs by designer Roberto Gil (the Offi Bebe Crib) can be found at www.modernseed.com.
* The Ouef crib, designed by a Brooklyn mother of two, is a gorgeous crib that converts to a toddler bed; www.ouef.com or 718-965-1216.
* Ikea even makes a very sleek and very affordable crib; www.ikea.com.

Top Seven Things to Know About Baby Clothes

1. Buy your layette, but wait to buy more clothes until all the gifts are in; you might not need as much as you think.
2. All clothes should be machine washable.
3. If you receive many gifts in small sizes, always exchange some for larger ones.
4. Use clothing with snaps around the bottom for easy changing.
5. Buy ahead when possible; winter coats, for example, are on sale in January.
6. Try to borrow expensive items like snowsuits and coats.
7. Patronize stores with liberal return policies.

Ten Tips for a Baby's Room

1. Good overhead lighting is key for convenience and safety.
2. A humidifier can be important in overheated New York apartments.
3. Have as many dressers, drawers, or shelves as possible—you'll need them.
4. Design the closet in the baby's room to allow for more toy than clothing space; baby clothes are tiny.
5. Baby proof the room (see page 192).
6. Have some toys placed within your baby's reach.
7. A glider or rocker can save the day (or night).
8. Curtains or shades help baby sleep.
9. If possible, leave a play space in the middle of the room.
10. Keep it simple—a busy or overdecorated room gets old quickly.

Here are the questions to ask when you shop for a crib:

❋ Do both sides, or just one, drop? One drop-side provides more stability and is easier to operate while holding a baby in the other arm.

❋ Can you raise or lower the crib's sides with one hand while holding the baby, or do you need both hands? Some American cribs have kickstands under the side rails, making them easier to raise and lower. More and more American companies (and most European companies) use an easy, leg-operated side-track mechanism.

❋ Is the crib stable when you shake it? A loose crib frame, or the sound of metal knocking against metal might indicate faulty construction or assembly.

❋ Does the crib include stabilizer bars, metal rods fastened to the endboards and located underneath the crib? These bars provide additional stabilization and protection for baby.

❋ Do the wheels have locks to prevent the crib from "walking"?

❋ Can the crib be converted into a youth bed (i.e. is one side completely removable)?

The crib you bring home should have a mattress that fits snugly (a gap of no more than one and a half inches between the mattress and the crib's sides and ends). Bumpers should be securely tied on with at least six ties or snaps. Keep the crib clear of any items—mobiles, clothing, and toys—that have strings longer than seven inches. Don't set up the crib near any potential hazards in the room, such as a heater, window, or cords from blinds.

Below are the crib manufacturers whose products are widely available in the New York area. Most of these lines are well known and established in the baby market, while others, like Mibb and Million Dollar Baby, are only a few years old. Some lines, like Legacy and Renaissance, are new, exclusive divisions of established lines (Child Craft and Simmons, respectively). The choice comes down to what you like and what you can afford. Shop around: prices range from less than $200 for a Cosco to more than $900 for a Bellini. (At Little Stars, we saw a line of sleek metal cribs from Bratt Decor that started at $1,000!) Ask whether the store delivers and what they charge for this service, and confirm they will assemble the crib in your home. They should.

- *Bassett*
- *Bellini*
- *Bonavita*
- *Child Craft**
- *Cosco*
- *Delta*
- *Legacy*
- *Mibb*
- *Million Dollar Baby*
- *Morigeau**
- *Pali*
- *Ragazzi*
- *Renaissance*
- *Simmons**

Changing Tables

Today's most popular changing tables are dressers with changing kits on top, built to grow with your child. The top of the dresser becomes a changing area when you place the changing kit, fitted with a pad, on top of the dresser. Remove the kit once you're beyond the diaper stage, and you have a standard chest of drawers that's great for a bigger kid's room. De Arthur, Morigeau, Bellini, Child Craft and several new, upscale companies carry this type of table. Prices start at about $200.

Conventional changing tables have a little pad with a small guardrail that goes all the way around the top (picture a rectangle) so your baby can't roll off. There are shelves underneath for storing diapers and wipes. However, you should never leave a baby unattended, no matter how secure your baby might seem. Popular brands for these tables include Simmons and Child Craft, and prices start at about $170.

Most crib manufacturers also carry coordinating changing tables as part of nursery suites that also include chests and cribs. These fancier tables generally cost between $100 and $200.

Gliders

A glider or rocking chair is optional, but if you have the space and the money, you may find having one helpful when you're feeding your baby or trying to get him to sleep. Dutalier gliders retail for about $500, and are practical for New York apartments. The popular sleigh glider is very compact. It comes in your choice of white or wood finishes, with different fabric patterns for the cushions. Matching ottomans are also available. Albee's, Cradle and All, and other baby superstores will custom-make a glider cover to match your decor. But beware: Alexander got trained to fall asleep while being rocked; as he got older, he expected to be rocked whenever he woke during the night. Angela did not have a glider in her room for this reason, and was a better sleeper from day one.

Carriages/Strollers

Newborns and toddlers alike spend many hours in the stroller going to the park, the supermarket, or window-shopping along the avenues. New York is a walking town, and your stroller is the equivalent of a suburban minivan. Whether you choose a carriage (a bassinetlike construction on wheels) or a stroller (easily collapsible) depends on your personal needs. While suburban mothers and fathers may be content with an inexpensive umbrella stroller that spends most of its time in the trunk of a car, city parents know a sturdy carriage is a must-have for babies and toddlers, especially since we use it to carry the groceries home, too.

All strollers sold today are safe (the JPMA sees to that), but not every type may be right for you. Consider what time of year your baby is due before you purchase your carriage or stroller. For winter babies, a carriage with a boot (an enclosed end) might be the best bet to keep your infant warm. For summer babies, look for a carriage with good ventilation and a sunshade. Also consider where you live. If your building has a doorman, you can usually get some help carrying a heavier stroller up the stairs and inside. If you're in a walk-up or nondoorman building, look for one that's light and portable, and practice folding it to get it down to a quick routine; you're going to be wrestling that stroller in and out of buses and cabs for a good couple of years.

Other desirable features include a stroller seat that reclines (a must for newborn to three-month-olds), plenty of storage space underneath, brakes on all four wheels, and a handle that reverses to allow the baby to face you or to face out. The latest innovation is the popular stroller/car seat combination. This is an infant car seat that straps and snaps into a stroller base. New moms swear by this for taxi travel and city walking. Popular models include the Snap 'N' Go by Baby Trend, Century 4-in-1 Plus by Century, the Circus and Sterling LiteRiders by Graco, the Evenflo Trendsetter by Evenflo, and the Kolcraft Secura Travel System by Kolcraft. The Snap 'N' Go is by far the most popular model, with prices ranging from $100 to $180. Practically all of the moms at Pamela's West Side New Mothers Luncheon use this model to get their babies around the city safely.

For umbrella strollers, the English-made Maclarens consistently have the lowest rate of returns or repairs of umbrella strollers and have withstood the test of time for parents who re-use them with their second child. It retails for $170 to $300, depending on the model. For a full carriage/stroller, it is generally agreed that the Peg Perego strollers are the best of the lot. We both used the Milano ($360) and loved it. These Italian-made strollers are so popular in New York, the playgrounds look like Peg Perego parking lots! They are sturdy, attractive, stand folded upright for storage, and have a multitude of features that make life easy for mom and baby (reversible handle, large removable storage basket, full boot, and large canopy).

Jogging strollers are also very popular with parents who exercise with their babies. The cost is between $100 and $400, depending on wheel size—the bigger the wheels, the more smoothly they roll. A marathon runner we know used one of these to run with his daughter for years. For parents of twins or two small children, side-by-side or tandem strollers might be good options. Side-by-sides are great for twins or children close to the same weight, while tandem strollers are great for kids of different sizes—with larger kids in front, and smaller in back. These two-seaters sell for an average price of $125.

When preparing to buy, tell the store clerk how you plan to use the carriage, and ask for a recommendation. Take the carriage for a "test drive" in the store to see whether it feels comfortable for you and your partner; check the height of the handles or bar, and make sure neither of you has to hunch over to reach it comfortably.

How can we discuss carriages and strollers without mentioning the Bugaboo Frog? This is the big orange stroller that moms either love or hate. There are even playgroups formed around moms without Bugaboos! That being said: this is an awesome-looking stroller, very stylish and very expensive. For our money, it's not the most practical, because it is quite large and does not fold up easily. It is quite popular though, and the dads seem to love it as much as the moms do.

Another new stroller worth mentioning is the Stokke Xplory. This expensive stroller is a strange-looking contraption but is known to be a great city stroller because baby sits high above the sidewalk.

Here is a list of popular brands sold in New York:

❊ Aprica
❊ Baby Trend
❊ Bugaboo Frog
❊ Century
❊ Chicco
❊ Combi*
❊ Emmaljunga
❊ Evenflo
❊ Graco
❊ Inglesina
❊ Kolcraft
❊ Maclaren*
❊ Peg Perego*
❊ Silver Cross
❊ Stokke

Car Seats

Even if you don't have a car, you must have a car seat. State law dictates that your newborn must leave the hospital in one, and while you could bor-

row a seat from a friend, purchasing your own will be a practical investment.

Babies must always ride in a car seat whenever in an automobile; it's the law. City taxis must come equipped with rear seat belts to attach over the car seat, so double check before you get into a cab. If you have any questions, call the New York Coalition for Transportation Safety at 516-571-5032. That said, it's very difficult to carry both a car seat and a stroller around with you. Hence, the new stroller/car seat combos, with the removable infant car seats that strap and snap into a base is a great alternative. Prices range from $100 to $180. Some city parents just use a baby carrier for infants, and hold toddlers on their laps.

The more ungainly convertible seats can be used from birth through the toddler years and have a reclining mechanism so they face rearward for infants and forward for toddlers and young children. With more features and an advanced five-point tethering system, the Britax Roundabout ($200) is by far the most popular model on the market right now. Other best-selling brands in Manhattan include Century and Evenflo. As of September 1999, all forward facing car seats had to be shipped with tether straps for extra protection. (They've been doing this in Europe for years.)

Three designs of restraining straps or harnesses are available in car seats: the five-point harness, the T-shield, and the bar shield. Most experts agree that the five-point harness is the safest, but all three are sound options. The five-point harness is also the most time-consuming to put on and off, which can be annoying to impatient toddlers. All of this will make sense once you see them in the stores.

Though convertible seats can be used from birth, experts advise you to buy an infant carrier car seat for babies from birth up to twenty pounds (these range in price from $40 to $80), and the convertible car seat when the child weighs more. Infant car seats are smaller, recline better, often come with a sunshade, and are more heavily padded than the convertible. They're portable and can easily be carried in and out of the car without disturbing a sleeping baby. Remember that these seats must be rear-facing in your vehicle; toddler seats forward-facing.

Booster seats and high-back boosters are designed for kids over forty pounds—too big for convertible seats, but still too small for regular seatbelts. They have a raised, rigid base that allows children to use adult belts. Prices range from around $25 to $150.

Many new parents are concerned that their car seat is not installed properly (and for good reason, because this is often the case). The National Highway Traffic Safety Administration provides a service through www.seatcheck.org that will check that your seat has been installed correctly. For those of you who live outside of the city, or who have relatives that do, local suburban police and fire stations will also do the car-seat checks at no cost.

Baby Swings

A swing might be your lifesaver during your baby's first few months—or maybe not. This is something your child either loves or hates. (Rebecca hated it, but Alexander loved it and never made a peep when he was in it.) We recommend you borrow one from a friend or relative before making the investment.

The Graco Swyngomatic is the only widely available swing. It's great. There are two models on the market—with and without the overhead bar. The

benefit of the Graco Advantage is that without the bar, you can't bump your baby's head on it. Graco Advantage retails for $120; the original Graco can be found for $79 to $109. Fisher-Price and Regalo also make baby swings ranging from $40 to $100.

Bouncy Seats

The bouncy seat is another potential lifesaver; in fact, we know women who would not have been able to shower for six months had they not made this investment. It's portable; you can move it from the living room to the kitchen to the bathroom so you can always see your baby and he can always see you. Plus, the newest bouncy seats are more plush than ever, and have a vibrating feature that can lull a fussy baby right to sleep. (Another new innovation we don't know how we lived without!) The bouncy seat is great for feeding your baby when he's starting to eat solid food but is still too small for a high chair. Combi's "Activity Rocker" is the one most people get ($69); it's well made, it vibrates—and it's fancier than other brands. The European style of rocker-bouncers is very popular as well, such as the one from Chicco. Prices range from $30 for a Kids II seat, and $64 for a Chicco. Here's a list of the bouncy seats available in New York:

* Chicco
* Combi*
* Evenflo
* Kids II
* Summer

High Chairs

When you are buying a high chair, it is advisable to:

1. Buy a chair with a wide base to limit the chances of the chair tipping over.
2. Find a chair with a one-hand tray-release mechanism, which makes it easier to take your baby in and out.
3. Look for a wrap-around tray—easier to eat from and keep clean.
4. Find a chair with a detachable seat cushion. These chairs become dirty easily and you will want it to last more than a year.

Most high-chair accidents occur (usually with children under one year) when a child has not been strapped in properly and tumbles out. Don't rely on the chair's tray to keep your baby enclosed; use the safety belt and never leave your baby unattended.

Before buying a high chair, decide if you want wood or metal and vinyl. Wooden high chairs are beautiful, but they don't collapse—so they are not ideal for those with limited apartment space. Also they require the use of both hands to take the tray off. Some models require you to flip the tray over the baby's head. If you're not careful, this can be a dangerous maneuver.

Right now, the most popular and functional high chairs are metal and vinyl. They have one-handed tray-release mechanisms, reclining and height features. They have easy-to-clean seats and comfy cushioning.

By far, the most popular high chair on the market is the Peg Perego Prima Pappa—with seven height adjustments and four recline positions, a thickly padded seat, a wrap-around tray, and a wide-

wheeled base, this high chair is ideal. This is also the most expensive model, at $170. High-chair prices start at $90 for a Million Dollar Baby.

First Years' Reclining Three Stage Feeding Seat is a great alternative to a high chair because, like a booster seat, it straps onto a regular chair (at $30, it's also an inexpensive alternative). This seat has three recline positions for each stage of early childhood: newborn, infant, and toddler. To adjust, you simply press two buttons and slide the seat. This product is ideal for traveling, as well as smaller apartments where space is limited.

Finally, we must repeat: Never leave your baby unattended in a high chair, even for a few seconds!

Here are some of the best and most popular brands:

- ❋ Baby Trend
- ❋ Evenflo
- ❋ Graco
- ❋ Stokke
- ❋ Peg Perego
- ❋ Chicco
- ❋ First Years
- ❋ Rochelle
- ❋ Million Dollar Baby

Booster Seats/Hook-On Seats

You may want to buy a portable chair to use when you take your baby or toddler to a restaurant or other place where no high chair is available.

Hook-on seats have a short life. (Rebecca couldn't sit comfortably in one after she was nine months old.) Also, if the seat is hooked incorrectly onto the table, or if the child can detach the seat from under the table with his foot, these seats can cause accidents. If you do use a hook-on seat, always place a chair under it. Manufacturers include Graco, Chicco, and Baby Trend, but Consumer Reports does not recommend using hook-on seats at all; the hazards are just too serious.

We have found booster seats to be safer and more practical than hook-ons. They can be used for children up to preschool age, and our favorite, the Safety 1st ($30), can be easily folded. Put this on a chair in your kitchen and you may be able to live without an expensive high chair! Other popular brands include Cosco, First Years, and Kids II, with prices ranging between $12 and $25.

Playpens/Portable Cribs

Playpens are a great place to park your baby when you need five minutes to yourself to shower, answer the door, talk on the phone, or make dinner. Some babies might amuse themselves in the playpen for up to thirty minutes at a time, but not all children like them. Kelly used a playpen for months with Alexander and yet Angela wouldn't stay ten minutes without screaming her head off. Playpens are also big and difficult to store and transport, so you might want to go for the portable crib instead. It can function as a playpen, but it's smaller and can easily be put away. Portable cribs have a thin mattress and sheets, so they can be used as a crib when you're traveling. Many of the playpens and cribs are fundamentally the same, but each brand offers different additional features. When shopping for a playpen, be sure to compare different brands to find the best features for your specific needs. Prices range from $80 for the Graco

Pack 'N' Play, to $175 for Arm's Reach Concepts's dual playpen/bassinet. Popular brands include:

* *Arm's Reach Concepts*
* *Century**
* *Fisher-Price*
* *Graco Pack 'N' Play**
* *Regalo*

Bathtubs/Bath Seats

At first, bathe your tiny baby in the kitchen or bathroom sink. When he's a little bigger and you'd prefer to use the bathtub, you may want to buy a special baby tub that fits into the big tub. Most baby tubs are similar; they come either with or without a sponge insert. The sponge tends to get a mildew odor, is hard to wring out, and takes days to dry—so we opt for without. The Cuddletub by Graco ($25) is a great bathtub that is carried by many stores. It has an adjustable foam cushion with mesh underneath for newborns to rest on. It can be removed once your baby can sit up on his own. The best-selling Evenflo Two-Year tub ($22) is the sturdiest of tubs and can be used for a child up to two years old. It has an insert for infants up to three months old, which can be easily removed as the child grows.

When your baby is old enough to sit up on his own, he's ready for a bath seat. The Safety 1st bath seat ($17) is a ring that attaches to your bathtub with suction cups. It is roomy enough to hold a two-year-old. We have both been happy with Safety 1st. Once she can sit up on her own, your baby will also enjoy the inflatable Kel-Gar Snug-Tub ($18). It looks like a mini pool and is lots of fun for older babies (over six months).

Baby Carriers

You see these pouchlike, soft cloth carriers strapped onto the fronts of mothers and fathers everywhere. They're often called "snuglis" for the company that invented them. While the actual Snuglis are attractive and functional, Baby Bjorn has surpassed them in quality and price. Pamela's Snugli went virtually unused for Rebecca, but a friend gave her a Baby Bjorn when Benjamin was born, and she used it every day.

This is another item that you'll use for only a short time. Kelly purchased one and then had a nine-and-a-half pound baby, who quickly became too heavy to carry strapped onto her shoulders. Try to borrow one from a friend and test it with your baby before purchasing to see if you're comfortable with it. Baby carriers are popular with second- or third-time moms who might have a stroller to push or other hands to hold.

Prices range from $25 for a Snugli to $79 for the best-selling Baby Bjorn. Nojo makes a popular Baby Sling (about $40), which allows you to hold your baby horizontally as well as vertically (allowing baby to sleep more comfortably). This product is wonderful for breastfeeding because you simply pull the fabric up over baby's head and you are guarded from exposure.

Backpacks

Women who use backpacks swear by them for comfort and convenience. Your baby is ready for a backpack once she can sit up on her own. Borrow one from a friend, and try it out with your baby on board before you decide to purchase your own.

The most popular brand is the Kelty backpack, which is strong and durable. Kelty is well known for its outdoor equipment and this product is just as heavy-duty. It costs slightly more than the other brands (about $100), but will last forever.

Gerry and Tough Traveler also make dependable backpacks starting at about $70.

Baby Monitors

Here's how to be in one room and hear your baby crying in another. These gadgets give you plenty of different options. Some monitors are battery-operated and can be carried throughout the apartment. It is difficult to say which brand is the most functional because of varying frequencies in different areas. The most secure method in buying the right monitor is to ask other parents in your neighborhood or building which monitors works best for them. Many New York buildings pick up "noise" from other apartments. You may hear another baby crying and think it's your own. Here are some of the most recent and popular additions to the monitor category:

* *900 Megahertz (MHz) monitors:* These offer greater range and clarity than earlier models. Options include First Years Crisp 'N' Clear ($50), and Safety 1st's Sensitive Sound ($50), or Grow with Me ($65).

* *Monitors with two receivers:* These are great and functional for larger living spaces because you can leave monitors in separate rooms. Graco makes the most popular model ($50).

❖ *Rechargeable Monitors:* Available from The First Years for $80, these work much like your portable or cellular phone, except it is a direct line to your little darling.

Safety 1st has Angel Care which is a sound and movement monitor created to guard against SIDS. It is an ultra-sensitive sensor pad that is placed under the baby's mattress. If the pad does not sense motion, including heartbeat and breath for twenty seconds an alarm sounds to alert you. It costs about $100. Beware: this can drive you crazy and keep you up at night, even when your baby is asleep.

Safety 1st has also created a Child View Monitor that has 2.4 Gigahertz (GHz) for clarity and additional privacy. It has a camera for sound and image as well as a little television monitor for $150.

You may have to try out a few different monitors before you settle on one product—sometimes you pick up your neighbors' conversations instead of the baby's cries.

Some new additions to this category are the video monitors where you can actually watch your baby from the comfort of your own bed while they are asleep. Two good ones are the MobiCam wireless video monitor (about $179) and the BebeSounds Portable Video and Sound monitor ($199 from BebeWing.com).

Diaper Bags

Diaper bags come in two basic styles: over-the-shoulder, which zips or snaps closed, and the increasingly popular backpack with a drawstring opening.

You won't believe how much stuff you have to carry for your baby. Find a roomy bag with lot of pockets (for bottles, wipes and the like) and a plastic lining. A changing pad is another great feature. The superstores have terrific selections. Babies Alley makes a popular Chanel look-alike in quilted black with gold chain straps. Peg Perego has patterns that match their carriages. Pierre Deux's pretty (and functional) bag comes in a variety of colors, and Baby Mania offers a funky, fake fur bag for $129.95. Chic designers like Kenneth Cole, Donna Karan, and Kate Spade have also gotten into the act with stylish, subdued bags (mostly in basic black), available at Bellini and other upscale stores. Prices range from $20 for a Babies Alley diaper bag to $200 for a Pierre Deux. Baby Bjorn and Evenflo make popular backpacks that don't even look like diaper bags.

This is another category that keeps getting better and better. Some of the newest diaper bags are both trendy, functional, and great-looking too. The Skip Hop (designed and developed by a new mom) is a practical, attractive bag with lots of pockets that hangs over your stroller and can be worn over your shoulder. It is extremely popular with new moms. Two other brands that are all the rage are bags by Pack Happy, Petunia Pickle Bottom, and Fleurville. A new diaper bag just for dad is by Diaper Dudes and is cool enough looking for hip dads to carry around the city.

the stores

Our baby superstores are not necessarily large in size, but we consider them super because they provide one-stop shopping. You can buy all the furniture you need (crib, changing table, dresser), as well as sheets, towels, diapers, nipples, bottles, layettes or clothing for newborns, strollers/carriages, high chairs, playpens, baby carriers/backpacks, and much, much more. You get the idea. We like them because they make your life easy. Most sell toys, too, but be aware that the selection is limited and the prices are often higher than at Toys "R" Us or other toy stores.

Some stores are ritzier than others, some more value oriented. The proximity of the store to your home should help you decide where to shop. Many expectant moms in New York visit too many stores in their quest for the perfect crib, sheets, and towels. You don't have to! Find a place that's convenient, and use it for all your needs. Patronize one store consistently, so the staff gets to know you and will go that extra mile when necessary. Also, buy in bulk. Many stores never "officially" discount, but may give you a better price if you are placing a large order. Don't be afraid to ask. And there's no harm in asking if they'll match a better price that you have seen somewhere else.

Also check out the store's delivery policy. Policies vary widely.

Superstores

✢ Albee's*

715 Amsterdam Avenue at 95th Street
662-8902
www.babyexpressstores.com
Return Policy: Refunds with receipt.
Albee's is not glamorous—fluorescent lighting, no carpeting, and lots of chaos give you an idea of the atmosphere—but we love it. Carla and Michael, the owners, are friendly, knowledgeable, and down-to-earth, and the store is

packed full of just about everything your baby could ever need. We also appreciate their honesty. Pamela was talked out of purchasing a slew of newborn sleepers that Carla said the baby would outgrow in a month. (And, she was right!) Prices here are the best in the city on many items including high chairs, playpens, and strollers. Yet it's not for the faint of heart. Albee's is always busy and so fully stocked that you have to navigate carefully. It carries Simmons, Child Craft, and Morigeau cribs, as well as some Ragazzi and Lexington brands, and all the carriage/stroller brands. What it doesn't have in stock can be ordered for you. Albee's also sells clothing, bedding, nipples, bottles, bottle racks, carriage accessories, tapes, videos, books, bibs, cloth diapers, and diaper bags, but not formula. There is a baby registry—great for people looking to purchase gifts for a new mom.

✢ Baby Depot

707 Sixth Avenue at 23rd Street
229-1300
www.coat.com
Return Policy: Store credit only.
Baby Depot is part of Burlington Coat Factory, a huge store at 23rd Street and Sixth Avenue. This neat and brightly lit department carries everything you'll want, including cribs, high chairs, strollers, clothes, and accessories. The prices are very good. Baby Depot carries a large selection of Simmons and Child Craft cribs. Its stroller selection includes Peg Perego, Aprica, Graco, Combi, Kolcraft, and Maclaren. There is a nice selection of books and videos

for babies and toddlers as well as all the nipples and bottles, bibs, cups, and spoons you could ask for. Its layette and clothing selection is great (it carries maternity clothing, too) and it has good prices on Carter's. The store manager is extremely knowledgeable and eager to help. But it's best to know what you're looking for when shopping at Baby Depot, because the service can be hit or miss. Still, it's worth the trip—the prices are some of the best in town.

❊ *Buy Buy Baby*

270 Seventh Avenue
bet. 25th and 26th streets
917-344-1555
www.buybuybaby.com
The addition of Buy Buy Baby to Manhattan has been a boon for Manhattan families. Buy Buy Baby offers everything from baby furniture, clothing for newborns to toddlers, and accessories, including toys, books, CDs, audio and video tapes, stuffed animals, infant seats, bassinets, playpens, high chairs, car seats, and more. Buy Buy Baby is also a great place to stock up on formula, diapers, wipes, and related items. There are seven other stores in the U.S. so it is a good place to register so out-of-town relatives can see what you really need for your new baby.

❊ *Planet Kids*

247 East 86th Street bet. Second
and Third avenues
426-2040
2688 Broadway bet. 102nd and 103rd streets
864-8705

www.planetkidsny.baweb.com
Return Policy: Return within 7 days, exchange within 12; after 12 days, store credit only.
Opened in July 1999 by the owner of Regine Kids, Shlomo Moskatel, this bright, spacious store contains everything your child needs. There are three floors filled with clothes, cribs, changing tables, car seats, strollers, and huge, colorful displays of toys and accessories. Cribs include those from Ragazzi, Bonavita, C & T, Status, and Child Craft. Strollers include Graco, Maclaren, Peg Perego, Kolcraft, Aprica, Combi, Baby Trend, and Century. Planet Kids also sells Dutailier gliders ($300 to $490). Children's clothing is by OshKosh B'Gosh, Le Top, Carter's, and Gerber (up to toddler sizes), and there is a full layette department as well.

❊ *Schneider's*

41 West 25th Street
bet. Broadway and Sixth Avenue
228-3540
www.schneidersbaby.com
Return Policy: No refund. Store credit or exchange with receipt on new merchandise in original package, within 20 days.
Schneider's is a neighborhood store that's been serving the downtown crowd for over fifty years. It carries brands such as Pali, Legacy, Vermont Precision, Maclaren, Peg Perego, Combi, Baby Bjorn, Century, Evenflo, and Tough Traveler. This well-stocked store carries a full line of accessories but no clothing.

Toys "R" Us

1514 Broadway at West 44th Street
(646) 366-8858
www.toysrus.com
Return Policy: Refund with receipt, otherwise store credit only.

We love Toys "R" Us. It sells furniture and accessories at the best prices in town. You'll find cribs for under $200, strollers, high chairs, playpens, bottles, bibs, and waterproof bed pads, as well as diapers and formula (available by the case). While Toys "R" Us favors the mass-market labels, you can find some of the better brands such as Peg Perego and Graco, plus Cosco, Evenflo, Kolcraft, Aprica, and Fisher-Price. Weekdays and evenings are your best bet for shopping; these stores are mobbed on the weekends. Delivery service is available; prices depend on the size of the items to be shipped.

Specialty Stores

ABC Carpet & Home

888 Broadway at 19th Street
473-3000
www.abchome.com
Return Policy: Refund with receipt, otherwise store credit only.

Style-conscious parents need not worry about outfitting their little one's room. ABC Carpet and Home stocks a small but carefully chosen selection of nursery furnishings in keeping with its antique and country chic theme. The look here is sophisticated rustic, evoking the nineteenth century. You'll find everything from Victorian-inspired cast iron cribs and cradles to fashionably distressed decorative accessories. In addition to home furnishings, there is an impressive selection of high-quality baby and toddler clothing, a huge range of plush and classic toys, and children's books and stationery. This is an excellent spot to pick up gifts.

Bella Zander

400 Chambers Street
917-309-4475 or 917-587-6386
email: bellazander@cs.com

Two Tribeca moms have teamed up to create a company that offers a personalized shopping experience for nursery and children's room decor. Customers can choose among hundreds of fabrics for bedding products, a handcrafted line of furniture (cribs, junior beds, changing tables, and dressers), decorative accesories, and more. Bella Zander carries Amy Coe, Pamela Kline, Bratt Decor, Clair de la Lune, and many other brand names, all at prices below retail. By appointment only, so call ahead.

Bellini

1305 Second Avenue bet. 68th
and 69th streets
517-9233
www.bellini.com
Return Policy: Store credit.

Customers who shop here rave about the top-of-the-line furniture and service at this Tiffany's of baby stores. The store is beautiful, with bright, muraled walls and the longest list of baby necessities we've ever seen! The staff will spend hours helping you select the perfect crib, (this is the only place in town to find a Bellini crib), and coordinating furniture, bedding, and accessories. It custom-makes bedding sets and has a library of fabrics you can choose from. Special knit items like sweaters and christening outfits are exquisite. Kelly got a wonderfully trimmed receiving blanket from Bellini with a matching diaper and bib. Delivery is a flat rate of $65; smaller items are shipped UPS. It says it will match prices if it can verify what another store charges.

❈ *Blue Bench*
159 Duane Street bet. Hudson Street
and West Broadway
267-1500
Return Policy: Store credit only.
This beautiful Tribeca store is spacious, clean, and bright, and displays exquisite solid-wood pieces such as cribs, rocking chairs, bureaus, and desks. Most items in the store are fashionably distressed with an heirloom quality about them. Blue Bench carries toys, books, and stuffed animals as well. Susan, the store's owner, provides a full interior decorating service, and will come to your home to take pictures and measurements, and help you choose everything from colors to fabric, rugs, and curtains. The rooms are classic, making them a one-time investment.

❈ *Chelsea's Kids Quarter*
33 West 17th Street bet. Fifth and Sixth
avenues
627-5524
Return Policy: Store credit only.

When a child has outgrown his crib, it is time to venture into the world of children's beds, and this store provides the next step. Chelsea Kids supplies you with all you will need to furnish a child's room—tables and chairs, beautiful toy chests, plush toys, bedding, and lighting. We saw a gorgeous red toy chest for $299. All of the furniture is made of solid wood and will easily withstand the tests of time and usage. A basic wood bed costs about $400, and there are many add-ons to choose from, such as storage drawers, a trundle bed, a bunk bed, or bookcases, as well as a large variety of wood finishes. This store will also do interior design, helping you to choose fabrics and wallpaper, and do general color coordination.

❈ *Just for Tykes*
83 Mercer Street bet. Spring
and Broome streets
274-9121
Return Policy: Store credit only
with receipt within 10 days.
Just for Tykes is a high-end hybrid of a superstore and specialty store. While it doesn't stock nipples and diapers, it offers high-end baby furniture and baby bedding. Brands include Liz Wain, Sleeping Partners, Designer's Guild, and Bellisimo. It stocks car seats (Britax and Century), strollers, toys, swings, and more. It also has infant and toddler clothing by designers such as Portofino, Petit Boy, Deux Par Deux, and more. Just for Tykes was opened by Erika O'Brien, a downtown mom frustrated by the lack of high-quality merchandise in her neighborhood.

Karin Alexis

490 Amsterdam Avenue bet. 83rd
and 84th streets
769-9550
www.karinalexis.com
Return Policy: Store credit or exchange.
An eclectic shop replacing a furniture store reflects the Upper West Side's practical, yet funky sensibility. Karin is the owner and operator of this shop specializing in clothing, accessories, and gifts for children newborn and up. She designs many of the items in her store, and they are usually boldly patterned and brightly colored. This is also a great spot for baby gifts and accessories.

Kid's Supply Co.

1343 Madison Avenue at 94th Street
426-1200
www.kidssupplyco.com
Return Policy: Quite restrictive,
call store for details.
Kid's Supply Co. is a small, high-end store brimming with an eclectic mix of timeless, sophisticated furniture, and unusual accessories. Befitting its tony neighborhood, Kid's Supply is quite pricey, and designs and manufactures its own line of high-quality goods. The staff will work closely with you to create the room of your dreams. Beds convert from bunk beds to twins, and they come as day beds and trundle beds. They can be custom-finished, too. Cribs and changing tables, which convert into dressers, are available as well. Linens can be customized, and it has an especially wide selection of boys' bedding. Kid's Supply Co. also has

a larger store with beautiful displays in Greenwich, Connecticut (203-422-2932), one hour outside of New York City.

Pamela Scurry's Wicker Garden

1327 Madison Avenue bet. 93rd
and 94th streets
410-7001
Return Policy: Store credit only.
This top-of-the-line boutique is exquisite, and the baby furniture, much of which is hand-painted, is some of the loveliest (and most expensive) in town. You'll find finishing touches, such as coordinating wastepaper baskets, diaper pails, chests, and changing tables to match a crib. It has books of linens to choose from, will custom-make anything, and carries top brands such as Blauen. The main floor has a full layette selection; most of the clothing is imported from France and Italy, all with the Wicker Garden label. This is the place for beautiful children's clothes and hand-painted furniture when you choose to go first class.

Room and Board

105 Wooster Street bet. Prince and Spring
streets
334-4343
www.roomandboard.com
Room and Board is a great new four-story furniture store located in Soho. It offers functional yet stylish furniture for every room in your home. It also offers unique options for the nursery and kids' rooms. Selections include cribs, gliders, mini tables and chairs, even bedding.

❋ *The Upper Breast Side*

220 West 71st Street, Suite 1

bet. Broadway and West End Avenue

873-2653

www.upperbreastside.com

Return Policy: Exchange only within two weeks of purchase.

This boutique for breastfeeding moms is all the rage with Upper West Siders. This is a one-of-a-kind place offering every accoutrement for breastfeeding. Bras, breast pumps, nursing pillows, and more. The owner is extremely knowledgeable, and committed to finding the best products for nursing. She also carries some baby accessories.

Superstores Outside of New York City

❋ *The Baby and Toy Superstore**

11 Forest Street, Stamford, CT 06901

203-327-1333

www.kidshomefurnishings.com

Return Policy: Refund within fifteen days with receipt and original packaging, otherwise store credit only.

The store is clean, bright, and big, and offers all the best brands at some of the best prices around. Roz, Harvey, and Seth, the owners, work closely with customers and know their merchandise. It offers every Pali and Ragazzi crib and set of furniture, and carry items that aren't available anywhere else in the New York area. Other brands include Legacy, AP Industries, Morigeau, Moosehead, and Michael's Wicker. They sell ready-made linens,

but will custom-make beautiful crib sets as well. New York residents pay no sales tax, but delivery is $85 and up (assembly is included). Kelly loves Baby and Toy Superstore and uses the store to this day.

❋ *Buy Buy Baby*

Several Tristate Area locations

www.buybuybaby.com

Return Policy: Refund within 30 days if the item is unused; after 30 days, store credit only.

These stores are huge (40,000 square feet and over 20,000 products), and known for their top-notch personalized service and guaranteed low prices. Product brands include Peg Perego, Maclaren, Graco, Century, Britax, Cosco, Evenflo, Simmons, Child Craft, Dutalier, and more. Clothing is available from Baby Lulu, Carter's, Little Me, Calvin Klein, Nautica, Baby Dior, and Flapdoodles, among others. Aside from offering just about anything a parent could want, Buy Buy Baby also has three artists on staff to customize furniture; an electronic baby registry; nursing rooms; and free gift-wrapping. Delivery to Manhattan is $70, plus an extra $25 for assembly, and smaller items can be shipped through UPS. This store can get crowded, especially during the weekends—so go early or check out the website instead.

Furniture, Clothing, and Donations

You will see how quickly your child outgrows everything from bassinet to rocking chairs, cribs, and clothing. Two terrific outlets to donate your gently used gear are:

Baby Buggy

736-1777

www.babybuggy.com

Baby Buggy, a nonprofit organization founded by Jessica Seinfeld in 2001, is dedicated to collecting and distributing gently used and new gear, clothing, and products for infants and young children in need throughout the five boroughs of New York City. Since 2001, Baby Buggy has given hundreds of thousands of essential items to thousands of families through its network of qualified social service partners. Check its website for information about donating items.

Room to Grow

54 West 21st Street, Suite 401

620-7800

www.roomtogrow.org

Started in 1988 by Julie Burns, Room to Grow is a nonprofit organization providing low-income parents with clothing, books, toys, and other baby essentials from birth to three years old. Room to Grow gladly accepts new and nearly new items.

Interior Design and Decoration

Ready to get creative? The following New York stores sell children's wallpaper and accessories to help you pull together your baby's room. Many have in-store consultants with experience or degrees in interior design. We have also listed a few interior designers and consultants who specialize in children's rooms. We have seen their work, and it is truly special.

Charm and Whimsy

Esther Sadowsky, Allied ASID

114 East 32nd Street

683-7609

Esther has found her niche designing nurseries and children's rooms. From a small room to a suite of rooms, she will create a fun, delightful space for your child to grow up in. She can design furniture, select fabrics and carpeting, and hand-paint your chairs and benches. She can even paint a mural on your child's ceiling; the cost is based on a case-by-case appraisal. Custom, hand-painted furniture, murals, and finishes are all specialties of Charm & Whimsy. Esther designs rooms for the parents, too.

Gracious Home

1217/1220 Third Avenue at 70th Street

517-6300

1992 Broadway at 67th Street

231-7800

Gracious Home sells beautiful coordinated borders, wallpaper, and paint. It has a children's section offering beautiful bumper sets and bedding. It carries area rugs, wastepaper baskets, lamps, and bathroom accessories. Gracious Home will make up any window treatment you desire, or coordinate an entire room. The entire selection is quite beautiful.

Janovic Plaza*

Many locations throughout Manhattan

772-1400

Janovic Plaza offers a wide selection of wallpaper, borders, paints, and window treatments, and designers there will help plan your room and coordinate everything. There's a broad selection of reasonably priced fabrics suitable for a child's room. Ask about Janovic's classes on painting and wallpapering. Pamela has used the Janovic Plaza store on West 72nd Street for borders and window treatments, with happy results.

✣ Kids Digs

Carol Maryan Architects
212 West 79th Street, Suite 1C
787-7800

Owner Carol Maryan is an architect and designer who specializes in child-oriented spaces. Her room designs can be adapted to your child's needs as the years go by. A consultation, which is a problem-solving session and includes a sketch of the proposed room, depends on job size and scope. Carol will complete a design project at an hourly rate based on the job specifications.

✣ Laura Beth's Baby Collection

321 East 75th Street bet. First and Second avenues
717-2559

A former buyer in the famed Baby Department at Barneys New York, Laura Beth meets one-on-one with stylish moms-to-be to help them pick out linens and accessories for the wee one's room at her chic store. She offers one-stop personal shopping for crib linens, custom bedding, and a variety of accessories for the nursery, including mobiles, frames, bookends, and more. Laura has great taste, and carries only the finest collections the baby market has to offer at prices better than retail. The new location has a great collection of nursery items for stylish

moms-to-be plus a huge selection of stylish baby announcements, thank-you notes, birthday invitations, stickers, and gift enclosures.

✣ MB Discount Furniture

2311 Avenue U bet. East 23rd
and East 24th streets
718-332-1500
Return Policy: Store credit, exchange, or refund.

Hands-down, MB is the best merchandised store in Brooklyn (and nicer than many in Manhattan). It stocks everything from cribs and strollers to bedding, accessories, gift items, clothes, swings, high chairs, playpens, and car seats. Unique model rooms are set up on one side of the store and custom bedding is a specialty here. Agnes, the owner, says they "will make anything you want," even adult bedding. Crib brands include Morigeau-Lepine, Bonavita, C & T, Pali, Tracer, and Ragazzi; strollers include Peg Perego, Baby Trend, Combi, and Inglesina. The store also carries bottles, nipples, diaper bags, and layettes from brands like Absorba, Baby Steps, Mini Clasix, and Carter's. MB Discount Furniture has a price guarantee, and will match the lowest prices found elsewhere.

✣ Plain Jane

525 Amsterdam Avenue at 85th Street
595-6916
www.plainjanekids.com
Return Policy: Store credit only.

If you want to put together a 40s/50s retro look, this eclectic store sells decorative accessories, furniture, and bedding for the home, especially for a baby's room (which, of course, is exactly what you're looking for). It does a wonderful job with custom bedding and furniture, and has a knack for arranging items in displays that will give you lots of ideas.

❊ *Robin Weiss*

Paint Your World

917-751-4412

www.paint-your-world.com

Robin Weiss, founder of Paint Your World, specializes in custom-painted wall murals. She does beautiful, creative murals for children's rooms (and for other parts of the home as well). Check out her website for some samples of her work.

❊ *SmartStart*

Susan Weinberg

334 West 86th Street, Suite 6C

580-7365

Susan, an interior designer, starts with a consultation to focus on your needs and to analyze the space. She shops for you, starting from a list of your basic needs, then helps you select the furniture. The consultation fee varies (whether in the city or outside the city). Her hourly rate is around $100; for large projects, her fee is 20 percent of the cost. She can also help order birth announcements.

❊ *YoyaMart*

15 Gansevoort Street (at Hudson Street)

242-5511

www.yoyamart.com

YoyaMart is a hip store designed to bring par-ents high-quality imported furniture and accessories. It also carries Netto cribs, Kiehl's baby products, and fun toys, too.

Best Places for Gift Items

Sometimes finding a great baby gift is tough to do—especially if you are really busy (and who isn't these days?). These are three no-fail places to get the perfect gift for your friend's new addition—or your own!

❊ *Cocoa Crayon*

917-750-1117

www.cocoacrayon.com

Cocoa Crayon is a New York–based gift business that was born out of a passion for finding hip, well-designed, useful things for kids. Creator Lisa Moss features a fabulous selection of gifts for new moms, babies, kids, and adults, too. Pamela used Cocoa Crayon to purchase teachers' holiday gifts this year with great results.

❊ *Go To Baby*

315 East 57th Street bet. First and Second avenues

223-8090

www.gotobaby.com

Go To Baby's unique baby gifts and baby gift baskets are high quality and well-priced. It offers a wide selection of baby gifts including clothing, stuffed animals, books, personalized gift items, and more. Its website is easy to use and it also has a retail store that carries many of the same things.

✳ *Fill-R-Up Gift Baskets*

197 East 76th Street

452-3026

www.fill-r-up.com

Fill-R-Up is a customized gift basket service and retail store located on Manhattan's Upper East Side. The company is the brainchild of Amanda Moses, who, as an event planner at a top fashion company, was often looking for gift baskets for VIP clients and events. Amanda offers great baskets for new moms, new babies, birthday parties, and more.

baby proofing

Little did you know your apartment was a danger zone. Beware if you have—as do most of us—a glass or sharp-edged coffee table, electrical outlets, lamps, lamp cords, drawers, cleaning solutions and cosmetics under sinks/vanities, or anything sitting on a table. Baby proofing your home is one of the most important tasks you'll undertake. By the time your child begins to creep and crawl, all potentially dangerous objects must be covered, secured, removed, or replaced.

Here are ways to get baby-proofing help:

✳ Buy a book or video such as *Mr. Baby Proofer*, a thirty-minute video that shows parents how to create a safe environment for newborns.

✳ Ask for advice at any of the baby superstores. A salesperson will talk you through what you need in order to create a safe home.

✳ Hire a baby-proofing expert. Howard Applebaum

of Baby Proofers Plus (628-8052 or 800-880-2191) will come to your home for a free consultation, determine what you need, prepare an estimate, and install everything. We have both used Howard, who gives seminars on child safety at local hospitals, and we highly recommend him. Another excellent baby proofing company is All Star Baby Safety, Inc. (396-1995), run by Tom Treanor, who will come to your home for a consultation and price estimate for the full service. He will also travel to Long Island and Westchester if you want to baby proof a beach or country house. Tom is a distributor of the magnetic Tot-Lok safety system and a member of the International Association for Child Safety.

Many people baby proof their own apartments. Howard Applebaurn provides the following safety suggestions:

✳ Poisons or toxic materials (i.e. all cleaners) should not be stored under the sink; place them high up, out of your baby's reach.

✳ Attach all busy boxes, mirrors, or crib toys on the wall side of the crib, so that your baby cannot use the objects to climb out of the crib. Do not mount a wall hanging above the crib, where your child can pull it down and perhaps dislodge nails.

✳ Toilet lids should be locked closed.

✳ Keep all trash containers locked up and out of baby's way.

✳ Remove tall lamps or coat racks or block them with furniture to ensure that your baby can't pull them over.

✳ When cooking, all pot handles should be

turned inward so your baby cannot reach them. Use back burners when possible.

❈ Separate plants and babies. Some plants are poisonous, and a young child may eat the leaves or pull the whole plant on top of himself.

❈ Hanging cords from answering machines, phones, lamps, and appliances should be out of your baby's reach.

❈ Do not take pills or medication in front of children; they mimic what they see.

❈ Remove all soaps, razors, and shampoos from around the edge of the bathtub.

❈ Do not use tacks or staples to secure electrical cords to walls; they can fall out or be pulled out and swallowed. Use tape.

❈ Discard plastic dry cleaner bags before entering the house. Babies can suffocate in them or pull off pieces and choke on them.

❈ Keep emergency phone numbers, including the poison control center, near all telephones.

❈ To prevent carpeting from sliding, use a foam grid padding beneath it.

❈ Babies like to pull off the tips from doorstops. Place some glue inside the cap, then stick the cap back onto the doorstop.

❈ Remove magnets from your refrigerator door. If they fall to the floor and break, a child may pick up the pieces and swallow them. Invest in baby magnets or plastic non-breakable ones.

❈ If you have a fireplace, place a piece of carpet or foam on the whole base so your child won't bang into the brick.

❈ Get a bathtub spout cover to prevent your child from hitting his head against it.

❈ If you have a home gym, keep that room closed when you're not in it. Babies can get their fingers stuck in the spokes of exercise bikes, put their fingers in the gears, or pull weights onto themselves.

❈ Glass panels in coffee tables can break under the weight of a child. Replace with acrylic.

❈ Mobiles should be removed when a child is five to seven months old. A baby of that age can pull the mobile down, or be injured if the little strings from the mobile can be wrapped around his fingers.

❈ Cords for window blinds should be lifted high and out of reach. Babies can accidentally wrap the cords around themselves.

❈ Wash out cleaning fluid bottles before putting them in your recycling bin. Just a drop of cleaning fluid can cause serious injury to a baby.

❈ Never leave infants alone in the bathtub. Ignore telephone calls and doorbells. Babies can drown in just an inch of water. Never leave a tub with water standing in it.

❈ Check the underside of upholstered furniture for loose staples or sharp points.

baby and
toddler clothing

If you've always thought baby clothing was the cutest thing in the world—well, you are going to love this chapter! New York stores have all the baby clothing you need, want, or have dreamt of. There's tons of adorable stuff to choose from, but don't bring all of it home at once. Babies grow very, very quickly, and the outfit that fit the last time you put it on may not even come close a few weeks later. We'll tell you about some of the best clothing shops in the city to help you save time, energy, and money.

What a difference a second child made in our shopping habits! The first time around, only the "best"—meaning most expensive—would do for our little ones. From dresses to pajamas, we spared no expense. Now, with our second children, Benjamin and Angela, we've opted for a different strategy: Buy on sale! Shop at the Gap, Children's Place, and Old Navy. Pamela swears by Greenstones 50-percent-off sales in January and June, and Kelly has been known to travel down to Baby Depot for bargain-priced turtlenecks. And Century 21 can't be beat for socks and underwear.

shopping tips

If your shower gifts include too many outfits in three- and six-month sizes, return most of them for a credit, or exchange them for twelve- or eighteen-month sizes. Don't dawdle, either. If you put it off, you'll find the stores won't take them back or they'll have been marked down. Also, wait until all the baby gifts are in—you may not need as much as you think.

❋ Pay attention to a store's return policy. Most of the shops—especially the European-style boutiques, such as Jacadi and Bonpoint—

Best Department Stores for Style and Selection

Lord & Taylor
Saks Fifth Avenue
Bloomingdale's
Macy's

are very strict when it comes to returns. Department stores tend to be the most lenient; goods can usually be brought back for cash or credit for up to one year.

❋ Ask about the sales. Small shops often have January and June/July special pricing events; some have quarterly sales. Department stores always seem to have sales. In some shops, you won't be able to use gift certificates on sale items.

❋ If you plan to shop with your little one in tow, use a baby carrier or small stroller. Some of these stores are small, crowded, and you may have to walk up a flight of stairs.

❋ Onesie outfits are practical. You can't have too many of these pullover, short sleeve T-shirts with bottom snaps to layer under winter clothes or to use as-is in hot weather. All the stores carry onesies, in a variety of price ranges. Buy the least expensive ones you can find, and always in 100-percent cotton.

❋ Think cotton. It's cozy, soft, and easily washable. (Your pediatrician will probably tell you to wash your baby's clothes for the first year in the non-detergents Dreft or Ivory Snow, which do not irritate a baby's sensitive skin.)

❋ You'll find it convenient to have many sleeping outfits, but test several before buying a bunch to see which your baby prefers. Pamela bought half a dozen Carter's sleeping gowns with draw-string bottoms, but found that Rebecca was uncomfortable with her feet restricted. She exchanged them for open sleeper bag paja-mas, and Rebecca was much happier. (All sleepwear must be 100-percent polyester to be flame retardant.)

❉ Don't buy any infant clothes with strings around or near the neck, which can be dangerous. Most manufacturers have stopped making baby clothes with strings.

❉ Use clothing with snaps around the bottoms, for easy changing.

❉ Give some thought to how and when you'll do laundry. Your baby will go through several out-fits a day. If you have a washer and dryer in your apartment, and it's easy to throw in a load at odd moments, a large layette may be unneces-sary. If you use a machine in your building's basement or take clothing to a neighborhood laundromat, it may be more convenient and easier on your pocketbook to stock a relatively large supply of clothing. Either way, all clothing should be machine washable.

❉ Buy ahead whenever possible. (Winter coats are often on sale in January.) Also, try to borrow expensive items, such as snowsuits.

❉ If you receive many gifts in small sizes, always exchange some for larger ones.

❉ Many stores have prepared an essential layette list for you—some of them incredibly long! Take such lists with a grain of salt, keeping in mind your own budget and storage space.

❉ Because store hours can change frequently, we suggest calling before making a trip. Most stores are open seven days a week, from 10 or 11 a.m. until 6 p.m.

Here's a practical layette:

For Baby

❉ 6 onesies
❉ 2 side-snap or side-tie shirts (until umbilical cord separates)
❉ 6 stretchies or coveralls, which cover your baby from neck to feet, and have snaps (these in heavier material are good for sleeping)
❉ 4 sleep gowns or sleeper bags (Kelly favors the sleeper bags—great in cold weather and with air-conditioning)
❉ 2 caps
❉ 6 pairs of socks
❉ 1 snowsuit (for winter babies)
❉ 4 receiving blankets (to lay the baby down on and wrap her up in)
❉ 2 heavier waffle weave blankets (one for stroller, one for crib)
❉ 3 hooded towel/washcloth sets
❉ 12 cloth diapers (for burping the baby)
❉ 4 bibs
❉ 1 outdoor hat (keeps winter babies warm, protects summer babies from sun)
❉ 1 pair cotton mittens (to prevent your baby from scratching her face)
❉ 1 pair outdoor mittens (for winter babies) baby scissors, nail clipper, non-glass thermometer, nasal aspirator, hairbrush/comb
❉ bath tub

For Crib

* 2 quilted mattress pads
* 2 waterproof liners
* 3 to 4 fitted crib sheets
* 6 crib bibs (to protect sheets from baby spit up)
* 1 bumper pad

the stores

From expensive designer boutiques to discount department stores, children's shops dot the retail landscape of New York. We can't even begin to explain the prices at some of these European boutiques found on Madison Avenue. (Neither of us would pay $100 for a child's T-shirt from France, but apparently someone does.) Meanwhile, Sixth Avenue, from 16th to 23rd streets, is home to terrific bargain shopping: Baby Depot in the Burlington Coat Factory, Old Navy, and Daffy's.

* babyGap*

Many locations around New York
and the tristate area
www.gapkids.com
Return Policy: Lenient.
Who doesn't love the Gap? There are over twenty babyGap stores in town, usually within grown-up Gap stores. Nothing outrageous here. The Gap's baby clothing is often 100-percent cotton, and in traditional colors and styles. But the sales are great! Comfortable play clothes hold up well after repeated washings. (Just be prepared to see other babies at the playgroup wearing the exact same outfit.) For extra special events, try Baby Lux located at the Gap at 680 Fifth Avenue at 54th Street (977-7023), where cashmere, silk, linen, and leather are the materials of the day.

* Baby Moves Boutique

139 Perry Street at Greenwich Street
255-1685
www.babymovesnyc.com
This boutique, located within the Baby Moves center (a center for early childhood classes), offers a carefully chosen selection of children's clothing (infants to six years), accessories, baby gear, and developmental toys. Bring your kids along, because they can play in the playroom here while you shop.

* Bambini

1088 Madison Avenue at 83rd Street
717-6742
Return Policy: Store credit within seven days.
The epitome of the Upper East Side shop. Bambini offers fine Italian clothing for children from three months to eight years old. The selection is formal and pricey; this is a good place to purchase a holiday or special occasion outfit for a boy or girl.

* Barneys

660 Madison Avenue at 61st Street
826-8900

Prettiest (and Priciest!) Layettes in Town

La Layette
Bonpoint
Spring Flowers

Return Policy: Refund with receipt.

The children's department at Barneys is small but well stocked. Just as you'd expect, most of the clothes and accessories—for newborns to children age four—are stylish and expensive. The department also carries pretty linens, shoes, albums, hand-painted pillows, stuffed animals, toys, and Kate Spade diaper bags. Brands Carried: Grain de Lune, Paul Smith, Maharishi, Bonpoint, Lilly Pulitzer, Burberry's for Kids, flora and henri, Metropolitan Prairie, and Barneys private label.

❋ Bloomingdale's*

1000 Third Avenue bet. 59th and 60th streets

705-2000

www.bloomingdales.com

Return Policy: Lenient.

The sprawling children's department on the eighth floor has one section for layettes, newborns, and toddlers, then separate sections for girls, boys, and teens. You'll also find accessories, toys, and gifts—and end-of-season sales. We have shopped here for years. Brands Carried: Carter's, Little Me, Baby Dior, Classic Pooh, Miniclasix, Absorba, Ralph Lauren Baby, Esprit, Flapdoodles, Baby B'Gosh, Baby Guess, and its private label, Next Generation.

❋ Bombalulus

101 West 10th Street bet. Sixth

and Greenwich avenues

463-0897

www.bombalulus.com

Return Policy: Store credit only.

Bombalus is an African word that loosely translates

as "a group of artists working together." Most of the clothes are handmade and moderately priced. You'll find hand-painted onesies, T-shirts, shorts, leggings, sweatshirts, and hand-sewn jackets and hats. The store imports colorful clothing, as well as unique toys and collectibles from Bali and Guatemala.

❋ Bonpoint

1269 Madison Avenue at 91st Street

722-7720

811 Madison Avenue at 68th Street

879-0900

Return Policy: Store credit only; no returns on sale items.

All clothes have the Bonpoint label and are imported from Paris—but so are the prices! Sizes begin at newborn and go up to size sixteen for preteen girls, and size twelve for boys. The store has a wide selection and is easy to shop in. Styles range from casual to dressy, with fabrics from cotton to silk. The atmosphere is formal, but if you (or Grandma) are looking for only the best, its beautifully tailored French clothing is perfect.

❋ Bu & The Duck

106 Franklin Street bet. Church Street

and West Broadway

431-9226

www.buandtheduck.com

Return policy: Store credit only.

This lovely Tribeca shop carries clothing for newborn to six years old. Susan Lane, the owner, designs and sews most of the clothing herself—beautiful rayon sundresses with lace trim, striped leggings, flowery knit cardigans, and much more. The prices range from moderate to expensive; you can purchase a T-shirt for $30 or a special winter coat for over $200. Along with clothing, Bu offers imported children's shoes as well as a special selection of accessories, toys, and gift items. Brands Carried: Lalalou, Quincy, Melagrano, Boofoowoo, Pom D'Api, Naturino, and Magnolia.

✳ CALYPSO Enfant

426 Broome Street
bet. Lafayette and Crosby streets
966-3234
These two boutiques offer fine one-of-a-kind children's clothing from a variety of European, American, and in-house designers. You can find knit booties and hats, cashmere sweaters (even for newborns), silk and corduroy bustles, and adorable dresses—all in a wide array of Calypso colors—as well as great heirloom blankets and wooden toys. On weekends every kid gets a free balloon. Holidays bring in Santa, the Easter Bunny, and the Halloween Witch!

✳ Catimini

1125 Madison Avenue at 84th Street
987-0688
Return Policy: Store credit only; no returns on sale items.
Catamini's stylish French clothing is bright and colorful and available in sizes ranging from newborn to age twelve. (Catamini's label is carried at Saks Fifth Avenue, Neiman Marcus, and Nordstrom.)

✳ Century 21 Department Store

22 Cortlandt Street bet. Broadway and Church Street
227-9092
www.c21stores.com
Return Policy: Refund within 30 days with receipt and price tag attached.
Century 21, the discount department store, has a large children's department. It's not difficult to find a bargain, with prices that hover around 25-percent below retail. Accessories include diaper bags, cloth diapers, and bibs. It's crowded, especially on weekends; it's best to shop here without your baby. Brands Carried: Carter's, Little Me, Ralph Lauren, Gerber, and Absorba.

✳ The Children's Place*

Locations throughout Manhattan
529-2201
www.childrensplace.com
Return Policy: No sale is ever final.
This growing chain with shops in Manhattan and many across the tristate area is a real find, and could well be the next Gap. The store is clean, its return policy is flexible, and the clothing is comfortable, high quality, stylish, and affordable. The collections are basic and come in bright and traditional colors, with some fashion sense. We've seen beautiful fall/winter corduroys in rich, royal colors—deep blue, ruby red, and emerald green—as well as bright, multi-colored summer clothing and bathing suits. You can also find socks, hats, headbands, scrunchies, and adorable sunglasses.

❊ Cremebebe

68 Second Avenue bet. 3rd and 4th streets

979-6848

Return Policy: Store credit only.

This store is funky and cheerful, with a wide selection of colorful American and Italian clothes in sizes ranging from ages newborn to five years. The owner creates some of the items herself, scanning bright designs of apples, trains, and the Cremebebe logo, onto T-shirts that sell for $8. She also sells her own plastic bibs and hand-knit sweaters. Racks of vintage jeans for kids (around $20 a pair), fancier silk dresses (for about $50), and a selection of toys, stuffed animals, and accessories complete the mix. Brands Carried: Malina and Shortcake.

❊ Daffy's

111 Fifth Avenue at 18th Street

529-4477

335 Madison Avenue at 44th Street

557-4422

125 East 57th Street at Lexington Avenue

376-4477

1311 Broadway at 34th Street

736-4477

Return Policy: Refund within fourteen days, otherwise store credit only.

Daffy's is a discount store for the whole family. Its children's department is particularly good, and our bargain-hunting friends swear by Daffy's for some of the best deals in town. Like Loehmann's, be prepared to pick through racks and hunt for infant clothes that were misplaced in the toddler section. Pamela picked up Flapdoodle leggings here for $5.99; Daffy's also

Funkiest Kids' Clothes

Space Kiddets

Z'Baby Company

Peanut Butter and Jane

stocks Rebecca's favorite brand, Le Tout Petit, which can sometimes be found here in the right size. Brands Carried: Mini Basix, Absorba, Wee Play, Little Me, Baby Incorporated, and Flapdoodles.

❊ flora and henri

931 Madison Avenue bet. 74th and 75th streets

249-1694

www.florahenri.com

flora and henri offers a unique line of vintage-inspired children's clothing, for sizes newborn to twelve years. The clothing is simple and classic and uses cotton fabrics in soft, natural colors, often featuring floral prints. This is its first East Coast store.

❊ Greenstones

442 Columbus Avenue bet. 81st

and 82nd streets

580-4322

Greenstones, Too

1184 Madison Avenue bet. 86th

and 87th streets

427-1665

Return Policy: Store credit only; no returns on sale items.

These family-owned-and-operated stores contain a wide selection of European-imported clothing for boys and girls from newborn to age twelve, with an especially good selection of outer-wear. Prices are moderate for sportswear and more expensive for dressier designer items. Watch for their unbeatable 50-percent-off sales that take place in January and June. (Rebecca and Benjamin get their winter coats here every year.) Brands Carried: Catamini, I.K.K.S., Jean Bourget, Miniman, Kenzo, Naf Naf, and Petit Boy.

❖ Gymboree

1120 Madison Avenue bet. 83rd
and 84th streets
717-6702
1049 Third Avenue at 62nd Street
688-4044
1332 Third Avenue at 76th Street
517-5548
2015 Broadway bet. 68th and 69th streets
595-7662
2271 Broadway bet. 81st and 82nd streets
595-9071
www.gymboree.com
Return Policy: Lenient.

The large, roomy Gymboree stores specialize in play clothes and active wear for boys and girls from newborn to eight years. The moderately priced clothes are 100% cotton and come in brightly colored designs, with new collections arriving every six to eight weeks. Kelly shops the 83rd Street location often, and loves it.

❖ H&M

1328 Broadway at Herald Square (34th Street)
www.hm.com
H&M, the Swedish sensation, has many stores around Manhattan now, but only the Broadway store offers clothing for babies and kids. New Yorkers have fallen in love with H&M for its appealing range of products and reasonable prices.

❖ Ibiza Kidz

46 University Place bet. 9th and 10th streets
533-4614
Return Policy: Exchange or store credit only.

This is the shop for cool downtown kids. Located within the Ibiza women's store, it offers a great selection of colorful print clothes for newborn children to size twelve. Ibiza carries the Malina line of beautiful silk suits and jackets, for age newborn to eighteen months, not to mention elaborate tutus with matching wings and wands, funky suitcases, hats, and a good selection of shoes. Prices are moderate to expensive. Brands Carried: Kenzo, I.K.K.S., Petit Boy, Zutano, Pompolina, Malina, and Chevignon.

❖ Jacadi

787 Madison Avenue at 67th Street
535-3200
www.jacadiusa.com
Return Policy: Store credit only within seven days; no returns on sale items.

The Jacadi store in New York (more in outlying suburbs) is independently owned and operated. The merchandise is imported from France and is mostly the Jacadi label. Both dressy and play clothes are available for newborns to twelve-year-olds, as well as towels, nursery furniture (by Pali, Pereculture, and Peg Perego), and wallpaper. Be discriminating about what

Best Places for Sale Items Under $10

The Children's Place

Talbots Kids

Old Navy

you buy because returns are next to impossible. Watch for semiannual sales from December through February and May through August.

❊ Julian & Sara

103 Mercer Street bet. Spring

and Prince streets

226-1989

Return Policy: Store credit with receipt;

no returns on sale items.

This tiny boutique imports most of its clothing from Europe and features an incredible selection for girls, with everything from party dresses to play clothes in sizes for newborns to twelve-year-olds. There are also shoes and accessories, plus a beautiful line of pajamas by Arthur. Brands Carried: Jean Bourget, Lili Gaufrette, Petit Bateau, Mona Lisa, Confetti, Petit Boy, Charabia, Kenzo, and Arthur.

❊ Kendall's Closet

162 West 84th Street

bet. Columbus and Amsterdam avenues

501-8911

Kendall's Closet is a small store with great personal service. It offers clothes for boys and girls ages three months to six years. Great girls' clothes are pretty easy to find, while stylish boys' clothes are usually more difficult.

Kendall's Closet does much to rectify this with some of the cutest boys' clothes around.

❊ Kidstown

10 East 14th Street

243-1301

This baby and kids emporium offers a large selection of reasonably priced (even inexpensive) layettes, infant and toddler clothes, and more. If you are in the neighborhood, it's definitely worth popping in here.

❊ Koh's Kids

311 Greenwich Street bet. Chambers

and Reade streets

791-6915

Return Policy: Store credit only.

This intimate little store has served the Tribeca area for over ten years. With funky clothes for children ages newborn to seven years old, Koh's Kids clothing goes from dressy to casual. Store owner Grace Koh is famous for her knit outfits. She handknits sweaters, dresses, blankets, and onesies which run on the expensive side, but are high-quality and last for years. Grace stocks sparkly sequined shoes, adorable knit hats, and toys and accessories too. Brands Carried: Baby Armadillo, Flapdoodles, and Petit Bateau.

❊ La Layette . . . Et Plus Ltd.*

170 East 61st Street bet. Third

and Lexington avenues

688-7072

Return Policy: Store credit only.

This tiny boutique near Bloomingdale's specializes

in personalized service (an appointment is recommended) and layettes. Almost everything is made especially for La Layette, and the selection is exquisite. These layettes can be rather expensive, however: from $500 to $5,000, with an average price of $800. Go see their beautiful (many one-of-a-kind) bris and christening outfits and custom clothing for older children (a girl's party dress for $350). Hand-painted cribs ($1,250) are sold with coordinating sheets, bumpers, and pillows. Everything is exquisite!

❊ *Les Petits Chapelais*

142 Sullivan Street bet. Houston and Prince streets
505-1927
www.lespetitschapelais.com
This adorable boutique is charming and fun. It offers its own brand, Les Petits Chapelais, and all of the clothes are designed by the owner. The style is high-end, brightly colored French clothing from newborn sizes to size ten.

❊ *Lester's**

1522 Second Avenue at 80th Street
734-9292
Return Policy: Refund with receipt within seven days, otherwise store credit only.
This discount store has a wide variety of play clothes, accessories, and shoes for newborns to

Best Stores for Value
Little Folks
Macy's
Baby Depot
The Children's Place

teens. Lester's enjoys putting layettes together, and appointments are preferred. Much of the merchandise is trendy, yet is priced below its competitors, making this a definite find on the Upper East Side. Brands Carried: Petit Bateau, Little Me, Mini Basix, I.K.K.S, Juicy, Tractor, Mini Man, and Flapdoodles.

❊ *Lilliput SoHo Kids*

240 Lafayette Street bet. Prince and Spring streets
965-9201
www.lilliputsoho.com
The larger of the two Lilliputs (the smaller store is across the street and slightly north) is a charming small boutique featuring fanciful clothing, shoes, and accessories for children newborn to age eight.

❊ *Little Folks*

123 East 23rd Street bet. Park
and Lexington avenues
982-9669
Return Policy: Refund with receipt within seven days, otherwise store credit only.
Little Folks could fit in the superstore category, since it carries cribs, high chairs, and accessories, but we call it a clothing store because the large selection of discounted merchandise is terrific. Pamela bought Rebecca's snowsuit at Little Folks for $40 less than what she saw in another store. The staffpeople at Little Folks are particularly knowledgeable. Brands Carried: Brambilla, Carter's, Baby Guess, Weebok, and Sara's Prints.

Lord & Taylor

424 Fifth Avenue bet. 38th and 39th streets

391-3344

www.maycompany.com

Return Policy: Lenient.

Spacious and inviting, the children's department at this grand old department store is filled with a wide variety of quality layette items and clothing. It has recently added a Saturday morning story hour for children, too. There's also a wonderful selection of stuffed animals, diaper bags, backpacks, bedding sets, and christening outfits. The staff at Lord & Taylor always seems to be exceptionally helpful. Brands Carried: Nautica, Ralph Lauren, Carter's, Little Me, Absorba, DKNY, and OshKosh B'Gosh, and Lord & Taylor's private label.

Macy's

Herald Square, 151 West 34th Street

bet. Broadway and Seventh Avenue

695-4400

www.macys.com

Return Policy: Lenient.

The largest kids floor in the world sells everything from baby skin cream to Sam & Libby leopard print shoes, and offers a changing room for your baby. Macy's carries a huge variety of clothing for newborns and older children. The prices are generally moderate, and you can always find something on sale. Huge, bright gumball machines, televisions, and sticker and postcard stations help to keep kids entertained while you shop. Brands Carried: OshKosh B'Gosh, Esprit, Disney, Mickey & Co, Sam & Libby, Tommy Hilfiger Kids, and Polo Ralph Lauren Kids.

Magic Windows*

1186 Madison Avenue bet. 86th

and 87th streets

289-0028

www.magic-windows.com

Return Policy: Store credit only;

no returns on sale items.

Magic Windows specializes in the unique. Petit Bateau is a large part of its layette business, along with other truly special lines. This is the place to find baby clothes with handmade smocking, Periwinkle cribs, changing tables, and bureaus. You can also find children's clothes up to size sixteen. Brands Carried: Petit Bateau, Absorba, Baby Steps, Agabang, Florence Eiseman, Sophie Dess, L'Agneau, D'Or, and Anavini.

Oilily

820 Madison Avenue

bet. 60th and 69th streets

772-8686

www.oililyusa.com

Return Policy: Refund with receipt

within two weeks, otherwise store credit only.

Exclusively carrying its own designs, this Dutch store's trademark is bright colors and eye-catching patterns. Children's sizes start at three months. It sells sportswear, play clothes, and shoes. It also sells women's clothing if you desire that "mother/daughter" matching look. Prices are comparable to other Madison Avenue European clothing stores.

Old Navy Clothing Co.*

610 Sixth Avenue at 18th Street

645-0663

150 West 34th Street at Seventh Avenue

594-0049

503/511 Broadway bet. Broome
and Spring streets

226-0838

300 West 125th Street bet. Eighth Avenue
and Frederick Douglass Boulevard

531-1544

www.oldnavy.com

Return Policy: Refund with receipt
within thirty days.

The Old Navy Clothing Co. is owned by the Gap and is a lower-priced alternative. These warehouselike stores are great to visit, even if you don't need kiddie clothes. The Sixth Avenue store and the 34th Street location have their own cafe (with quite a few strollers parked next to the tables) and lots of candy, gadgets, candles, and lotions, plus basic jeans and other essentials for grown-ups. At all of the locations, you will find reasonably priced, 100-percent cotton items for newborns to adults. There are adorable overalls for $10, infant dresses for $10 to $16, and onesies in bright colors for $5.50, in addition to sunglasses, socks, hats, bathing suits, and whatever else is currently fashionable. A word of warning: Old Navy is a mob scene on weekends.

Patagonia

426 Columbus Avenue bet. 80th and 81st
streets

917-441-0011

101 Wooster Street bet. Prince and Spring streets

343-1776

www.patagonia.com

Patagonia has some great cold-weather gear for infants and kids: sturdy and warm outerwear, plus thermals that our little ones can wear close to their bodies to keep them extra toasty. It also carries warm hats and mittens.

Peanut Butter & Jane*

617 Hudson Street bet. Jane
and West 12th streets

620-7952

Return Policy: Store credit only.

This store is filled to the brim with all types of clothes, from everyday to funky or dressy. Prices are reasonable, with T-shirts for $20 and up, dresses for $50 and up, onesies for $15 and up, and rompers from $25 and up. There is a small selection of shoes as well. You can find mint vintage pieces in all sizes, along with unusual gift items like puppets, Curiosity Kits for making anything and everything (from jewelry to exploding volcanoes), and a wide range of developmental toys for newborns and up. This is also the place to find great costumes for holidays and parties. Brands Carried: Petit Bateau, Flapdoodles, Wizard of Oz, and Les Tout Petits.

Petit Bateau

110 Madison Avenue at 82nd Street

988-8884

www.petit-bateau.com

The ubiquitous Petit Bateau onesie is seen on many of the Upper East Side's most well-turned-out babies! This shop offers a complete layette, baby, and children's selection with a

French flair. The T-shirts are great (you'll love them yourself), as are the beautifully designed pajamas and outfits.

La Petite Etoile

746 Madison Avenue bet. 64th and 65th streets
744-0975
This European boutique offers fine French and Italian children's dress and casual clothing from newborn to size fourteen. The store also carries a small selection of shoes and accessories.

Planet Kids

2688 Broadway bet. 102nd and 103rd streets
864-8705
Return Policy: Refund with receipt within 7 days. Uptown moms swear by Planet Kids as the only place in the neighborhood to pick up baby supplies and quality clothing. The store carries clothes from sizes newborn to fourteen and sixteen. It also sells furniture and accessories for babies. Brands Carried: Flapdoodles, OshKosh, Healthtex, and Levi's.

Prince & Princess

41 East 78th Street at Madison Avenue
879-8989
www.princeandprincess.com
Return Policy: Store credit only.
With prices such as $275 for a knit onesie, this European children's boutique is truly for princes and princesses or just the place to find a special holiday suit or dress. It also carries high-end sportswear and accessories such as headbands, bags, and hats. The store carries clothing for newborns to children age fourteen, but will take special orders for women up to age twenty. Be prepared to browse on your own.

Ralph Lauren

867 Madison Avenue at 72nd Street
606-2100
Ralph Lauren has opened a separate shop on Madison Avenue to showcase his clothing for kids newborn to age twelve. His classic traditional clothing is a must for preppy moms and dads. If you are looking for an unbelievable baby gift (and don't have a budget), check out the cashmere sweaters and pants for newborns!

Robin's Nest

1168 Lexington Avenue bet. 80th
and 81st streets
737-2004
Return Policy: Store credit only;
no returns on sale items.
Robin's Nest is tiny but well stocked with clothes for newborns to children up to age twelve. Most styles found here are casual. The store also carries an array of accessories such as backpacks, barrettes, bibs, hats, and specialty picture frames, as well as handmade toys and blankets. Prices range from moderate for T-shirts to expensive for a large selection of sweaters. Robin's Nest also sells hand-knit sweaters with pewter buttons and matching hats; these can be specially ordered in the customer's choice of colors. Robin's Nest schedules private appointments, and will also come to your home or hospital to help you with your layette needs. Brands Carried: Lili Gaufrette, Kenzo, Jean Bourget, I.K.K.S., Pappa & Ciccia, Petit Bateau, and Chevignon.

Rockstarbaby

298 Elizabeth Street

995-8638

Do you want to dress your baby the way all of the celebs do? Look no further than Rockstarbaby. This trendy shop offers layette, playwear, and accessories in sizes newborn to twenty-four months. The clothing is fun, with a real downtown L.A. sensibility. If you are looking for a leather jacket for your six-month-old, this is the place.

Saks Fifth Avenue*

611 Fifth Avenue at 50th Street

753-4000

www.saksfifthavenue.com

Return Policy: Lenient.

This top-notch department store has an excellent infant and toddler department and carries a variety of brands, including a number of designers not found elsewhere. The department is wonderfully laid out and extremely easy to shop, and the salespeople are very helpful and courteous. There are also great sales at Saks—all the best labels for less. Brands Carried: Absorba, Petit Bateau, DKNY, Ralph Lauren, Heartstrings, Florence Eiseman, Sylvia White, Baby Lulu, Monkey Wear, Catamini, Simonetta, Joan Calabrese, Zoe, and Magil.

Small Change

1196 Lexington Avenue at 81st Street

772-6455

Return Policy: Exchange and store credit only.

This small store has a diverse selection of European clothing in sizes newborn to sixteen years. The merchandise runs the gamut from the classic to the more avant-garde. Small Change also sells shoes, socks, tights, hair accessories, hats, gloves, and more. Brands Carried: I.K.K.S., Petit Bateau, Magil, Sophie Dess, Sonia Rykiel, Lili Gaufrette, and Mini Man.

Space Kiddets*

46 East 21st Street bet. Park Avenue South and Broadway

420-9878

Return Policy: Store credit only.

Most of the clothing here is funky but moderately priced. Space Kiddets has a little of everything, including toys, table and chair sets, fantasy play clothes, even Elvis memorabilia! Brands Carried: Maxou, Mouse Feathers, Mini Thallion, and I.K.K.S.

Spring Flowers*

538 Madison Avenue at 55th Street

717-8182

1050 Third Avenue at 62nd Street

758-2669

905 Madison Avenue at 72nd Street

717-8182

Return Policy: Store credit only.

Spring Flowers is especially known for its extensive collection of top-quality French and Italian clothes for children newborn to ten years old. (A Spring Flowers Layette store adjoins the Third Avenue store.) Spring Flowers carries play clothes and an outstanding selection of party and holiday clothes for boys and girls. Dresses are sold with matching hats, tights, purses, and accessories. Boys' navy blazers and flannel pants are beautifully tailored. Spring Flowers also has a wide selection of European shoes, including the Sonnet brand from England—popular first walkers. Prices are high, as you'd expect, and the service is excellent. Brands Carried: Sophie Dess, Sonia Rykiel, Florian, Petit Bateau, Giesswien, Cacharel, Joan Calabrese, Magil, and Pappa & Ciccia.

❋ Talbots Kids & Babies*

1523 Second Avenue at 79th Street
570-1630
www.talbots.com
Return Policy: Refund with receipt,
otherwise store credit only.
This large, well-lit store sells attractive clothes for boys and girls from newborn to size sixteen. Its high-quality, preppy style of clothing is worth a look. Classic polo shirts and elastic waist khakis are perfect for husky boys. The store concentrates on toddlers and older children; the layette and infant/toddler section is smaller. It has excellent sales, with prices often half the original. This is one of Kelly's favorites.

❋ Tartine et Chocolat

1047 Madison Avenue at 82nd Street
717-2112
www.tartine-et-chocolat.com
This expensive Madison Avenue boutique features dressy items for children ages newborn to about ten. It has a nice (if pricey) layette selection, but if you are a fan of European style, you will love it here.

❋ Tigers, Tutu's & Toes

128 Second Avenue bet. St. Mark's Place
and 7th Street
228-7990
Return Policy: No refunds; exchange
or store credit only within six months.
This East Village shop has a jungle theme, with a faux leopard rug, fake trees, and a giant stuffed tiger sitting on the floor. Of course there are tutus—in red, pink, yellow, and orange—as well as shoes both classic and outrageous. You can also find a large selection of casual Zutano clothing—some leopard print items are in keeping with the motif. Everything is well priced. Also, look for stuffed animals, animal backpacks, puppets, puzzles, crayons, and other jungle-theme toys. Brands Carried: Elefanten, Skechers, Aster, Venettini, Zutano, I.K.K.S., Rubbies, and Petit Bateau.

❋ Tutti Bambini

1480 First Avenue at 77th Street
472-4238
Return Policy: Store credit only;
no returns on sale items.
Tutti Bambini is a small boutique that carries a full line of clothing and accessories for newborns to preteens. You'll also find some sumptuous (and expensive) Penny Candy sweaters. Brands Carried: Petit Boy, I.K.K.S., Confetti, Chevignon, Lorilyn, Les Tout Petits, Catamini, Cotton Caboodle, Penny Candy, and Suss Designs.

❊ Z'Baby Company*

100 West 72nd Street at Columbus Avenue
579-BABY
996 Lexington Avenue at 72nd Street
472-BABY
Return Policy: Store credit within 10 days of purchase with receipt. No returns on sale items. At Z'Baby Company, you'll find a particularly good layette department—and the store's buyer and head layette specialist, a mom herself, will work with you to put together the layette of your dreams. It's best to make an appointment! Z'Baby carries a wide range of clothing, shoes, and accessories from France, Italy, and New York—for boys from newborn to eight and girls to age sixteen. Store services include phone orders, a baby shower registry, personal shopping, and layette by appointment. Brands Carried: Grain de Lune, Petit Bateau, Bienvenue sur Terre, Kenzo, Petit Industrie, Sonya Rykiel, Charabia, Cacherel, Aster, Pom Dapi, Buckle My Shoe, and Primigi.

❊ Zitomer

969 Madison Avenue bet. 75th
and 76th streets
737-2037
www.zittles.com
Return Policy: Refund with receipt
within ten days.
With Zitomer's convenient shopping hours and flexible return policy, every neighborhood would be lucky to have a store like this one. This is a mini department store with toys, clothes, chocolates, and lingerie, as well as children's clothing, ranging from newborn to four-

teen years. The service is good and the selection is excellent. You can open a charge account here, which comes in handy when filling prescriptions at its full-fledged pharmacy. Brands Carried: Petit Bateau, Florian, Aletta, Carter's, Sophie Dess, Mini Basix, Mini Man, Joseph Baby, and Galipette.

trunk shows and private boutiques

This section includes makers of high-quality children's clothing that is either not readily available in stores, new to the U.S., or sold at trunk shows two to three times a year as well as in stores. At some shows you will have to custom-order pieces; others display racks of clothing you can buy that day. Get on these designers' mailing lists to be invited.

❊ Bodyscapes, Inc.

20 West 22nd Street, Suite 411
243-2414
www.bodyscapeskids.com
Henrietta Drewes has been designing clothes for over thirty years and, for the last fifteen, bright, whimsical clothing for children ages six months through eight years. Henrietta has a unique and loyal following of people she's worked with for years; she's dressed many of the daughters of her original clients, and just recently dressed one of their granddaughters! Most of her pieces are reversible and made of 100 percent cotton, corduroy, flannel, or any combination of the above. She has a huge array of prints to choose from. In fact, whatever you

could imagine to interest a child, she's got it. You might find a black corduroy pant that reverses into plaid flannel, a colorful farm print, or any number of other fun combinations. Parents are welcome to visit Henrietta's Chelsea loft (be sure to make an appointment) to pick out their own. Prices range from $16 for a bib to $175 for a leather jacket.

Judy's Fancies
689-8663
Judith Correa handsews clothing for newborns to toddlers from the finest fabrics (and creates beautifully tailored christening gowns for $150 and up). Other prices range from $45 for a simple cotton dress to $60 for a velvet outfit. Her clothing is pastel-colored and very European in style. She will custom-make clothes for children of all ages and sizes, and parents are welcome to contribute to the design (or even design the clothing themselves).

Little Follies
12 East 86th Street
(800) 242-7881
www.littlefollies.com
email: info@littlefollies.com
Known for its pretty, classic hand-smocked rompers, dresses, and shortalls, Little Follies has recently expanded its line to include pants, shorts, shirts, and hand-knit sweaters. Almost all of the clothing is machine washable, and made of either 100-percent cotton or a cotton/polyester blend. Sizes start at three months and go up to size eight (shortalls stop at five), and prices average between $65 and $85 for cotton outfits, $100 for velvet shortalls, and $125 and up for velvet dresses. Little Follies holds trunk shows at the Mark Hotel (77th Street between Fifth and Madison avenues) two to three times a year; call the 800 number for catalogs and show dates.

Papo d'Anjo
(888) 660-6111
Praça Luis de Camões n.36 3° Esq.
1200-243 Lisbon Portugal
tel.: 011 351 21 865-0290
fax: 011 351 21 868-0172
www.papodanjo.com
e-mail: papodanjo@papodanjo.com
Portugal-based designer Catherine Connor travels all over Europe selecting fine, unusual fabrics for this high-end children's clothing line. Her clothes are all handmade, and the style is classic European. Sizes range from ages six months to twelve years; prices start at $49 for an oxford or vyella long-sleeved shirt, and go up to $300 for a traditional wool tweed coat. These clothes are sold in stores such as Saks, Small Change, Magic Windows, and other fine children's clothing boutiques, as well as in twice-yearly trunk shows at various locations in New York. E-mail for trunk-show information.

resale shops

On the other end of the scale, here's where you'll find real bargains—the big names, hardly worn, at prices way below those of the boutiques.

First & Second Cousin New and Resale Children's Shop

142 Seventh Avenue South bet. 10th and Charles streets

929-8048

Return Policy: Store credit only.

This shop offers mostly new (and hip) clothing with brands like Flapdoodles and Mulberry Bush for newborns to size fourteen. It also has fun handmade clothing such as batik and tie-dyed pieces. First and Second Cousin also sells pajamas, and baby carriers made by Baby Bjorn and Sara's Ride. The selection of resale clothing is small, but clean—and prices are about half of what the new merchandise costs.

Jane's Exchange

207 Avenue A bet. 12th and 13th streets

674-6268

Return Policy: Store credit only.

This Alphabet City consignment shop is brimming with top-quality one-of-a-kind clothing and accessories for children ages newborn to ten years, with ages newborn to five being its strong point. Adorable dresses, onesies, and shirts fill the walls. Prices can range anywhere from $3 to $100 for a single outfit, but most are under $20. You'll find everything from simple Gap basics to hip European styles. It also carries children's furniture, accessories, books, games, and toys, and maternity wear in good condition for $5 to $25. Most of the items sold here are gently worn, but there are also brand-new pieces. This store carries only in-season clothes, so there are no end-of-season sales—but with prices like these who needs them?

malls

Consider the possibility of leaving town from time to time to do your children's clothes shopping—find bargains, skip the sales tax (in New Jersey), or enjoy strolling your baby around an air-conditioned mall on a hot and sticky New York day. Mall shopping makes for a good outing, and the food courts will keep the kids happy. We list malls in the tristate area that have several children's stores and are within an hour of the city. All driving directions are from New York City.

Many of the mall stores have been described throughout this chapter. Most, if not all, of these malls have large department stores with wonderful children's departments. Make a day of it. Pop into FAO Schwarz, Zany Brainy, or the Disney Store to start the day off right, and then feed the kids an early lunch at the food court. (And while they nap in the stroller, you can shop for yourself!)

Northern New Jersey

Fashion Center

Route 17 and Ridgewood Avenue

Paramus, NJ

201-444-9050

Directions: Take the George Washington Bridge to Route 4 West. Take Route 4 to Route 17N and Ridgewood Avenue.

Stores:

Denny's • Zany Brainy • Jenny John Shoes

The Mall at Short Hills

Short Hills, NJ

973-376-7350

www.shopshorthills.com

Directions: Take the George Washington Bridge to the Garden State Parkway and continue to exit 142—Interstate 78. Then take 78 West to Route 24 West and exit at 7C—JFK Parkway. Follow signs to the Mall at Short Hills. The mall will be on your right-hand side.

Stores:

A Pea in The Pod • Benneton Kids • Eileen Fisher • GapKids • Gymboree • Limited Too • Talbots Kids • Oilily

Paramus Park Mall

Route 17 North

Paramus, NJ

201-261-8000

Directions: Take the George Washington Bridge to Route 80 West, stay on Route 80 until you reach the Garden State Parkway North (Exit 163). Take the Garden State to Route 17N. Go half a mile, and you will see two entrances to the mall in the northbound lane.

Stores:

The Children's Place • GapKids • Gymboree

Garden State Plaza

Route 17 South

Paramus, NJ

201-843-2404

www.westfield.com

Directions: Take the George Washington Bridge to Route 4 West. Take Route 4 to Route 17 South, go 100 yards past the Route 4 interchange, and make a right into the mall entrance.

Stores:

Baby Place • Bambini Italiani • Brooks Brothers • The Children's Place • Finish Line • GapKids • babyGap • Gymboree • Jacadi • JCPenney • Lord & Taylor • Macy's • Motherhood Maternity • Mimi Maternity • Neiman Marcus • Nordstrom • Old Navy • Talbots Kids & Babies

Riverside Square Mall

Route 4 West

Hackensack, NJ

201-489-2212

www.shopriverside.com

Directions: Take the George Washington Bridge to Route 4. The mall is on the right-hand side of the street, past the Hackensack exit.

Stores:

A Pea in the Pod • babyGap • Benetton • Bloomingdale's • Eileen Fisher • GapKids • Gymboree • La Petite Gaminerie • Saks Fifth Avenue

Westchester/Rockland

Palisades Center

West Nyack, NY

845-348-1000

Directions: Take the George Washington Bridge to the Palisades Interstate Parkway North. Exit 9E to the New York State Thruway. Take 87 South to 287 East, then take Exit 12, West Nyack Palisades Center.

Stores:

babyGap • Barnes & Noble • Disney

Store • GapKids • Gymboree • JCPenney
Kids Footlocker • Limited Too • Lord &
Taylor • Old Navy • The Children's Place
Waldenbooks

❊ The Westchester

Bloomingdale Road
White Plains, NY
914-683-8600
www.simon.com
Directions: Take the Hutchinson River Parkway
or I-95 North to 287 West. Take 287 to
Westchester Avenue (Exit 8). Make a left onto
Bloomingdale Road for parking at The
Westchester.
Stores:
A Pea In The Pod • babyGap • Brooks
Brothers • The Children's Place •
Disney Store • Eileen Fisher • GapKids
Gymboree • Hannah Andersson •
Jacadi • KB Toys • Kids Footlocker •
Limited Too • Neiman Marcus •
Nordstrom • Oilily • Stride Rite Shoes •
Talbots Kids & Babies

❊ Woodbury Common Premium Outlet

Harriman, NY
845-928-7467
www.premiumoutlets.com
Directions: Take the upper level of the George
Washington Bridge heading west; make a right
onto the Palisades Parkway North. Take the
Palisades to Exit 9 West. Follow thruway for 30
minutes, exit at Harriman (Exit 16). First right
after the tollbooth.
Stores: *All stores here are

discount stores and/or outlets.
Carter's Childrenswear • The Children's
Place • JM Originals • KB Toy
Liquidators • Maternity Works •
Neiman Marcus Last Call • Off 5th
Oilily • OshKosh B'Gosh • Patagonia •
World of Fun

Long Island

❊ Roosevelt Field Shopping Center

Glen Cove, NY
516-742-8000
Directions: Take the Long Island Expressway to
the Northern State Parkway (Exit 38). Take the
Northern State to the Meadowbrook Parkway,
and get off at Exit M2, Mall Exit. The mall will
be directly in front of you.
Stores:
Bloomingdale's • The Children's Place •
Disney Store • FAO Schwarz • Gap
Kids • Gymboree • JCPenney • Jordan
Marie • KB Toys • Kids Footlocker •
Limited Too • Macy's • Noodle Kidoodle
Nordstrom • The Right Start • Stern's •
Stride Rite • United Colors of Benetton

❊ Sunrise Mall

Sunrise Highway
Massapequa, NY
516-795-3225
Directions: Take the Long Island Expressway to
Route 110 South. Get off at Sunrise Highway
(Exit 27 West). Go down two streetlights and
make a right. The mall is on Sunrise Highway.
Stores:

The Children's Place • Disney Store •
GapKids/babyGap • JCPenney • KB Toys
Kids Footlocker • Limited Too
Lobel's • Stride Rite • Macy's • Mother-
hood Maternity • Noodle Kidoodle •
Old Navy • Stern's

❊ *Walt Whitman Mall*

Dix Hills, NY
631-271-1741
Directions: Take the Long Island Expressway to
Route 110 (Exit 49 North). Take Route 110 north
five miles; the mall is on the right-hand side of
Route 110.
Stores:
Bloomingdale's • The Children's Place
Disney Store • GapKids • Gymboree
Lord & Taylor • Macy's • Mimi Maternity
Saks Fifth Avenue • Warner Bros. Store

Connecticut

❊ *Stamford Town Center*

Tresser Boulevard
Stamford, CT
203-324-0935
Directions: Take I-95 North to Exit 8. Make a left
at the first light, Atlantic Street. Go to the third
traffic light and make a right onto Tresser
Boulevard. From Tresser Boulevard, make a left
into the mall entrance.
Stores:
Brooks Brothers • Disney Store •
Elizabeth Wood • FAO Schwarz •
GapKids • Gymboree • KB Toys •
Kids Footlocker • Limited Too •
Mimi Maternity • Motherhood Maternity
Macy's • Saks Fifth Avenue • Waldenkids

toys, toys, toys...

You're about to rediscover the magic of toys, because you're going to be playing with them more than you can imagine. Having a baby is a great excuse to act like a kid again, and New York's toy stores, from the venerable FAO Schwarz to the tiniest neighborhood specialty shop, will help you to remember what it was like when a toy store was the greatest place in the world. Of course, the world of toys has changed since you were a kid, so here are some tips to get you started on picking the right toys, including where to find them.

Jennifer Bergman from West Side Kids (one of our favorite toy stores) believes that play is a child's version of work. Healthy, happy, imaginative play is crucial to a growing child's development. The more creative playtime a child has, the more likely she or he will become a creative, well-rounded adult. Creative thinking is important whether you are a doctor, an accountant, an actor or a painter. Be creative with your child, play with abandon . . . but remember: no toy can replace you, and you can only enhance the toy.

❄ Toys must be safe, durable, and age-appropriate; that means no buttons, long strings, ribbons, or small parts for children under three years of age. If a toy or toy part can fit through the cardboard center of a toilet paper roll then it's too small.

❄ If you're looking for a specific item, call ahead. Some stores will gift wrap and deliver nearby, so you might be able to shop over the phone.

❄ There are a few websites (see the Website Directory) that are excellent for ordering toys. Once you know what you want, check the web for the best prices.

❄ Pay attention to return policies and store credits. Some stores, like FAO Schwarz and Toys "R" Us, have an "anything, anytime" return policy, which can be useful if your youngster, like Alexander on his first birthday, receives three Barney dolls.

age-specific toys

Jennifer Bergman suggests these toys for the specific age groups, but remember, more does not equal better. Stick to one or two toys that your child enjoys for each stage:

1st Month

At this age, babies are just beginning to focus on the face, and they can see high-contrast images. So you might want to consider black-and-white toys for a newborn.

❄ Stim-Mobile (Wimmer Ferguson)
❄ Pattern-Play Cards (Wimmer Ferguson)
❄ B&W crib bumper books
❄ B&W Board Books
❄ B&W Gymini (Tiny Love) Hang one item at a time! Don't overwhelm your little one. By hanging single items you can learn what their favorites are.
❄ Infant Mirror (Wimmer Ferguson)
❄ Tracking Tube (Early Start) Great for the stroller.
❄ Lullaby Light Show (Tomy) or IRC Lullaby Dream Show (Tomy)

2nd Month

Baby can now grasp a rattle, and will begin to lift her head and roll over. Continue with above toys and introduce:

- ✳ Pat Mat: We recommend a pat mat with bright color objects rather than pastels.
- ✳ Activity Blanket (Discover & Go Playmat, Wimmer Ferguson)
- ✳ Bumper Books (Whoozit, Lamaze) Hang as low as you can in the crib so the baby can focus on the graphics.
- ✳ Small Rattles (Ambi, Haba, Sassy, etc.) Place the rattle in the palm of the baby's hand and watch him or her grasp it.
- ✳ Foot & Wrist rattles (Manhattan Baby, Eden)
- ✳ Whoozit (B&W Side) (Manhattan Toy)

3rd Month

As your baby begins to turn in the direction of voices or other sounds, it is a great time to introduce musical toys.

- ✳ Rattles with bells (i.e., Geo Rattles from Imagiix)
- ✳ Wiggly Giggler Rattle (Hands On Toys)
- ✳ Pull down musical toys (i.e. Winnie-the-Pooh from Gund)
- ✳ Whoozit Musical (Manhattan Toy)

4th Month

Now the baby is beginning to raise her chest, and is reaching and teething.

- ✳ Crib Activity Gym (Fisher-Price Busy Box, Kick & Play Piano)
- ✳ Soft multitextured blocks
- ✳ Clack Rattle (Lamaze)
- ✳ Smiley Face Mirror (Sassy)
- ✳ Discovery Links (Lamaze)
- ✳ Teethers
- ✳ 123 Discovery Lane (Tiny Love)
- ✳ Activity Arch (Tiny Love)
- ✳ Happy Sounds Ball (Tomy)
- ✳ Videos: Baby Mozart, Baby Bach, Baby Beethoven, Baby Einstein, So Smart series

5th Month

Your baby can now hold her head steady, roll over, reach for objects, grasp a rattle, raise herself up on her arms, and sit. And put everything in her mouth, as well.

- ✳ You no longer need black and white toys. Your baby should be able to focus on more detail.
- ✳ In addition to the above toys, introduce more manipulative toys, such as:
- ✳ Twin Rattle (Ambi)
- ✳ Stroller Fun (Early Years)
- ✳ Fisher-Price Soft Snap & Lock Beads

6th - 7th Month

Now your child can sit, bear his own weight when held up, and comprehend cause and effect. He may pass object from hand to hand or look for objects dropped on the floor. To help with separation anxiety, play lots of hide and seek games using cups, puppets, boxes, and your hands. Your baby will begin to understand that if the toy always comes back so will you.

* Stacking Cups (Small World Toys, Sassy, Galt, etc)
* Fascination Station (Sassy)
* Activity Spiral (Early Years)
* Bath toys: squirts, sieve, cups, floating toys, bath books
* Sand toys: small shovel, sieve, and bucket
* Neobaby Pick 'n' Pull (Tomy)
* Cloth and Vinyl Books
* Baby Shakespeare video

8th - 9th Month

Now your baby can bear weight on her legs. She'll work to get a toy out of reach, look for a dropped object, pull herself up to standing position, play patty-cake, and nest.

* Babysongs video series
* Balls in a Bowl (Early Learning)
* Lift-the-Flap books
* Chuckling Charlie

10th - 11th month

You baby's becoming aware of his environment, and is beginning to interact with toys as well as becoming more independent. He may be pulling himself up, cruising, and making a razzing sound.

* Baby's First Blocks (TC Timber)
* Bouncing Billy (Tomy)
* Mozart Magic Cube
* Tommy Toot (Ambi)
* Plastic kazoo

1 Year

Your baby may be walking, responding to your voice, cruising, making razzing sounds, and trying to nest, stack, and sort. It may be time to introduce:

* Simple Peg Puzzles
* Pull Toys Battat's Spinning Bus, Troller, Ambi Max, World on Wheels (Bozart)
* Push Toys: Fisher-Price Corn Popper
* Activity Cube (Anatex)
* Pounding Bench (either plastic or wood) or Pound a Ball (many versions)
* First Dolls (Corolle Calin, bath babies, Raggedy Ann, etc.)
* Stacking Rings (Fisher-Price, Sassy, Lamaze, Brio, etc.)
* Pop-up Friends (many versions) (creature pops up when correct manipulation is done)
* Umbrella Stroller
* Sound Puzzle Box (Battat)
* Flashcards

18 months

Your baby is gaining more control of fine motor skills, and is beginning to follow your direction.

* Lock Box (Tag Toys)
* Pathfinder (Anatex)
* Shape Sorter (Gazoobo)
* Brio Builder Pounding Board

2 Years

At two years of age, your child is beginning to build and create, and is interested in how things work.

She's becoming verbal, reciting her ABCs and 123s.

✤ Picture Cube Puzzles (Selecta)
✤ Magic Sound Blocks (Small World Toys)
✤ See Inside Puzzles (Ravensburger)
✤ Tricycle
✤ Figure 8 wooden train set (TC Timber, Brio, Thomas)
✤ Tomy Bring-Along CD Player
✤ Object recognition puzzles
✤ Bop Bag
✤ Trucks of all sizes
✤ Beginning phonics toys like Leapfrog's Phonics Bus
✤ Play pretend toys
✤ Art supplies
✤ I Spy Preschool Game
✤ Brio Builder level 1

3 Years

Can you believe it? Your child's a preschooler! His construction and manipulative skills are increasing, and he's learning to play well with others. He is beginning to understand the concept of counting and reciting the ABCs. His fantasy world is expanding, and he's able to make associations.

✤ Tangrams (Mr. Mighty Mind)
✤ Marble Maze (Quercetti)
✤ Pretend & Play Cash Register
✤ Gearations (Tomy)
✤ Flashlight (Playskool)
✤ Leap Frog Think 'n' Go phonics
✤ Bingo Bears
✤ Floor puzzles (approx. 12 to 25 pieces)

✤ Games: Barnyard Boogie Woogie, Hi-Ho Cherri-o, Footloose, Kids on Stage, Colorforms Silly Faces, Maisy's ABC Game, Four First Games, Snail's Pace, Lotto
✤ Sequencing games: Things I Can Do (Educa), Tell-a-Story (Ravensburger), Step-by-Step (Educa), Magnetic Letters & Numbers
✤ Animal Ball Park (Tomy)
✤ Art Supplies
✤ Lacing aids: Lacing cards, beads, shoes

the stores

✤ A Bear's Place*

789 Lexington Avenue bet. 61st
and 62nd streets
826-6465
www.abearsplace.com
Return Policy: Store credit only.
This friendly shop features educational toys for children under twelve. There are spelling board games, a Velcro rainbow board, musical instruments, puzzles, and a wonderful puppet theater. All toys sold here are JPMA approved. Gift-wrapping is available. A Bear's Place also has a large selection of upholstered furniture, and it offers customized and handpainted pieces as well, such as cribs, changing tables, and beds.

✤ The Children's General Store

Grand Central Station
107 East 42nd Street Lexington passage
682-0004
Return Policy: Store credit only.

These shops carry an appealing selection, from puppets to cards, books, and tutus. For older children there are musical instruments, how-to kits, dollhouse furniture by Ambi, and Plan toys. Free gift-wrapping.

❊ Classic Toys

218 Sullivan Street bet. Bleecker
and West 3rd streets
674-4434
Return Policy: Store credit only.
A unique mix of vintage and new toys, including toy soldiers, miniature cars, figurines, and well-known characters (Star Trek, Disney), as well as a selection of dinosaurs, farm animals, and stuffed animals.

❊ Cozy's Cuts for Kids*

1125 Madison Avenue at 84th Street
1416 Second Avenue at 74th Street
448 Amsterdam Avenue at 81st Street
www.cozyscutsforkids.com
Besides haircuts, Cozy's also sells toys and party favors, such as mini-Play-Doh kits, toy cars, barrettes, beach balls, pencils, stickers, and egg slime, as well as more educational material like books and puzzles. You can also find children's videos, handmade costumes, board games, and artist aprons—Pamela has found many party favors here for Rebecca and Benjamin's birthdays.

❊ Cute Toonz

372 Fifth Avenue at 34th Street
967-6942
Return Policy: Store credit and exchange only within three weeks.

Lots of great Disney, Sesame Street, and other cartoon characters in all shapes and forms. Shop here for T-shirts, backpacks, cups, stuffed animals, watches, and Hello Kitty accessories. A great place for small gifts and party favors.

❊ Didi's Children's Boutique

1196 Madison Avenue at 88th Street
860-4001
www.didis.com
Didi's is a new addition to the Upper East Side and has a nice selection of educational and wooden toys. Didi's specializes in classic toys (no Fisher-Price here) and has many building-block sets. The store is colorful, well-laid-out, and makes for easy shopping.

❊ Dinosaur Hill

306 East 9th Street bet. First
and Second avenues
473-5850
www.dinosaurhill.com
Return Policy: Lenient.
This specialty toy and clothing store has quality marbles, marionettes, mobiles, T. C. Timber toys, and handcrafted toys. It also carries clothing, including an extraordinary selection of hats, mostly for children ages newborn to six. Free gift-wrapping.

❊ E.A.T. Gifts

1062 Madison Avenue at 80th Street
861-2544
Return Policy: Store credit, or exchange only with receipt for item in original packaging.
This Upper East Side store is full of fantastic

things, including all sorts of stuffed animals, toy cars, bath toys, puzzles, puppets, and an excellent selection of children's books. Beware—this is not a spot for bargain-hunters! There are also gift items for older children—from funky jewelry to activity kits and journals. This store is excellent for party planning, offering paper goods and balloons. There are tons of little toys, ideal for filling party bags, and a great selection of piñatas, in the shapes of ballet slippers and basketballs. Kelly loves its selection of hard plastic bowls and plates featuring Arthur, Classic Pooh, Curious George, Madeline, and many other favorite characters. The famous E.A.T. restaurant is just next door.

FAO Schwarz*

767 Fifth Avenue bet. 58th and 59th streets
644-9400
www.fao.com
Return Policy: Lenient.
FAO Schwarz is a city landmark and major tourist attraction. But that is because it has the best and largest range of toys in the world: from wonderful dolls (see the Barbie Boutique), board games, a jungle of stuffed animals, and an endless selection of arts and crafts. Whether you are looking for classic toys or modern favorites you will find it here. All the hottest fads and rages are generally in stock. This is an exciting place for children. They will love it, and so will Grandma. Yes, it's expensive, but you can find many gift items for $50 or less. Gift-wrapping is free. During the holiday season, the lines of people waiting to get in wrap around the block!

Gepetto's Toy Box

10 Christopher Street bet. Greenwich Avenue and Gay Street
620-7511
www.nyctoys.com
Return Policy: Store credit only.
Gepetto's carries toys by manufacturers like Ambi, Playmobil, Sigikid, and others. It features a nice selection of musical mirrors, photo albums, and other specialty gifts. Free gift-wrapping.

Hom Boms

1500 First Avenue bet. 78th and 79th streets
717-5300
Return Policy: Refund within 30 days with original packaging and receipt.
Among other things, Hom Boms carries soft, plush toys for infants, wooden pull-along toys for toddlers, and activity kits for older children, and features major brands like Playmobil, Brio, and Madame Alexander. Of course, no toy store is truly complete without an art-supply section. You will find everything from basic Crayola crayons to glitter pens and stickers here. Hom Boms offers free gift-wrapping and delivery in the area.

KB Toys

901 Avenue of the Americas bet. 32nd and 33rd streets
629-5386
2411 Broadway at 89th Street
595-4389
www.kbtoys.com
Return Policy: Refund with receipt within thirty days, otherwise store credit only.

KB Toys is a chain, with shops in many malls. It carries the most popular name brands such as Fisher-Price and Playskool, as well as arts and crafts and water toys. This is the place to find the hot toy of the moment. Prices are usually discounted, the sales are wonderful, and if you need a quick $5 toy for your child who went on the potty for the first time, this is the place.

❊ *Kidding Around**

60 West 15th Street bet. Fifth and Sixth avenues

645-6337

Return Policy: Store credit only.

Kidding Around has a nice infant section with rattles, mobiles, and squishy toys, and a larger selection of toys for one- to eight-year-olds. There are unique puppet theaters, musical instruments, Native American and African American dolls, and a nice French doll line. You'll find Brio, Ambi, Battat, and Playmobil here, as well as beach balls, and books. It will also supply you with personalized party bags. Free gift-wrapping.

❊ *Kid O*

123 West 10th Street (Greenwich Avenue)

366-5436

www.kidonyc.com

This newly opened children's boutique features modernist toys, books, and even furniture for kids. Much of the merchandise is imported from Europe and is artist-inspired. (A Calder-like mobile is one example.) The furniture is quite unique and expensive—but it will make for a beautiful and one-of-a-kind baby's room.

❊ *Kidrobot*

126 Prince Street bet. Wooster and Greene streets

966-6688

www.kidrobot.com

This tiny store in the heart of Soho is quite busy on the weekends with kids (and adults!) looking to add to their action-figure collections. Kidrobot specializes in collectible vinyl toys, twelve-inch action figures, mini figures, mini remote-controlled cars, and more! Pamela even spotted some cute party favor items here.

❊ *Little Extras**

676 Amsterdam Avenue at 93rd Street

721-6161

Return Policy: Refund if the item is in sellable condition.

Pretty, roomy, and inviting, Little Extras is a great source for gifts. It stocks black-and-white toys for newborns, bibs with cute sayings, and the educational New Beginnings line. In addition, the store carries some furniture, including stools, tables and chairs, and toy chests, as well as the best quality bathrobes and towels (which can be monogrammed) for children. Free gift-wrapping and personalizing.

❊ *Mary Arnold Toys*

1010 Lexington Avenue bet. 72nd and 73rd streets

744- 8510

Return Policy: Refunds with a receipt within thirty days; otherwise store credit only.

A neighborhood favorite for decades, here you'll find the fine brands from Fisher-Price to

Madame Alexander, as well as videos, games, dolls, puppets, and arts and crafts galore. The staff can create party-favor bags or a special gift basket. Free gift-wrapping and local delivery.

New York Doll Hospital

787 Lexington Avenue bet. 61st and 62nd streets
838-7527

The New York Doll Hospital has been in New York City since 1900. It will repair any broken, damaged, and worn stuffed animals and dolls. It also carries a nice selection of dolls and is popular with collectors of antique dolls.

New York Firefighter's Friend

263 Lafayette Street bet. Prince and Spring streets
226-3142
www.nyfirestore.com
Return Policy: Store credit or exchange with receipt within 7 days.

Located just a few doors from the Ladder twenty fire station, Firefighter's Friend offers all the things an aspiring little firefighter might need. You can find books, and toys like fire trucks, stuffed fire bears, and fire helmets. This store also offers clothing items such as rain boots, raincoats, and baseball caps—all in firefighter fashion. No gift-wrapping here, but it will ship anything via UPS or priority mail. Also, go next door to its police-themed store, New York 911—it is a great place to find gifts for your little law enforcer.

Penny Whistle Toys*

448 Columbus Avenue bet. 81st and 82nd streets
873-9090
Return Policy: Store credit only.

This is a terrific toy store known for its commitment to high quality and its unique toys and games. Penny Whistle carries many top-of-the line brands like Brio, Tiny Love, Playmobil, Koosh, and Sassy. Great games, puzzles, and art and crafts kits are available, too. The friendly, easygoing staff will help you find the perfect age-appropriate gift, and gift-wrapping is free. There is also a location on Route 27 in Bridgehampton.

Promises Fulfilled

1592 Second Avenue bet. 82nd and 83rd streets
472-1600
Return Policy: Store credit only.

You'll find a varied selection for babies and lots of choices when you need a birthday present for an older child (from costumes to construction kits). You can also buy personalized and coordinated accessories for your child's room: toy chests, benches, frames, bookends, clocks, coat racks, mirrors, and lamps. The most popular items are the hand-painted rocking chairs, and personalized birthday party favors. Cute baby books and photo albums are a specialty. Free gift-wrapping. The East Hampton location is a favorite of the Weinberg kids!

❋ Toys "R" Us

1514 Broadway at 44th Street

(646) 366-8858

www.toysrus.com

Return Policy: Refund with a receipt, otherwise store credit only.

Toys "R" Us discounts every well-known brand-name toy. It carries a lot of Fisher-Price, Safety 1st, Playskool, and Mattel; it also has all the latest toys, and the prices and selection on books, videos, and Barbie dolls are usually the best in town.

❋ West Side Kids*

498 Amsterdam Avenue at 84th Street

496-7282

Return Policy: Store credit only.

This is a terrific neighborhood store, with excellent service and a varied selection of educational toys, quality books, and "imagination" items for playing pretend, such as miniature brooms, rakes, and kitchen utensils. There is also a selection of puzzles, games, and art supplies, plus a great assortment of small toys for party favors. Check out the array of Halloween and dress-up costumes, too. It offers free gift-wrapping.

❋ Zittles*

969 Madison Avenue bet. 75th and 76th streets, 3rd floor of Zitomer

737-2040

www.zittles.com

Return Policy: Refund with receipt within ten days, otherwise store credit only.

It looks like a pharmacy downstairs, yet upstairs it is a treasure trove of children's commercial, educational, and specialty toys. You'll find dolls, puzzles, books, arts and crafts, videos, games, computer games, "dress up" items, and toys from brands like Battat, Ambi, Brio, Fisher-Price, and Leap Frog. The store will ship and deliver locally. Free gift-wrapping. Get on the mailing list or go to the website, where it advertises its "playdates." Eight to ten times per year, representatives from companies like Lego, Brio, and Thomas come and let children play with their new toys. It's a nice way to spend an afternoon.

Costumes

At least once a year (more if you have a child like Benjamin who loves to dress up like a superhero), you will need to pick up a costume for your little one. You can easily find selections at your regular toy stores, clothing stores, and department stores. The following specialty stores, however, are the authorities when it comes to Halloween and costume parties. These are great stores to check out:

❋ Abracadabra Superstore

19 West 21st Street between Fifth and Sixth avenues

627-5194

www.abracadabra.com

This is truly a superstore of all things scary—monsters, skeletons, ghosts, and ghouls. Also, you can find clown supplies, makeup, horror props, masks, and costumes. Children's costumes for sale include characters from Powerpuff Girls, Disney classics, Star Wars, and much more. For infants, it has costumes like bunnies, angels, and Teletubbies. This store is not for the weak of heart. If your child is easily frightened, we suggest leaving your little trick-or-treater at home. Abracadabra has excellent magic shows two or three times each weekend; call for show times.

Gordon Novelty

52 West 29th Street bet. Broadway and Sixth Avenue
254-8616
Gordon Novelty is a warehouse of props and costumes. It carries over a thousand different hats, wigs, and masks portraying celebrities like Einstein, Elvis, and Michael Jackson, as well as monsters and other characters like Spiderman, Superman, Cinderella, and Snow White.

Halloween Adventure

104 Fourth Avenue bet. 11th and 12th streets
673-4546
www.halloweenadventure.com
Open year-round, Halloween Adventure is crammed with beautiful costumes, novelties, and accessories. It has a magic department (with a professional magician to give demonstrations on Saturdays) and a professional makeup department. Children's costumes range from Disney and Star Wars characters to knights, wizards, angels, fairies, and princesses.

books, videos/dvds, audios, catalogs, and magazines

No doubt about it: city babies—and their moms—love city bookstores! Together they can listen to stories, pick out videos and CDs, and, best of all, discover the joys of children's books. This multimedia universe is one of the most exciting aspects of baby culture today. In every case, talented writers, artists, and musicians are creating lasting treasures for your children.

This section lists the best children's bookstores in New York and all they hold, from the classic must-haves, like *Goodnight Moon* or *Where the Wild Things Are*, to useful adult titles such as *Practical Parenting Tips*. We have recommended our favorite audio tapes and CDs (essential for those long car rides) and videos, not only to entertain the kids but to provide you with a few moments of peace. We have also listed some of the best parenting magazines, along with a selection of catalogs to assist you with at-home shopping.

Of course, the web has totally changed and enriched the way we get our parenting information. Don't fail to read through the many great sites listed in the Website Directory at the end of the book.

best bookstores for children

❋ Bank Street Bookstore*

610 West 112th Street at Broadway
678-1654
www.citysearch.com/nyc/bankstbooks
Return Policy: Store credit only.
With more than 40,000 titles for children, parents, and educators, Bank Street Bookstore is perhaps the best resource in the city for children's books. The knowledgeable staff can help you find an age-appropriate books.

❋ Barnes & Noble Discount Store

105 Fifth Avenue at 18th Street
807-0999
www.bn.com
Return Policy: Generous.
The second floor of this discount branch has a nice selection of children's books. It's a good destination for party-favor books for children's birthdays. Kelly likes to give a small book as a party favor instead of those plastic bags filled with lots of silly items.

❋ Bookberries

983 Lexington Avenue at 71st Street
794-9400
Return Policy: Hardcover returns for credit, or an exchange; paperbacks cannot be returned.
This intimate bookstore has a great selection of books for all ages, with a darling elevated section for kids in the back. The area is carpeted with plenty of space to sit down and read. The selection includes all of the classics, from *Curious George* to *Eloise*, and everything is clearly marked by age group. The staff is very friendly.

Best Reading Tip We've Ever Heard

Carry a book with you and read to your child whenever and wherever you can:
 ❋ over breakfast in the morning
 ❋ on a bus
 ❋ in the pediatrician's office

Books of Wonder

18 West 18th Street bet. Fifth and Sixth avenues
989-3270
www.booksofwonder.com
Return Policy: Store credit only.
This is a very special children's bookstore carrying new, out-of-print, vintage, and rare books, with an entire section devoted to the Wizard of Oz—not to mention a great selection of illustrated books. No television or movie tie-ins here, (meaning no Barney- or Sesame Street–type books). Call for information on story hours.

Borders Books & Music

550 Second Avenue bet. 32nd and 33rd streets
685-3938
461 Park Avenue at 57th Street
980-6785
www.borders.com
Return Policy: Refund or exchange with receipt within 30 days.
Borders has a lovely children's department with small tables to sit at as you peruse your and your child's favorite books. Like Barnes & Noble, Borders has everything; a coffee bar, the latest magazines, and a newspaper rack make this store complete. Call ahead for the monthly children's calendar.

Corner Bookstore

1313 Madison Avenue at 93rd Street
831-3554
This is Pamela's neighborhood bookstore and she loves it! It is a charming spot where you truly want to sit and browse. It has a terrific selection of books for children and parents, and a very knowledgeable and friendly staff who are always willing and happy to provide recommendations.

Integral Yoga Bookstore

227 West 13th Street
929-0586
Don't let the name fool you—this bookstore has books on prenatal and postpartum care, many parenting titles, and health-related child nonfiction books. Instructional videos and audio tapes as well as lullaby music is also available. It has everything you could need for doing yoga too!

Lenox Hill Bookstore

1081 Lexington Avenue between 72nd and 73rd streets
472-7170
Return Policy: Store credit only.
This brightly lit store has a small but adequate selection of kids' books tucked in a back corner. It includes everything from board books by Sandra Boynton to *Madeline*. There is a roomy floor and bench to read on and the staff is extremely friendly and helpful.

Logos Bookstore

1575 York Avenue bet. 83rd and 84th streets
517-7292
Return Policy: Store credit only.
Logos is a very neighborhood-oriented little bookstore, and a popular place to take your kids. There is a wide selection of books for children of

all ages, on topics including religion, poetry, science, nature, and history. Logos also offers special events for children, including birthday parties and reading groups. The owner, Harris Healy, is very knowledgeable and hands-on.

※ *Rizzoli Bookstore*

31 West 57th Street bet. Fifth and Sixth avenues
759-2424
Rizzoli bookstore is very upscale and is a great place to buy gifts. It also boasts a nice selection of children's and parenting books, as well as some educational toys and gift items.

※ *The Scholastic Store*

557 Broadway bet. Prince and Spring streets
343-6166
This is a store that makes us uptown parents jealous! It is huge, with plenty of space to maneuver around with your stroller and toddler. It has special events often on weekends and holidays featuring costumed characters like Clifford—even story hours for parents and babies. It carries the entire line of Scholastic products including books, toys, stuffed animals, puzzles, cd-roms, and more. There are lots of things to play with around the store too.

※ *Shakespeare and Company*

993 Lexington Avenue
bet. 68th and 69th streets
570-5148
716 Broadway at Washington Place
529-1330
137 East 23rd Street
220-5199

These homey bookstores offer a nice selection of books for babies and children, as well as some parenting books. The staff is always willing to lend a hand in choosing quality books for your child.

※ *The Strand Bookstore*

828 Broadway at 12th Street
473-1452
www.strandbooks.com
Return Policy: Refund within three days with receipt.
This family-owned bookstore is famous for its "eighteen miles of books," and has been since 1927. There is a huge selection of discounted books, mainly used and out-of-print, but also some publishers' overstock and reviewers' copies—all at fabulous prices. The children's department is mostly in the basement, where kids can lose themselves in the nooks and crannies with shelves crammed with books. On the third floor you'll also find a nice selection of rare children's books.

choosing a book for your child

There are so many benefits to reading with your child: it will familiarize him with speaking patterns, increase his vocabulary, develop his attention span, introduce him to new concepts, and most importantly, help him learn to enjoy reading. Books provide influences that will be key in forming his personality. As a New York parent, you have an abundance of resources available to help you find the newest in children's literature and give you an opportunity to rediscover old classics. Sometimes all of this information can be overwhelming, but there are a few pointers we can give you to make the process of choosing a book for you and your child to share as smooth as possible. We have searched high and low throughout the city, visiting bookstores and libraries, and speaking with the experts. Here is what we've come up with:

* Don't be afraid to ask for help from the children's department at your favorite bookstore or from the children's librarian at your local New York Public Library branch. That's what the staff is there for and they will be more than happy to help you!
* Especially for very small children, pick books that are durable (cloth books and board books are very popular) and with pages that little fingers will be able to turn. Bright, simple illustrations are always great!
* For slightly older children, be sure to follow your child's interests. If he likes sports or history, choose books with simple story lines in these areas. Children especially enjoy books about kids their own age in different historical periods. (The American Girl series is a favorite of Rebecca's.)
* Books should be challenging and stimulating—they should give children a chance to ask questions, think about possible solutions, use their imaginations, and have fun!
* Read your child the books that you read as a child. It will be more enjoyable for both of you if you like what you are reading too.
* Most importantly, let your child be active in

choosing the books she wants to read. She might feel ready to start exploring simple chapter books (like Winnie-the-Pooh, Pippi Longstocking, or the Ramona series from Beverly Cleary) when she is about five or six years old and first learning how to read. Take turns reading aloud (you'll probably have to do most of the reading at first). Your child will grow into the book and enjoy the challenge.
* Many suppliers and carriers of children's books maintain websites. You can go to these to find new releases, locate places to borrow or purchase a specific book, and even order a book!
* Barnes and Noble publishes a great book for choosing reading material for your child: *The Barnes and Noble Guide to Children's Books*. It can be purchased in the children's section of any Barnes and Noble store.

Making the Most of Reading with Your Child

When reading aloud with your child, set aside a certain time each day and make it part of his daily routine. Snuggle up together and make it a time that you share. We suggest reading a story at night right before bedtime. This is an easy habit to develop, helps your child wind down at the end of the day, and can become a life-long love. Let him be active in the reading process: encourage him to point out and describe pictures, suggest possible endings, and ask questions. Older babies can participate by pointing and helping to turn the pages. Use silly voices for the characters—it will make storytelling more enjoyable for all involved. Introduce your child to the reading process early on, and tell short, simple stories to your newborn. A parent's voice evokes special responses from a child and it is never too early to take advantage of this. Also, don't be afraid to read just one or two words per page and skip the rest. This is how a one- or two-year-old reads. Toddlers like to jump around a lot, and the constant stimulation is good for them. Turn those pages quickly!

best books for young children

There are so many great books out there for children of all ages! For newborn babies to children ages five or six, there are three main categories to use as guidelines. Baby books (infant–2 years) are simple and repetitive with lots of pictures. These books are bright and colorful, and connected to the baby's surroundings in some way. They should be sturdy and are rounded at the corners for safety. The most popular forms: bath books (great in the tub), cloth books (perfect for the crib), board books, and touch and feel books.

Once your child is around two, you can introduce her to preschool books. These books are concept-based and should be helpful in developing a sense of humor. They also begin to teach children about social interaction and the difference between right and wrong. They should be easy, fun, and colorfully illustrated. Preschool books are especially popular in pop-up form.

Finally, picture books should have slightly more complex story lines and illustrations. They often address a key life issue: siblings, sharing, potty training, starting school, and so on. These come in hardcover and paperback and some have plush figures as well. Classic books have been kept in a separate category—they're great for all ages. We've also included some special needs books that explain issues like divorce or adoption to young children.

It is important to remember that reading levels are just recommended ages and that what may be right for one three-year-old may be too advanced, or too simple for another. Your child will let you know when she is ready to move on by showing interest in more difficult concepts and reading material. The age ranges given for the following books are generally appropriate for most children in that age group. Use your judgment and enjoy.

Baby books

Board Books:

❋ *Little Spot Board Books*
  by Eric Hill
  (Spot's First Words, Spot at Home,
  Spot in the Garden, Spot's Toy Box)
  These books tell simple stories that are easy for small children to follow. Spot helps children learn to associate words and images.

❋ *Click, Clack, Moo: Cows That Type*
  by Dauren Cronin
  Farmer Brown has a problem, his cows like to type. A New York Times best-seller.

❋ *Counting Kisses*
  by Karen Katz
  All about how many kisses you can give your baby.

❋ Sesame Street Board Books

(Elmo's Guessing Game, Ernie and
Bert Can . . . Can You?, Ernie Follows
His Nose, Hide and Seek With Big Bird)
Sesame Street has been entertaining and edu-
cating children for years, and these books help
even the youngest children learn useful con-
cepts. Hide and Seek with Big Bird was one of
Benjamin's favorites.

❋ Neil Ricklen Board Books

(Daddy and Me, Mommy and Me,
Baby's Clothes, Baby's Colors, etc.)
These books use one word per picture to describe
familiar situations. They are adorable and use real
baby photographs rather than illustrations.

❋ Sandra Boynton Board Books

(Snoozers, A to Z, Moo,
BAA, La La La!, Doggies, etc.)
Kids love the rhyming sentences with cute cartoon pictures. Pamela's kids loved these books,
and came back to them time and time again.

❋ Anne Geddes Board Books

(Garden Friends, Colors, Dress-ups, Faces)
There's nothing babies love more than looking
at other babies, and photographer Anne
Geddes shows them in a whole new light.
There are baby mushrooms, baby flowers, and
many baby animals.

❋ Helen Oxenbury Board Books

(Working, Dressing, Friends)
These great books teach little ones about the
basics with simple illustrations and single words.

❋ Just Like You

by Jan Fearnley
All about how a little mouse and his mother see
the animals in the forest getting ready to go to
sleep for the night.

❋ Thomas and the Freight Train

This is an early introduction to the beloved little train.

Cloth Books:

❋ Thomas the Tank Engine Says Good Night

This cute book is perfect for the crib.

❋ Cloth Books by Eric Hill

(Animals, Clothes, Home)
These charming books by the creator of Spot
are perfect for little ones.

Bath Books:

❋ Bath Books by Eric Hill

(Spot Goes Splash, Spot's Friends, Spot's Toys)
Make a splash with Spot, the adorable puppy!

❋ Bath Books by Beatrix Potter

(Benjamin Bunny, Jemima Puddle-Duck,
Mr. Jeremy Fisher, Mrs. Tiggy-Winkle,
Peter Rabbit)
Looking at these classic characters will make
baths more enjoyable for your little one.

❋ Babar's Bath Book

This elephant makes a great companion in the tub.

Sesame Street Bath Books
(Elmo Wants a Bath, Ernie's Bath Book)
No one knows bath time like the experts, Ernie
and his rubber ducky.

Preschool Books

The Clifford Books
by Norman Bridwell
(Clifford the Big Red Dog, Clifford and the
Big Storm, Clifford and the Grouchy Neighbors,
Clifford Goes to Hollywood, Clifford the Small
Red Puppy, Clifford's Big Book of Stories)
Everybody loves the Big Red Dog! Follow him
and Emily Elizabeth through their adventures in
this popular series by Norman Bridwell.

The Arthur Books by Marc Brown
(Arthur's Really Helpful Word Book, Arthur Goes
to School, Arthur's Neighborhood)
Starring the adorable aardvark Arthur, these
books help small children learn about word
association and social interaction.

Grandfather Twilight
by Ben Berger
This lovely story of grandfather night walking
through the woods is thoroughly enchanting.

Kiss Good Night
by Hest/Jeram
A teddy bear reads a story to a little boy at bedtime.

My Very First Mother Goose
by Iona Opie
This is a great rhyming book for the very young.

Spot Books
by Eric Hill
(Where's Spot?, Spot Goes to a Party,
Spot Goes to School, Spot Goes to the Beach,
Spot Goes to the Farm, Spot Sleeps Over,
Spot's Birthday Party, Spot's First Christmas,
Spot's First Walk)
These books are great for every preschooler.
Kids can lift the flaps to accompany Spot as he
makes his way through many of his big firsts.

Peter Rabbit Books
by Beatrix Potter
(Peter Rabbit and Friends: A Stand-Up Story
Book, Peter Rabbit: A Lift-the-Flap Rebus Book,
Peter Rabbit's ABC 123)
These books make learning interactive and fun.

Sesame Street Preschool Books
by various authors
(The Sesame Street Word Book, Elmo's Lift-
and-Peek Around the Corner Book, Tickle Me
My Name is Elmo, Sesame Street Lift-and-Peek
Party!, Lift and EEEEK! Monster Tales: There's
a Monster in the Closet, The Monster at the
End of This Book)
Kids love reading about characters from their
favorite show—and everyone loves Elmo!

Time for Bed
by Fox/Dyer
This new bedtime story is a great hit. Simple
text and great illustrations.

Everyone Poops
by Taro Gomi

This book uses simple illustrations and explanations, showing kids that going to the bathroom is perfectly natural. (You will love this book, as well.)

❋ Going to the Potty
by Fred Rogers

Mr. Rogers patiently and supportively explains potty training to parents and children.

Classics

❋ Beatrix Potter books
(The Complete Tales, The Tale of Benjamin Bunny, The Tale of Peter Rabbit, The Tale of Squirrel Nutkin, The Tale of Tom Kitten, The Tale of Two Bad Mice)

For generations, children have enjoyed the cute, trouble-making little animals in Beatrix Potter's stories.

❋ Curious George
by H. A. Rey

(The Adventures of Curious George, Curious George Gets a Medal, Curious George Learns the Alphabet, Curious George Rides a Bike, Curious George Takes a Job, Curious George Flies a Kite, Curious George Goes to the Hospital)

Curious George loves life in the city with the man in a yellow hat, but his curiosity for new things can get him into trouble!

❋ Dr. Seuss Books
(One Fish, Two Fish, Red Fish, Blue Fish, etc.)

These are silly, rhyming stories with amusing drawings and creative characters with the power to bring you back to your own childhood as well.

❋ The Giving Tree
by Shel Silverstein

(Giraffe and a Half, The Missing Piece, The Missing Piece Meets the Big O)

This is the story of the life-long friendship between a little boy and a very generous tree.

❋ Goodnight Moon*
by Margaret Wise Brown

Everyone loves this timeless, charming picture book about a little rabbit who says goodnight to everything, including the moon outside his window.

❋ Harold and the Purple Crayon
by Crockett Johnson

(Harold's ABC, Harold's Purple Crayon)

Join Harold as he draws his way through adventures.

❋ The Little Engine That Could*
by Watty Piper

This inspiring tale about the brave little engine has been popular for over seventy years for good reason.

❋ Madeline
by Ludwig Bemelmans

(Madeline and the Bad Hat, Madeline and the Gypsies, Madeline in London, Madeline's Rescue, Mad About Madeline)

Follow Madeline and her friends on their adventures in Paris.

Make Way for Ducklings

by Robert McCloskey

(Blueberries for Sal, One Morning in Maine, Time of Wonder)

This classic book tells the tale of Mrs. Mallard and her eight ducklings crossing a busy Boston street.

Olivia

by Ian Falconer

(Olivia Saves the Circus, Olivia and the Missing Toy, Olivia Counts)

This little pig has lots of adventures.

Pat the Bunny, Pat the Cat, Pat the Puppy

by Dorothy Kunhardt

Your child will love touching the soft bunny and Daddy's scratchy face.

The Very Hungry Caterpillar*

by Eric Carle

(The Grouchy Ladybug, The Very Busy Spider, The Very Lonely Firefly)

This is a beautiful, interactive picture book about a caterpillar, who eats and eats until eventually, turning into a butterfly.

Guess How Much I Love You

by Mcbratney and Jeram

The story of a mommy and baby hare that has become a classic. We have read this to our children many times.

Where the Wild Things Are

by Maurice Sendak

(Alligators All Around: An Alphabet, Chicken Soup With Rice: A Book of Months—one of Rebecca's favorites, One Was Johnny: A Counting Book, Pierre: A Cautionary Tale in Five Chapters and a Prologue, In the Night Kitchen)

When Max gets sent to his room without dinner, he sails off to the land of the Wild Things, where he can misbehave as much as he wants. But is this as great as it sounds? Also, check out Chicken Soup with Rice. This is how Rebecca and Benjamin learned the months of the year.

Other great reading recommendations:

Goodnight, Gorilla

by Peggy Rathmann

Brown Bear, Brown Bear, What Do You See?

by Bill Martin, Jr. (illustrated by Eric Carle). Also, Polar Bear, Polar Bear, What Do You See? Jamberry by Bruce Degan Time for Bed by Mem Fox (illustrated by Jane Dyer)

Snowy Day

by Ezra Jack Keats

Bus Stops

by Gomi

Lady with the Alligator Purse

by Nadine Bernard Westcott

Jesse Bear, Jesse Bear, What You Will Wear
by Nancy White Carlstrom

Peek-A-Boo
by Jan Olmerod

Silly Sally
by Audrey Wood

10, 9, 8
by Molly Bang

Eating the Alphabet: Fruits and Vegetables from A to Z
by Lois Ehlert

Special Needs Books

Adoption Is for Always
by Linda Walvoord Girard

At Daddy's on Saturdays
by Linda Walvoord Girard

Dinosaurs Divorce: A Guide for Changing Families
by Laurence Krasny Brown

I'd Rather Laugh
by Linda Richman
An inspirational look at how one mother survived losing a child.

Let's Talk About It: Divorce
by Fred Rogers

Lifetimes: The Beautiful Way to Explain Death to Children
by Bryan Mellonie

Over the Moon: An Adoption Tale
by Karen Katz

Tell Me Again About the Night I Was Born
by Jamie Lee Curtis

We Adopted You, Benjamin Koo
by Linda Walvoord Girard

What's Heaven?
by Maria Shriver

When a Pet Dies
by Fred Rogers

When Dinosaurs Die: A Guide to Understanding Death
by Laurence Krasny Brown

best books for parents

As a new mother, you'll want to stock your shelves with books by experts such as Penelope Leach, Dr. Spock, and T. Berry Brazelton. Here are a few more titles. You can get these books at any of the major bookstores or order them online. Also, don't forget to take advantage of your local library!

General

* The Baby Book: Everything You Need to Know About Your Baby from Birth to Age 2
  by William Sears, MD, and Martha Sears, RN

* Games Babies Play*
  by Julie Hagstrom and Joan Morrill

* How to Calm and Soothe Your Baby
  by Harvey Karp, MD

* Mother's Almanac*
  by Marguerite Kelly and Elia S. Parsons

* The Parent's Guide to Baby and Child Medical Care
  by Terril H. Hart, MD

* The Pediatrician's Best Baby Planner for the First Year of Life
  by Daniel W. Dubner, MD and D. Gregory Felch, MD

* Practical Parenting for the 21st Century*
  by Julie Ross

* Practical Parenting Tips
  by Vicki Lansky
  Solve Your Children's Sleep Problems*
  by Richard Ferber
  Pamela couldn't have survived the last seven years without this book! It's not for everyone, but it's definitely worth a close look.

* 25 Things Every New Mother Should Know*
  by Martha Sears, RN, and William Sears, MD

* What to Expect the First Year*
  by Arlene Eisenberg, Heidi E. Murkoff, and Sandee E. Hathaway
  This is referred to as the bible—as it should be. This is the month-by-month guide to your baby's first year.

* Your Amazing Newborn
  by M. Klaus and J. Kennell

* Your Baby's First Three Years by Dr. Paula Kelly

Breastfeeding

* Breastfeeding: The Nursing Mother's Problem Solver
  by Claire Martin, Nancy Funnemark Krebs, ed.

* The Breastfeeding Book: Everything You Need to Know About Nursing Your Child From Birth to Weaning
  by Martha Sears, RN

* The Complete Book of Breastfeeding
  by Marvin S. Eiger, MD and Sally Wendklos Olds

* Successful Breastfeeding
  by Nancy Dana and Anne Price

* The Womanly Art of Breastfeeding*
  by La Leche League

Toddlers

❋ *The Girlfriends' Guide to Toddlers*

by Vicki Iovine

The Vicki Iovine books are hilarious! Written for mothers by a mother who has seen it all with her four children.

❋ *Kids Book to Welcome a New Baby*

by Barbara J. Collman

❋ *How to Take Great Trips with Your Kids*

by Sanford and Joan Portnoy

❋ *The Smart Parents' Guide to Kids T.V.*

by Milton Chen, PhD

❋ *Your One-Year-Old to Your Four-Year-Old series*

by Louise Bates Ames, PhD, and Frances L. Ilg, MD

A series of books for each year of a child's life that highlights growth, development, and what to expect. Both of the series authors have taught and lectured at the Yale Child Study Center in New Haven.

Special Interests

❋ *Twins from Conception to Five Years*

by Averil Clegg and Anne Woolett

❋ *The Single Mother's Book: A Practical Guide to Managing Your Children, Career, Home, Finances, and Everything Else*

by Joan Anderson

❋ *In Praise of Single Parents*

by Shoshana Alexander

❋ *New York's 50 Best Places to Take Children*

by Allan Ishac

❋ *Overachieving Parents and Underachieving Children*

by Dorothy Bodenburg, MFCC

Particularly relevant to NYC moms who find they have their baby in five or six classes a week during the first year of life.

❋ *The 7 O'Clock Bedtime*

by Inda Schaenen

Discover the benefits of an early bedtime for the whole family!

❋ *The Manhattan Family Guide to Private Schools*

by Victoria Goldman and Catherine Hausman

❋ *The Parent's Guide to New York City's Best Public Elementary Schools*

by Clara Hemphill

videos/dvds

Almost all the superstores and many toy stores carry both children's entertainment and grown-up videos/dvds, covering a range of topics concerning new parents—breastfeeding, child development, and baby proofing. Also, don't forget your local library, HMV, Tower Records, Coconuts, Blockbuster Video, and Champagne Video, all of which sell and/or rent children's and parenting videos/dvds. Champagne Video is especially reasonable—two movies for $1.50, with a well-stocked children's section. There are four locations in Manhattan—three on the Upper East Side and one on the West Side. For a location near you, call 517-8700. We must add that children under two should not spend much time in front of the television. Experts recommend no more than one hour of TV per day!

Best Videos/DVDs for Children

During your child's first two or three years, he is going to fall madly in love with Barney, Big Bird, Ernie, Winnie-the-Pooh, or some character that hasn't even been invented yet. You'll be renting or buying any number of videos featuring these lovable creatures, even if, like Kelly, you once swore no child of yours would ever watch a purple dinosaur sing.

Here's a listing of videos/dvds based on popular television series (the titles give you an idea of what each is about). All the tapes/discs listed here offer either fun or instruction:

❋ *Barney*
(Best for nine months and up)
Children love sharing adventures with Barney and Baby Bop. Your child will love the sing-a-long songs, even if they drive you crazy.
Barney's Alphabet Zoo
Barney's Birthday*
Let's Pretend with Barney*
Riding in Barney's Car
Barney and Mother Goose*
And more . . .

❋ *Disney Spot Series*
(Best for newborns to nine months)
The Spot series is just as charming as Eric Hill's books.
Spot Goes to the Farm
Spot Goes to School*
Spot Goes to a Party
Where's Spot?*
Sweet Dreams Spot

❋ *Disney Classics*
(Best for ages two or three and up)
Everybody loves the Disney classics, even Mom and Dad. The animation is enjoyable for all ages and the tales are timeless.
A Bug's Life
Aladdin
A Goofy Movie
Bambi
Cinderella and Cinderella 2
The Fox and the Hound
The Great Mouse Detective
The Lion King
Mulan
Pocahontas
Sleeping Beauty
Snow White and the Seven Dwarfs
The Three Musketeers starring Mickey Mouse

Toy Story and Toy Story 2
One-Hundred-and-One Dalmatians
One-Hundred-and-Two Dalmatians
The Aristocats
And more...

❊ Disney's Winnie-the-Pooh Series

(Best for eighteen months and up)
Follow Winnie, Piglet, Tigger, and the others as
they make their way from adventure to adven-
ture. These are great because, aside from being
fun, they teach valuable lessons.
Pooh Party
Pooh Learning
Cowboy Pooh
Sharing and Caring
Making Friends*
Winnie-the-Pooh and the Blustery Day
Winnie-the-Pooh and a Day for Eeyore
Winnie-the-Pooh and Tigger Too*
Winnie-the-Pooh and the Honey Tree

❊ Richard Scarry

(Best for toddlers ages two to four)
Join the little worm Lowly and his friends in
their animated adventures.
Richard Scarry's Learning Songs
Best Sing-along Mother Goose Video Ever!
Best Busy People Video Ever!
Best Counting Video Ever!
Best ABC Video Ever!
Best Silly Stories and Songs Ever!
Best Birthday Party Ever!

❊ Sesame Street

(Best for twelve months and up)
Sesame Street videos/dvds are as educational as
the television show. Elmo, Bert, Ernie, Big Bird,
and other beloved characters will help teach your
little one how to sing, spell, and say his or her ABCs.
My Sesame Street Home Video
Play-Along
Sesame Street Sing Along
Big Bird Sings
The Best of Bert and Ernie
Do the Alphabet
The Best of Elmo
Sing, Hoot & Howl with the
    Sesame Street Animals
Sesame Street's 25th Birthday Celebration

❊ Julie Angier-Clark's Baby Series

(Best for newborn to age two)
What's better than cultural enrichment that's
fun, too? This series was not around when our
kids were newborns, but our new mommy
friends swear by them as the only videos/dvds
their newborns will focus on.
Baby Bach
Baby Einstein
Baby Mozart
Baby Shakespeare

Miscellaneous

(Eighteen months and up)
Here are some additional favorites of ours:
Baby Songs
Shari Lewis's "Don't Wake Your Mom!"
Wee Sing Grandpa's Magical Toys

Other New Releases

Bedknobs and Broomsticks

Leap Frog—Letter Factory, Talking
Words Factory

Rugrats in Paris, the Movie

The SpongeBob SquarePants Movie

The Wild Thornberry's Movie

Videos and DVDs for Parents

Videos/dvds are an easy, convenient way to pick up parenting tips and gain some know-how. They will save you precious time by allowing you to stay at home with your little one. The Lifetime cable channel also offers some interesting parenting programming. Check your local listings.

Baby's Early Growth, Care, and Development

❋ *Baby's First Months "What Do We Do Now?"* Developed by twelve pediatricians, it leads parents from birth through their baby's first few months. New parents are instructed on the daily care of a newborn.

❋ *The First Two Years: A Comprehensive Guide To Enhancing Your Child's Physical and Mental Development* This award-winning video observes babies involved in everyday activities. The developmental periods are divided by age: one day to three months, three to six months, six to twelve months, and twelve to twenty-four months. Other topics include breastfeeding, early child care, infant nutrition, physical growth, and mobility/motor skills.

❋ *Dr. Jane Morton's Guide to Successful Breastfeeding* Using a case study and graphics, this video shows the critical steps to comfortable, effective breastfeeding, including how to avoid common problems.

❋ *Touchpoints: The Definitive Video Series on Parenting, Volume 1: Pregnancy, Birth, and the First Weeks of Life** This practical guide to child development defines touchpoints as periods preceding rapid growth in learning, which are significant to future development. Points covered include pregnancy, delivery, preparation for birth, and the first weeks of your baby's life to three months.

❋ *Your Baby—A Video Guide to Care and Understanding with Penelope Leach* A comprehensive and practical guide to newborn baby care and development, this video demonstrates techniques of everyday care in a variety of situations.

❋ *What Every Baby Knows—A Guide To Pregnancy* An instructive video/dvd with sensible information concerning the development of children from birth to three months. It also explores a father's emotional involvement during pregnancy, gives a detailed profile of one couple's delivery, and looks at typical issues that arise in the early months after birth.

Exercise/Well-Being

❋ *Jane Fonda's Pregnancy, Birth, and Recovery* This exercise program demonstrates pregnancy and recovery workouts, baby massage, and infant care, and skills to physically prepare for birth.

*Kathy Smith's Pregnancy Workout** Both mothers-to-be and three different childbirth experts instruct mothers on how to maintain their energy and strength. Divided into prenatal and postnatal sections, the ninety-minute tape covers exercise for the new mothers up to six weeks after giving birth. Pamela used this tape to exercise at home, and found it challenging.

The Nursing Mothers Companion by Kathleen Hugging A how-to guide to nursing available on video and DVD.

Safety Videos

Barney Safety Barney and friends instruct little ones on safety with cars, traffic, and in the home.

Fire Safety for Kids with Beasel the Easel Endorsed by educators and firefighters, it teaches basic fire safety to children ages two and up. Children will enjoy the cast of characters and an original soundtrack.

*CPR To Save Your Child or Baby** This award-winning video carefully explains the step-by-step procedures of CPR, including instructions on the Heimlich maneuver and choking rescue. If you haven't had a chance to take a CPR-instruction class, this is the next best thing.

Infant and Toddler Emergency First Aid (Volume 1: Accidents, Volume 2: Illnesses) These are endorsed by the American Academy of Pediatrics. They explain emergency medical services including the proper procedures and actions to take when giving CPR or dealing with choking or poisoning.

Mr. Baby Proofer Designed to teach parents how to make their home a baby-safe environment, this hands-on guide also describes key safety products.

Choosing Quality Child Care It answers questions such as how to recognize quality child care, how to make sure a child is safe, and what to ask during an interview.

audiocassettes and cds for children

Just because you have a baby doesn't mean you have to spend the next few years listening to terrible, sappy music. There's some great music being written for children these days; don't be amazed when you find yourself humming the tunes to yourself (even in the company of other adults). In fact, you can find a lot of the adult music you like re-recorded for children. Much of the music recommended here is in Baby's Best by Susan Silver, or the Music for Little People catalog (800-409-2757). Also, don't hesitate to listen to your own music in the car. Pamela's friend Elizabeth only listened to classical music on car rides with her son, and he not only became accustomed to it, but he enjoys it, even now as a seven-year-old!

Raffi
Baby Beluga
Bananaphone*
Grocery Corner Store and Others
Singable Songs for the Very Young

✤ *Joanie Bartel*

Joanie Bartel's award-winning sound really appeals!

Lullaby Magic*

Bathtime Magic

Dancin' Magic*

Morning Magic

Sillytime Magic

✤ *Sesame Street*

The Best of Elmo

Ernie's Side by Side

Family and Friends

Sesame Street Silly Songs

Sing-Along Travels

Sing the Alphabet

Other Suggestions

✤ A Child's Gift of Lullabies
  by Someday Baby
✤ Dance on a Moonbeam
  by David Grover
✤ G'Night Wolfgang by Ric Louchard
✤ Hap Palmer's Follow Along Songs*
✤ Hush-A-Bye Dreamsongs
✤ Lullabies of Broadway by Mimi Bessette
✤ Lullaby Berceuse by XYZ
✤ Peter, Paul, and Mommy
  by Peter, Paul, and Mary*
✤ Shakin' It by Parachute Express
✤ Sleep, Baby Sleep by Nicolette Larson*
✤ The Lullaby and Goodnight Sleep Kit
✤ Sugar Beats* The Car Tunes is especially
  popular
✤ Toddlers Sing Storytime by Jerry Butler

✤ The Beatles for Kids
✤ Music by Laurie Berkner and David Grover are popular right now.

children's catalogs

Shopping by catalog can be the world's greatest convenience; there are loads of them, all filled with great things for babies and children, and all of these great things can be delivered right to your doorstep. Most of these catalogs also have websites, which makes shopping online easier than ever. Here are a few of our favorites offering one-of-a-kind accessories, toys, and practical imported clothing not available in stores.

✤ *Chinaberry Book Service**

2780 Via Orange Way, Suite B

Spring Valley, CA 91978

(800) 776-2242

www.chinaberry.com

Chinaberry has wonderful books for children, with the most detailed descriptions we've ever come across!

✤ *Constructive Playthings**

13201 Arrington Road

Grandview, MO 64030

(800) 832-0572

www.ustoy.com

An array of colorful, entertaining toys for young boys and girls, with a section called "First Playthings" that's especially good for newborns to one-year-olds.

The Disney Catalog of Children's Clothing

www.disneydirect.com
(800) 328-0612
All of the merchandise from your child's favorite Disney characters and movies.

Hanna Andersson*

1010 NW Flanders Street
Portland, OR 97209
(800) 222-0544
www.hannaandersson.com
Hanna Andersson carries moderately priced, superior quality cotton play clothes for young children, including swimwear and hats, plus some matching outfits for parents. These clothes last forever!

L.L. Bean Inc.

Freeport, ME 04033-0001
(800) 441-5713
www.llbean.com
Casual clothes for rugged kids. Great for outerwear. L.L. Bean is one of the few companies to offer clothing for larger body types.

Lilly's Kids

Lillian Vernon Corp.
Virginia Beach, VA 23479-0002
(800) 285-5555
www.lillianvernon.com
From Lillian Vernon, a catalog with well priced toys, games, and costumes.

The Natural Baby Catalog

7835 Freedom Avenue
North Canton, OH 44720
www.kidsstuff.com
The Natural Baby Catalog carries natural, ecological, and health-minded products, including cloth diaper covers, bedroom furniture, many beautifully crafted wooden toys, and books.

Ecobaby Organics, Inc.

332 Coogan Way
El Cajon, CA 92020
(888) ECO-BABY
www.ecobaby.com
This catalog has more than organic baby accessories—it also has non-toxic furniture, and a selection of breast pumps. It augments Natural Baby Catalog very nicely.

One Step Ahead*

75 Albrecht Drive
Lake Bluff, IL 60044
(800) 274-8440
www.onestepahead.com
One Step Ahead is good for baby products, including carriers/strollers, car seats, cribs, bottle holders, and some toys and clothing. Safety, travel, and mealtime helpers are also available.

OshKosh B'Gosh

1112 Seventh Avenue, P.O. Box 2222
Monroe, WI 53566-8222
(800) MY BGOSH (800-692-4674)
www.oshkoshbgosh.com
OshKosh is simple, all-American kids' wear, including classic denim overalls and jeans for

your toddler or young child, in both boys' and girls' sizes. It has a store on Fifth Avenue.

※ **Parenting and Family Life**
P.O. Box 2153, Dept. PA7
Charleston, WV 25328
(800) 468-4227
www.cambridgeeducational.com
Extensive selection of videos on parenting, discipline, and health-and-safety issues.

※ **Patagonia Mail Order**
P.O. Box 8900
Bozeman, MT 59715
(800) 336-9090
www.patagonia.com
Patagonia is known for its own brand of rugged everyday clothing and parkas, as well as its cozy fleece jackets.

※ **Perfectly Safe***
7245 Whipple Avenue, NW
North Canton, OH 44720
(800) 837-KIDS (800-837-5437)
www.kidsstuff.com
Safety gates, bathtub spout covers, and other items to child-proof a home.

※ **Play Fair Toys**
1690 28th Street
Boulder, CO 80302
(800) 824-7255
www.playfairtoys.com
Games, blocks, nesting animals, videos, and many other play items that just may help your little one learn to play fair.

※ **Talbots for Kids**
One Lakeville, MA 02348
(800) 543-7123
www.talbotskids.com
This is Kelly's favorite children's catalog and she buys lots of Angela's clothing from it. Amazing sales at the end of each season. The basics are as good as the Gap if not better.

※ **Toys to Grow On**
P.O. Box 17
Long Beach, CA 90801
(800) 542-8338
www.ttgo.com
Every kind of toy you can think of, for newborns to pre-teens.

※ **Troll's Learn & Play**
100 Corporate Drive
Mahwah, NJ 07430
(800) 247-6106
www.magiccabin.com
Creative toys, costumes, activity books, videos, art supplies, and counting toys, mostly for ages two and up.

magazines for parents

There's always something to do with children in New York. Check these publications for monthly calendars plus services and helpful articles just for New York parents. Many are free at local shops. Here are some of the better ones.

New York Parents

❊ Big Apple Parent
889-6400
www.parentsknow.com
This monthly publication features topical articles on parenting and kids. It has been around for over ten years and is an invaluable resource for Manhattan parents.

❊ New York Family
914-381-7474
www.parenthoodweb.com
Started by two moms, this monthly magazine offers useful event calendars as well as features on everything from children's health to traveling with kids.

❊ Parent Guide
213-8840
www.parentguidenews.com
This monthly magazine is for New York families with young children offering information on schools, camps, entertainment, and more.

National Magazines

Two of our favorite magazines are Parents and Child, but all of the magazines listed offer practical advice and information on parenting and child development.

❊ American Baby
557-6600
www.americanbaby.com
A monthly magazine for expectant parents and parents of children one and under.

❊ Baby Talk
522-8989
www.babytalk.com
A monthly magazine for expectant parents and parents of children two and under.

❊ Child*
(800) 777-0222
www.childmagazine.com
A popular, authoritative magazine full of information for parents of newborns through teens.

❊ Parents*
515-244-1832
www.parents.com
The most popular and informative magazine out there for parents. A favorite of Kelly's! The website is super too.

❊ Twins Magazine
(888) 55-TWINS (888-558-9467)
www.twinsmagazine.com
The only bimonthly national magazine for parents of twins.

❊ Working Mother
800-627-0690
www.workingmother.com
A monthly magazine for parents of infants through teens.

website directory

The Internet has revolutionized our lives as parents. What follows is a list of websites, organized by topic, which we found particularly useful. But sites open up and close down with frequency, so use this list as a point of reference, but update it with your own discoveries. For city parents who enjoy surfing the web, some of these listings may be familiar.

General

www.citybabyny.com
Keeps you up-to-date on what's new for parents in New York City.

www.babyzone.com
Offers a community resource for pre- and postnatal women.

www.babycenter.com
All-purpose website for expectant and new moms.

www.newyork.citysearch.com
What's happening in the greatest city in the world, including kids activities within designated areas.

www.ci.nyc.ny.us
The official New York City website for general information, event listings, and much more.

www.gocitykids.com
Go City Kids costs $19.95 to join to get a year's worth of family-friendly events and activities, but you can access the main site for free to get lots of great information.

www.metmuseum.org
The Metropolitan Museum of Art's official website.

www.cuny.edu
City University of New York—listings range from museums and restaurants to cultural and theater events.

www.nyckidsarts.org
Arts and arts education programming in New York City. Click on Kids Culture Catalog, for lists of over 230 arts and cultural organizations that offer programs for children. Also an events calendar, and listings of after-school classes.

www.urbanbaby.com
A website that is a reference guide for parents in many cities. Its message boards are popular.

Parenting

www.babycenter.com
A wealth of information on everything baby-related, i.e. maintaining fitness during pregnancy.

www.abcparenting.com
Comprehensive parenting site.

www.familywonder.com
A site for family entertainment, with activities, news, parenting tips, and a huge selection of toys.

Medical, Nutrition, and Fitness

www.acog.org

The American College of Obstetrics and Gynecology. Current information, doctors listings.

www.my.webmd.com

Articles on pregnancy, childbirth preparation, normal deliveries, alternative medicine, and nutrition.

www.ivillage.com

Fantastic site for pregnant women and new moms. A month-by-month chart on what to expect throughout your pregnancy.

www.cfmidwifery.org

The Citizens for Midwifery, promoting a Midwifery Model of Care. State-by-state information, contacts, and a helpful news directory.

www.mana.org

The Midwife's Alliance of North America.

www.midwiferytoday.com

Midwifery, birthing, books, products, feature articles, and a weekly newsletter.

www.moonlily.com/obc

The Online Birth Center offers loads of information on midwifery, pregnancy, birth, breastfeeding, and nannies.

www.nukitchenfood.com

A food delivery service that specializes in prepared food for pregnant or nursing mothers. About $34.99 a day.

www.bradleybirth.com

The Bradley Method of Natural Childbirth's website includes a national directory of instructors, and a suggested diet for pregnant women.

www.lamaze-childbirth.com

Locates a Lamaze educator in your area, and describes this style of birth preparation.

www.childbirth.org

Everything you need to know about birthing—from complications and cesareans to VBAC and postpartum stress.

www.thebabycorner.com

A complete resource for childbirth, breastfeeding, and parenting information.

www.birthcenters.org

From the National Association of Childbearing Centers, everything you need to know about birth centers.

www.birthpsychology.com

Articles on the psychological and emotional effects of pregnancy.

www.nutrio.com

A comprehensive nutrition and fitness resource.

www.expectingfitness.com

Exercise guidelines and suggested regimens for pregnant women.

ChildCare: Pediatricians, Nannies

www.kidsgrowth.com
Pediatric advice by topic, from abdominal pains to vision disorders. Very current information.

www.childbirth.org
Information about doulas.

www.dona.com
Doulas of North America. Locate a doula in your area.

www.webnannies.com
A good place to find and discuss issues pertaining to childcare.

www.liveandlearn.com
Good pointers on what to look for in a caregiver.

www.ci.nyc.ny.us
The New York City Department of Health Bureau of Day Care's website offers tips on choosing a licensed day-care program.

Just for Moms

www.athomemothers.com
The official website of the magazine *At Home Mother*.

www.clubmom.com
"If you're a mom, you're a member."

www.girlfriendsguide.com
By far, the hippest web page for moms and moms-to-be.

www.mothering.com
A new website for mothers.

www.hipmama.com/talk/cgi-bin/talk.cgi
Chat with other moms on topics ranging from health, adoption, single parenting, and more.

www.momsonline.oxygen.com
Chat with other moms and get some hot parenting tips.

And one for Daddies

www.fathersworld.com
A web ring with links to all kinds of sites for fathers, including resources for single dads, at-home dads, and fathering in general.

Baby Gifts

www.artictulip.com
BabyGund sterling silver gifts like rattles, bracelets, and other lovely baby gifts are all available here.

Party Planning

www.birthdayexpress.com
A complete resource for all things birthday-related.

www.birthdaypartyideas.com
Get tons of ideas for elaborate, original, and just plain fun birthday parties for your kids.

www.amazingmoms.com
All kinds of advice for planning an unforgettable birthday party for your little one.

www.greatentertaining.com

This site offers party supplies, party themes, recipes, and all kinds of other advice on throwing a great birthday party for your child.

Birth Announcements, Portraits and Other Novelties

www.amandakphoto.com

Creates a scrapbook of your baby's life that can begin during your pregnancy and follow through the first year. Prices start at $600.

www.bluemountain.com

From this electronic greeting card service you can e-mail birth announcements around the globe for free.

www.hallmark.com

Find e-cards here announcing your baby's birth.

www.ecards.com

Another fun e-card site, with cards announcing pregnancy or your baby's arrival.

www.sears-portrait.com

This site from Sears Portrait Studio has games, parenting advice, greeting cards, tips for getting better portraits of your kids, and much more.

www.familyheirlooms.com

A service that transforms baby's first shoes into bronzed heirlooms.

www.e-stork.com

Another place where you can create a personal web page announcing your baby's birth and include photos, birth stats, and more.

online shopping
Maternity Clothing

www.babystyle.com

Shop by basics and by style.

www.gap.com

Click on the Gap's online-only maternity line: basics and a splash of fun.

www.imaternity.com

The Maternity Everything Store. Stylish and comfortable clothing and accessories, with free shipping.

www.lizlange.com

Chic maternity clothing for all seasons. Liz will design it for you if need be.

www.pokkadots.com

It's a virtual boutique of stylish baby items for baby and Mom. It was voted *Forbes* magazine's Best of the Web for baby shopping sites.

www.maternitymall.com

Links to Motherhood Maternity, Motherhood Nursing Wear, A Pea in the Pod, and others.

www.maternityzone.com

A great site for moms-to-be, with the Belly Basics Pregnancy Survival Kit, diaper bags, lingerie, nursing clothes, and tons of fashionable maternity wear.

www.mothers-in-motion.com

Exercise clothing for moms-to-be.

www.maternityclothes.com

Your source for Maternity Vintage Levi's, and other hip maternity fashions.

Baby Necessities

www.babyage.com

A broad range of baby products at great prices.

www.babystyle.com

Great nursery items.

www.babyuniverse.com

Baby Universe has a wealth of information on subjects from bathing to shopping for your child.

www.buybuybaby.com

Accessories, cribs and cradles, strollers, car seats, and more.

www.thebabylane.com

Slings, baby blankets, and other items.

www.babygear.com

An amazing source for all things baby-related from a large listing of products by category.

www.ebrick.com

Everything for your baby, including diapers, strollers, cribs, and clothes.

www.baby-express-stores.com

Baby furniture and much more.

www.bumkins.com

It has super big, bright mommy bags. You can choose a grande, demi, or poco size to carry your kid's sippy cups, diapers, or other supplies. Made from waterproof fabric with many pockets, they are hip enough that they don't look like a classic diaper or maternity supply bags.

www.popoverbaby.com

For colorful and superwarm fleece to bundle your baby in on cold New York days. They are water-repellant and come in six different colors for $90.

www.rideonthesafeside.com

How to install car seats and information on car seat brands, etc.

www.interiordec.about.com/homegarden/ interiordec/msubchilddecor.htm

Articles on decorating your child's room—including creative ideas, trends, and safety tips.

www.upperbreastside.com

Line of nursing bras and baby clothing.

www.verybestbaby.com

This is the website for Nestle's Good Start infant iron formula.

www.walgreens.com

Order diapers, bottles, and all baby supplies from this discount chain.

Baby Furniture

www.casakids.com

Furniture designed by Roberto Gil

www.dreamshopforkids.com

Sleeping bags, super soft pillow cases, and everything your kid needs for a sleepover. Items are child-safe and durable plus easy to travel with and clean. Call 303-674-4246.

www.directbuy.com

Infant and baby furnishings, bedding, strollers, etc.

www.ikea.com

The Swedish furniture company offers well-priced and neatly designed cribs and other furniture for the nursery.

www.olivekids.com

Great bedding, rugs, decorations, and personalized products for children's rooms. There are many possible themes to choose from.

www.potterybarnkids.com

Stylish, reasonably priced baby and children's furniture and bedding sold online.

Baby Clothing and Accessories

www.babygap.com

It's the classic Gap basic clothes for babies and toddlers.

www.bestnco.com

Beautiful high-end baby and children's clothes. At Bergdorf's in the city.

www.blueberrybabies.com

An extensive website featuring layette, infant, and toddler clothing, gifts, and more.

www.bodenUSA.com

Adorable baby and children's clothing from London.

www.frenchkids.com

French Kids Online carries the best French and European brands for children's apparel.

www.olliebollen.com

Great selection of clothing and accessories for kids.

www.pokkadots.com

It's a virtual boutique of stylish baby items for baby and Mom. It was voted *Forbes* magazine's Best of the Web for Baby Shopping Sites.

www.poshbaby.com

Upscale website offering a concise mix of stylish clothing and accessories.

www.kidsdirectory.com

A great resource listing stores in forty different U.S. cities.

www.thebabyoutlet.com

Great baby wear and free shipping for your purchases.

www.designeroutlet.com

Shop for designer overstocks.

www.rainbee.com

Over 10,000 children's products from over 250 designers and manufacturers.

www.urbanmonster.com

There are two Urban Monster stores in Brooklyn, but

if you can't make it there, the website has some of the hippest baby gear around.

www.webclothes.com
Beautiful infant and children's clothing.

www.hannaandersson.com
Beautiful clothes made from soft fabrics in fun and elegant patterns.

www.zutano.com
Colorful and fun baby clothes for infants to toddlers as advertised in *Martha Stewart Kids*.

www.babyuniverse.com
A nice source for layettes and clothing.

Toys

www.amazon.com
Good selection of toys.

www.crayola.com/colorwonder
If your child wants to experience the wonder of fingerpaints without experiencing the mess, this is the site to explore. These fingerpaints are the kind that appear on Crayola's special paper so they won't color skin, walls, or anything else moms worry about staining.

www.homegrownkids.com
This is the site of the creators of the Toy Taco, the 36-inch circular themed playmat that folds up and goes with you. The theme includes taking the cars to the lake, through the town, to the gas station, and lots more.

www.makitfun.com
The website for Makit Products, which lets kids use Disney templates to draw, paint, or color their favorite Disney characters. There's Mickey Mouse and Winnie-the-Pooh as well as other favorites.

www.smarterkids.com
Awesome site that helps children learn, discover, and grow.

www.smarttoys.com
Games, puzzles, plush toys, Beanie Babies, and everything else.

www.shopping.yahoo.com/toys
Yahoo! has an extensive selection of toys, classified by age and category.

www.boardgames.com
All your favorite board games for rainy afternoons.

www.playthings.com
Presents the latest toy news, best-sellers, and coming attractions.

Books and Bookstores

www.bn.com
Barnes and Noble's website.

www.citysearch.com/nyc/bankstbooks
Bank Street Bookstore lists new books, featured authors, and events.

www.booksofwonder.com
Information about New York's largest children's bookstore.

www.nypl.org/branch/kids

The New York Public Library's "On-Lion" site for kids. Recommended reading, events in the city, magazine links and other New York kids links.

www.alanbrown.com

Book reviews for and by kids.

www.bookhive.org

Search for any kind of book on this site.

www.cataloglink.com

Hundreds of catalogs are at your fingertips here.

www.storknet.org/bkstore/index.html

A wonderful source for parenting books.

www.amazon.com

www.borders.com

www.childrensbooks.about.com

Great information and articles on choosing children's books; provides picks for books with strong female characters, books for reluctant readers, and recent award winners.

the city baby
yellow pages

aquariums

The Brooklyn Aquarium at Coney Island, Surf Avenue and Coney Island Boardwalk at W. 8th Street, 718-265-3400

au pair agencies

Au Pair in America, River Plaza, 9 West Broad Street, 06902, 800-9AU-PAIR (1-800-928-7247)

Au Pair Childcrest, 111 East 12700 South, Draper, UT 84020, 800-574-8889; 888-287-2471

Au Pair USA/Interexchange, 161 Sixth Avenue, 10th Floor, 800-AUPAIRS (800-287-2477)

baby nurses/doulas

Absolute Best Care, 850 Seventh Avenue at 55th Street, 481-5705

All Metro Health Care, 50 Broadway, Lynbrook, NY 11563, 516-887-1200

Beyond Birth (Doulas), 1992 Commerce Street, Suite 40, Yorktown Heights, NY 10598, 914-245-2229, 888-907-BABY

Bohne's Baby Nursing, 16 E. 79th Street, Suite G-4, 879-7920

Doula Care, Ruth Callahan, 70 W. 93rd Street, 749-6613

Fox Agency, 30 E. 60th Street, Suite 904, 753-2686

Frances Stuart Agency, 1220 Lexington Avenue, Suite 2B, 439-9222

In a Family Way, 124 W. 79th Street, Suite 9-B, 877-8112

Mother Nurture Doula Service, P.O. Box 284, Glen Oaks, NY 11004, 718-631-BABY (718-631-2229)

baby products,
see super stores

baby proofing

All Star Baby Safety, Inc., 877-668-7677
Babyproofers Plus, 628-8052

baby-sitting services

Avalon, 245-0250
Baby Sitters Guild, 682-0227
Bank Street College, 875-4400; 875-4404
Barnard Baby-Sitting Service, 854-2035
NYC Babysitters Club, 396-4090
New York City Explorers, 591-2619
Pinch Sitters, 260-6005
Sitter City, 888-211-9749

ballet,
see children's classes, dance

balloons

Balloon Bouquets of New York, 457 W. 43rd Street, 265-5252
Balloon Saloon, 133 W. Broadway at Duane Street, 227-3838
Birthday Express, 800-424-7843

bathrooms

East Side

Barneys, Madison Avenue at 61st Street, 826-8900

Bergdorf Goodman, Fifth Avenue at 57th Street, 753-7300

Bloomingdale's, Third Avenue at 59th Street, 705-2000

Bendel's, Fifth Avenue at 55th Street, 247-1100

FAO Schwarz, 767 Fifth Avenue at 58th Street, 644-9400

The Hotel Pierre, 2 E. 61st Street bet. Madison and Fifth avenues, 838-8000

Lord & Taylor, Fifth Avenue at 39th Street, 391-3344

The New York Palace Hotel, 455 Madison Avenue at 50th Street, 800-697-2522

The Regency Hotel, 540 Park Avenue at 60th Street, 759-4100

Saks Fifth Avenue, Fifth Avenue at 50th Street, 753-4000

Tiffany & Company, 727 Fifth Avenue at 57th Street, 755-8000

The Waldorf-Astoria, 301 Park Avenue at 50th Street, 355-3000

West Side

Macy's, Herald Square, 151 W. 34th Street bet. Broadway and Seventh Avenue, 695-4400

Manhattan Mall, 100 W. 32nd St. at Sixth Avenue, 465-0500

New York Hilton, 1335 Sixth Avenue at 53rd Street, 586-7000

Time Warner Center,
59th Street at Columbus Circle

Downtown

ABC Carpet & Home, 888 Broadway at 19th Street, 473-3000

Bed, Bath & Beyond, 620 Avenue of the Americas at 18th Street, 255-3550

Millenium Hilton, 55 Church Street bet. Fulton and Dey streets, 693-2311

SoHo Grand Hotel, 310 W. Broadway bet. Grand and Canal streets, 965-3000

South Street Seaport (The Fulton Market), 11 Fulton Street, 732-7678

Tribeca Grand Hotel, 2 Avenue of the Americas bet. White and Walker streets, 519-6600

World Financial Center, The Winter Garden, West Street bet. the World Trade Center and the Hudson River, 945-0505

birth announcements

Blacker & Kooby, 1204 Madison Avenue at 88th Street, 369-8308

Hudson Street Papers, 357 Bleecker Street between 10th and Charles streets, 229-1064

Hyde Park Stationers, 1070 Madison Avenue at 80th Street, 861-5710

Jamie Ostrow, 54 West 21st Street, 2nd Floor, 734-8890

Jill M. Cooper, 799-8317

Kate's Paperie,
561 Broadway at Prince Street, 941-9816;
8 W. 13th Street at Fifth Avenue, 633-0570;
1282 Third Avenue at 74th Street, 396-3670

Laura Beth's Baby Collection, 300 E. 75th Street, 717-2559

Lauren Wittels, Excellent Paper Place,
235 West 76th Street, Apt. 4A, 580-0921

Lincoln Stationers, 1889 Broadway at 63rd Street, 459-3500

Little Extras, 676 Amsterdam Avenue at 93rd Street, 721-6161

Papyrus Cards & Stationery,
1270 Third Avenue at 73rd Street, 717-1060;
852 Lexington Avenue bet. 64th and 65th streets, 717-0002;
107 E. 42nd Street at Lexington Avenue (Grand Central Station), 490-9894;
2157 Broadway bet. 75th and 76th streets, 501-0102

Rebecca Moss, Ltd., 510 Madison Avenue at 53rd Street, 832-7671

Mrs. John L. Strong, Barneys, 660 Madison Avenue at 61st Street, 2nd Floor, 833-2059

Tiffany & Co.,
727 Fifth Avenue at 57th Street, 755-8000

Venture Stationers, 1156 Madison Avenue at 85th Street, 288-7235

birthday cakes, cupcakes and cookies

BeautifulCookies.com, 866-FUN-GIFT (866-386-4438)

Cakes 'N' Shapes, Ltd., 403 W. 39th Street bet. Ninth and Tenth avenues, 629-5512

Carvel, 1091 Second Avenue bet. 57th and 58th streets, 308-4744; 800-322-4848

CBK Cookies of New York, 226 E. 83rd Street bet. Second and Third avenues, 794-3383

Creative Cakes, 400 East 74th Street bet. First and York avenues, 794-9811

Cupcake Cafe, 522 Ninth Avenue at 39th Street, 465-1530

Dean & Deluca, 1150 Madison Avenue, 717-0800; 560 Broadway at Prince Street, 226-6800

Flour Girl, 87th Street and Columbus Avenue, 595-9505

Grace's Market Place, 1237 Third Avenue at 71st Street, 737-0600

Haagen-Dazs, 187 Columbus Avenue bet. 68th and 69th streets, 787-0265; 33 Barrow Street bet. Seventh Avenue and Bleecker Street, 727-2152

Lafayette Bakery, 26 Greenwich Avenue between Tenth and Charles streets, 242-7580

Magnolia Bakery, 401 Bleecker Street at 11th Street, 462-2572

My Most Favorite Dessert Company, 120 W. 45th Street bet. Sixth Avenue and Broadway, 997-5032/997-5130

The Perfect Cake, 481-7467

Soutine, 104 W. 70th Street bet. Columbus and Amsterdam avenues, 496-1450

Sylvia Weinstock Cakes, 273 Church Street bet. White and Franklin streets, 925-6698

Veniero Pasticceria, 342 E. 11th Street bet. First and Second avenues, 674-7264

William Greenberg Desserts, 1100 Madison Avenue bet. 82nd and 83rd streets, 861-1340

birthday parties

Central Park Carousel, 736-8700

Chelsea Piers Gymnastics, Pier 62, 23rd Street at Twelfth Avenue, 336-6500

Circus Gymnastics, 2121 Broadway at 74th Street, 799-3755

Craft Studio, 1657 Third Avenue, 831-6626

Eli's Vinegar Factory, 431 E. 91st Street at York Avenue, 987-0885, ext. 4

Gymtime, 1520 York Avenue at 80th Street, 861-7732

Jodi's Gym, 244 E. 84th Street bet. Second and Third avenues, 772-7633

Linda Kaye's Birthday Bakers PartyMakers, 195 E. 76th Street bet. Third and Lexington avenues, 288-7112

Our Name Is Mud, 1566 Second Avenue bet. 81st and 82nd streets, 570-6868; 506 Amsterdam Avenue bet. 84th and 85th streets, 579-5575; 59 Greenwich Avenue, 647-7899

Party Poopers, 100 Greenwich Street, 274-9955; 104 Reade Street at Broadway, 587-9030

Regency Hotel, 540 Park Avenue bet. 61st and 62nd streets, 339-4132

74th Street Magic, 510 E. 74th Street bet. York Avenue and the East River, 737-2989

birthday party entertainers

Arnie Kolodner, 265-1430

Bobby DooWah, 914-762-2421/772-7633 (Jodi's Gym)

Clown Magic, 544-8153

Hollywood Pop Gallery, 777-2238

Leanne DeCamp, 971-8765

Little Maestros, 744-3194

Madeline the Magician, 475-7785

Magical Marion, 917-922-9880

Marcia the Musical Moose, 567-0682 or 914-358-8163

New York Sketches, 646-452-9946

Only Perfect Parties, 869-6988

Send in the Clowns, 718-353-8446

Silly Billy, 645-1299

birthing centers

The Birthing Center (affiliated with St. Luke's-Roosevelt Hospital Center), 1000 Tenth Avenue bet. 58th and 59th streets, 523-BABY

bookstores

Bank Street Bookstore, 610 W. 112th Street at Broadway, 678-1654

Barnes & Noble, locations throughout the city, 807-0099 (main store)

Books of Wonder, 18 W. 18th Street bet. Fifth and Sixth avenues, 989-3270

Bookberries, 983 Lexington Avenue at 71st Street, 794-9400

Borders Books & Music, 550 Second Avenue bet. 32nd and 33rd streets, 685-3938; 461 Park Avenue at 57th Street, 980-6785

Corner Bookstore, 1313 Madison Avenue at 93rd Street, 831-3554

Integral Yoga Bookstore, 227 W. 13th Street, 929-0586

Lenox Hill Bookstore, 1081 Lexington Avenue between 72nd and 73rd streets, 472-7170

Logos Bookstore, 1575 York Avenue bet. 83rd and 84th streets, 517-7292

Rizzoli Bookstore, 31 W. 57th Street bet. Fifth and Sixth avenues, 759-2424

The Scholastic Store, 557 Broadway bet. Prince and Spring streets, 343-6166

Shakespeare and Co., 993 Lexington Avenue bet. 68th and 69th streets, 570-5148; 716 Broadway at Washington Place, 529-1330; 137 E. 23rd Street, 220-5199

The Strand Bookstore, 828 Broadway at 12th Street, 473-1452

breastfeeding consultants and resources

Beth Israel Medical Center,
Lactation Program, 420-2939
Màire Clements, RN, IBCLC, 595-4797
La Leche League, 794-4687

breast pump rentals

Upper East Side

Caligor Pharmacy, 1226 Lexington Avenue at 83rd Street, 369-6000
Cherry's, 207 E. 66th Street bet. Second and Third avenues, 717-7797
Falk Drug, 259 E. 72nd Street at Second Avenue, 744-8080
Goldberger's Pharmacy, 1200 First Avenue at 65th Street, 734-6998
Timmerman Pharmacy, 799 Lexington Avenue bet. 61st and 62nd streets, 838-6450

Upper West Side

Apthorp Pharmacy, 2201 Broadway at 78th Street, 877-3480
Chateau Drug, 181 Amsterdam Avenue bet. 68th and 69th streets, 877-6390
Joseph Pharmacy, 216 W. 72nd Street and West End Avenue, 875-1718
Planet Kids, 2688 Broadway bet 102nd and 103rd streets, 864-8705
Suba Pharmacy, 2721 Broadway at 104th Street, 866-6700

Midtown

NYU Medical Center, 560 First Avenue at 32nd Street, 263-BABY
St. Luke's-Roosevelt Hospital Center, 1000 Tenth Avenue at 58th Street, 523-4000

Downtown

Barren Hospital Medical Center, 49 Delancey Street bet. Eldridge and Forsyth streets, 226-6164
C.O. Bigelow Apothecaries, 414 Sixth Avenue bet. 8th and 9th streets, 533-2700
Elm Drugs, 298 First Avenue bet. 17th and 18th streets, 777-0740
Kings Pharmacy, 5 Hudson at Reade Street, 791-3100
Little Folks, 123 E. 23rd Street bet. Park and Lexington avenues, 982-9669
Miriam Goodman, Home Delivery, 219-1080

cakes,
see birthday cakes

camps

A.C.T Summer Camp Program, The Cathedral of St. John the Divine, 1047 Amsterdam Avenue bet. 110th and 111th streets, 316-7530
Ballet Academy East, 1651 Third Avenue, 3rd Floor, bet. 92nd and 93rd streets, 410-9140
Bank Street Summer Camp, 610 W. 112th Street bet. Broadway and Riverside Drive, 875-4420
Chelsea Piers Summer Sports Camp, W. 23rd Street at the Hudson River, Pier 62, 336-6666
Columbia Grammar Summer Camp, 26 W. 94th

Street bet. Columbus Avenue and Central Park West, 749-6200, ext. 225

Columbus Gym Summer Camp, 606 Columbus Avenue bet. 89th and 90th streets, 721-0090

Corlears Summer Camp, 324 W. 15th Street bet. Eighth and Ninth avenues, 741-2800

Dalton Day Camp, 53 E. 91st Street bet. Park and Madison avenues, 423-5431

Discovery Programs, 251 W. 100th Street at West End Avenue, 749-8717

Hi Art!, 362-8190

Jodi's Gym, 244 E. 84th Street bet. Second and Third avenues, 772-7633

Language Workshop for Children, Summer Day Camps, 888 Lexington Avenue at 66th Street, 396-1369

Little Red School House, 272 Sixth Avenue at Bleecker Street, 477-5316, ext. 239

The Lucy Moses School for Music and Dance, 129 W. 67th Street bet. Broadway and Amsterdam Avenue, 501-3360

Marymount Summer Day, 1026 Fifth Avenue bet. 83rd and 84th streets, 744-4486

Montessori International Day Camp, 347 E. 55th Street bet. First and Second avenues, 223-4630

New Town Day Camp at Sol Goldman Y, 344 E. 14th Street bet. First and Second avenues, 780-0800, ext. 241

92nd Street Y, 1395 Lexington Avenue at 92nd Street, 415-5536

The Poppyseed Pre-Nursery, 424 West End Avenue at 81st Street, 877-7614

Renanim Pre-School and Summer Camp, 336 E. 61st Street bet. First and Second Avenues, 750-2266; 133-35 E. 29th Street bet. Lexington and Third avenues, 685-3330

Rhinelander Children's Center, 350 E. 88th Street bet. First and Second avenues, 876-0500

Rodeph Sholom Camp and School, 70 W. 83rd Street bet. Central Park West and Columbus Avenue, 362-8800

Summer Breeze Day Camp, 1520 York Avenue at 80th Street, 734-0922

Summer Days Camps, 510 E. 74th Street bet. York Avenue and the East River, 737-2989

Trinity Day Camp, 101 W. 91st Street bet. Amsterdam and Columbus avenues, 932-6983

West Side YMCA Kinder Camp, 5 W. 63rd Street at Central Park West, 875-4112

catalogs

Chinaberry Book Service, 2780 Via Orange Way, Suite B Spring Valley, CA 91978, 800-776-2242

Constructive Playthings, 13201 Arrington Road, Grandview, MO 64030, 800-832-0572

The Disney Catalog of Children's Clothing, 800-328-0612

Ecobaby Organics, 332 Coogan Way, El Cajon, CA 888-ECO-BABY

Hanna Andersson, 1010 NW Flanders Street, Portland, OR 97209, 800-222-0544

L.L. Bean Inc., Freeport, ME 04033-0001, 800-441-5713

Lilly's Kids, Lillian Vernon Corp., Virginia Beach, VA 23479-0002, 800-285-5555

The Natural Baby Catalog, 7835 Freedom Avenue, North Canton, OH 44720

One Step Ahead, 75 Albrecht Drive, Lake Bluff, IL 60044, 800-274-8440

OshKosh B'Gosh,
 1112 Seventh Avenue, P.O. Box 2222,
 Monroe, WI 53566-8222,
 800-MY BGOSH (800-692-4674)
Parenting and Family Life, P.O. Box 2153, Dept.
 PA7, Charleston, WV 25328, 800-468-4227
Patagonia Mail Order, P.O. Box 8900, Bozeman,
 MT 59715, 800-336-9090
Perfectly Safe, 7245 Whipple Avenue, NW, North
 Canton, OH 44720, 800-837-KIDS
 (800-837-5437)
Play Fair Toys, 1690 28th Street, Boulder, CO
 80302, 800-824-7255
Talbots for Kids, One Lakeville, MA, 02348, (800)
 543-7123
Toys to Grow On, P.O. Box 17, Long Beach, CA
 90801, 800-542-8338
Troll's Learn & Play, 100 Corporate Drive, Mahwah,
 NJ 07430, 800-247-6106

child cpr & safety instruction

Downtown Babies, Various locations, 217-2716
Fern Drillings, Various locations, 744-6649
Got CPR, 691-5989
Mindful Parenting, 980 Madison Avenue,
 561-6400
Save-A-Tot, 317 E. 34th Street, 725-7477
Tot-Saver, 5 E. 98th Street, 241-8195

child proofing,
see baby proofing

childbirth educators

**Association of Labor Assistants and Childbirth
 Educators**, 888-22ALACE
Choiceful Birth and Parenting,
 Ellen Krug, CSW, C.C.E., 718-768-0494
Ellen Chuse, C.C.E., 718-789-1981
Doulas of North America, www.dona.org
Fern Drillings, Various locations, 744-6649
Expectant Parenting, 744-3194
Tara Fallin, 917-282-1699
Mary Lynn Fiske, C.C.E., AAHCC, 718-855-1650
Judith Halek, 309 W. 109th Street bet. Broadway
 and Riverside Drive, 222-4349
Martine Jean-Baptiste, C.N.M., C.C.E., 769-4578
Jewish Community Center, 334 Amsterdam
 Avenue, 646-505-4444
Fritzi Kallop, 517-4488
Risa Lynn Klein, 1490 Second Avenue bet. 77th
 and 78th Streets, 249-4203
Mama Nurture, 165 W. 86th Street, 877-2005
Gayatri Martin, R.N., Choices for Childbirth,
 220 E. 26th Street, 725-1078
Realbirth, 54 West 22nd Street, 367-9006
Diana Simkin, Upper East Side locations, 348-0208
Marcy Perlman Tardio, 220 E. 26th Street,
 725-1078
Wellcare Center, 161 Madison Avenue bet. 32nd
 and 33rd streets, 696-9256

children's classes
Art

After-School Art, Inc., 510 E. 74th Street bet. York
 Avenue and the East River, 431-1026
ARTKIDS, (646) 201-9168

Art-N-Orbit, Reebok Sports Club East, 160 Columbus Avenue at 67th Street; Reebok Sports Clubs West, 330 E. 61st Street bet. First and Second avenues; Jewish Community Center of the Upper West Side, 334 Amsterdam Avenue at 76th Street; The Children's Museum of Manhattan, 212 W. 83rd Street bet. Broadway and Amsterdam Avenue, 420-0474

Gymtime/Rhythm and Glues, 1520 York Avenue at 80th Street, 861-7732

Hi Art!, 362-8190

Kids at Art, 1349 Lexington Avenue at 89th Street, 410-9780

Computers

Futurekids, 1628 First Avenue bet. 84th and 85th streets, 717-0110

The Techno Team Lab, Reebok Sports Club, 160 Columbus Avenue at 67th Street, 501-1425

Dance

The Ailey School, 405 W. 55th Street, 405-9143

American Youth Dance Theater, 434 E. 75th Street, #1C, bet. First and York avenues, 717-5419

Ballet Academy East, 1651 Third Avenue, 3rd floor, bet. 92nd and 93rd streets, 410-9140

Bridge for Dance, 2726 Broadway at 104th Street, 749-1165

Broadway Dance Center, 221 W. 57th Street at Broadway, 582-9304 ext. 25

Chinese Folk Dance Company, 390 Broadway bet. Walker and White streets, 334-3764

Dance for Children, 19 Murray Street bet. Broadway and Church Street, 608-7681

Djoniba Dance and Drum Center, 37 E. 18th Street, 477-3464

Greenwich House Music School, 44-46 Barrow Street bet. Bleecker and Bedford streets, 242-4770

In Grandma's Attic, Various locations, 726-2362

Judy Lasko Modern Dance, 131 W. 86th Street; 124 W. 95th Street, 864-3143

Kids Co-Motion, 579 Broadway bet. Prince and Houston streets; 280 Rector Place; 37 W. 26th Street, 431-8489

Kinderdance®, Various locations, 579-5270

Manhattan Ballet School, 149 E. 72nd Street bet. Lexington and Third avenues, 535-6556

The Lucy Moses School for Music and Dance, 129 W. 67th Street bet. Broadway and Amsterdam Avenue, 501-3360

Perichild Program, 132 Fourth Avenue, 2nd Floor, bet. 13th and 12th streets, 505-0886

The School for Education in Dance and the Related Arts, 254-3194

Shake, Rhythm and Roll, 357 West 36th Street, 3rd Floor, 563-6781

Steps on Broadway, 2121 Broadway at 74th Street

Drama

The Drama Zone, 220 E. 86th Street, (917) 690-0789

Gymnastics

Asphalt Green, 555 E. 90th Street bet. York and East End avenues, 369-8890 for catalog

Chelsea Piers, Pier 62, 23rd Street at Twelfth Avenue, 336-6500

Circus Gym, 2121 Broadway, 2nd Floor, at 74th Street, 799-3755

Columbus Gym, 606 Columbus Avenue bet. 89th and 90th streets, 721-0090

Gymtime Gymnastics, 1520 York Avenue at 80th Street, 861-7732

Jodi's Gym, 244 E. 84th Street bet. Second and Third avenues, 772-7633

Life Sport Gymnastics, West Park Presbyterian Church, 165 W. 86th Street at Amsterdam Avenue, 769-3131

Sokol New York, 420 E. 71st Street bet. First and York avenues, 861-8206

Tumble Town Gymnastics, 104 E. 19th Street, 387-1420

Wendy Hillard Foundation, Rhythmic Gymnastics NY, 792 Columbus Avenue, Suite 17T, at 100th Street, (646) 587-5421

Music

Bloomingdale School of Music, 323 W. 108th Street bet. Broadway and Riverside Drive, 663-6021

Campbell Music Studio, 305 West End Avenue at 74th Street; 436 E. 69th Street bet. York and First avenues, 496-0105

Church Street School for Music and Art, 74 Warren Street bet. W. Broadway and Greenwich Street, 571-7290

Diller-Quaile School Of Music, 24 E. 95th Street bet. Madison and Fifth avenues, 369-1484, www.diller-quaile.org

Family Music Center, Various locations, 864-2476

French-American Conservatory of Music, 154 W. 57th Street, 246-7378

Greenwich House Music School, 46 Barrow Street bet. Bleecker and Bedford streets, 242-4770

Mary Ann Hall's Music for Children, 2 E. 90th Street bet. Fifth and Madison avenues, 800-633-0078

The Lucy Moses School for Music and Dance, 129 W. 67th Street bet. Broadway and Amsterdam Avenue, 501-3360

Mozart for Children, 129 W. 67th Street bet. Broadway and Amsterdam Avenue; 15 Gramercy Park on 20th Street off Park Avenue; 120 E. 87th Street bet. Lexington and Park avenues, 942-2743

Music, Fun & Learning, 339 E. 84th Street bet. First and Second avenues; 263 W. 86th Street at West End Avenue, 717-1853

School for Strings, 419 W. 54th Street bet. Ninth and Tenth avenues, 315-0915

Third Street Music School Settlement, 235 E. 11th Street bet. Second and Third avenues, 777-3240

Turtle Bay Music School, 244 E. 52nd Street bet. Second and Third avenues, 753-8811

Pottery

Greenwich House Pottery, 16 Jones Street bet. Bleecker and W. Fourth streets, 242-4106

Cooking

Miette Culinary Studio, 109 MacDougal Street, Suite 2, 460-9322

Sports Training

Baseball Center of NYC, 202 W. 74th Street bet. Broadway and Amsterdam Avenue

Super Soccer Stars, 877-7171

Swimming

Asphalt Green, 555 E. 90th Street bet. York and East End Avenues, 369-8890

New York Health and Racquet Club, 60 W. 23rd

Street, 989-2300

Take Me to the Water, 10 locations, 828-1756

Yoga

B.K.S. Iyengar Yoga Association, 150 W. 22nd Street, 691-9642

Goodson Parker Wellness Center, 30 E. 76th Street, 4th Floor, at Madison Avenue, 717-5273

Next Generation Yoga, 200 W. 72nd Street, Fifth Floor, bet. Broadway and West End Avenue, 595-9306

Etiquette

Nicole De Vault, 415 E. 37th Street, 481-7280

Language

Big Apple Kids, 221 W. 82nd Street, 579-0301

China Institute in America, 125 E. 65th Street, 744-8181 ext. 142

La Croisette French Language Center, 861-7723

La Escuelita, 302 W. 91st Street, 877-1100

Language Workshop for Children, 888 Lexington Avenue at 66th Street, 396-0830

clothing stores
Baby and Toddler

babyGap, Various locations

Baby Moves Boutique, 139 Perry Street, 255-1685

Bambini, 1088 Madison Avenue, 717-6742

Barneys, 660 Madison Avenue at 61st Street, 826-8900

Bloomingdale's, 1000 Third Avenue bet. 59th and 60th streets, 705-2000

Bombalulus, 101 W. 10th Street bet. Sixth and Greenwich avenues, 463-0897

Bonpoint, 1269 Madison Avenue at 91st Street, 722-7720; 811 Madison Avenue at 68th Street, 879-0900

Bu & The Duck, 106 Franklin Street bet. Church Street and W. Broadway, 431-9226

CALYPSO Enfant, 426 Broome Street, 966-3234

Catimini, 1125 Madison Avenue at 84th Street, 987-0688

Century 21 Department Store, 22 Cortlandt Street, bet. Broadway and Church Street, 227-9092

The Children's Place, Various locations, 529-2201

Cremebebe, 68 Second Avenue bet. 3rd and 4th streets, 979-6848

Daffy's, 111 Fifth Avenue at 18th Street, 529-4477; 335 Madison Avenue at 44th Street, 557-4422; 125 E. 57th Street at Lexington Avenue, 376-4477; 1311 Broadway at 34th Street, 736-4477

Greenstones, 442 Columbus Avenue bet. 81st and 82nd streets, 580-4322; Greenstones, Too, 1184 Madison Avenue bet. 86th and 87th streets, 427-1665

Gymboree, 1120 Madison Avenue bet. 83rd and 84th streets, 717-6702; 1049 Third Avenue at 62nd Street, 688-4044; 1332 Third Avenue at 76th Street, 517-5548; 2015 Broadway bet. 68th and 69th streets, 595-7662; 2271 Broadway bet. 81st and 82nd streets, 595-9071

H&M, 1328 Broadway

Ibiza Kidz, 46 University Place bet. 9th and 10th streets, 533-4614

Jacadi, 787 Madison Avenue at 67th Street, 535-3200

Julian & Sara, 103 Mercer Street bet. Spring and Prince Streets, 226-1989

Kendall's Closet, 162 W. 84th Street, 501-8911

Kidstown, 10 E. 14th Street, 243-1301

Koh's Kids, 311 Greenwich Street bet. Chambers and Reade streets, 791-6915

La Layette . . . Et Plus Ltd., 170 E. 61st Street bet. Third and Lexington avenues, 688-7072

Lester's, 1522 Second Avenue at 80th Street, 734-9292

Lilliput SoHo Kids, 240 Lafayette Street bet. Prince and Spring streets, 965-9201

Little Folks, 123 E. 23rd Street bet. Park and Lexington avenues, 982-9669

Lord & Taylor, 424 Fifth Avenue bet. 38th and 39th streets, 391-3344

Macy's, Herald Square, 151 W. 34th Street bet. Broadway and Seventh Avenue, 695-4400

Magic Windows, 1186 Madison Avenue bet. 86th and 87th streets, 289-0028

Oilily, 870 Madison Avenue bet. 70th and 71st streets, 772-8686

Old Navy Clothing Co., 610 Sixth Avenue at 18th Street, 645-0663; 150 W. 34th Street at Seventh Avenue, 594-0049; 503/511 Broadway bet. Broome and Spring streets, 226-0838; 300 W. 125th Street bet. Eighth and Frederick Douglass Boulevard, 531-1544

Patagonia, 426 Columbus Avenue bet. 80th and 81st streets; 101 Wooster Street bet. Prince and Spring streets, 917-441-0011

Peanut Butter & Jane, 617 Hudson Street bet. Jane and W. 12th streets, 620-7952

Petit Bateau, 110 Madison Avenue at 82nd Street, 988-8884

Les Petite Chapelais, 142 Sullivan Street bet. Houston and Prince streets, 505-1927

La Petite Etoile, 746 Madison Avenue bet. 64th and 65th streets, 744-0975

Planet Kids, 2688 Broadway bet. 102nd and 103rd streets, 864-8705

Prince & Princess, 33 E. 78th Street at Madison, 879-8989

Ralph Lauren, 867 Madison Avenue at 72nd Street, 606-2100

Robin's Nest, 1168 Lexington Avenue bet. 80th and 81st streets, 737-2004

Rockstarbaby, 298 Elizabeth Street, 995-8638

Saks Fifth Avenue, 611 Fifth Avenue at 50th Street, 753-4000

Small Change, 1196 Lexington Avenue at 81st Street, 772-6455

Space Kiddets, 46 E. 21st Street bet. Park Avenue South and Broadway, 420-9878

Spring Flowers, 538 Madison Avenue at 55th Street, 717-8182; 1050 Third Avenue at 62nd Street, 758-2669; 905 Madison Avenue at 72nd Street, 717-8182

Talbots Kids & Babies, 1523 Second Avenue at 79th Street, 570-1630

Tartine et Chocolat, 1047 Madison Avenue at 82nd Street, 717-2112

Tigers, Tutu's & Toes, 128 Second Avenue bet. St. Mark's and 7th Street, 228-7990

Tutti Bambini, 1480 First Avenue at 77th Street, 472-4238

Z'Baby Company, 100 W. 72nd Street at Columbus Avenue, 579-BABY; 996 Lexington Avenue at 72nd Street, 472-BABY

Zitomer, 969 Madison Avenue bet. 75th and 76th streets 737-2037

Clothing, Maternity

A Pea in the Pod, 625 Madison Avenue bet. 58th and 59th streets, 826-6468

A Second Chance, 1109 Lexington Avenue bet. 77th and 78th streets, 2nd Floor, 744-6041

Barneys New York Maternity Department, 660 Madison Avenue at 61st Street, 6th Floor, 826-8900

Cadeau Maternity, 254 Elizabeth Street, 994-1810

Eileen Fisher, 521 Madison Avenue bet. 53rd and 54th streets, 759-9888; 1039 Madison Avenue bet. 79th and 80th streets, 879-7799; 341 Columbus Avenue at 76th Street, 362-3000; 103 Fifth Avenue bet. 17th and 18th streets, 924-4777; 314 E. Ninth Street bet. First and Second avenues, (Outlet Store) 529-5715; 395 W. Broadway bet. Spring and Broome streets, 431-4567

H&M, 1328 Broadway, 646-473-1165

Jelly Bean Maternity, 2449 Broadway at 90th Street, 769-9099

Liz Lange Maternity, 958 Madison Avenue bet. 75th and 76th streets, 879-2191

Maternity Works Outlet, 16 W. 57th Street bet. Fifth and Sixth avenues, 399-9840

Michele Saint-Laurent, 1028 Lexington Avenue bet. 73rd and 74th streets, 542-4200

Mimi Maternity, 1021 Third Avenue bet. 60th and 61st streets, 832-2667; 2005 Broadway bet. 68th and 69th streets, 721-1999

Motherhood Maternity, The Manhattan Mall, 32nd Street bet. Sixth and Seventh avenues, 564-8813; 1449 Third Avenue bet. 82nd and 83rd streets, 734-5984; 641 Avenue of the Americas at 20th Street, 741-3488; 16 W. 57th Street bet. Fifth and Sixth avenues, 399-9840

Old Navy, 150 W. 34th Street, 594-0049

Veronique Delachaux, 1321 Madison Avenue at 93rd Street, 831-7800

Clothes, Resale Shops

First & Second Cousin New and Resale Children's Shop, 142 Seventh Avenue South bet. 10th and Charles streets, 929-8048

Jane's Exchange, 207 Avenue A bet. 12th and 13th streets, 674-6268

Clothes, Trunk Shows & Private Boutiques

Bodyscapes, Inc., 20 W. 22nd Street, Room 502, 243-2414

Judy's Fancies, 689-8663

Little Follies, P.O. Box 111, Englewood, NJ 07631, 800-242-7881/212-585-1940

Papo d'Anjo, 396-9668 (voice mail), Praça Luis de Camões n.36 3° Esq., 1200-243 Lisbon Portugal, 011 351 21 324-1790

coffee bars

DT:UT, 1626 Second Avenue bet. 84th and 85th streets, 327-1327; 41 Avenue B bet. E. 3rd and E. 4th streets

Starbucks, Various locations, 613-1280

concerts, plays, & puppet shows

The Little Orchestra Society, The Lolli Pops Concert Series, 971-9500

New York Theater Ballet, Florence Gould Hall, 355-6160

The Paper Bag Players, 362-043

The Puppet Company, 741-1646

Puppetworks 718-965-6058

The Swedish Cottage Marionette Theater,
    Central Park at W. 81st Street, 988-9093

TADA!, 627-1732

Tribeca Performing Arts Center, 346-8510

costumes

Abracadabra Superstore, 19 West 21st Street
    between Fifth and Sixth avenues, 627-5194

Halloween Adventure, 104 Fourth Avenue bet.
    11th and 12th streets, 673-4546

M. Gordon Novelty, 933 Broadway bet. 21st and
    22nd streets, 254-8616

day-care center information

Child Care Inc., 275 Seventh Avenue, 929-4999

The Daycare Council of New York,
    10 E. 34th Street, 213-2423

The Department of Health,
    442-9666 (Childcare Info Line)

diaper services

Tidy Diapers, 50 Commerce Street,
    Norwalk, CT 06850, 800-732-2443

doll hospitals

New York Doll Hospital,
    787 Lexington Avenue, 838-7527

doulas,
see baby nurses/doulas

emergency numbers

Police, Ambulance, Fire Department, 911

Poison Control, 340-4494/764-7667/800-222-1222

fitness/health clubs

Bally Total Fitness, 45 E. 55th Street, 688-6630;
    144 E. 86th Street, 722-7371, 641 Sixth
    Avenue, 645-4565

David Barton, 30 E. 85th Street bet. Madison and
    Fifth avenues, 517-7577; 215 W. 23rd Street
    bet. Seventh and Eighth avenues, 414-2022

Body by Baby, Jane Kornbluh, 344 E. 14th Street,
    780-0800 ext. 236

Core Fitness, 12 East 86th Street, bet. Fifth and
    Madison avenues

Equinox, 10 Columbus Circle at 60th Street, 871-
    0425; 1633 Broadway at 50th Street, 541-7000;
    420 Lexington Avenue at 44th Street, 953-
    2499; 97 Greenwich Street, 620-0103; 14 Wall
    Street at Nassau Street, 964-6688; 54 Murray
    Street at West Broadway, 566-6555

Jewish Community Center, 334 Amsterdam
    Avenue at 76th Street, 646-505-4444

Maternal Fitness, 108 E. 16th Street, 4th floor,
    between Park Avenue and Irving Place,
    353-1947

New York Health & Racquet Club,
    Various locations, 800-HRC-BEST

New York Sports Clubs,
    Various locations, 800-796-NYSC

92nd Street Y, 1395 Lexington Avenue at 92nd Street, 415-5729

Peggy Levine, 2726 Broadway bet. 104th and 105th streets, 3rd Floor, 222-3637

Pure Power Boot Camp, 38 W. 21st Street, 2nd Floor, 414-1886

Reebok Sports Club/NY, 160 Columbus Avenue at 67th Street, 362-6800; 330 E. 61st Street bet. First and Second avenues, 355-5100; 45 Rockefeller Plaza bet. 50th and 51st streets, and Fifth and Sixth avenues, 218-8600

Diana Simkin, 348-0208

Strollercize, Inc., 800-Y-STROLL

Vanderbilt YMCA, 224 E. 47th Street bet. Second and Third avenues, 756-9600

YWCA, 610 Lexington Avenue at 53rd Street, 735-9750

furniture,
see super stores

hair salons

Astor Place Hair Designers, 2 Astor Place bet. 8th Street and Broadway, 475-9854

Cozy's Cuts for Kids, 1416 Second Avenue at 74th Street; 1125 Madison Avenue at 84th Street; 448 Amsterdam Avenue at 81st Street; 585-COZY

The Hair's Castle, 1470 York Avenue at 78th Street, 744-2177

Kids Cuts, 201 E. 31st Street bet. Second and Third avenues, 684-5252

Paul Molé Haircutters, 1031 Lexington Avenue at 74th Street, 988-9176

SuperCuts, Various locations, 800-SUPERCUT/ (800-787-3728)

Whipper Snippers, 106 Reade Street bet. W. Broadway and Church Street

hospitals

Beth Israel Hospital, 16th Street at First Avenue, 420-2000 (General), 420-2999 (Classes), 420-3895 (Patient Care)

Columbia Presbyterian Hospital/Babies Hospital/Sloane Hospital for Women, 3959 Broadway at 166th Street, 305-2500 (General), 305-2040 (Parent Ed.)

Lenox Hill Hospital, 100 E. 77th Street bet. Lexington and Park avenues, 434-2000 (General), 434-2273 (Parent Ed.), 434-3152 (Babies' Club)

The Mount Sinai Medical Center, 1176 Fifth Avenue at 98th Street, 241-6500 (General), 241-7491 (Women's and Children's Office), 241-6578 (Breastfeeding Warm Line)

NY Presbyterian Hospital, at the NY Weill Cornell Center, 525 E. 68th Street bet. York Avenue the East River, 746-5454 (General), 746-3215 (Parenthood Prep.)

New York University Medical Center, 560 First Avenue at 32nd Street, 263-7300 (General), 263-7201 (Classes)

Roosevelt Hospital, 1000 Tenth Avenue at 59th Street 523-4000 (General), 523-6222 (Classes)

St. Luke's Hospital, 1111 Amsterdam Avenue at 114th Street, 523-4000 (General), 523-6222 (Parent/Family Ed.)

St. Vincent's Hospital and Medical Center, 170 W. 12th Street at Seventh Avenue, 604-7000 (General), 604-7946 (Maternity Ed.)

hotlines, warmlines, & other special help

Adoption

Adoptive Parents Committee, 304-8479
Adoptive Parents Support Group, 475-0222

Hotline Help

Child Abuse and Maltreatment
    Reporting Center, 800-342-3720
Emergency Children's Service, 341-0900 (general),
    966-8000 (nights, weekends, holidays)
First Candle/National SIDS Resource Center,
    800-221-SIDS (800-221-7437)
National AIDS Hotline, 800-342-AIDS
New York Foundling Hospital Crisis,
    Intervention Nursery 472-8555
Poison Hotline, 340-4494/764-7667

Single Parents

Parents Without Partners, 800-637-7974
Single Mothers By Choice, 988-0993
Single Parents Support Group, 780-0800 ext. 239

Twins or More

M.O.S.T. (Mothers Of Super Twins), 631-859-1110
National Organization of Mothers
    of Twins Clubs, Inc., 877-540-2200

Special Needs Groups

Cystic Fibrosis Foundation, 986-8783
Educational Alliance, 780-0800
League for the Hard of Hearing, 917-305-7700
The Lighthouse/New York Association
    for the Blind, 821-9200

National Down Syndrome Society, 460-9330
Pregnancy and Infant Loss Center, 612-473-9372
    (Bereavement Group)
Resources for Children with Special Needs,
    677-4650
Spina Bifida Information and Referral,
    800-621-3141
United Cerebral Palsy of New York City,
    677-7400,
Williams Syndrome Hotline, 248-541-3630
YIA Early Intervention Program, 418-0335

indoor play space

Sydney's Playground, 66 White Street at Broadway,
    431-9125

interior design & decoration

Charm and Whimsy, Esther Sadowsky, Allied
    A.S.I.D, 114 E. 32nd Street, 683-7609
Gracious Home, 1217/1220 Third Avenue at 70th
    Street, 517-6300, 1992 Broadway at 67th
    Street, 231-7800
Janovic Plaza, Various locations, 772-1400
Kids Digs, Carol Maryan Architects, 212 W. 79th
    Street, Suite 1C, 787-7800
Laura Beth's Baby Collection, 300 E. 75th Street,
    Suite 24E; 321 E. 75th Street bet. First and
    Second avenues 717-2559
MB Discount, 2311 Avenue U bet. E. 23rd and 24th
    streets
Plain Jane, 525 Amsterdam Avenue at 85th Street,
    595-6916

Robin Weiss, 917-751-4412

SmartStart, Susan Weinberg, 334 W. 86th Street, Suite 6C, 580-7365

YoyaMart, 15 Gansevoort Street at Hudson, 242-5511

lactation consultants,
see breastfeeding

lamaze,
see childbirth educators

layette, see
clothing stores

libraries

Upper East Side

96th Street, 112 E. 96th Street bet. Park and Lexington avenues, 289-0908

67th Street, 328 E. 67th Street bet. First and Second avenues, 734-1717

Webster, 1465 York Avenue bet. 77th and 78th streets, 288-5049

Yorkville, 222 E. 79th Street bet. Second and Third avenues, 744-5824

Upper West Side

Bloomingdale, 150 W. 100th Street at Amsterdam Avenue, 222-8030

Columbus, 742 Tenth Avenue bet. 50th and 51st

streets, 586-5098

Riverside, 127 Amsterdam Avenue at 65th Street, 870-1810

St. Agnes, 444 Amsterdam Avenue at 81st Street, 877-4380

Midtown

Donnell Library Center, 20 W. 53rd Street bet. Fifth and Sixth avenues, 621-0636

Downtown

Epiphany, 228 E. 23rd Street bet. Second and Third avenues, 679-2645

Hudson Park, 66 Leroy Street at Seventh Avenue, 243-6876

Jefferson Market, 425 Sixth Avenue at 10th Street, 243-4334

Kips Bay, 446 Third Avenue at 31st Street, 683-2520

Lower East Side

New Amsterdam, 9 Murray Street bet. Broadway and Church Street, 732-8186

Tompkins Square, 33 E. 10th Street bet. Avenues A and B, 228-4747

magazines, national

American Baby 557-6600

Baby Talk 522-8989

Child 800-777-0222

Parents 515-244-1832

Twins Magazine 888-55-TWINS (888-558-9467)

Working Mother, 800-627-0690

magazines, new york

Big Apple Parents' Paper, 889-6400
New York Family, 914-381-7474
Parent Guide, 213-8840

magicians,
see birthday party entertainers

malls

Northern New Jersey

Fashion Center, Route 17 and Ridgewood Avenue, Paramus, NJ, 201-444-9050
Garden State Plaza, Route 17 South, Paramus, NJ, 201-843-2404
The Mall at Short Hills, Short Hills, NJ, 973-376-7350
Paramus Park Mall, Route 17 North, Paramus, NJ, 201-261-8000
Riverside Square Mall, Route 4 West, Hackensack, NJ, 201-489-2212

Westchester/Rockland

Palisades Park Center, West Nyack, NY, 914-348-1000
The Westchester, Bloomingdale Road, White Plains, NY, 914-683-8600
Woodbury Commons Mall, Harriman, NY, 914-928-4000

Long Island

Roosevelt Field Shopping Center, Glen Cove, NY, 516-742-8000
Sunrise Mall, Sunrise Highway, Massapequa, NY, 516-795-3225

Walt Whitman Mall, Dix Hills, NY, 516-271-1741

Connecticut

Stamford Town Center, Tresser Boulevard, Stamford, CT, 203-324-0935

massage

Carapan, 5 W. 16th Street bet. Fifth and Sixth avenues, 633-6220
Laura Favin, 220 W. 71st Street, Suite 2A, 501-0606, 917-209-6534
The Medical Massage Group, 328 E. 75th Street, Suite 3, 472-4772
Mother Massage and More, 108 E. 16th Street, Suite 401, 533-3188
Prenatal Massage Center, 123 W. 79th Street, Suite LL2, 330-6846
The Quiet Touch, 317 W. 35th Street, 246-0008, 800-946-2772
Wellpath, 1100 Madison Avenue at 83rd Street, 737-9604

maternity clothing,
see clothing, maternity

midwives

Beth Israel Women's Health Center, 16th Street and First Avenue, 420-2000
CBS Midwifery, Inc., Barbara Sellars, (affiliated with St. Luke's Roosevelt), 103 Fifth Avenue at 17th Street, 366-4699
Midwifery Services, Inc., (affiliated with St. Luke's-Roosevelt), 135 W. 70th Street bet. Broadway and Columbus Avenue, 877-5556

mommy & me classes

Aha! Learning Partners, 1624 First Avenue bet. 84th and 85th streets, 517-8292

Art Farm in the City, 419 E. 91st Street bet. York and First avenues, 410-3117

Asphalt Green Inc., The A.G.U.A. Center, 1750 York Avenue at 91st Street, 369-8890

Baby Fingers, 165 W. 86th Street at Amsterdam Avenue; 167 W. 89th Street bet. Columbus and Amsterdam avenues, 874-5978

Bloomingdale School of Music,
323 W. 108th Street bet. Broadway and Riverside Drive, 663-6021

Broadway Babies, 184 E. 76th Street at Lexington Avenue; 160 Columbus Avenue; 52 Mercer Street, 472-0703

C.A.T.S. (Children's Athletic Training School), The Jewish Center, 131 W. 86th Street, 5th Floor, bet. Amsterdam and Columbus avenues; Turtle Bay Music School, 235 E. 49th Street bet. Second and Third avenues, 832-1833

Chelsea Piers, Pier 62, 23rd Street at Twelfth Avenue, 336-6500

Children's Studio, 307 E. 84th Street bet. First and Second avenues, 737-3344

Child's Play, Central Presbyterian Church, 593 Park Avenue at 64th Street, 838-1504; Rutgers Presbyterian Church, 236 W. 73rd Street at Broadway, 877-8227

Children's Tumbling, Suellen Epstein, 9 Murray Street at City Hall, 233-3418

Church Street School for Music and Art,
74 Warren Street at W. Broadway, 571-7290

Circus Gymnastics, 2121 Broadway at 74th Street, 799-3755

Columbus Gym, 606 Columbus Avenue bet. 89th and 90th streets, 721-0090

Diller-Quaile School of Music, 24 E. 95th Street bet. Madison and Fifth avenues, 369-1484

Discovery Programs, 251 W. 100th Street at West End Drive, 749-8717

Do Re Mi, 504 E. 63rd Street at York Avenue, 35 W. 26th Street bet. Fifth and Sixth avenues, 505-3456

The Early Ear, 48 W. 68th Street bet. Central Park West and Columbus Avenue; 353 E. 78th Street bet. First and Second avenues; 110 W. 96th Street bet. Amsterdam and Columbus avenues, 877-7125

Educational Alliance Parenting and Family Center at The Sol Goldman YMHA,
344 E. 14th Street bet. First and Second avenues, 780-0800 ext. 239

Free to Be Under Three,
24 St. Mark's, Suite 8 253-2040

Funworks for Kids, 201 E. 83rd Street at Third Avenue, 917-432-1820

Gymtime/Rhythm and Glues, 1520 York Avenue at 80th Street, 861-7732

Hands On! A Musical Experience, Inc., 1365 First Avenue bet. 73rd and 74th streets, 628-1945; 529 Columbus Avenue bet. 85th and 86th streets, 496-9929

Imagine Swimming, 253-9650

JAMS, Ansche Chesed Synagogue, W. 100th Street bet. Broadway and West End Avenues; 165 W. 91st Street

Jewish Community Center, 334 Amsterdam Avenue at 76th Street, 646-505-4444

Jodi's Gym, 244 E. 84th Street bet. Second and Third avenues, 772-7633

Judy Stevens Playgroup, 77 Franklin Street at Church Street, 941-0542

Kids Co-Motion, 579 Broadway bet. Prince and Houston streets; 280 Rector Place; 37 W. 26th Street, 431-8489

Kidville, 163 E. 84th Street bet. Third and Lexington avenues, 848-9415

Kindermusik®, The Greenwich Village Center/The Children's Aid Society, 219 Sullivan Street at W. 3rd Street, 254-3074

The Language Workshop for Children, 888 Lexington Avenue at 66th Street, 396-0830

Life Sport Gymnastics, West Park Presbyterian Church, 165 W. 86th Street at Amsterdam Avenue, 769-3131

Little Maestros, 344 E. 69th Street bet. First and Second avenues, 347-400-3977

The Lucy Moses School for Music and Dance, 129 W. 67th Street bet. Broadway and Amsterdam Avenue, 501-3360

Mama Nurture, 165 W. 86th Street, 877-2005

Mary Ann Hall's Music for Children, The Church of Heavenly Rest, 2 E. 90th Street bet. Madison and Fifth avenues, 800-633-0078

Mixing Bowl, 243 E. 82nd Street, 585-2433

Mommy and Me, The Greenwich Village Center/ The Children's Aid Society, 219 Sullivan Street at W. 3rd Street, 254-3074 ext. 19

Musical Kids, 1296 Lexington Avenue, 996-5898

Music Together, Various locations 244-3046 (East Side); 219-0591 (West Side); 358-3801 (Lower Manhattan); 718-369-3099 (Brooklyn)

New York Kids Club, 265 W. 87th Street bet. Broadway and West End Avenue, 721-4400

New York Swims, 75 West End Avenue at 63rd Street, 265-8200

Once Upon a Baby, Various locations, 769-3670

Rhinelander Children's Center, 350 E. 88th Street bet. First and Second avenues, 876-0500

74th Street Magic, 510 E. 74th Street bet. York Avenue and the East River, 737-2989

Sokol New York Gym, 420 E. 71st Street bet. First and York Avenues, 861-8206

The Sports Club/L.A. Fun 'n' Fit, 330 E. 61st Street bet. First and Second avenues, 917-286-9730

The Sunshine Kids' Club: A Preschool of Music, 230 E. 83rd Street bet. Second and Third avenues, 439-9876

Swim Jim, 749-7335

Take Me to the Water, 828-1756

Tumble Town Gymnastics, 118 E. 28th Street, Room 708, bet. Park and Lexington avenues, 889-7342

Turtle Bay Music School, 244 E. 52nd Street bet. Second and Third avenues, 753-8811

YWHA 92nd Street, 1395 Lexington Avenue at 92nd Street, 415-5600

museums

The American Museum of Natural History, 79th Street at Central Park West, 769-5100

The Children's Museum of Manhattan, 212 W. 83rd Street bet. Broadway and Amsterdam Avenue, 721-1234

The Children's Museum of the Arts, 182 Lafayette Street, 274-0986

Dahesh Museum of Art, 580 Madison Avenue bet. 56th and 57th streets, 759-0606

Metropolitan Museum of Art, Fifth Avenue at 82nd Street, 535-7710

Scandinavia House, 58 Park Avenue bet. 37th and 38th streets, 879-9779

nanny advertisments/ newspapers

Irish Echo, 14 E. 47th Street, 686-1266

Irish Voice, 875 Avenue of the Americas, Suite 2100, 684-3366

The New York Times, 229 W. 43rd Street, 354-3900

The Polish Daily News, Nowy Dziennik, 333 W. 38th Street, 594-2266, ext. 31

nanny agencies

A Choice Nanny, 850 Seventh Avenue, Suite 305, 246-KIDS (246-5437)

Absolute Best Care, 850 Seventh Avenue at 55th Street, 481-5705

Best Domestic Placement, 10 E. 39th Street at Fifth Avenue, Suite 1118, 683-3060

Domestic Job Picks, 545 Fifth Avenue, Suite 309, 986-2102

The Fox Agency, 30 E. 60th Street, 753-2686

Frances Stuart Agency, 1220 Lexington Avenue, 439-9222

The London Agency, 767 Lexington Avenue, 755-5064

My Child's Best Friend, 35 W. 35th Street at Sixth Avenue

Nannies Plus, P.O. Box 603, Chester, NY 10918, 800-752-0078

Pavillion Agency, 15 E. 40th, Suite 400, 889-6609

Professional Nannies Institute, 501 Fifth Avenue, 692-9510

Robin Kellner Agency, 2 W. 45th Street, 997-4151

Sitter City, 213 W. Institute Place, Suite 410, Chicago, IL, 60610, 888-211-9749

Town and Country, 250 W. 57th Street, 245-8400

nanny surveillance, background checks & training

Babywatch, 889-1494

Care Check, 1056 Fifth Avenue, 360-6640

Homestep, 760-5959, 516-375-8492

Kid View, 800-624-2930 (Code 00)

Mind Your Business, P.O. Box 4434, Warren, NJ 07040, 888-869-2462

new mother classes—hospitals

Beth Israel Hospital, 16th Street at First Avenue, 420-2000 (General), 420-2999 (Classes)

Columbia Presbyterian Hospital, Babies Hospital/ Sloane Hospital for Women, Broadway at 166th Street, 305-2500 (General), 305-2040 (Parent Education Program)

The Mount Sinai Medical Center, One Gustave L. Levy Place, Fifth Avenue at 98th Street, 241-6500 (General), 241-7491 (Women & Children's Office), 241-6578 (Breastfeeding Warm Line)

New York Hospital/Cornell Medical Center, 525 E. 68th Street, 746-5454 (General), 746-3215 (Preparation for Parenthood Office)

New York University Medical Center, 560 First Avenue at 32nd Street, 263-7200 (General), 263-7201 (Classes)

Roosevelt Hospital, 1000 Tenth Avenue at 58th Street, 523-4000 (General), 523-6222 (Parent/ Family Education)

St. Luke's Hospital, 1111 Amsterdam Avenue at 114th Street, 523-4000 (General), 523-6222 (Parent/Family Education),

St. Vincent's Hospital and Medical Center, 153 W. 11th Street, 604-7000 (General), 604-7946 (Maternity Education)

nutritionists

Joanne Diamond, RD, Women's Health Beth Israel, 844-8620

Allyson Mechaber, 718-797-0310, 201-615-6143

Lauren Slayton, Food Trainers, 769-4300

Bonnie Taub-Dix, MA, RD, CDN, New York City and Long Island, 737-8536; 516-295-0377

parenting classes & groups

Colleen Campo, 744-3700 ext. 49

The Early Childhood Development Center, 163 E. 97th Street, 360-7803

Educational Alliance Parenting and Family Center at the Sol Goldman, YM-YWHA, 344 E. 14th Street bet. First and Second avenues, 780-0800, ext. 236

Elizabeth Bing Center for Parents, 164 W. 79th Street, 362-5304, 646-456-3266, 718-856-5677

Sandra Jamrog, 866-8527

The Jewish Community Center, 334 Amsterdam Avenue at 76th Street, 646-505-4444

Phyllis LaBella, CSW, BCD, Adoption Specialist, Domestic and International, 987-0077

Mindful Parenting, 980 Madison Avenue bet. 76th and 77th streets, 561-6400

"New Parents' Get Together," 92nd Street YM-YWHA, 1395 Lexington Avenue, 996-1100

New Mommies Network, Lori Robinson, 769-3846

New Mothers Luncheons, East and West Side locations, Ronni Soled, 744-3194

The Parent Child Center, 247 E. 82nd Street, 879-6900

Parenting Horizons, 109 E. 50th Street and Park Avenue; 165 W. 86th Street at Amsterdam Avenue, 765-2377

The Parenting Program, Temple Shaaray Tefila, 250 E. 79th Street at Second Avenue, 535-8008, ext. 248

The Parent's League, 115 E. 82nd Street, 737-7385

Rhinelander Children's Center, 350 E. 88th Street bet. First and Second avenues, 876-0500

Nancy Samalin, RN, MS, 787-8883

Kiki Schaffer, CSW, Mother/Infant Counseling, 529-9247

Lisa Schuman, CSW, CASAC, 590 West End Avenue, Suite 1A, 874-1318

Elizabeth Silk, MSSW, CSW, BCD, 873-6435

The SoHo Parenting Center, 568 Broadway, Suite 205, 334-3744

Uptown Mommies, Sarah Klagsbrun, MD, 996-4300

parks & recreation

New York Parks Department, 360-8111

Recreation Office, 408-0243

party entertainers,
see birthday party entertainers

party favors

HomeFront Kids, 202 E. 29th Street, 3rd Floor, bet. Second and Third avenues, 545-1447 ext. 1302

Jill M. Cooper, Personalize It!, 799-8317

Party Gifts by BETHiE, 877-371-0932

pharmacies,
see breast pump rentals

photographers

A Perfect Portrait, Nancy Ribeck, 476 Broome Street, Suite 6A, bet. Wooster and Greene streets, 534-3433

Jami Beere Photography, 646-505-5636; 917-903-4212

Barry Burns, 260 W. 36th Street, 2nd Floor, bet. Seventh and Eighth avenues, 713-0100

Kate Burton Photography, 316 E. 84th Street, 717-9958

Nina Drapacz, 500 E. 85th Street at York Avenue, 772-7814

Kate Engelbrecht, 55 Washington Street, Brooklyn, 718-858-5165

Fromex, 182 E. 86th Street bet. Third and Lexington avenues, 369-4821

JordonElyse Photography, 917-757-0703

Brian Kao, 646-552-8965 or 201-583-1003

Rachel Klein, 595-1444

Jennifer Lee, 40 W. 72nd Street, Suite 53, bet. Central Park West and Columbus Avenue, 799-1501

Sarah Merians Photography & Company, 104 Fifth Avenue, 4th floor, at 16th Street, 633-0502

Karen Michele, 721 Fifth Avenue at 56th Street, 355-7576

Nancy Pindrus Photography, 21 W. 68th Street bet. Central Park West and Columbus Avenue, 799-8167

Paloma Sendrey, 917-428-2843 or 718-432-2365

Gail Sherman, 88 Central Park West at 69th Street, 877-7210

plays,
see concerts, plays, & puppet shows

private trainers

Jane Kornbluh, 677-6165

Ana Learner, 355-3109

Debby Peress, 249-3972

Diana Simkin, 348-0208

puppet shows,
see concerts, plays, & puppet shows

resale shops,
see clothes, resale shops

restaurants

Upper East Side

Barking Dog Luncheonette, 1453 York Avenue at 77th Street, 861-3600; 1678 Third Avenue at 94th Street, 831-1800

California Pizza Kitchen, 201 E. 60th Street bet. Second and Third avenues, 755-7773

China Fun, 1221 Second Avenue at 64th Street, 752-0810; 246 Columbus Avenue at 71st Street, 580-1516

Googies, 1491 Second Avenue at 78th Street, 717-1122

Hi-Life Bar and Grill, 1340 First Avenue at 72nd Street, 249-3600; 477 Amsterdam Avenue at 83rd Street, 787-7199

Il Vagabondo, 351 E. 62nd Street bet. First and Second avenues, 832-9221

Lili's Noodle Shop and Grill, 1500 Third Avenue bet. 84th and 85th streets, 639-1313

Nick's, 1814 Second Avenue bet. 93rd and 94th streets

Serendipity 3, 225 E. 60th Street bet. Second and Third avenues, 838-3531

Tony's Di Napoli, 1606 Second Avenue at 83rd Street, 861-8686

Upper West Side

Alice's Tea Cup, 103 W. 73rd Street at Columbus Avenue, 799-3006

@SQC, 270 Columbus Avenue bet. 72nd and 73rd streets, 579-0100

Gabriela's, 685 Amsterdam Avenue at 93rd Street, 961-0574

Josephina, 1900 Broadway bet. 63rd and 64th streets, 799-1000

Louie's Westside Cafe, 441 Amsterdam Avenue at 81st Street, 877-1900

Popover Cafe, 551 Amsterdam Avenue at 87th Street, 595-8555

Ruby Foo's, 2182 Broadway at 77th Street, 724-6700; 1626 Broadway at 49th Street, 489-5600

Sambuca, 20 W. 72nd Street bet. Central Park West and Columbus Avenue, 787-5656

Midtown East and West

Benihana, 120 E. 56th Street bet. Park and Lexington avenues, 593-1627; 47 W. 56th Street bet. Fifth and Sixth avenues, 581-0930

Broadway Diner, 590 Lexington Avenue at 52nd Street, 486-8838; 1726 Broadway at 55th Street, 765-0909

Ellen's Stardust Diner, 1650 Broadway at 51st Street, 956-5151

Hamburger Harry's, 145 W. 45th Street bet. Broadway and Sixth Avenue, 840-0566

Metropolitan Cafe, 959 First Avenue bet. 52nd and 53rd streets, 759-5600

Chelsea/Flatiron

America, 9 E. 18th Street bet. Fifth Avenue and Broadway, 505-2110

Chat 'n' Chew, 10 E. 16th Street bet. Union Square West and Fifth Avenue, 243-1616

West Village

Arturo's Pizzeria, 106 W. Houston Street at Thompson Street, 677-3820

Cowgirl Hall of Fame, 519 Hudson Street at 10th Street, 633-1133

East Village

Miracle Grill, 112 First Avenue bet. 6th and 7th streets, 254-2353; 415 Bleecker Street between Bank and W. 11th streets, 924-1900

Two Boots, 37 Avenue A bet. 2nd and 3rd streets, 505-2276; Two Boots to Go-Go, 74 Bleecker at Broadway, 777-1033; Two Boots to Go West, 201 W. 11th Street at Seventh Avenue, 633-9096; Two Boots Pizzeria, 42 Avenue A at 3rd Street, 254-1919

Central Village/NoHo

Noho Star, 330 Lafayette Street at Bleecker Street, 925-0070

Tribeca

Bubby's, 120 Hudson Street at North Moore Street, 219-0666

The Odeon, 145 W. Broadway bet. Duane and Thomas streets, 233-0507

SoHo

Peanut Butter & Co., 240 Sullivan Street, 677-3995

Tennessee Mountain, 143 Spring Street at Wooster, 431-3993

The Chains

Carmine's, 2450 Broadway at 91st Street, 362-2200; 200 W. 44th Street bet. Broadway and Eighth Avenue, 221-3800

Dallas BBQ, 1265 Third Avenue at 73rd Street, 772-9393; 27 W. 72nd Street bet. Columbus Avenue and Central Park West, 873-2004; 132 Second Avenue at 8th Street, 777-5574; 132 W. 43rd Street between Sixth Avenue and Broadway, 221-9000; 21 University Place at 8th Street, 674-4450

EJ's Luncheonette, 1271 Third Avenue at 73rd Street, 472-0600; 447 Amsterdam Avenue bet. 81st and 82nd streets, 873-3444; 432 Sixth Avenue bet. 9th and 10th streets, 473-5555

Jackson Hole Burgers, 1611 Second Avenue bet. 83rd and 84th streets, 737-8788; 232 E. 64th Street bet. Second and Third avenues, 371-7187; 517 Columbus Avenue at 85th Street, 362-5177; 521 Third Avenue at 35th Street,

679-3264; 1270 Madison Avenue and 91st Street, 427-2820

John's Pizzeria, 260 W. 44th Street bet. Broadway and Eighth Avenue, 391-7560; 408 E. 64th Street bet. First and York avenues, 935-2895; 278 Bleecker Street bet. Sixth and Seventh avenues, 243-1680

La Cocina, 217 W. 85th Street bet. Broadway and Amsterdam Avenue, 874-0770; 2608 Broadway bet. 98th and 99th streets, 865-7333

Ollie's Noodle Shop & Grille, 200 W. 44th Street at Seventh Avenue, 921-5988; 1991 Broadway bet. 67th and 68th streets, 595-8181; 2315 Broadway at 84th Street, 362-3712; 2957 Broadway at 116th Street, 932-3300

Patsy's, various locations, 688-9707 (East Side)

Theme Restaurants

Hard Rock Cafe, 221 W. 57th Street bet. Broadway and Seventh Avenue, 489-6565

Jekyll & Hyde, 91 Seventh Avenue South bet. W. 4th and Barrow streets, 989-7701

Mars 2112, 1633 Broadway at 51st Street, 864-2553

Mickey Mantle's, 52 Central Park South bet. Fifth and Sixth avenues, 688-7777

Planet Hollywood, 1540 Broadway at W. 45th Street, 333-7827

shoes

East Side Kids Inc., 1298 Madison Avenue at 92nd Street 360-5000

Great Feet, 1241 Lexington Avenue at 84th Street, 249-0551

Harry's Shoes, 2299 Broadway at 83rd Street, 874-2035

Ibiza Kidz, 42 University Place at 9th Street, 505-9907

Lester's, 1522 Second Avenue at 80th Street, 734-9292

Little Eric, 1118 Madison Avenue at 83rd Street, 717-1513

Shoofly, 42 Hudson Street at Duane Street, 406-3270

TipTop Kids, 149 W. 72nd Street, 874-1004

summer activities,
see camps

superstores—
Baby Products, Furniture
In New York

Albee's, 715 Amsterdam Avenue at 95th Street, 662-8902

Baby Depot, 707 Sixth Avenue at 23rd Street, 229-1300

Buy Buy Baby, 270 Seventh Avenue bet. 25th and 26th streets, 917-344-1555

Planet Kids, 247 E. 86th Street bet. Second and Third avenues, 426-2040; 2688 Broadway bet. 102nd and 103rd streets, 864-8705

Schneider's, 20 Avenue A at E. 2nd Street, 228-3540

Toys "R" Us, 1514 Broadway at 44th Street, 646-366-8858

Outside of New York

The Baby and Toy Superstore, 11 Forest Street, Stamford, CT, 203-327-1333

Buy Buy Baby, Various locations

specialty stores

ABC Carpet & Home, 888 Broadway at 19th Street, 473-3000

Bella Zander, 400 Chambers Street, 917-309-4475 or 917-587-6386

Bellini, 1305 Second Avenue bet. 68th and 69th streets, 517-9233

Blue Bench, 159 Duane Street bet. Hudson Street and W. Broadway, 267-1500

Chelsea's Kids Quarter, 33 W. 17th Street bet. Fifth and Sixth avenues, 627-5524

Just for Tykes, 83 Mercer Street bet. Spring and Broome streets, 274-9121

Karin Alexis, 490 Amsterdam Avenue bet. 83rd and 84th streets, 769-9550

Kid's Supply Co., 1325 Madison Avenue at 94th Street, 426-1200

Pamela Scurry's Wicker Garden, 1327 Madison Avenue bet. 93rd and 94th streets, 410-7001

Room and Board, 105 Wooster Street bet. Prince and Spring streets, 334-4343

Upper Breast Side, 220 W. 71st Street, Suite 1, bet. Broadway and West End Avenue, 873-2653

toy stores

A Bear's Place, 789 Lexington Avenue bet. 61st and 62nd streets, 826-6465

The Children's General Store, Grand Central Station, 107 E. 42nd Street Lexington passage, 682-0004

Classic Toys, 218 Sullivan Street bet. Bleecker and W. 3rd streets, 674-4434

Cozy's Cuts for Kids, 1125 Madison Avenue at 84th Street, 744-1716; 448 Amsterdam Avenue at 81st Street, 579-2600

Cute Toonz, 372 Fifth Avenue at 34th Street, 967-6942

Didi's Children's Boutique, 1196 Madison Avenue at 88th Street, 860-4001

Dinosaur Hill, 306 E. 9th Street bet. First and Second avenues, 473-5850

E.A.T. Gifts, 1062 Madison Avenue at 80th Street, 861-2544

FAO Schwarz, 767 Fifth Avenue bet. 58th and 59th streets, 644-9400

Gepetto's Toy Box, 10 Christopher Street bet. Greenwich Avenue and Gay Street, 620-7511

Hom Boms, 1500 First Avenue bet. 78th and 79th streets, 717-5300

KB Toys, 901 Avenue of the Americas bet. 32nd and 33rd streets, 629-5386; 2411 Broadway at 89th Street, 595-4389

Kid O, 123 W. 10th Street at Greenwich Avenue, 366-5436

Kidrobot, 126 Prince Street bet. Wooster and Greene streets, 966-6688

Kidding Around, 60 W. 15th Street bet. Fifth and Sixth avenues, 645-6337

Little Extras, 676 Amsterdam Avenue at 93rd Street, 721-6161

Mary Arnold Toys, 1010 Lexington Avenue bet. 72nd and 73rd streets, 744- 8510

New York Firefighter's Friend, 263 Lafayette Street bet. Prince and Spring streets, 226-3142

Penny Whistle Toys, 448 Columbus Avenue bet. 81st and 82nd streets, 873-9090

Promises Fulfilled, 1592 Second Avenue bet. 82nd and 83rd streets, 472-1600

Toys "R" Us, 1514 Broadway at 44th Street, 646-366-8858

West Side Kids, 498 Amsterdam Avenue at 84th Street, 496-7282

Zittles, 969 Madison Avenue bet. 75th and 76th streets, 3rd floor of Zitomer, 737-2040

the Y associations

McBurney YMCA, 124 W. 14th Street at Sixth Avenue, 741-9210

Vanderbilt YMCA, 224 E. 47th Street bet. Second and Third avenues, 756-9600

West Side YMCA, 5 W. 63rd Street bet. Central Park West and Broadway, 875-4112

YWCA of the City of New York, 610 Lexington Avenue at 53rd Street, 755-4500

yoga classes, adult

Baby Om, Various locations, 615-6935

Mary Ryan Barnes, Yoga for Two, 175 W. 93rd Street at Amsterdam Avenue, 666-2237

Be Yoga, Various locations, www.beyoga.com

Beth Donnelly Caban, 718-604-0104

Integral Yoga Institute, 227 W. 13th Street bet. Seventh and Eighth avenues, 929-0586

Iyengar Yoga Institute of New York, 150 W. 22nd Street, 11th Floor, bet. Sixth and Seventh avenues, 691-9642

Jivamukti Yoga Center, 404 Lafayette Street, 3rd Floor, bet. Astor Place and 4th Street, 353-0214; 853 Lexington Avenue, 2nd floor, bet. 64th and 65th streets, 396-4200

Gayatri Martin, RN, Choices for Childbirth, 220 E. 26th St., 725-1078

Next Generation Yoga, 200 W. 72nd Street, Suite 58, 595-9306

Prenatal Yoga Center, 251 W. 72nd Street, Suite

2F, bet. Broadway and West End Avenue, 362-2985

Mikelle Terson, 37 W. 76th Street bet. Central Park West and Columbus Avenue, 362-4288

Elana Weiss, 452-2922 or 917-882-1643

Yoga Zone, 138 Fifth Avenue bet. 18th and 19th streets 647-9642, 160 E. 56th Street, 12th Floor, bet. Third and Lexington avenues, 935-9642

ZOOS

The Bronx Zoo, 185 Street at Southern Boulevard, 718-220-5100

Central Park Wildlife Conservation Center, Fifth Avenue at 64th Street, 439-6500

index

A

ABC Carpet & Home, 137, 185
Abingdon Square Park, 103
Abracadabra Superstore, 226–27
Absolute Best Care, 51, 54, 62
Adoption Is for Always (Girard), 239
adoptive parents support groups, 76
Adventure Playground, 100
After-School Art, Inc., 112–13
after-school programs, 110–23
   see also personal enrichment
   programs
age-specific toys, 218–22
Aha! Learning Partners, 85–86
The Ailey School, 114
Albee's, 183
Alice in Wonderland Statue, 100
Alice's Tea Cup, 128
All Metro Health Care, 51
All Star Baby Safety, 192
America, 130–31
American Baby, 249
American Girl Place, 105
American International Security, 57
American Museum of Natural
   History, 105, 146
American Youth Dance Theater, 114
Angier-Clark, Julie, 243
Applebaum, Harold, 192
Apthrorp Pharmacy, 80
art classes, 112–14
The Art Farm in the City, 86
Arthur books, 236
ARTKIDS, 113
Art-N-Orbit, 113
Arturo's Pizzeria, 131
Asphalt Green, 86, 111, 120, 122
Astor Place Hair Designers, 154
At Daddy's on Saturdays (Girard),
   239
audiocassettes and cds, 244–45
au pairs, 59–60

B

Babar's Bath Book, 235
Baby Book, The (Sears and Sears),
   240
baby books, 234–36
BabyBucks Card, 164
Baby Buggy, 189
baby carriers, 181
baby clothing, 196–215
Baby Depot, 183–84
Baby Fingers, 86–87
baby furniture and accessories,
   172–93
   see also baby's room; specific
   furniture and accessories
babyGap, 198
baby monitors, 181–82
Baby Moves Boutique, 198
baby nurses/doulas, 26, 29–30, 50,
   51–52
Baby Om, 41, 99
baby proofing, 192–93
*Baby's First Months "What Do We
   Do Now?"*, 244
baby-sitters, 61–63
baby's room, 174, 189–91
baby swings, 178
Baby Talk, 249
Baby Time Chef, 45
The Baby and Toy Superstore, 188
Babywatch, 58
backpacks, 181
Ballet Academy East, 114
balloons and decorations, 149–50
Bally Total Fitness, 34
Bambalulus, 199
Bambini, 198
Bank Street Bookstore, 230
Barking Dog Luncheonette, 126
Barnes, Mary Ryan, 39
Barnes and Noble, 105, 136, 230
The Barnes Method, 39
Barneys New York, 166, 198
Barney videos and dvds, 242, 245

Barren Hospital Medical Center, 81
Bartel, Joanie, 246
The Baseball Center NYC, 121
bassinets, 172–73
bath books, 235–36
bathrooms, public, 136–38
bathtubs/bath seats, 180
Battery Park, 102–3
Bauer, Nina, 162
A Bear's Place, 221
BeautifulCookies.com, 150
Bella Zander, 185
Bellini, 185–86
Belly Basics Survival Kit, 164
Benihana, 130
Bergman, Jennifer, 218
Best Domestic Placement, 54
Beth Israel Hospital, 16, 20, 67, 76
Be Yoga, 40–41, 99
Beyond Birth, 51
Big Apple Kids, 123
Big Apple Parent, 249
Big City Moms, 75
Bilek, Jennifer, 155
birth announcements, 140–43
birth attendants, 12–16
Birth Balance, 26–27
birthday cookies and cakes, 150–54
Birthday Express, 150
birthday parties, 143–54
birthing centers, 19
The Birthing Center, 19
birth place, 16–23
B.K.S. Iyengar Yoga Association, 122
Blacker & Kooby, 141
Bloomingdale's, 199
Bloomingdale School of Music, 87,
   117
Blue Bench, 186
board books, 234–35
Boat Pond, 100
Bobby Doo-Wah, 147
Body by Baby, 34
Bodyscapes, Inc., 210–11

Bohne's Baby Nursing, 51
Bonpoint, 199
Bookberries, 230
books, 232–41
    baby, 234–36
    for parents, 239–42
Books of Wonder, 231
bookstores, 230–32
booster seats/hook-on seats, 179–80
Borders Books & Music, 231
bouncy seats, 178
Boynton, Sandra, 235
Bradley Method, 24, 26–29
breastfeeding:
    books on, 204
    supplies for, 80–81
    support groups for, 76–77
Breastfeeding: The Nursing Mother's Problem Solver (Martin and Krebs), 240
Breastfeeding Book, The (Sears), 240
The Breastfeeding Salon, 76–77
The Bridge for Dance, 114
Bright Horizons Center, 60
Broadway Babies, 87
Broadway Dance Center, 114
Broadway Diner, 130
Bronx Zoo, 105
Brown Bear, Brown Bear, What Do You See? (Martin and Carle), 23
Bu & The Duck, 199–200
Bubby's, 132
Burns, Barry, 158
Bus Stops (Gomi), 238
Buy Buy Baby, 184, 188

C

Caban, Beth Donnelly, 39
Cadeau Maternity, 166
Cakes 'N' Shapes, Ltd., 151
California Pizza Kitchen, 126
Caligor Pharmacy, 80
CALYPSO Enfant, 200
Campbell Music Studio, 117–18

Campo, Colleen K., 70
Carapan, 42
Care Check, 58–59
caregivers, 48–63
Carl Schurz Park, 101
Carmine's, 133
Carmine Street Recreation Center, 111
carriages/strollers, 175–77
car seats, 177–78
Catimini, 200
C.A.T.S. (Children's Athletic Training School), 87
CBK Cookies of New York, 151
CBS Midwifery, Inc., 16
celebrating "big firsts," 140–62
Central Park, 148–49, 100–101
Central Park Zoo, 99, 101, 146
Central Presbyterian Church, 88
Century 21, 200
changing tables, 175
Charm and Whimsy, 189
Chateau Drug, 80
Chat 'n' Chew, 131
Chelsea Piers, 88, 111, 120
Chelsea Piers Gymnastics, 144
Chelsea's Kids Quarter, 186
Cherry's Pharmacy, 80
Child, 249
childbirth educational resources, 25–30
childbirth methods, 24–25
Child Care Inc., 61
The Children's General Store, 221–22
Children's Museum of Manhattan, 105–6
Children's Museum of the Arts, 106
The Children's Place, 200
The Children's Studio, 88
Children's Tumbling, 88–89
Child's Play, 88
Chinaberry Book Service, 246
China Fun, 126–27

China Institute in America, 123
Chinese Folk Dance Company, 115
Choiceful Birth and Parenting, 26
A Choice Nanny, 54
Choices for Childbirth, 28, 40
Choosing Quality Child Care, 245
Church Street School for Music and Art, 89, 118
Chuse, Ellen, 25
Circus Gymnastics, 89, 121, 144
classes:
    for children, see after-school programs
    for parents, see parenting classes
Classic Toys, 222
Clements, Màrie, 76
Click, Clack, Moo: Cows That Type (Cronin), 234
Clifford books, 236
cloth books, 235
clothing:
    baby, 196–215
    catalogs, 246–48
    maternity, 164–69
Clown Magic Party Entertainment, 147
C.O. Bigelow Apothecaries, 81
Cocoa Crayon, 191
coffee bars, 135–36
Columbia Presbyterian Hospital, 20, 67
Columbus Gym, 89, 121
Complete Book of Breastfeeding, The (Eiger and Olds), 240
computer classes, 122
Constructive Playthings, 246
convertible car seats, 177
cooking classes, 120
Cooper, Jill M., 141, 148
Core Fitness, 34–35
Corner Bookstore, 231
co-sleepers, 173
costumes, 226–27
Counting Kisses (Katz), 234

Cowgirl Hall of Fame, 131
Cozy's Cuts for Kids, 154–55, 222
CPR classes, 68–69
CPR To Save Your Child or Baby, 245
The Craft Studio, 144
Creative Cakes, 151
Cremebebe, 201
cribs, 173–75, 198
Crumbs, 151
Cry Baby Matinee, 75
Cupcake Cafe, 151
Curious George books, 237
Cute Toonz, 222

D

Daffy's, 201
Dahesh Museum of Art, 106
Dallas BBQ, 133
dance classes, 114–17
Dance for Children, 115
David Barton, 34
day-care centers, 60–61
Dean & Deluca, 152
DeCamp, Leanne, 90, 147
De Vault, Nicole, 122–23
Diamond, Joanne, 44
Diana Ross Playground, 100
diaper bags, 812
diaper services, 79
Didi's Children's Boutique, 222
Diller-Quaile School of Music, 89,
    118
Dinosaur Hill, 222
Dinosaurs Divorce (Brown), 239
Discovery Programs, 90, 111
Disney Catalog of Children's
    Clothing, 247
Disney videos and dvds, 242–43
Divalysscious Moms, 75
Djoniba Dance and Drum Center,
    115
Documents Reference Check, 57
Domestic Job Picks, 55
Do Re Mi, 90

Doula Care, 51
doulas, see baby nurses/doulas
Doulas of North America, 29–30
Downtown Babies, 68
drama classes, 117
The Drama Zone, 117
Drapacz, Nina, 160
Drillings, Fern, 26, 68
*Dr. Jane Morton's Guide to
    Successful Breastfeeding*, 244
Dr. Seuss books, 237
DT:UT, 135
Duane Park, 103
Dylan's Candy Bar, 75, 126
Dynasty Tailors, 165

E

E.A.J. Gifts, 222–23
The Early Childhood Development
    Center, 70
The Early Ear, 90
East 96th Street Playground,
    100–101
East River Park, 101
East Side Kids Inc., 156
Eating the Alphabet (Ehlert), 239
Ecobaby Organics, Inc., 247
Educational Alliance Parenting and
    Family Center, 71, 79, 90
Eileen Fisher, 166–67
EJ's Luncheonette, 133
Eli's Vinegar Factory, 144–45
Elizabeth Bing Center for Parents,
    70
Ellen's Stardust Diner, 130
Elm Drugs, 81
emergencies hotlines, 77
entertainment:
    for kids and moms, 84–107
    for new mothers, 74–75
Equinox, 35
etiquette lessons, 122–23
Everyone Poops (Gomi), 236–37
Evie's Organic Edibles, 45

Excellent Paper Place, 142
exercise, 32–38
    prenatal, 32–41
    videos and dvds, 244–45
    see also massage; spas; yoga
Exhale Spa, 69, 73–74
Expectant Parenting Seminars, 27

F

Fairway Cafe, 128
Falk Drug, 80
Fallin, Tara, 28
Family Music Center, 118
FAO Schwarz, 136, 223
Favin, Laura, 42
Fill-R-Up Gift Baskets, 192
Firehouse, 128
*Fire Safety for Kids with Beasel the
    Easel*, 245
First & Second Cousin New and
    Resale Children's Shop, 212
First Two Years, The, 244
Fiske, Mary Lynn, 26
fitness and health clubs, 33–38
flora and henri, 201
Flower Girl, 152
food delivery, 45
Food Trainers, 44–45
Fox Agency, 51, 55
Framex, 158
Frances Stuart Agency, 51, 54
Fred's, 129
Free To Be Under Three, 91
The French-American Conservatory
    of Music, 118
Fritzi Kallop's Birth Book (Kallop), 24
Fun 'n' Fit programs, 97
Funworks for Kids, 91
Futurekids Computer Learning
    Center, 122

G

Gabriela's, 129
Games Babies Play (Hagstrom and

Morrill), 240
Geddes, Anne, 235
Gepetto's Toy Box, 223
gift items, 191–92
Girlfriends' Guide to Toddlers, The (Iovine), 241
Giving Tree, The (Silverstein), 237
gliders, 175
Going to the Potty (Rogers), 237
Goldberger's Pharmacy, 80
Goldman, Victoria, 241
Goodnight, Gorilla (Rathmann), 238
Goodnight Moon (Brown), 237
Goodson Parker Wellness Center, 122
Googie's, 127
Gordon Novelty, 227
GotCPR, 68–69
Go To Baby, 191
Grace's Market Place, 152
Gracious Home, 189
Grandfather Twilight (Berger), 236
Gravity Fitness & Spa, 46
Great Feet, 156
Greenhouse Agency, 55
Greenhouse Spa, 46
Greenstones, 201–2
Greenwich House, 115, 118–19, 120
Grilled Cheese NYC, 132
Guess How Much I Love You (Mcbratney and Jeram), 238
Gymboree, 202
gymnastics programs, 120–21
Gymtime/Rhythm and Glues, 91, 113, 121, 145

H

haircuts, 154–56
The Hair's Castle, 155
Halek, Judith Elaine, 25, 26–27
Halloween Adventure, 227
Hamburger Harry's, 130
H&M, 167, 202
Hands On! A Musical Experience,

Inc., 91–92
Hanna Andersson, 247
Hard Rock Cafe, 135
Harold and the Purple Crayon (Johnson), 237
Harry's Shoes, 156–57
Hi Art!, 113
high chairs, 179
high risk pregnancies, 15, 19
Hi Life Bar and Grill, 127
Hippo Park Playground, 102
Hollywood Pop Gallery, 147
Hom Boms, 223
HomeFront Kids, 148
home organizers, 45–46
Homestep, 59
hospitals, 20–23
    classes at, 18, 19, 24, 67–68
    common questions about, 18
    costs of stay in, 17–18
    evaluating, 16, 18
    LDR rooms, 16–17, 18
    midwives on staff of, 19
    nursery levels of, 19
hotlines and support groups, 76–79
How to Calm and Soothe Your Baby (Karp), 240
How to Take Great Trips with Your Kids (Portnoy and Portnoy), 241
Hudson River Park Playground, 102
Hudson Street Papers, 141
Hugh Park Stationers, 141

I

Ibiza Kidz, 157, 202
I'd Rather Laugh (Richman), 239
Il Vagabondo, 127
Imagine Swimming, 92
In a Family Way, 51
indoor play space, 104
Infant and Toddler Emergency First Aid, 245
In Grandma's Attic, 115
In Praise of Single Parents

(Alexander), 241
Integral Yoga Institute, 39, 231
Iyengar Yoga Institute of New York, 39–40

J

Jacadi, 202–3
Jackson Hole Burgers, 133
James J. Walker Park, 103
James Michael Levin Playground, 100
Jami Beere Photography, 159
Jamie Ostrow, 141
Jamrog, Sandra, 71
JAMS, 92
Jane Fonda's Pregnancy, Birth, and Recovery, 244
Jane's Exchange, 212
Janovic Plaza, 189–90
JBB Midwifery, 28
Jean-Baptiste, Martine, 28
Jekyll & Hyde, 135
Jelly Bean Maternity and Children, 167
Jesse Bear, Jesse Bear, What You Will Wear (Carlstrom), 239
Jewish Community Center, 27, 35, 71, 92, 111–12, 113
Jivamukti Yoga Center, 40
Jodi's Gym, 92, 121, 145
jogging strollers, 176
John Jay Park, 101
John's Pizzeria, 134
JordanElyse Photography, 159
Josephina, 129
Joseph Pharmacy, 81
Judy Lasko Modern Dance, 116
Judy's Fancies, 211
Judy Stevens Playgroup, 93
Julian & Sara, 203
Just for Tykes, 186
Just Like You (Fearnley), 235
Juvenile Products Manufacturers Association (JPMA), 173, 175

city baby new york

K

Kallop, Fritzi, 24, 26
K & T birth announcements, 140
Kao, Brian, 158
Karin Alexis, 187
Karma Yoga, 41
Kate Burton Photography, 159–60
Kate Engelbrecht Photography, 160
Kate's Paperie, 141–42
Kathy Smith's Pregnancy Workout, 245
KB Toys, 223–24
Kendall's Closet, 203
Kidding Around, 224
Kid O, 224
Kidrobot, 224
Kids at Art, 114
Kids Book to Welcome a New Baby (Collman), 241
Kids Co-Motion, 93, 116
Kids Cuts, 155
Kids Digs, 190
Kid's Supply Store Co., 187
Kidstown, 203
Kid View, 59
Kidville, 46, 93
Kinderdance, 116
Kindermusik, 93–94
Kings Pharmacy, 81
Kiss Good Night (Hest and Jeram), 236
Klein, Rachel, 161
Klein, Risa Lynn, 28
Koh's Kids, 203
Kolodner, Arnie, 147
Kornbluh, Jane, 38
Krug, Ellen, 26

L

LaBella, Phyllis, 74
labor delivery rooms (LDR), 16–17, 18
La Cocina, 134
La Croisette French Language Center, 123
lactation consultants, 29, 76–77
   see also breastfeeding
Lady with the Alligator Purse (Westcott), 238
La Escuelita, 123
Lafayette Bakery, 152
La Layette...Et Plus Ltd., 203–4
La Leche League, 76, 240
Lamaze consultants and classes, 24, 26–29
language courses, 123
Language Workshop for Children, 94, 123
La Petite Etoile, 207
Laura Beth's Baby Collection, 142, 190
Lauren Wittels, 142
layettes, 197–99
Lee, Jennifer, 159
Lenox Hill Bookstore, 231
Lenox Hill Hospital, 21
Lerner, Ana, 38
Les Petits Chapelais, 204
Lester's, 157, 204
Let's Talk About It: Divorce (Rogers), 239
Levine, Peggy, 37
Life Sport Gymnastics, 94, 121
Lifetimes: The Beautiful Way to Explain Death to Children (Mellonie), 239
Lili's Noodle Shop and Grill, 127
Lilliput SoHo Kids, 204
Lilly's Kids, 247
Lincoln Stationers, 142
Linda Kaye's Birthday Bakers Partymakers, 145–46
Little Engine That Could, The (Piper), 237
Little Eric, 157
Little Extras, 142, 224
Little Folks, 81, 204
Little Follies, 211
Little Maestros, 94, 147
Little Spot board books (Hill), 234
Liz Lange Maternity, 167
L. L. Bean Inc., 247
Logos Bookstore, 231–32
The London Agency, 55
Lord & Taylor, 205
Louie's Westside Cafe, 129
Love A Lot Preschool, 61
The Lucy Moses School for Music and Dance, 94, 116

M

McBurney YMCA, 99
Macy's, 137, 205
Madeleine the Magician, 147
Madeline (Bemelmans), 237
magazines for parents, 248–49
Magical Marion, 147
Magic Windows, 205
Magnolia Bakery, 152
Make Way for Ducklings (McCloskey), 238
malls, 212–15
Mamallama Munch, 75
Mama Nurture, 27, 95
Manhattan Ballet School, 116
Manhattan Directory of Private Nursery Schools, 161
Manhattan Family Guide to Private Schools, The (Goldman and Hausman), 241
Marcia the Musical Moose, 147
Margarita Moms gatherings, 38
Mars 2112, 135
Martin, Gayatri, 28–29, 39, 40
Mary Ann Hall's Music for Children, 94–95, 119
Mary Arnold Toys, 224–25
massage, 41–43
Maternal Fitness, 35–36
Maternity Basics, 167
maternity clothing, 164–69
   alternative stores for, 165

rentals, 164
    stores for, 165–69
Maternity Works Outlet, 168
MB Discount Furniture, 190
Mechaber, Allyson, 44
Medela Lactina, 80
Medical Massage Group, 41, 43
Metropolitan Cafe, 130
Metropolitan Moms, 74
Metropolitan Museum of Art, 106
Meyer, Carolyn, 69
Michele, Karen, 159
Michele Saint-Laurent, 168
Mickey Mantle's, 135
Midwifery Services, Inc., 16
midwives, 15–16, 19
The Miette Culinary Studio, 120
Mimi Maternity, 168
Mindful Parenting, 69, 73–74
Mind Your Business, 59
Miracle Grill, 131
Miriam Goodman, 81
The Mixing Bowl, 95
Mommy and Me programs, 84–99
Mommy and Me The Greenwich
    Village Center, 95
More Than a Moms Group, 70
Motherhood Maternity, 168–69
Mother Massage and More, 42–43
Mother Nurture, 51–52
Mother's Almanac (Kelly and
    Parsons), 240
Mothers and Menus, 45
Mount Sinai Medical Center, 21, 67,
    69
Mozart for Children, 119
Mr. Baby Proofer, 245
Mr Baby Proofer video, 192
Mrs. John L. Strong, 142
Museum Adventures NYC, 113
Music, Fun & Learning, 119
Musical Kids, 96
music classes, 117–20
Music Together, 95–96

My Child's Best Friend, 55, 62
My Most Favorite Dessert Company,
    153
My Very First Mother Goose (Opie),
    236

n
Nancy Pindrus Photography, 160
nannies, 52–59
    checking references of, 57
    employer tax and insurance
    responsibilities for, 59
    getting started with, 58–59
    interviewing of, 56–57
    placing ads for, 52–54
Nannies Plus, 55
National AIDS Hotline, 77
National Association of Mothers
    Centers, 77
The Natural Baby Catalog, 247
New Mommies Netork, 72–73
New Mom/Newborn circle, 26
New Mother Luncheons, 72
new mothers, motherhood:
    adjusting to, 66–81
    classes for, 66–74
    entertainment for, 74–75
    hotlines and support for, 76–79
    important supplies for, 79–81
New Parents' Get Together at 92nd
    Street Y, 71–72
newspaper classifieds, 52–54
New York City Explorers, 63
New York Coalition for
    Transportation Safety, 177
New York County Medical Society,
    13
New York Doll Hospital, 225
New York Family, 249
New York Firefighter's Friend, 225
New York Foundling Hospital Crisis
    Intervention Nursery, 77
New York Health & Racquetball
    Club, 36, 122

New York Hospital/Cornell Medical
    Center, 67
New York Independent Schools
    Directory, 161
New York Kids Club, 96
New York's 50 Best Places to Take
    Children (Ishac), 241
New York Sketches.com, 148
New York Sports Club, 36
New York State Dietetic Association,
    44
New York Swims, 96
New York University Medical Center,
    22, 67, 81
New York Yoga, 99
Nick's, 127
92nd Street Y, 36, 71–72, 98–99,
    112, 162
NoHo Star, 132
nursery levels, at hospitals, 19
Nursing Mothers Companion, The,
    245
nutrition, 43–45
nutritionists, 44–45
NY Presbyterian Hospital, 21–22

o
obstetricians, 12–15
    interview questions for, 13–14
    specializing in high risk pregnan-
    cies, 15
The Odeon, 132–33
Oilily, 205
Old Navy, 169, 206
Olivia books, 238
Ollie's Noodle Shop & Grille, 134
Once Upon a Baby, 96
One Step Ahead, 247
Only Perfect Parties, 148
Opaline Cafe, 106
OshKosh B'Gosh, 247–48
Our Name Is Mud, 146
Overachieving Parents and
    Underachieving Children

(Bodenburg), 241
Over the Moon: An Adoption Tale
    (Katz), 239
Oxenbury, Helen, 235

P

Paint Your World, 191
Pamela Scurry's Wicker Garden, 187
Papa d'Anja, 211
Papyrus Cards & Stationery, 142–43
The Parent Child Center, 69
Parent Guide, 249
Parenting and Family Life, 248
parenting classes:
    for CPR, 68–69
    at hospitals, 18, 19, 24, 67–68
    for new mothers, 66–74
    see also childbirth educational
        resources
Parenting Horizons, 69–70
The Parenting Program, 73
Parents, 249
*Parent's Guide to Baby and Child
    Medical Care, The* (Hart), 240
*Parent's Guide to New York City's
    Best Public Elementary Schools,
    The* (Hemphill), 241
Parent's League Toddler Book, 73
The Parent's League, 73, 110, 144,
    161–62
Parents Without Partners, 77
parks, 100–103
    see also specific parks
Parks Department, N.Y., 99–100, 148
Party City, 150
party favors, 148
Party Gifts by BETHiE, 148
party places and entertainment,
    144–48
Party Poopers, 146
Patagonia, 206, 248
Patsy's, 134
Pat the Bunny (Kunhardt), 238
Pat the Cat (Kunhardt), 238

Pat the Puppy (Kunhardt), 238
Paul Molé Haircutters, 155
Pavillion Agency, 55
A Pea in the Pod, 165–66
Peanut Butter & Co., 132
Peanut Butter and Jane, 206
pediatricians, 48–50
    interview questions for, 49–50
*Pediatrician's Best Baby Planner for
    the First Year of Life, The* (Dubner
    and Felch), 240
Peek-A-Boo (Olmerod), 239
Penny Whistle Toys, 225
Peress, Debby, 38
The Perfect Cake, 153
Perfectly Safe, 248
A Perfect Portrait, 158
Perichild Program, 116
personal enrichment programs,
    122–23
Personalize it!, 141, 148
Peter Rabbit books, 236, 237
Petit Bateau, 206–7
photographs, 158–61
Pinch Sitters, 63
Plain Jane, 190–91
Planet Hollywood, 135
Planet Kids, 81, 184, 207
Play Fair Toys, 248
playgrounds, 99–103
    see also parks; specific play-
        grounds and parks
playpens/portable cribs, 180
Poison Hotline, 77
Popover Cafe, 129
pottery classes, 120
*Practical Parenting for the 21st
    Century* (Ross), 240
Practical Parenting Tips (Lansky), 240
pregnancy:
    common tests during, 14–15
    nutrition during, 33, 43–45
premature infants, support groups
    for parents of, 77

prenatal classes, *see* parenting classes
prenatal exercise, 32–41
    see also exercise
Prenatal Massage Center, 43
Prenatal Yoga Center, 41, 99
preschool books, 236–37
preschools, 161–62
Prince and Princess, 207
private boutiques, 210–11
private trainers, 38
Professional Nannies Institute, 55
Promises Fulfilled, 225
P.S. 40 playground, 13
P.S. 87 Playground, 102
public bathrooms, 136–38
public libraries, 103–4
Pure Power Boot Camp, 37

Q

Quiet Touch, 42

R

Raffi, 245–46
Ralph Lauren, 207
Realbirth, 25, 26
Rebecca Kelly Dance Studio, 116
Rebecca Moss, Ltd., 143
Reebok Sports Club NY/Sports Club
    LA, 37, 87, 97, 113, 122
Reel Moms, 75
resale shops, 211–12
restaurants, kid-friendly, 126–36
    theme, 134–35
    see also coffee bars
Rhinelander Children's Center, 72,
    96–97, 112
Ricklen, Neil, 235
Right Start catalog, 80
River Run Playground, 102
Riverside Park, playgrounds of, 102
Rizzoli Bookstore, 232
Robin Kellner Agency, 55
Robin's Nest, 207
Rockstarbaby, 208

Room and Board, 187
Room to Grow, 189
Roosevelt Hospital, 22–23, 25, 67, 81
Rosenbaum, Alice, 69
Ruby Foo's, 129
Rustic Playground, 99

S

safety videos, 245
St. Catherine's Playground, 101–2
St. Jean's Community Center, 87
St. Luke's Hospital, 23, 68, 81
St. Vincent's Hospital and Medical Center, 23, 68
Saks Fifth Avenue, 208
Samalin, Nancy, 74
Sambuca, 129–30
Sarah Merians Photography & Company, 161
Save-A-Lot, 69
Scandinavia House, 106–7
Scarry, Richard, 243
Schneider's, 184
The Scholastic Store, 232
The School for Education in Dance and Related Arts, 115
The School for Strings, 119
Schuman, Lisa, 74
A Second Chance, 166
Send in the Clowns, 148
Sendrey, Paloma, 160
Serendipity 3, 127–28
Sesame Street:
    audiocassettes and cds, 246
    books, 235–36
    videos and dvds, 243
7 O'Clock Bedtime, The (Schaenen), 241
74th Street Magic, 97, 112, 146–47
Shake, Rhythm and Roll, 117
Shakespeare and Company, 232
Sherman, Gail, 159
shoes, 156–57

Shoofly, 157
Silk, Elizabeth, 73
Silly Billy, 148
Silly Sally (Wood), 239
Simkin, Diana, 28, 37, 38
Single Mother's Book, The (Anderson), 241
single parent support groups, 77–78
Sitter City, 55–56, 63
Slayton, Lauren, 44–45
Small Change, 208
Smart Parents' Guide to Kids T.V., The (Chen), 241
SmartStart, 191
Snowy Day (Keats), 238
The Soho Parenting Center, 70
Sokol New York Gym, 97, 121
Sol Goldman YM-YWHA, 71, 79, 90
The Soundings, 116
Soutine, 153
Space Kiddets, 208
spas, 46
special events, 107
special interest books, 241
special needs children:
    books for, 239
    support groups for parents of, 78–79
Spector Playground, 100
sports training classes, 121
Spot books, 236
Spot videos and dvds, 242
Spring Flowers, 208–9
SQC, 128
Stamford Town Center, 215
Starbucks, 135–36
State News, 150
Steps on Broadway, 117
stores:
    baby clothing, 198–210
    baby furniture and accessories, 183–88
    for books, 230–32
    in malls, 212–15

maternity clothing for, 165–69
    superstores outside NYC, 188
    for toys, 221–26
The Strand Bookstore, 232
Strollercize, 38
Suba Pharmacy, 81
Successful Breastfeeding (Dana and Price), 240
The Sunshine Kids' Club, 97
SuperCuts, 155–56
Super Soccer Stars, 121
superstores, 188
support groups, see hotlines and support groups
Swim Jim, 98
swimming lessons, 121–22
Sydney's Playground, 104
Sylvia Weinstock Cakes, 153

T

Take Me to the Water, 98, 122
Talbots Kids & Babies, 209, 248
Tardio, Marcy Perlman, 29
Tartine et Chocolate, 209
Taub-Dix, Bonnie, 45
The Techno Team, 122
Tell Me Again About the Night I Was Born (Curtis), 239
Tennessee Mountain, 132
10, 9, 8 (Bang), 239
Terson, Mikelle, 40
Third Street Music School Settlement, 120
Thomas the Tank Engine series, 235
Tidy Diapers, 79
Tiffany & Co., 137, 143
Tigers, Tutu's & Toes, 209
Time for Bed (Fox and Dyer), 236
Timmerman Pharmacy, 80
Tip Top Kids, 157
toddlers, books for, 241
Tony's Di Napoli, 128
Tot-Saver, 69
Touchpoints video series, 244

city baby new york

Town and Country, 56
toys, 218–26
    age-specific, 218–21
    stores for, 221–26
Toys "R" Us, 185, 226
Toys to Grow On, 248
Treanor, Tom, 192
Troll's Learn & Play, 248
trunk shows, 210–11
Tumble Town, 98, 121
"Tupler Technique" exercises, 35–36
Turtle Bay Music School, 98, 120
Tutti Bambini, 209
25 Things Every New Mother Should Know (Sears and Sears), 240
Twins from Conception to Five Years (Clegg and Woolett), 241
Twins Magazine, 249
twins/multiples support groups, 78
Two Boots, 131–32

U

umbilical cord blood, 30
umbrella strollers, 176
Union Square Park, 103
The Upper Breast Side, 188
Uptown Mommies, 74

V

Vanderbilt YMCA, 38, 99
Veniero Pasticceria, 153
Venture Stationers, 143
Veronique Delachaux, 169

Very Hungry Caterpillar, The (Carle), 238
Viacord, 30
videos and dvds, 242–45

W

Washington Square Park, 103
water labor and birth, 25, 27
We Adopted You, Benjamin Koo (Girard), 239
Weinberg, Susan, 191
Weiss, Elana, 41
Weiss, Robin, 191
Weisshappel, Sonya, 45–46
Wellcare Center, 29
Wellpath, 42
Wendy Hillard Foundation-Rhythmic Gymnastic NY, 121
West Park Presbyterian Church, 86
West Side Dance Project, 117
West Side Kids, 226
What Every Baby Knows--A Guide to Pregnancy, 244
What's Heaven? (Shriver), 239
What to Eat When You're Expecting, 43
What to Expect the First Year (Eisenberg, Murkoff, and Hathaway), 240
What to Expect When You're Expecting (Murkoff), 43
When a Pet Dies (Rogers), 239
When Dinosaurs Die (Brown), 239

Where the Wild Things Are (Sendak), 238
Whipper Snippers, 156
William Greenberg Desserts, 153–54
Winnie the Pooh videos and dvds, 243
Womanly Art of Breastfeeding, The, 240
Working Mother, 249

Y

YMCA, YWCA, 38, 99
    see also specific branches
yoga, 38–41, 99
Yoga for Two, 39, 99
Your Amazing Newborn (Klaus and Kennell), 240
Your Baby--A Video Guide to Care and Understanding with Penelope Leach, 244
Your Baby's First Three Years (Kelly), 240
Your One-Year-Old to Your Four-Year-Old series (Ames and Ilg), 241
YoyaMart, 191

Z

Z'Baby Company, 210
Zitomer, 210
Zittles, 226

neighborhood index

Bronx, Bronx Zoo, 105
Brooklyn, MB Discount Furniture, 190

Central Park:

Adventure Playground, 100
Alice in Wonderland Statue, 100
Boat Pond, 100
Carousel, 101, 149
Diana Ross Playground, 100
East 96th Street Playground, 100–101
The Great Lawn, 149
James Michael Levin Playground, 100
Sheep Meadow, 100, 149
Spector Playground, 100
Strawberry Fields, 100, 149
Zoo, 99, 101, 146

Chelsea/Flatiron:

ABC Carpet & Home, 137, 185
Abracadabra Superstore, 226–27
America, 130–31
Baby Depot, 183–84
Bally Total Fitness, 34
Bed, Bath and Beyond, 137
B.K.S. Iyengar Yoga Association, 122
Bodyscapes, Inc., 210–11
Books of Wonder, 231
Buy Buy Baby, 184, 188
Carapan, 42
Chat 'n' Chew, 131
Chelsea Piers, 88, 111, 120

Chelsea Piers Gymnastics, 144
Chelsea's Kids Quarter, 186
David Barton, 34
Djoniba Dance and Drum Center, 115
Epiphany Branch Library, 104
Gordon Novelty, 227
Iyengar Yoga Institute of New York, 39–40
Jamie Ostrow, 141
Kidding Around, 224
Maternal Fitness, 35–36
Pure Power Boot Camp, 37
Realbirth, 25, 26
Room to Grow, 189
Schneider's, 184
Space Kiddets, 208

Downtown:

Abingdon Square Park, 103
Barren Hospital Medical Center, 81
Battery Park, 102–3
Bella Zander, 185
Blue Bench, 186
Carmine Street Recreation Center, 111
Century 21, 200
Children's Tumbling, 88–89
Chinese Folk Dance Company, 115
Church Street School for Music and Art, 89, 118
C.O. Bigelow Apothecaries, 81
Dance for Children, 115
DT:UT, 135

Duane Park, 103
Elm Drugs, 81
Equinox, 35
Hudson Park Branch Library, 104
Hudson River Park Playground, 102
Judy Stevens Playgroup, 93
Kings Pharmacy, 81
Little Folks, 81, 204
Love A Lot Preschool, 61
Miriam Goodman, 81
P.S. 40 playground, 13
Shoofly, 157
Sydney's Playground, 104
Whipper Snippers, 156

East Side:

After-School Art, Inc., 112–13
Aha! Learning Partners, 85–86
American Girl Place, 105
American Youth Dance Theater, 114
The Art Farm in the City, 86
Asphalt Green, 86, 111, 120, 122
Ballet Academy East, 114
Bally Total Fitness, 34
Bambini, 198
Barking Dog Luncheonette, 126
A Bear's Place, 221
Bellini, 185–86
Benihana, 130
Blacker & Kooby, 141
Bloomingdale's, 199
Bonpoint, 199
Bookberries, 230
Borders Books & Music, 231

Bright Horizons Center, 60
Broadway Babies, 87
Broadway Diner, 130
California Pizza Kitchen, 126
Caligor Pharmacy, 80
Campbell Music Studio, 117–18
Carl Schurz Park, 101
Catimini, 200
CBK Cookies of New York, 151
Central Presbyterian Church, 88
Cherry's Pharmacy, 80
The Children's General Store,
    221–22
The Children's Studio, 88
Child's Play, 88
China Fun, 126–27
China Institute in America, 123
Core Fitness, 34–35
Corner Bookstore, 231
Cozy's Cuts for Kids, 154–55, 222
The Craft Studio, 144
Creative Cakes, 151
Crumbs, 151
Cry Baby Matinee, 75
Cute Toonz, 222
Dahesh Museum of Art, 106
David Barton, 34
Dean & Deluca, 152
Didi's Children's Boutique, 222
Diller-Quaile School of Music, 89, 118
Do Re Mi, 90
The Drama Zone, 117
DT:UT, 135
Dylan's Candy Bar, 75, 126
E.A.J. Gifts, 222–23
The Early Childhood Development
    Center, 70
The Early Ear, 90
East River Park, 101
East Side Kids Inc., 156
EJ's Luncheonette, 133
Eli's Vinegar Factory, 144–45
Equinox, 35
Exhale Spa, 69, 73–74

Falk Drug, 80
FAO Schwarz, 136, 223
Fill-R-Up Gift Baskets, 192
flora and henri, 201
Funworks for Kids, 91
Futurekids Computer Learning
    Center, 122
Goldberger's Pharmacy, 80
Goodson Parker Wellness Center, 122
Googie's, 127
Go To Baby, 191
Grace's Market Place, 152
Gracious Home, 189
Great Feet, 156
Gymtime/Rhythm and Glues, 91,
    113, 121, 145
The Hair's Castle, 155
Hands On! A Musical Experience,
    Inc., 91–92
Hom Boms, 223
Hugh Park Stationers, 141
Il Vagabondo, 127
Jacadi, 202–3
Jane's Exchange, 212
Janovic Plaza, 189–90
Jivamukti Yoga Center, 40
Jodi's Gym, 92, 121, 145
John Jay Park, 101
John's Pizzeria, 134
Kate's Paperie, 141–42
KB Toys, 223–24
Kids at Art, 114
Kids Cuts, 155
Kid's Supply Store Co., 187
Kidville, 46, 93
La Layette...Et Plus Ltd., 203–4
Language Workshop for Children,
    94, 123
La Petite Etoile, 207
Laura Beth's Baby Collection, 142,
    190
Lenox Hill Bookstore, 231
Lenox Hill Hospital, 21
Lester's, 157, 204

Lili's Noodle Shop and Grill, 127
Linda Kaye's Birthday Bakers
    Partymakers, 145–46
Little Eric, 157
Little Follies, 211
Little Maestros, 94, 147
Liz Lange Maternity, 167
Logos Bookstore, 231–32
Magic Windows, 205
Manhattan Ballet School, 116
Mary Ann Hall's Music for Children,
    94–95, 119
Mary Arnold Toys, 224–25
Medical Massage Group, 41, 43
Metropolitan Cafe, 130
Metropolitan Museum of Art, 106
Michele Saint-Laurent, 168
Mimi Maternity, 168
Mindful Parenting, 69, 73–74
The Mixing Bowl, 95
Mount Sinai Medical Center, 21, 67, 69
Music, Fun & Learning, 119
Musical Kids, 96
New Mother Luncheons, 72
New York Doll Hospital, 225
New York Hospital/Cornell Medical
    Center, 67
New York Presbyterian Hospital,
    21–22
Nick's, 127
92nd Street Y, 36, 71–72, 98–99,
    112, 162
96th Street Library, 103
Oilily, 205
Our Name Is Mud, 146
Pamela Scurry's Wicker Garden, 187
Papyrus Cards & Stationery, 142–43
Parenting Horizons, 69–70
The Parenting Program, 73
The Parent's League, 73, 110, 144,
    161–62
The Parent Child Center, 69
Paul Molé Haircutters, 155
A Pea in the Pod, 165–66

Petit Bateau, 206–7
Prince and Princess, 207
Promises Fulfilled, 225
Ralph Lauren, 207
Rebecca Moss, Ltd., 143
Reebok Sports Club NY/Sports Club
    LA, 37, 87, 97, 113, 122
Rhinelander Children's Center, 72,
    96–97, 112
Robin's Nest, 207
Rustic Playground, 99
St. Agnes Branch Library, 104
St. Catherine's Playground, 101–2
St. Jean's Community Center, 87
Saks Fifth Avenue, 208
Save-A-Lot, 69
Scandinavia House, 106–7
A Second Chance, 166
Serendipity 3, 127–28
74th Street Magic, 97, 112, 146–47
Shakespeare and Company, 232
67th Street Library, 103
Small Change, 208
Sokol New York Gym, 97, 121
Spring Flowers, 208–9
State News, 150
The Sunshine Kids' Club: A
    Preschool of Music, 97
Talbots Kids & Babies, 209, 248
Tartine et Chocolate, 209
Timmerman Pharmacy, 80
Tony's Di Napoli, 128
Tot-Saver, 69
Turtle Bay Music School, 98, 120
Tutti Bambini, 209
Two Boots, 131
Vanderbilt YMCA, 38, 99
Venture Stationers, 143
Veronique Delachaux, 169
Webster Branch Library, 103
Wellpath, 42
William Greenberg Desserts, 153–54
Yorkville Branch Library, 103
YWCA of the City of New York, 38, 99

Zitomer, 210
Zittles, 226

East Village:
Astor Place Hair Designers, 154
Cremebebe, 201
Dinosaur Hill, 222
Free To Be Under Three, 91
Grilled Cheese NYC, 132
Halloween Adventure, 227
Kidstown, 203
Miracle Grill, 131
Perichild Program, 116
Third Street Music School
    Settlement, 120
Tigers, Tutu's & Toes, 209
Two Boots Pizzeria, 131–32
Veniero Pasticceria, 153

Grammercy Park/ Murray Hill:
Beth Israel Hospital, 16, 20, 67, 76
HomeFront Kids, 148
Kips Bay Branch Library, 104
New York University Medical Center,
    22, 67, 81
Tumble Town, 98, 121
Wellcare Center, 29

Long Island, NY:
Roosevelt Field Shopping Center, 214
Sunrise Mall, 214–15
Walt Whitman Mall, 215

Lower East Side:
New Amsterdam Branch Library, 104
Tompkins Square Branch Library, 104

Northern New Jersey:
Fashion Center, 212
Garden State Plaza, 213
The Mall at Short Hills, 212–13
Paramus Park Mall, 213
Riverside Square Mall, 213

Soho/Tribeca:
Bu & The Duck, 199–200
Bubby's, 132
CALYPSO Enfant, 200
Downtown Babies, 68
Equinox, 35
Gepetto's Toy Box, 223
Jivamukti Yoga Center, 40
Kidrobot, 224
Koh's Kids, 203
Lilliput SoHo Kids, 204
New York Firefighter's Friend, 225
The Odeon, 132–33
Peanut Butter & Co., 132
restaurants, 132–33
The Soho Parenting Cente, 70
Tennessee Mountain, 132
Tribeca Perfoming Arts Center, 107

Stamford, Conn.:
The Baby and Toy Superstore, 188
Stamford Town Center, 215

Union Square:
Body by Baby, 34
Educational Alliance Parenting and
    Family Center, 71, 79, 90
McBurney YMCA, 99
Mother Massage and More, 42–43
Sol Goldman YM-YWHA, 71, 90
Union Square Park, 103

Westchester/ Rockland:
Palisades Center, 213–14
The Westchester, 214
Woodbury Common Premium
    Outlet, 214

West Side:
The Ailey School, 114
Albee's, 183
Alice's Tea Cup, 128
American Museum of Natural

History, 105
Apthrorp Pharmacy, 80
Art-N-Orbit, 113
Baby Fingers, 86–87
Balloon Bouquets of New York, 149
Bank Street Bookstore, 230
Barneys New York, 166, 198
The Baseball Center NYC, 121
Big Apple Kids, 123
Birth Balance, 26–27
The Birthing Center, 19
Bloomingdale Branch Library, 103
Bloomingdale School of Music, 87,
    117
The Bridge for Dance, 114
Broadway Dance Center, 114
Cakes 'N' Shapes, Ltd., 151
Campbell Music Studio, 117–18
Carmine's, 133
C.A.T.S (Children's Athletic Training
    School), 87
Chateau Drug, 80
Children's Museum of Manhattan,
    105–6
China Fun, 126–27
Circus Gymnastics, 89, 121, 144
Columbia Presbyterian Hospital, 20,
    67
Columbus Branch Library, 103
Columbus Gym, 89, 121
Cozy's Cuts for Kids, 154–55, 222
Crumbs, 151
Cupcake Cafe, 151
Dean & Deluca, 152
Discovery Programs, 90, 111
Donnell Library Center, 104
The Early Ear, 90
EJ's Luncheonette, 133
Elizabeth Bing Center for Parents,
    70
Ellen's Stardust Diner, 130
Equinox, 35
Excellent Paper Place, 142
Fairway Cafe, 128

Firehouse, 128
First & Second Cousin New and
    Resale Children's Shop, 212
Flower Girl, 152
Fred's, 129
The French-American Conservatory
    of Music, 118
Gabriela's, 129
The Gravity Fitness & Spa, 46
Greenstones, 201–2
H&M, 167, 202
Hamburger Harry's, 130
Hands On! A Musical Experience,
    Inc., 91–92
Hard Rock Cafe, 135
Harry's Shoes, 156–57
Hi Life Bar and Grill, 127
Hippo Park Playground, 102
JAMS, 92
Jekyll & Hyde, 135
Jelly Bean Maternity and Children,
    167
Jewish Community Center, 27, 35,
    71, 92, 111–12, 113
John's Pizzeria, 134
Josephina, 129
Joseph Pharmacy, 81
Judy Lasko Modern Dance, 116
Karin Alexis, 187
Kendall's Closet, 203
La Escuelita, 123
Life Sport Gymnastics, 94, 121
Lincoln Stationers, 142
Little Extras, 142, 224
Lord & Taylor, 205
Louie's Westside Cafe, 129
The Lucy Moses School for Music
    and Dance, 94, 116
Macy's, 137, 205
Mama Nurture, 27, 95
Manhattan Mall, 137
Mars 2112, 135
Maternity Works Outlet, 168
Mickey Mantle's, 135

Mimi Maternity, 168
Mozart for Children, 119
My Most Favorite Dessert Company,
    153
New Mother Luncheons, 72
New York Kids Club, 96
New York Swims, 96
Old Navy, 169, 206
Ollie's Noodle Shop & Grille, 134
Our Name Is Mud, 146
Papyrus Cards & Stationery, 142–43
Patagonia, 206, 248
Penny Whistle Toys, 225
Plain Jane, 190–91
Planet Hollywood, 135
Planet Kids, 81, 184, 207
Popover Cafe, 129
Prenatal Massage Center, 43
Prenatal Yoga Center, 41, 99
P.S. 87 Playground, 102
Quiet Touch, 42
Reebok Sports Club NY/Sports Club
    LA, 37, 87, 97, 113, 122
River Run Playground, 102
Riverside Branch Library, 104
Riverside Drive playgrounds, 102
Rizzoli Bookstore, 232
Roosevelt Hospital, 19, 22–23, 25,
    67, 81
Ruby Foo's, 129
St. Luke's Hospital, 19, 23, 68, 81
Sambuca, 129–30
The School for Strings, 119
Shake, Rhythm and Roll, 117
Soutine, 153
SQC, 128
State News, 150
Steps on Broadway, 117
Suba Pharmacy, 81
The Techno Team, 122
Tiffany & Co., 137, 143
Tip Top Kids, 157
Toys "R" Us, 185, 226
The Upper Breast Side, 188

Wendy Hillard Foundation-Rhythmic
  Gymnastic NY, 121
West Park Presbyterian Church, 86
West Side Dance Project, 117
West Side Kids, 226
West Side YMCA, 99
Yoga for Two, 39, 99
Z'Baby Company, 210

West Village:

Lafayette Bakery, 152
Arturo's Pizzeria, 131
Baby Moves Boutique, 198
Balloon Saloon, 149–50
  Bambalulus, 199
Cadeau Maternity, 166
Children's Museum of the Arts, 106
Classic Toys, 222
Cowgirl Hall of Fame, 131
EJ's Luncheonette, 133
Equinox, 35

Greenwich House Music School,
  115, 118–19
Greenwich House Pottery, 120
H&M, 167
Hudson Street Papers, 141
Ibiza Kidz, 157, 202
Integral Yoga Institute, 39, 231
James J. Walker Park, 103
Jefferson Market Branch Library, 104
John's Pizzeria, 134
Julian & Sara, 203
Just for Tykes, 186
Kate's Paperie, 141–42
Kid O, 224
Kids Co-Motion, 93, 116
Kindermusik, 93–94
La Cocina, 134
Les Petits Chapelais, 204
Magnolia Bakery, 152
The Miette Culinary Studio, 120
Mommy and Me The Greenwich

Village Center, 95
NoHo Star, 132
Our Name Is Mud, 146
Party City, 150
Party Poopers, 146
Peanut Butter and Jane, 206
Rebecca Kelly Dance Studio, 116
Rockstarbaby, 208
Room and Board, 187
St. Vincent's Hospital and Medical
  Center, 23, 68
The Scholastic Store, 232
Shakespeare and Company, 232
The Soundings, 116
The Strand Bookstore, 232
Sylvia Weinstock Cakes, 153
Two Boots to Go-Go, 131
Two Boots to Go West, 131
Washington Square Park, 103
YoyaMart, 191

About the Authors

KELLY ASHTON holds a B.A. from Yale University and an M.B.A. from Harvard University. She is the mother of Alexander and Angela, and she writes and speaks on child-related topics.

PAMELA WEINBERG graduated from Brandeis University and is the mother of Rebecca and Benjamin. She runs the West Side New Mother's Luncheon series and frequently speaks on parenting issues.

Visit Kelly and Pam on the web at www.citybabyny.com